⓵

**advanced
history
core texts**

THE SCHOOLS HISTORY PROJECT · OFFICIAL TEXT ·

S·H·P

THE REIGN
OF ELIZABETH
ENGLAND 1558–1603

advanced
history
core texts

advanced
history
core texts

THE REIGN
OF ELIZABETH

ENGLAND 1558–1603

Barbara Mervyn

Series Editor: Ian Dawson

HODDER
EDUCATION
PART OF HACHETTE LIVRE UK

In the same series

The Early Tudors: England 1485–1558	David Rogerson, Samantha Ellsmore and David Hudson	ISBN 978 0 7195 7484 9
Britain 1790–1851	Charlotte Evers and Dave Welbourne	ISBN 978 0 7195 7482 5
Communist Russia under Lenin and Stalin	Terry Fiehn and Chris Corin	ISBN 978 0 7195 7488 7
Fascist Italy	John Hite and Chris Hinton	ISBN 978 0 7195 7341 5
Weimar and Nazi Germany	John Hite with Chris Hinton	ISBN 978 0 7195 7343 9

The Schools History Project

This project was set up in 1972, with the aim of improving the study of history for students aged 13–16. This involved a reconsideration of the ways in which history contributes to the educational needs of young people. The project devised new objectives, new criteria for planning and developing courses, and the materials to support them. New examinations, requiring new methods of assessment, also had to be developed. These have continued to be popular. The advent of GCSE in 1987 led to the expansion of SHP approaches into other syllabuses.

The Schools History Project has been based at Trinity and All Saints' College, Leeds, since 1978, from where it supports teachers through a biennial bulletin, regular INSET, an annual conference and a website (www.tasc.ac.uk/shp).

Since the National Curriculum was drawn up in 1991, the project has continued to expand its publications, bringing its ideas to courses for Key Stage 3 as well as a range of GCSE and A level specifications.

This book is dedicated to the memory of my mother, Joan A. Mortensen, who died before its completion but who taught me to aim high and to persevere. Also, for all their help during the writing of this book, my special thanks go to my husband Philip, for his encouragement, patience, sense of fun, and technical support, and my son Christopher, for his unfailing good humour and willingness to turn down his music.

© Barbara Mervyn 2001

First published in 2001
by Hodder Education, part of Hachette Livre UK
338 Euston Road
London NW1 3BH

Reprinted 2003, 2004, 2006, 2006, 2007, 2008 (twice)

Papers used in this book are natural, renewable and recyclable products. They are made from wood grown in sustainable forests. The logging and manufacturing processes conform to the environmental regulations of the country of origin.

Layouts by Janet McCallum
Artwork by Oxford Designers & Illustrators
Typeset in 10/12pt Walbaum by Wearset, Boldon, Tyne & Wear
Printed and bound in Great Britain by Martins the Printers, Berwick upon Tweed

A catalogue entry for this book is available from the British Library

ISBN 978 0 7195 7486 3

Contents

Photo credits

Cover *main* © The British Museum, London; *inset* By courtesy of the National Portrait Gallery, London; **p.1** *l* By courtesy of the National Portrait Gallery, London, *c* Scala, *r* Corsham Court Collection; **p.2** *t* Hulton Archive, *b* Fotomas Index; **p.3** *t* © National Maritime Museum, London, *b* The British Library (Add. 48027 f.650); **p.4** *t* Private Collection/Bridgeman Art Library, London, *b* © The British Museum, London; **p.6** The Royal Collection © 2001, Her Majesty Queen Elizabeth II; **p.7** The Royal Collection © 2001, Her Majesty Queen Elizabeth II; **p.9** Reproduced by permission of the Marquess of Bath, Longleat House, Warminster, Wiltshire, Great Britain (photo: Photographic Survey, Courtauld Institute of Art); **p.10** Reproduced by kind permission of Viscount De L'Isle, from his private collection; **p.11** *both* By courtesy of the National Portrait Gallery, London; **p.12** *t* Hulton Archive, *c* Private Collection (photo: Mr Jason Revell), *b* By permission of the Master and Fellows of St. John's College, Cambridge; **p.13** *both* By courtesy of the National Portrait Gallery, London; **p.23** By courtesy of the National Portrait Gallery, London; **p.34** The Royal Collection © 2001, Her Majesty Queen Elizabeth II; **p.35** Private Collection/Bridgeman Art Library, London; **p.36** Beauchamp Collection, Devon/Bridgeman Art Library, London; **p.38** The Royal Collection © 2001, Her Majesty Queen Elizabeth II; **p.40** The British Library (Eger. 3320 f.5); **p.42** His Grace the Duke of Norfolk (photo: Photographic Survey, Courtauld Institute of Art); **p.44** By courtesy of the National Portrait Gallery, London; **p.45** *all* By courtesy of the National Portrait Gallery, London; **p.46** *all* By courtesy of the National Portrait Gallery, London; **p.47** Mary Evans Picture Library; **p.49** © Staatliche Museen Kassel; **p.52** Hulton Getty; **p.58** Scottish National Portrait Gallery; **p.98** *t* Private Collection/Bridgeman Art Library, London, *b* © National Maritime Museum, London; **p.109** *t* Reproduced by permission of the Marquess of Bath, Longleat House, Warminster, Wiltshire, Great Britain, *b* Norfolk Record Office, Norwich City Records, Case 20 c (1); **p.125** *t* Andrew Lambert, *b* National Trust Photographic Library/Mike Thurstan; **p.126** National Trust Photographic Library/ Mike Williams; **p.134** *both* Fotomas Index; **p.135** *t & c* Fotomas Index, *b* Hulton Archive; **p.139** Fotomas Index; **p.146** Fotomas Index; **p.150** The British Library (Roy.2.A.XVI, f.3); **p.154** Palazzo Barberini, Rome/Bridgeman Art Library, London; **p.159** *t* By courtesy of the National Portrait Gallery, London, *c & b* Mary Evans Picture Library; **p.164** Mary Evans Picture Library; **p.174** Scottish National Portrait Gallery; **p.180** The British Library (Add. 48027 f.650); **p.188** *t* Mary Evans Picture Library, *b* Hulton Archive; **p.200** Mary Evans Picture Library; **p.202** Mary Evans Picture Library; **p.203** By courtesy of the National Portrait Gallery, London; **p.209** St Faith's Church, King's Lynn, Norfolk/ Bridgeman Art Library, London; **p.214** By courtesy of the National Portrait Gallery, London; **p.218** Scottish National Portrait Gallery; **p.219** Mary Evans Picture Library; **p.220** Mary Evans Picture Library; **p.221** *t* The Art Archive, *b* By courtesy of the National Portrait Gallery, London; **p.229** *l* Hermitage, St. Petersburg/Bridgeman Art Library, London, *r* By courtesy of the National Portrait Gallery, London; **p.230** *l* Hulton Archive, *r* Mary Evans Picture Library; **p.237** *t* Mary Evans Picture Library, *b* By courtesy of the National Portrait Gallery, London; **p.244** © National Maritime Museum, London; **p.245** *t & bl* © National Maritime Museum, London, *br* © The British Museum, London; **p.246** *t* Royal Armouries, *b* Woburn Abbey, Bedfordshire/ Bridgeman Art Library, London; **p.254** Hulton Archive; **p.258** *all* By courtesy of the National Portrait Gallery, London; **p.260** *t & c* AA Photo Library, *b* By courtesy of the National Portrait Gallery, London; **p.261** *t* Mary Evans Picture Library, *b* Hulton Archive; **p.263** Shakespeare Birthplace Trust; **p.264** *t* Fotomas Index, *b* AA Photo Library; **p.265** *all* Mary Evans Picture Library; **p.266** *tl* © V&A Picture Library, *tr* Mary Evans Picture Library, *b* Fotomas Index; **p.267** *t* Mary Evans Picture Library, *b* Hulton Archive; **p.268** *t* Hulton Archive, *b* © Donald Cooper; **p.269** *l* © Simon Warner, *r* © Ivan Kyncl; **p.274** *t* Mary Evans Picture Library, *b* Hulton Archive; **p.275** Private Collection/Bridgeman Art Library, London; **p.278-9** © The British Museum, London; **p.280** Fotomas Index; **p.281** Fotomas Index; **p.284** Walker Art Gallery Liverpool, Merseyside/Bridgeman Art Library, London; **p.285** By courtesy of the National Portrait Gallery, London; **p.286** courtesy the Marquis of Salisbury (photo: Fotomas Index); **p.287** Woburn Abbey, Bedfordshire/ Bridgeman Art Library, London; **p.288** By courtesy of the National Portrait Gallery, London; **p.289** courtesy the Marquis of Salisbury (photo: Fotomas Index); **p.290** Scala; **p.295** © BBC; **p.296** *t* © BBC, **p.296-7** *b* The British Library, London/ Bridgeman Art Library, London; **p.297** *t* Moviestore Collection.

Using this book

This is an in-depth study of Elizabeth I's reign. It contains everything you need for examination success and more. It provides all the content you would expect, as well as many features to help both independent and class-based learners. So, before you wade in, make sure you understand the purpose of each feature.

Focus route

For every topic throughout the book, this feature guides you to produce the written material essential for understanding what you read and, later, for revising the topic (e.g. pages 250, 298–99). These focus routes are particularly useful if you are an independent learner working through this material on your own, but they can also be used for class-based learning.

Activities

The activities offer a range of exercises to enhance your understanding of what you read and prepare you for examinations. They vary in style and purpose. There are:

- a variety of essay questions, for both AS exam-style structured essays (e.g. pages 169, 192) and more discursive A level essays (e.g. pages 144, 282)
- source investigations (e.g. pages 130, 247–48)
- examinations of historical interpretations which are now central to A level history (e.g. page 37)
- decision-making exercises which help you see events from the viewpoint of people at the time (e.g. pages 152, 176)
- exercises to develop key skills such as communication (e.g. pages 136,182), ICT (e.g. pages 136, 167,177) and much more.

These activities help you to analyse and understand what you are reading. They address the content through the key questions that the examiner will be expecting you to have investigated.

Overviews, summaries and key points

In such a large book on such a massive topic, you need to keep referring to the big picture. Each section and chapter begins with an overview and each chapter ends with a review that includes a key-points summary of the most important content.

Learning trouble spots

Experience shows that time and again some topics cause confusion for students. This feature identifies such topics and helps you to avoid common misunderstandings (e.g. pages 10, 53, 113). In particular, this feature addresses some of the general problems encountered when studying history, such as assessing sources (e.g. pages 118, 193); analysing the provenance, tone and value of sources (e.g. page 20); handling statistics (e.g. page 141); and assessing historians' views (e.g. page 104).

Charts

The charts are our attempts to summarise important information in note or diagrammatic form (e.g. pages 231, 253). There are also several grid charts that present a lot of information in a structured way (e.g. pages 68–70). However, everyone learns differently and the best charts are the ones you draw yourself! Drawing your own charts in your own way to summarise important content can really help understanding (e.g. page 44) as can completing assessment grids (e.g. page 189).

Glossary boxes

This book has been written in an accessible way, but occasionally it has been necessary to use advanced vocabulary. These words are often explained in brackets in the text but sometimes you may need to use a dictionary. You will meet a number of general historical terms, as well as some that are specific to the study of sixteenth-century England. You won't find all of these in a dictionary, but they are defined in glossary boxes (e.g. page 8) and are listed in the Index in bold. The first time a glossed word appears in the text it is in SMALL CAPITALS like this.

Talking points

These are asides from the normal pattern of written exercises. They are discussion questions that invite you to be more reflective and to consider the relevance of this history to your own life. They might ask you to voice your personal judgement (e.g. pages 7, 133, 183); to make links between the past and the present (e.g. pages 36, 93, 261); or to highlight aspects of the process of studying history (e.g. pages 66, 157, 272).

The reign of Elizabeth is far distant in time, but this does not mean it is irrelevant to us today. Key developments, such as the growth in Parliament's rights, still have an impact. Understanding sixteenth-century attitudes, to religious toleration for example, helps us to analyse our own attitudes. Finally, the actual process of studying history is very relevant to the modern world. Throughout this book you will be problem solving, working with others, and trying to improve your own performance as you engage with deep and complex historical issues. Our hope is that by using this book you will become actively involved in your study of history and that you will see history as a challenging set of skills and ideas to be mastered, rather than an inert body of factual material to be learned.

Introduction:
Elizabeth – myth and reality

'Oh Lord, the Queen is a woman!'

(a London woman on seeing Elizabeth for the first time)

SOURCE 1 Coronation portrait of Queen Elizabeth I by an unknown artist

'I will have but one mistress and no master.'

(Elizabeth, 1566)

SOURCE 2 A portrait of Queen Elizabeth I by Zuccari Federico

'My sex cannot diminish my prestige.'

(Elizabeth, 1603)

SOURCE 3 An allegorical portrait of Queen Elizabeth I painted in the 1620s (*detail*)

In 1588, as the Spanish Armada threatened to invade England, Elizabeth rode among her troops at Tilbury. There she proclaimed: 'I know I have the body of a weak and feeble woman, but I have the heart and stomach of a king, and of a King of England too.'

This is one of Elizabeth's most famous sayings and, together with the three quotations on page 1, it has passed into popular culture. An image has been created of Elizabeth as a powerful monarch who inspired her people and led them through one of the Golden Ages of English history. This image is still portrayed today, in books, plays and particularly films. But how true is it?

The main thrust of this book is an investigation into Elizabeth's success as monarch. Did Elizabeth and her government bring stability and prosperity to England between 1558 and 1603? How close to reality is the image of an Elizabethan Golden Age; or is it a myth, created by Elizabeth and her councillors, which has proved too strong for historians to destroy? These questions underpin the five main areas of enquiry in this book, which are:

- What sort of monarch did Elizabeth promise to be? (Section 1)
- Was Elizabeth in control of government? (Section 2)
- Did Elizabeth's government bring prosperity to her people? (Section 3)
- How far did religion affect stability at home and abroad? (Sections 4 and 5)
- To what extent can the reign of Elizabeth be described as a cultural Golden Age? (Section 6).

SOURCE 4 Edmund Campion, a Jesuit priest, was executed for treason by Elizabeth in 1581
- Was stability enhanced or endangered by the Elizabethan Religious Settlement?

R. P. Edmundus Campianus, Soc. JESV pro Fide occisus Londini in Anglia, Anno M D LXXXI. Die j. Dec:

SOURCE 5 A vagabond being flogged for begging
- What effects did inflation and economic policy have on stability?

SOURCE 6 Fighting the Spanish Armada, 1588
- Was foreign policy determined by religious principle or national security?

ACTIVITY

1 What can you learn about Elizabeth from Sources 1–3, the three quotations on page 1 and the Tilbury quotation?
2 Using Sources 1–9 and your existing knowledge of Elizabeth, brainstorm an answer to the question: Did Elizabeth and her government bring stability and prosperity to England between 1558 and 1603?

SOURCE 7 The execution of Mary, Queen of Scots, 1587
- How effectively did the government react to threats to national security?

Dolose agunt filij iniquitatis

Tyrone defired a parley with the Lord Lieutenant.

SOURCE 8 The Earl of Tyrone, leader of the Irish Rebellion of the 1590s, desires a parley with the Lord Lieutenant at Kinsale in 1601
- Did Elizabeth's policies serve to increase or decrease stability both at home and abroad?

SOURCE 9 The Globe theatre
- Was Elizabeth's reign a Golden Age for culture, and if so why?

What sort of monarch did Elizabeth promise to be?

Section 1 enables you to evaluate the sort of ruler Elizabeth promised to be when she became Queen in 1558. You will consider the following details:

- Elizabeth's character and upbringing, which is particularly crucial in view of her political inexperience

- the power and responsibilities of a sixteenth-century monarch

- the public's expectations of Elizabeth in 1558 and of the monarchy in general

- the situation she inherited in 1558 resulting from the policies of Henry VIII, Edward VI and Mary I.

This is not an area about which you are likely to be set an A level examination question. For this reason, Section 1 contains more decision-making activities of a hypothetical nature than factual focus routes. It will, however, give you a flavour of Elizabeth's personality, the problems she faced in 1558, and what was expected of her.

Above all, this section should make you think about the development of historical interpretation. The reign of Elizabeth I has long been seen as a **Golden Age**, where the Queen – by associating herself with the positive achievements of the period – acquired an almost mystical status amongst her subjects. You need to look at the extent to which this image was a deliberate product of the Tudor propaganda machine, and ask yourself why it has been accepted with so little questioning by historians across the intervening centuries.

FOCUS ROUTE

As you work through Section 1, prepare a SWOT analysis of the situation facing the government on Elizabeth's accession in 1558.

A SWOT analysis is a way of listing the different sorts of factors in a particular situation. You should list your findings in a table under the four headings as follows:

Strengths	Weaknesses
Opportunities	Threats

Bear in mind that some factors can be seen in more than one way. For example, a poor economic situation could be seen as a weakness, but it might also offer an opportunity to make quick improvements; the opportunity to expand trade could bring with it a potential threat from another power.

You may wish to add to this table after reading Section 2, which focuses on the government institutions and officials available to help the monarch.

A portrait of Elizabeth as a young girl, painted in 1545 (*detail*)

1

How did Elizabeth's early life shape her character?

CHAPTER OVERVIEW

COURT

An institution of government centred on the monarch as he/she moved between royal palaces. The monarch displayed his/her power at court in elaborate ceremonials, while courtiers tried to secure patronage and influence.

Although the reign of Mary I is no longer described as completely disastrous, the picture has persisted of an unloved and unpopular queen, who was followed by Elizabeth, her younger, more attractive and ultimately far more successful half-sister. Much has been made of the differences in their personalities and the extent to which their characters were the result of their childhood experiences. Both had seen their father put their mothers aside for another woman, both had been declared illegitimate and sent away from COURT, both had grown up during a period of turbulent change and both had experienced some personal danger. Yet the effect of these experiences on the two was very different.

The aim of this chapter is, therefore, to investigate Elizabeth's childhood so that you will gain an understanding of how her early experiences influenced the decisions she made as Queen.

A What was Elizabeth's inheritance? (pp. 8–10)

B Who influenced the young Elizabeth? (pp. 11–15)

C Review: How did Elizabeth's early life shape her character? (p. 16)

TALKING POINT

Is it useful for historians to understand the childhoods of rulers and politicians?

SOURCE 1.1 The family of Henry VIII: (from left to right) Mary, Edward, Henry, Jane Seymour, Elizabeth. This picture was painted in about 1545 by an unknown artist (*detail*)

ROMAN CATHOLICISM
The branch of the Christian Church under the leadership of the Pope. It was the main religion of Western Europe before the Protestant Reformation.

PROTESTANTISM
A Christian movement which began in Germany and broke away from the Catholic Church after Martin Luther attacked Papal corruption in the 1520s.

PRIVY COUNCIL
A body of advisers chosen by the monarch, who also had responsibility for carrying out royal decisions.

 ## What was Elizabeth's inheritance?

When Mary became Queen in the summer of 1553, at the age of 37, she was known to be:

- determined to honour the memory of her mother, Catherine of Aragon
- proud of her Spanish descent
- passionate about ROMAN CATHOLICISM
- determined to return England to Roman Catholicism
- set on making a marriage alliance with her Spanish relative.

In contrast, far less was known about Elizabeth when she became Queen at the age of 25. It would have been generally assumed that she would marry and share political power with her husband. And, although she was viewed at home and abroad as a PROTESTANT, she was not seen as passionately religious.

The situation Elizabeth inherited in 1558 was not an easy one. She was the last of Henry VIII's three legitimate children to inherit the throne and, as both her brother Edward VI and her sister Mary I had died childless, the continuity of the Tudor dynasty rested on her shoulders. She therefore had to come to a decision over the most eligible candidate for a husband. Other decisions needed to be made more urgently in order to ensure some degree of continuity in governing the country. The size and composition of the PRIVY COUNCIL and the appointment of ministers were immediate priorities and the issues of foreign alliances and religious doctrine could not be delayed for long.

SOURCE 1.2 The Tudor family tree

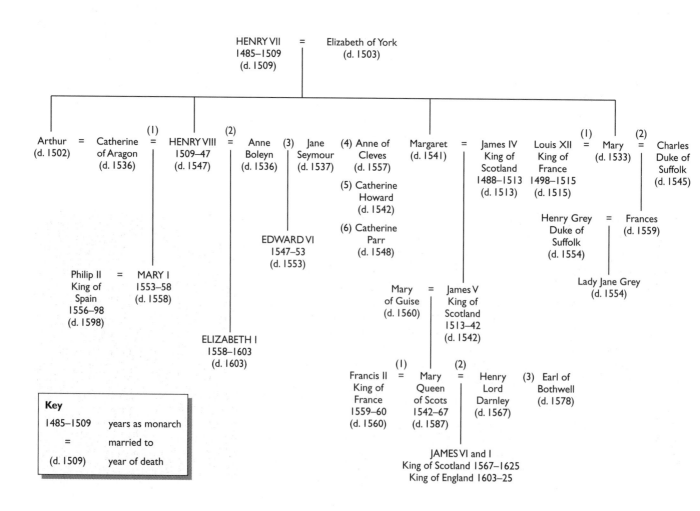

The religious situation Elizabeth faced was difficult as a result of the changes made during the previous three reigns. In the 1530s, Henry VIII had tried to gain permission from the Pope to divorce his first wife, Catherine of Aragon. When this was not forthcoming, he broke with Rome. The English Church remained Catholic in doctrine, but Henry VIII became Head of the Church instead of the Pope. This gave Henry the power to appoint his own Archbishop of Canterbury, Thomas Cranmer, who authorised the royal divorce. In 1533 Henry married Anne Boleyn, who was already pregnant with Elizabeth.

On Henry's death in 1547, his young son Edward VI, with the support of the Duke of Somerset and then the Duke of Northumberland, changed the faith and doctrine of the English Church from Roman Catholic to Protestant. The speed of the changes, however, meant that not all English people were Protestant by Edward's death in 1553. Many, particularly older people, still preferred Catholic services in Latin, decorated churches and celebrating saints' days as holy days, all of which had been abolished. When Mary became Queen in 1553 she quickly re-introduced Roman Catholicism and the Pope's authority to the country. She burnt at the stake nearly 300 Protestants who would not conform, but her short reign did not allow her time to eradicate Protestantism completely. Elizabeth, therefore, took over a country which contained two committed groups, as well as a much larger group who were not fervent supporters of either Roman Catholicism or Protestantism.

For Elizabeth, the issue of the country's religion was entwined with the dynastic situation. Until Elizabeth produced a child of her own, the next in line to the English throne was her cousin Mary Stuart (Mary, Queen of Scots). Some Catholics, including the Pope, thought Mary should be Queen anyway, because they did not recognise the marriage of Elizabeth's parents, thus making Elizabeth illegitimate. Mary was a Catholic and was supported in her claims to the English throne by France, because her mother, Mary of Guise, was French and Mary herself was about to marry Francis, the son of Henry II, King of France. If Elizabeth followed her own faith and decided to establish a Protestant Church, Mary, with French and Papal support, would automatically become the natural leader for English Catholics wishing to rebel against Elizabeth.

The new, and politically inexperienced, Queen would not have much breathing space to settle into her new role before she had major decisions to make. And, she would need to rely both on the advice of her older and more experienced councillors, particularly Sir William Cecil, and on her own instincts and judgement.

LORD PROTECTOR
The title assumed by Edward Seymour, Duke of Somerset, to show his guardianship over Edward VI and to justify his use of kingly powers such as appointing and dismissing councillors.

ENCLOSURES
The hedging-off of land with common grazing rights, to allow private landlords to use the land for sheep farming.

Edward Seymour, Duke of Somerset
Using his position as Edward's uncle, in 1547 Somerset declared himself LORD PROTECTOR of the King and for two and a half years dominated the council established by Henry VIII's will. He supervised the change of religion and continued Henry's war against Scotland. Somerset's preoccupation with foreign policy bankrupted the country and prevented him from acting quickly when Kett's Rebellion, a protest against ENCLOSURES, broke out in 1549. This left the way open for John Dudley, Earl of Warwick and Duke of Northumberland, to defeat the rebellion and seize power.

Somerset was responsible for ordering the execution of his brother Thomas and the interrogation of Elizabeth in 1549 (see page 12).

ACTIVITY

1 List the decisions that Elizabeth would have had to make in 1558.
2 Which of these decisions would have been difficult and why?

John Dudley, Earl of Warwick and Duke of Northumberland

Dudley built up enough support on the Privy Council to make himself Lord President of the Council in 1549 and Duke of Northumberland in 1551. He continued the Protestant reformation and withdrew from foreign wars in order to rebuild the economy. His political power depended on his control of the young King. As Edward's health worsened, Northumberland devised a plot to marry his son to Lady Jane Grey, a granddaughter of Henry VIII, in order to retain control of the monarchy and country. The failure of this plot and subsequent accession of Mary Tudor in 1553 made Northumberland's execution inevitable.

■ **Learning trouble spot**

It is easy to assume that the Church in England became a fully Protestant Church in the 1530s when Henry VIII broke away from the Roman Catholic Church. However, Henry retained many features of Catholicism, despite making himself Head of the Church. Therefore, outwardly, Henry's Church was Catholic with a Protestant label. The major move towards a Protestant doctrine came during Edward VI's reign.

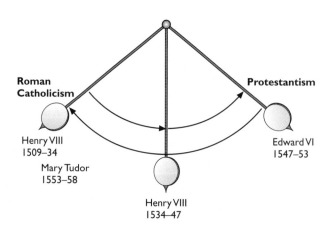

Roman Catholicism

Protestantism

Henry VIII 1509–34

Edward VI 1547–53

Mary Tudor 1553–58

Henry VIII 1534–47

ACTIVITY

Read through the descriptions on pages 11–13 of the seven people and their relationships with Elizabeth, then discuss:

a) how each person influenced Elizabeth as she grew up

b) which qualities and characteristics Elizabeth might have developed as a result of these relationships and experiences.

B Who influenced the young Elizabeth?

Elizabeth's childhood was unusual, even by the standards of sixteenth-century royal princesses. Most obviously, she lived with a governess at a distance from her father and had four stepmothers in eleven years. In addition, her status as a legitimate princess and her position in the line of succession changed according to her father's moods, his current marital status and the appearance or otherwise of healthy male heirs.

People who influenced Elizabeth's childhood

Seven people, in particular, featured prominently in Elizabeth's early life.

Henry VIII, Elizabeth's father and King of England 1509–47

Henry was intelligent, powerful, cruel and vain. He married Anne Boleyn in 1533 and had her executed, on charges of treason for adultery, in 1536. In the intervening years Anne had given birth to Elizabeth and a still-born child. Henry's third marriage to Jane Seymour produced a much wanted son, Edward. Elizabeth was made illegitimate and lost the title of princess. She became Lady Elizabeth.

Henry entrusted Elizabeth's upbringing to a governess and gave her a HOUSEHOLD of her own, which moved around the royal residences. He occasionally invited her to court, for events such as Edward's christening. In the Act of Succession of 1543–44 he named her as his heir after Edward and Mary, but did not make her legitimate. For most of Elizabeth's childhood he was a distant, powerful figure. She appears to have been proud of him and, although there are examples of his losing his temper with her, their meetings, though infrequent, were generally friendly.

This portrait of Henry VIII by an unknown artist was painted in 1536.

HOUSEHOLD
The personal staff of a monarch, a member of the royal family or a great noble. The monarch's household was part of the court.

Catherine Parr, Henry VIII's sixth and last wife

Catherine nursed Henry through his last years when his health was declining. She was an ideal stepmother and persuaded Henry to bring his daughters back to court. She kept an eye on Elizabeth's religious instruction, as well as her general education. Catherine was sympathetic towards further Protestant reform. Immediately after Henry's death she married Thomas Seymour and brought up Elizabeth in their household at Chelsea. They had an affectionate relationship and regarded each other as mother and daughter.

It was in Chelsea, however, that Thomas Seymour began his flirtation with Elizabeth, teasing and romping with her until Catherine was forced to send away Elizabeth and her household. Despite this, the two females remained on friendly terms until Catherine's death following childbirth in 1548.

Thomas Seymour, the Lord Protector's brother, Edward VI's uncle and Catherine Parr's widower

After the death of his wife in 1548, Thomas Seymour embarked on a dangerous plan. He wanted to marry Elizabeth and abduct Edward VI, to bring the young King under his personal control. At fourteen Elizabeth was flattered by his attentions and seemed more than a little attracted to him.

Seymour was arrested, along with Kat Ashley, Elizabeth's governess, and Thomas Parry, her steward. As it was treason for a royal heir to marry without the Privy Council's permission, Elizabeth herself was interrogated to discover if she was party to Seymour's plans. Although eventually cleared, Elizabeth was in grave danger during this period.

Seymour was executed by order of the Privy Council in 1549, having endangered the lives of both Elizabeth and her governess.

Kat Ashley, Elizabeth's governess

Kind, well-educated, naive and devoted, Kat was with Elizabeth from 1536. She supervised Elizabeth's education in mathematics, languages, geography, sewing, dancing, deportment and riding. She was arrested and interrogated by the Privy Council during Thomas Seymour's 'courtship' of Elizabeth in 1548, but was eventually released and restored to her former position.

Elizabeth loved Kat and remained closely attached to her throughout her childhood. She fiercely resisted attempts by Edward and Mary to replace Kat with governesses of their choosing. She showed her devotion by appointing Kat First Lady of the Bedchamber when she became Queen in 1558.

Roger Ascham, a scholar and Elizabeth's tutor

Ascham was a distinguished Latin scholar and educational expert. He was Elizabeth's tutor from 1548 to 1550 and returned in 1555 to concentrate on her studies of Greek.

By the age of fourteen, Elizabeth could speak fluent French, Italian and Latin. She read Greek daily and enjoyed listening to music. Ascham described his pupil as the 'brightest star'. While his influence on Elizabeth's childhood was obviously important, Ascham himself was not happy in the atmosphere of a royal household and, following a quarrel with Elizabeth's steward, he resigned his post and returned to his studies at Cambridge.

Edward VI, Elizabeth's half-brother and King of England 1547–53

Edward was precocious, arrogant, narrow-minded and a fervent Protestant. He and Elizabeth were originally close, despite living in separate households, but once he became King at the age of nine he was dominated by Edward Seymour, Lord Protector. He saw Elizabeth infrequently and, although Elizabeth continued to write to him regularly, the easy affection which they had shared as children had gone. He remained aloof during the investigation of Elizabeth's involvement in Thomas Seymour's plans and did not receive her at court for six months after the event. When the Duke of Northumberland was Master of the King's Household, he used his influence to ensure that Elizabeth did not meet her brother and that her letters did not reach him. Edward died in 1553, aged sixteen.

COUP D'ETAT
A violent or illegal seizure of power.

MASS
A Catholic church service in Latin where the priest transforms the bread and wine into the body and blood of Christ, thereby re-enacting the Last Supper.

Mary Tudor, Elizabeth's half-sister and Queen of England 1553–58

Mary was courageous, loyal and devout, but she sometimes lacked political judgement. She had little reason to be fond of Elizabeth, whose birth had meant that, at the age of eighteen, she had to give up her household and address her half-sister as princess, a title she considered her own. She also had very little in common with Elizabeth because she had remained attached to the Spanish inheritance and Roman Catholicism of her mother, Catherine of Aragon.

In 1553, after the defeat of Northumberland's COUP D'ETAT, when he had attempted to put his daughter-in-law Lady Jane Grey on the throne, the two sisters entered London together in triumph. However, Mary's suspicions of Elizabeth often resurfaced, usually on the prompting of Simon Renard, the Imperial ambassador. Mary saw Elizabeth as a possible figurehead for the enemies of Catholicism, as she believed Elizabeth was a Protestant despite Elizabeth's attendance at MASS. Elizabeth left court in December 1553. Relations with Elizabeth deteriorated further in 1554 when Mary sent Elizabeth to the Tower on suspicion of her involvement in Wyatt's Rebellion, an uprising against Mary's proposed marriage to Philip II of Spain. Elizabeth's life was once again in danger, as Mary and her councillors discussed whether she should be executed alongside Wyatt. After her eventual release, Elizabeth was kept under house arrest in Oxfordshire. The tensions in their relationship continued right to the end, with Mary refusing to proclaim Elizabeth heir to the throne on the grounds that Elizabeth was not her sister but the bastard daughter of a notorious woman who had replaced her mother, the rightful Queen.

This portrait of Mary was painted by Hans Eworth in 1554.

ACTIVITY

1 Read through the list of some of the key events (1–14) in Elizabeth's early life and put them into chronological order.
2 Read through the passages (A–N) describing or relating to the events and match them with the correct event.

Turn to page 300 for the answers.

Some of the key events in Elizabeth's early life

1 Elizabeth is threatened with execution

2 The arrest of Thomas Seymour

3 The death of Henry VIII

4 Elizabeth is interrogated in Edward's reign

5 Elizabeth learns that she is Queen

6 Elizabeth's flirtation with Thomas Seymour

7 Elizabeth's imprisonment in the Tower

8 Henry's marriage to Catherine Parr

9 The execution of Thomas Seymour

10 Henry's marriage to Jane Seymour

11 Elizabeth is interrogated in Mary's reign

12 The birth of Elizabeth

13 The birth of Edward

14 The execution of Anne Boleyn

Passages describing or relating to the key events

A It seems to me that she ought not to spare either of them, for while they are alive there will always be plots to raise them to the throne, and it would be just to punish them, as it is publicly known that they are guilty and deserve death. (Imperial Ambassador, March 1555)

B The King, who had abandoned his usual summer progress that year, contrived to hide his bitter disappointment. Orders were given for the birth to be celebrated with bonfires and the pealing of church bells. (Sunday, 7 September 1533)

C The King took his son into his arms and as he held him he was to be seen in tears. (October 1537)

D Much suspected by me,
Nothing proved can be,
    Quoth Elizabeth, prisoner (Summer 1555)

E They both tickled my lady Elizabeth in bed . . . and another time at Hanworth he romped with her in the garden, and cut her gown, being black cloth, into a hundred pieces and when [I] came up and chid Lady Elizabeth she assured me she could not strive withal, for the Queen held her while the Lord Admiral [Thomas Seymour] cut the dress. (Kat Ashley, 1548)

F Then she said, 'I have heard say that the executioner is very good and I have a very little neck'. (19 May 1536)

G And as for the traitor Wyatt, he might peradventure write me a letter but on my faith I never received any from him. (Elizabeth, March 1555)

H This day died a man with much wit and very little judgement. (Elizabeth, 20 March 1549)

I When the governor of her household, Sir Thomas Bryan, broke this news to Elizabeth, the child, not yet four years old, gravely asked, 'How haps it governor: yesterday my Lady Princess, and today but my Lady Elizabeth?' (Elizabeth, February 1537)

J It was reported afterwards that, disregarding the winter cold, she was sitting under the oak tree reading the Bible in Greek. It was also said that when told of her [fortune] she knelt on the grass and quoted in Latin these words from the 118th psalm: This is the Lord's doing; it is marvellous in our eyes. (November 1558)

K She will not confess any practice by Mrs Ashley . . . concerning my Lord Admiral [Thomas Seymour] yet I do see in her face that she is guilty. (Commissioner from the King's Council, January 1549)

L She was 31 at the time of her marriage to the King, an affectionate and understanding woman, good looking and good tempered. (1545)

M The boy burst into tears; so did his sister; they clung to each other uncontrollably. It was the last time they were to be close. Soon afterwards Edward was taken away to London to begin his unhappy reign. (1547)

N His conspiracy had been discovered and he had been taken to the Tower, precipitating the arrest of Mrs Ashley and Thomas Parry, his supposed accomplices in his designs upon the Lady Elizabeth. (January 1549)

The following ten events in Elizabeth's early life had an effect on her character. For each event decide which of the three possibilities, **a)**, **b)**, or **c)**, was the most likely effect. Explain the reasons for your choice.

1 The execution of her mother, on her father's orders, made Elizabeth:
   a) vindictive and determined to hate her father and refuse to have any dealings with him.
   b) obsessive and determined to clear her mother's name of the charge of adultery.
   c) dispassionate and determined to win her father's public support and respect.

2 The birth of Edward, which cost Elizabeth her legitimate claim to the throne, made her:
   a) resentful and determined to have nothing to do with her brother.
   b) affectionate towards her brother at first, but cautious in her dealings with him as they grew older.
   c) troublesome and she took advantage of every opportunity to regain her title.

3 A childhood spent in the care of a governess and at different locations made Elizabeth:
   a) loyal to her servants, because she was cut off from the normal ties of family and friendship.
   b) increasingly arrogant and detached, because she refused to chat with her inferiors.
   c) confused, and incapable of forming any close relationships.

4 Her education in the classics and humanism made Elizabeth:
   a) highly literate and articulate, and able to deal directly with foreign ambassadors.
   b) an intellectual, who enjoyed philosophical argument and debate with other great minds.
   c) scholarly and able to work out her politics and policies on the basis of her reading of the Greek and Latin classics.

5 Her governess had to write to Henry VIII to remind him that his daughter lacked decent clothes. This early need to be careful financially made Elizabeth:
   a) extremely extravagant. She spent rashly and impulsively.
   b) very thrifty and economical, and keen to find new ways of making and saving money.
   c) very mean. She refused to pay for anything that was not absolutely essential.

6 Catherine Parr's influence on her upbringing made Elizabeth:
   a) a fanatical and extreme Protestant, who was determined to follow and enforce the one true faith.
   b) open minded, but more likely to have Protestant rather than Catholic sympathies.
   c) fed up with religious teachings and determined to get away from it all as soon as she could.

7 The 'affair' with Thomas Seymour made Elizabeth:
   a) detached and determined to avoid future scandal in her personal life.
   b) flirtatious, as she realised her increasing attraction to the opposite sex.
   c) anxious, and keen to marry as soon as possible to fulfil her duty.

8 The accession of Catholic Mary I in 1553 made Elizabeth:
   a) hypocritical, because she asked for Catholic instruction and attended Mass but did not really want to become a true Catholic.
   b) clever, because by attending Mass, albeit infrequently, she kept in Mary's good books.
   c) scheming, because she knew that by being seen to be forced to attend Mass she would increase Mary's unpopularity and trigger a Protestant rebellion against Mary.

9 Her involvement in Wyatt's Rebellion and imprisonment in the Tower made Elizabeth:
   a) courageous, cool and determined to survive whatever the cost.
   b) fearful, depressed and determined to obey her sister in all things.
   c) angry, resentful and determined to lead another rebellion against Mary.

10 Elizabeth's childhood experiences had, by her accession in 1558, made her:
   a) relieved that she could now hand over decision making to her councillors and concentrate on having a good time.
   b) cautious, calculating, unwilling to display her emotions and aware of the need to create the right image as Queen.
   c) angry and revengeful, determined to get her own back on all those responsible for her harsh childhood.

Turn to page 300 for the answers.

C Review: How did Elizabeth's early life shape her character?

FOCUS ROUTE

1 Using the information in this chapter, construct a timeline showing the main events in Elizabeth's life up to her accession as Queen in 1558.
2 Elizabeth is often described as an extremely cautious queen. Which events in her childhood might have contributed to her becoming cautious?

TALKING POINT

Are the qualities necessary for women to be successful rulers the same as they are for men?

How far adults are the product of their childhood experiences is a matter for debate and it is difficult to draw definite conclusions. Certainly, it is easy to look back with the benefit of hindsight at the shrewd, cautious and detached ruler which Elizabeth became and to attribute such characteristics to certain events and relationships in her childhood. In reality, we cannot be sure.

Of the seven people described on pages 11–13, it seems reasonable to assume that those who affected Elizabeth most dramatically (but for very different reasons) were her father and Thomas Seymour, while, with the exception of Kat Ashley, her relationships with women were difficult. The influence of both Edward and Roger Ascham was more peripheral. Although obviously responsible for her education, Ascham seems to have had little influence over other areas of her life. Elizabeth's relationship with Edward, like her relationship with Mary, only became significant when each succeeded to the throne. Historians who have attempted to analyse Elizabeth's childhood have often focused on the possible impact of her father's six marriages.

SOURCE 1.3 J. Ross, *Suitors to the Queen*, 1975

Elizabeth saw how her royal father was the embodiment of power and manhood, wielder of fate for the women who married him, and thus she acquired abnormal experience of the impotence and disposability of married women.

There is little doubt that Elizabeth had a harsh upbringing. Her mother's execution, her interrogation during the Seymour affair and her imprisonment in the Tower by Mary were turbulent experiences, from which she will have drawn her own conclusions.

SOURCE 1.4 W. MacCaffrey, *Elizabeth I*, 1993, p. 29

Elizabeth had undergone a useful apprenticeship in the art of politics, but the skills she learned were necessarily those derived from her own circumstances of extreme vulnerability. She had developed a strategy of caution, of immobility, of playing as few cards as possible, waiting and hoping on events. She was yet to learn the skills required for the exercise of rulership – making decisions, giving commands and ensuring those commands were obeyed. ... Elizabeth's experience was very limited. Her life had been led almost exclusively in the seclusion of country houses, with only an occasional and short visit to the court.

ACTIVITY

Prepare a script for a four- or five-minute radio programme about Elizabeth's childhood and the extent to which it prepared her for government. Your script can be presented in written format, orally or on cassette. You can make use of the information in this chapter to help you, but also undertake some research of your own.

KEY POINTS FROM CHAPTER 1: How did Elizabeth's early life shape her character?

1 Elizabeth's upbringing was unusual, even by sixteenth-century royal standards, and its effect on her has been the source of considerable discussion. It was also unusual that she was still unmarried at the age of 25. Royal princesses (with the exception of Mary) were usually married off early for political advantage.
2 Elizabeth's relationships with her father, her half-brother and her half-sister were not always good, and Elizabeth's life was in danger twice through her links with Thomas Seymour and Thomas Wyatt.
3 Elizabeth's childhood experiences may have taught her to be cautious when making decisions, but they did not prepare her for running a country. And, when she became Queen in 1558, she had a series of important decisions to make.

2

What was expected of Elizabeth in 1558?

CHAPTER OVERVIEW   When Elizabeth became Queen on 17 November 1558 public expectations were high after the gloom of the final years of Mary's reign. The exact level of her personal popularity is hard to assess however, not least because there seems to have been a considerable amount of stage management and propaganda from the outset. Some foreign ambassadors reported that blessings were showered on Elizabeth as if 'she had been another Messiah'; but for many, their loyalty to the daughter of Henry VIII would have been mixed with a degree of caution.

SOURCE 2.1   W. MacCaffrey, *Elizabeth I*, 1993, p. 37

His [Henry's] son had not lived to assume the mantle of sovereignty, and his elder daughter wore it uneasily, anxious to shift its burden to her husband. Whether his younger daughter was equal to that task remained to be seen.

It was commonly expected that Elizabeth would marry quickly and produce an heir to safeguard the future of the Tudor dynasty. That was the duty of a royal princess. Elizabeth remaining unmarried was not an option many considered at all likely. Elizabeth's gender did not disqualify her from making the decisions necessary to rule by herself, but strong leadership tended to be equated with men, and therefore kings. Unless she chose to leave the decision making to a husband or minister, marriage would not necessarily mean a reduction in her powers.

It was certainly not envisaged that any future husband would automatically take over the running of the country. There were reasons for this. Before Mary's marriage to Philip of Spain, Parliament had drawn up a marriage treaty which severely limited Philip's political influence in England. It was also not unknown for one royal partner to be an absentee consort, living elsewhere and making the occasional visit. There were also several contemporary examples of competent female rulers: Mary of Guise in Scotland or Isabella of Castille in Spain who, although married, retained power in her own realm. In England, however, Elizabeth would need to work hard to prove to her subjects that she was capable of ruling successfully. Not all were convinced of the suitability of a female ruler after Mary's reign.

This chapter will look at what a Tudor monarch was expected to do and how Elizabeth's gender and her marital status affected this. Your knowledge of Elizabeth's childhood and personal qualities will help you to understand the motives and priorities which influenced her actions.

A   Gender and marriage (pp. 18–21)

B   What was expected of a Tudor monarch? (pp. 22–24)

C   Review: What was expected of Elizabeth in 1558? (p. 25)

FOCUS ROUTE

Read this chapter and make notes on the following questions.

1 Was Elizabeth expected to marry? Why?
2 What are the reasons given by different historians to explain why this expectation was not fulfilled?
3 What practical problems would Elizabeth face as a result of her gender? Think about the male-dominated political environment and the role of a monarch.

TALKING POINT

How might a female ruler use her gender to her advantage, even in a male-dominated society?

A Gender and marriage

There is some debate among historians as to whether Elizabeth made a conscious decision early on not to marry. This discussion is closely linked to the sixteenth-century view of the role of women.

SOURCE 2.2 C. Haigh, *Elizabeth I*, 1988, p. 9

In sermons and prescriptive literature, sixteenth-century Englishmen propounded an ideal of womanhood, and it was an ideal which left little room for an unmarried female ruler: a woman should be a wife, and she should be silent, obedient and domestic. A woman might rule her own kitchen, but surely not her own kingdom; outside the kitchen, she should be under the authority of a man, because she was physically, intellectually and emotionally inferior to men.

Yet despite the belief that women were secondary to men, not even her councillors believed that Elizabeth would hand over political power to her husband on her marriage; a view no doubt reinforced by the fear that they might be out of a job if that happened. Nevertheless, they continually pushed for marriage so that Elizabeth could produce a son to secure the succession and ensure political stability.

Christopher Haigh sees 1561 as a turning point in the saga of whether Elizabeth would marry or remain single. In that year, Elizabeth came close to marrying Robert Dudley, the Earl of Leicester, after his wife died 'in mysterious circumstances' in September. Although his wife's death was probably due to cancer, rumours abounded that Elizabeth and Dudley were lovers and they had plotted to poison her. Elizabeth finally heeded Cecil's advice not to marry Dudley.

SOURCE 2.3 C. Haigh, *Elizabeth I*, 1988, p. 13

He [Cecil] consigned Elizabeth to the role of Virgin Queen. It was probably at this point that Elizabeth decided not to marry ... there were still twenty years of international courtships to go, but with a brief exception in 1579, they were diplomatic manoeuvres for political advantage. ... Elizabeth probably intended to remain single.

Other historians, notably Susan Doran, have interpreted Elizabeth's single status differently.

SOURCE 2.4 S. Doran, *Monarchy and Matrimony, the Courtships of Elizabeth I*, 1996, p. 1

There is very little evidence to support the view, which appears in so many biographies, that from the beginning of her reign the Queen had made a conscious decision to remain unwed either because of her implacable hostility to matrimony or her determination to rule alone.

Doran also argues that Elizabeth was aware of her duty to provide her subjects with an heir to the throne, and that at no time in the first half of her reign did she rule out the prospect of marriage. She did not, therefore, choose to remain single at all. Doran also argues that the image of the Virgin Queen was not deliberately created in the 1560s by Elizabeth and her councillors in an attempt to compensate for the so-called disadvantages of her gender and her single status.

SOURCE 2.5 S. Doran, *Monarchy and Matrimony, the Courtships of Elizabeth I*, 1996, p. 9

Elizabeth ... did not have to remain unmarried and chaste to appear exceptional to her subjects, nor did she need to develop the secular cult of the Virgin to create for herself a special mystique.

TALKING POINT

The study of historians' interpretations is called historiography. Is examining historiography useful for A level students? How can two historians, who reach opposite conclusions, be helpful to you as a student?

ACTIVITY

Read Sources 2.6–2.11 which give you some idea of sixteenth-century attitudes towards female rulers.
a) What were the reactions of the authors of Sources 2.6–2.9 towards female rulers?
b) How are these views contradicted by Sources 2.10 and 2.11?
c) Is it possible to come to an agreement about contemporary views of female rulers on the basis of Sources 2.6–2.11?

SOURCE 2.6 Thomas Becon, a Norfolk clergyman, 1554

Thou hast set to rule over us a woman, whom nature hath formed to be in subjection to man . . . Ah, Lord, to take away the empire from a man and give it to a woman seemeth to be an evident token of thine anger towards us Englishmen.

SOURCE 2.7 From a speech to the House of Commons, 1563

God incline Your Majesty's heart to marriage, and that he will so bless and send such good success therein that we may see the fruit and child that may come thereof.

SOURCE 2.8 Philip II of Spain, 1559

It would be far better for the Queen and her kingdom if she would take a consort who might relieve her of those labours which are only fit for men.

SOURCE 2.9 Lord William Cecil, Principal Secretary of State, 1566

Pray God would send our mistress a husband, and by time a son, that we may hope our posterity shall have a masculine succession.

SOURCE 2.10 John Calvin, *Zurich Letters*

There were occasionally women [like Elizabeth] . . . raised up by divine authority . . . the nursing mothers of the Church.

SOURCE 2.11 John Aylmer, *An Harborowe for Faithful and Trew Subjectes*, 1559

Yea say you, God hath appoynted her to be subject to her husband . . . therefore she maye not be the heade. I graunte that, so farre as pertaining to the bandes of mariage, and the offices of a wife, she must be a subject; but as a Magistrate she maye be her husbande's head . . . Whie may not the woman be the husbande's inferiour in matters of wedlock, and his head in the guiding of the commonwelth.

When it became clear that Elizabeth was not going to marry and have children immediately, medical reasons were put forward to explain this unusual state of affairs. Since the sixteenth century, other theories have been developed to account for Elizabeth's unmarried state. Some argue that she had a psychological aversion to matrimony.

ACTIVITY

Read Sources 2.12–2.16.
a) What explanations have been put forward to explain why Elizabeth resisted her subjects' pleas to marry and provide an heir?
b) Why does Susan Doran argue that such speculations are suspect?
c) What assumptions do all these sources make?

SOURCE 2.12 A memorandum from William Cecil, 1579

Considering the proportion of her body, having no impediment of smallness of stature, of largeness in body, nor no sickness nor lack of natural functions in those things that properly belong to the procreation of children . . . the judgement of her physicians . . . show probability of her aptness to have children.

SOURCE 2.13 Alvaro de la Quadra, Spanish ambassador

It is the common opinion, confirmed by certain physicians, that this woman is unhealthy, and it is believed that she will not bear children.

SOURCE 2.14 A. Plowden, *Marriage with My Kingdom*, 1977, p. 160

It would hardly be surprising if by the time she was eight years old a conviction that for the women in her family there existed the inescapable correlation between sexual intercourse and violent death had taken root in her subconscious.

SOURCE 2.15 L. J. Taylor-Smith, 'Elizabeth I: a Psychological Profile', 1984

These childhood experiences taught Elizabeth that 'maleness mattered' and left her with a 'masculine identification' . . . as a result Elizabeth came to value and adopt the masculine qualities of dominance, aggression and fearlessness, which made it impossible for her to assume the subservient role expected of a wife.

SOURCE 2.16 S. Doran, *Monarchy and Matrimony, the Courtships of Elizabeth I*, 1996, p. 6

None the less, these arguments are simply psychological speculations, which, though fascinating, are suspect, based as they are on unproved models of human behaviour and inadequate evidence. There is no factual information at all to indicate how the deaths of her mother and stepmothers affected the young princess, and it could equally well be argued that their emotional impact was slight.

TALKING POINT

What do you think are the advantages and disadvantages for historians of using ambassadorial reports as evidence?

During the 1560s there were persistent rumours that Elizabeth was about to marry Robert Dudley, and even that she was expecting his child.

SOURCE 2.17 Alvaro de la Quadra, Spanish ambassador, 1560

He [Cecil] perceives the most manifest ruin impending over the Queen through her intimacy with Lord Robert [Dudley], Lord Robert has made himself master of the business of the state, and of the person of the Queen, to the extreme injury of the realm, with the purpose of marrying her.

SOURCE 2.18 Alvaro de la Quadra, Spanish ambassador, 1560

[The Queen and Dudley were] thinking of destroying Lord Robert's wife ... they have given out that she was ill, but she was not ill at all. She was very well and taking great care not to be poisoned. ... The Queen on her return from hunting (four days before Lady Dudley's death) told me that Lord Robert's wife was dead, or nearly so, and begged me to say nothing about it.

SOURCE 2.19 Robert Dudley, 1572

Her Majesty's heart is nothing inclined to marry at all, for the matter was ever brought to as many points as we could devise, and always she was bent to hold with the difficult test.

SOURCE 2.20 Elizabeth to Dudley, 1566

If you think to rule here, I will take a course to see you forthcoming. I will have but one mistress and no master.

SOURCE 2.21 Elizabeth talking about Dudley, 1575

Dost thou think me so unlike myself and unmindful of my royal Majesty that I would prefer my servant ... in the honour of a husband?

Elizabeth did not marry Dudley and for the remainder of her reign Parliament frequently requested her to choose a husband to ensure the succession. On several occasions marriage with foreign princes was discussed.

ACTIVITY

Read Sources 2.17–2.21.
a) What was it about Elizabeth's relationship with Dudley that caused so much gossip?
b) Do you regard Source 2.18 as a reliable source of information about Elizabeth's relationship with Dudley? Explain your reasons.
c) What reasons are suggested for Elizabeth's refusal to marry Dudley?

INFERENCE
Reaching a conclusion on the basis of given facts.

PROVENANCE
Where a source originated from. This will include date, author and purpose as well as the historical context.

■ **Learning trouble spot**

There is always a tendency for students to rewrite the contents of sources when answering source-based questions. Instead, you need to show the examiner that you can focus on the actual question, using skills of INFERENCE to work out the value or significance of a particular source. You may not be asked specifically to comment on a source's usefulness or reliability at this level, but you will be expected to have addressed this and such issues as PROVENANCE, tone of language, etc. when working out your answer.

ACTIVITY

Read Sources 2.22–2.24.

a) What reason does Susan Doran give to explain why Elizabeth never married?

b) Why had Mary's reign shown that a marriage treaty was not always a safeguard against a royal husband exercising power?

SOURCE 2.22 S. Doran, *Monarchy and Matrimony, the Courtships of Elizabeth I*, 1996, p. 210

Had her council ever united behind any one of her suitors, she would have found great difficulty in rejecting its proposal; likewise without strong conciliar backing Elizabeth would not or could not marry a particular candidate.

SOURCE 2.23 S. Doran, *Monarchy and Matrimony, the Courtships of Elizabeth I*, 1996, p. 213

Yet many at Court disliked the prospect of the Queen marrying a foreigner. Besides xenophobic prejudices, they shared a genuine apprehension about the practical political problems that seemed likely to arise from any union between Elizabeth and a foreign prince. Her consort, it was feared, might draw the Queen into wars of his own making and expect her subjects to pay the cost; he might take his wife abroad to live in his own territories, leaving England to be governed by a viceroy; worse still, the birth of a male child would put at risk England's national independence. Furthermore, if Elizabeth were to die in childbirth, her husband would act as regent with the authority to rule until the child reached maturity. Even though a number of these concerns could be dealt with in a carefully worded marriage contract, as indeed they had been in Mary I's matrimonial treaty, these alarming prospects influenced many to speak out against Elizabeth's foreign candidates.

SOURCE 2.24 C. Jordan, 'Woman's Rule in Sixteenth-Century British Political Thought', *Renaissance Quarterly*, Vol. 40, 1987, p. 429

The failure of the legislation intended to limit Philip's power seems to have been largely due to the Queen herself, who must have repeatedly declined to exercise the independence of mind that the law had authorised. Her fate doubtless weighed upon Elizabeth, who would have had to reflect on the extent to which such instruments of policy, when they relate to sexual politics, are only as binding as the strongest party to them determines they should be. By refusing to marry, Elizabeth avoided risking the loss of control that Mary had experienced.

Other historians have seen Elizabeth's decision not to marry as a result of her growing awareness of the advantages of remaining single. It meant that she would not have to consider the wishes of a husband, and that she could build on the image of Virgin Queen which elevated her above the ranks of ordinary female rulers, particularly her sister.

ACTIVITY

Read Sources 2.25–2.27. What advantages were there in Elizabeth's remaining single?

SOURCE 2.25 J. Hurstfield, *Elizabeth I and the Unity of England*, 1960, p. 40

Marriage and motherhood would deprive her temporarily – perhaps permanently – of the authority and power to rule. To share power she would hate. To renounce it she would find intolerable.

SOURCE 2.26 Sir James Melville, Scottish ambassador, 1564

Your Majesty thinks that if you were married you would be but Queen of England, and now you are both King and Queen.

SOURCE 2.27 C. Haigh, *Elizabeth I*, 1988, p. 19

Elizabeth sought to present herself, woman though she was, as a fit occupant of the throne of England, and she did not propose to confuse the issue by recruiting a husband or an heir. ... This was not done by an attack upon the sixteenth century stereotype of a woman. Elizabeth accepted the image and often derided her own sex ... she did not seek to change the ideal, but to escape from it, by suggesting that she was no ordinary woman.

TALKING POINT

Why is it impossible to be certain about when, if ever, Elizabeth decided not to marry?

B What was expected of a Tudor monarch?

Whether she married or remained single, Elizabeth had to decide how the country was going to be run. In the first few months of her reign, she therefore needed to develop her own style of monarchy.

■ 2A The responsibilities of a Tudor monarch

Deciding policy
- declaring war, going to war and making peace
- settling issues, including religious doctrine, arising from previous reigns
- ensuring the day-to-day running of the government, appointing officials
- determining relations with other countries
- ensuring the succession of the dynasty
- promoting economic growth and trade

Enforcing policy
- providing a framework of laws to protect people from crime and disorder
- dealing with threats to internal security, such as rebellions
- ensuring the courts work effectively

Raising revenue
- collecting money from the crown's ordinary sources of revenue, including rents from land, customs duties from imports, fines from legal rulings and feudal dues traditionally paid to the monarch by the nobility (when land changed hands for example)
- ensuring that extraordinary taxation, to meet the expenses of both going to war and defending the country against attack, was approved by Parliament and then collected

TALKING POINT

When studying the reign of a monarch is it necessary to know what happened in previous reigns? How far back is it necessary to go in Elizabeth's case?

SOURCE 2.28 Henry VII: painted in 1505 by an unknown artist

To help her to carry out her duties as monarch Elizabeth inherited a network of institutions and officials. These are described in detail in Section 2. There was, however, no written constitution defining her powers and rights as Queen; how Elizabeth chose to use the network was a matter of individual preference. Her four Tudor predecessors had each brought their own style and personality to the role, with very different results.

Henry VII, King of England 1485–1509
Henry VII was efficient, hardworking and respected, but not popular. He appointed able councillors and listened to their advice. He used force when he had to, and revived the role of Justices of the Peace (JPs). He rewarded those who were loyal and punished those who were not. He kept out of foreign commitments but increased England's prestige abroad. He increased sources of royal revenue and built up a large reserve but was seen as miserly. Happily married, he had two sons and two daughters who all made important political marriages.

Henry VIII
Henry VIII married Catherine of Aragon in 1509. He went to war against France, Scotland and Spain in the first part of his reign but achieved little. From 1515 to 1529, Cardinal Wolsey acted as his chief minister. By 1529, although he had a daughter, Mary, he was desperate for a son, but the Pope would not approve a divorce. On the advice of his new minister, Thomas Cromwell, he broke away from Rome, made himself Head of the Church in England and divorced Catherine to marry Anne Boleyn. In the 1530s he dissolved the monasteries and seized their land. In 1536 he defeated the Pilgrimage of Grace, a major rebellion in the North. By the 1540s Henry was often in pain. He gave way to pressure from his nobles and executed Thomas Cromwell. He spent the last seven years of his reign fighting expensive wars against Scotland and France and trying to stem the spread of extreme Protestantism at home. When he died the monarchy was short of money. He left a young son to succeed him.

Edward VI
Edward was only nine years old when he became King, so powerful nobles ran the country for him. The 1549 Act of Uniformity and the 1552 Prayer Book enforced a Protestant form of worship, but the removal of Catholic images and the introduction of an English Bible led to a rebellion in the West Country in 1549. Efforts to unite England and Scotland through a marriage between Edward and Mary Stuart failed, resulting in war between the two countries. Poverty increased as prices rose and there was a series of bad harvests. Consequently, landlords enclosed their land, which led to Kett's Rebellion in 1549. Edward died when he was sixteen. The government was still short of money, but attempts had been made to withdraw from foreign commitments and to stabilise the economy.

Mary I
Mary restored the Roman Catholic religion and the authority of the Pope, and married the Catholic King Philip II of Spain. The marriage treaty gave Philip the title of King of England but none of the powers and privileges normally associated with the title, apart from those he shared as joint sovereign with Mary. Nevertheless, the prospect of a Spanish marriage led to Wyatt's Rebellion in 1554. The rebels reached London but were defeated. Ninety rebels were executed and Princess Elizabeth was imprisoned in the Tower on suspicion of involvement.

Mary married Philip and tried to re-establish Catholicism by publicly burning nearly 300 Protestants who refused to conform. In 1558, Mary and her council committed England to helping Spain in its war against France. During this war England lost Calais, its last European stronghold. By the end of Mary's reign English people were suffering from poor harvests, inflation and flu epidemics. Mary died leaving large debts and no child to succeed her. The quieter achievements made by her councillors in the fields of administration and local government were, however, to benefit her successor.

ACTIVITY

In a group, discuss the following questions, then report back to the class.
a) Who was the most successful of the early Tudors and who was the least successful? Why?
b) Did gender play a role in the success or failure of a monarch?
c) Which examples from earlier reigns would Elizabeth definitely copy, and which would she definitely avoid? Why?

■ Learning trouble spot

The chances are that you will use the internet as a resource during your AS and A level history course. Using the internet can be very helpful – provided you don't forget all those questions you've been taught to ask about sources and textbooks.

The biggest issues are:

a) Is the information on a website accurate? For example, are the dates right? Are the descriptions of events accurate?

b) Are the interpretations on a website up to date? For example, does the analysis of Elizabeth's motives or policies taking the latest research into account?

If you use a book like this, you can reach your own conclusions about whether it is accurate and up to date. You can check when the book was published and find out about the author from the information on the back of the book. If you read the Acknowledgements (page 303) you will also see that this book has been read by one of the leading historians of Elizabeth. You can do this check with any book you use in history – but can you with websites?

The major problem with the web is that there is no quality control on websites. Anyone can create a website on Tudor history without needing to get it checked out by a historian to make sure it's accurate and up to date. So you need to ask questions about websites:

- When was it created and is it updated regularly?
- Does it say anything about who created it? How accurate and reliable is it likely to be?
- Who is it aimed at? Primary schools? A level and university students? The general public? How does its target audience affect what's on the site?
- Does it have a book list or bibliography showing where the author got his or her information? How recent are the books on the list?
- Is it providing the analysis and sources you need for A level or simply information about dates and events? If it's just information, then reading everything on the site may not be a good use of your own valuable time.
- And finally – is this website really of any use to you? Some are, some are not, so don't feel you have to say there's something useful in every site!

Two of the best reasons for using websites are to find sources and portraits and other illustrations which are often in colour. Here are a handful of the best (April 2001):

www.luminarium.org/renlit/eliza.htm
Excellent for portraits of Elizabeth, although there is no information about artists or analysis of the portraits. Also contains biographical outlines and links.

www.fordham.edu/halsall/mod/modsbook03.html
Probably the best provider of primary sources. You can find much of *Harrison's Description of England*, extracts from Elizabeth's speeches and material on the voyages of Drake, Raleigh and others.

http://renaissance.dm.net
A very detailed site with many aspects of everyday life, as well as politics and Elizabeth's court.

Other sites you may find useful:

www.tudorhistory.org
Wide-ranging site with good links.

http://e3.uci.edu/~papyri/camden
The full text of William Camden's *Annales Rerum Gestarum Angliae et Hiberniae Regnante Elizabetha.*

http://www.historyplace.com/speeches/elizabeth.htm
Online reproduction of the speech delivered by Queen Elizabeth I when she visited her soldiers in the field as they prepared for battle.

http://hiwaay.net/~crispen/tudor/chronology/
Detailed chronology of key events beginning with the ascent of Henry VII to the throne, and ending with the death of Elizabeth I in 1603.

http://www.English.swt.edu/Elizabeth1/html
View the coronation portrait and a small collection of lesser-known portraits. Gives the names of the artists, and current locations of the paintings.

http://tudor.simplenet.com
View portraits, wax figures, woodcuts, and sketches of Queen Elizabeth, the last of the Tudor monarchs.

http://www.nmm.ac.uk
Site of the National Maritime Museum. Examines Drake's around-the-world voyage, his run-ins with the Spanish, and his relationship with Queen Elizabeth I as well as other maritime topics.

http://www.royal.gov.uk/history/tudor.htm
Official site offers profiles of Henry VII, Henry VIII, Edward VI, Mary I, and Elizabeth I. Includes a collection of portraits.

And finally…
Remember – you don't believe everything you read in the newspapers. You shouldn't believe every interpretation you read in a history book. So don't just print out or paste in what you find on the web – think like a historian and check its accuracy and reliability!

ACTIVITY

Divide the websites above and any others you can identify amongst your class.
    Analyse each site and report back to your class on:
a) who produced the site, and when, and who its target audience appears to be
b) the main content of the site with examples, e.g. information, sources, analysis
c) whether the site can help you with your study of Elizabeth and in what ways
d) whether you think the site is a reliable source for the reign of Elizabeth and why.

C Review: What was expected of Elizabeth in 1558?

a) Using Chart 2A on page 22 list the skills and qualities Elizabeth would need to bring to the post of monarch.

b) Do you think Elizabeth had the necessary skills and qualities to be a successful monarch? Refer back to Chapter 1.

In the very first months of her reign Elizabeth had to develop her own style of monarchy. This was not easy because a female ruler was seen by many as unnatural, even 'monstrous'. As the Lord Deputy in Ireland said in 1592, 'God's wounds, this it is to serve a base, bastard, pissing kitchen woman! If I had served any Prince in Christendom I had not been so dealt withal!'

Elizabeth's marital status was of considerable significance throughout her reign. If she remained single she alone could determine the style of monarchy but would, conceivably, face some practical problems as a result of her gender, such as how to lead her army into battle in pursuit of honour, or to be Head of the Church and, above all, how to maintain effective methods of leadership in a male-dominated environment. If she married, the choice of candidate had to be acceptable to the Privy Council and her people, and a watertight marriage treaty would have to be drawn up to exclude her husband from political power in England and safeguard English interests.

Whether Elizabeth ever intended to marry or not, the fact remains that when she ascended the throne she was female, single and responsible for ruling a kingdom. Beyond the advice of her councillors and a network of institutions, she had only her own skills and intuition to guide her.

KEY POINTS FROM CHAPTER 2: What was expected of Elizabeth in 1558?

1 In the sixteenth century, women were very much secondary to men. Government and society were male dominated.

2 A female ruler was unusual in England and some contemporaries viewed it as a recipe for disaster.

3 Elizabeth's failure to marry immediately has been the cause of considerable debate, both then and now. We do not know when, or even if, she made a decision not to marry.

4 Elizabeth's marital status would have implications for her style of government and the way in which she used her powers as a monarch.

3

What choices did Elizabeth face in 1558?

CHAPTER OVERVIEW   It is reasonable to assume that once Elizabeth became Queen she could do much as she liked, that she could determine solutions to the problems of the day and then impose them through the existing framework of government institutions. This, however, suggests a freedom of action which Elizabeth did not have. The system of government that she had inherited was certainly a way of exercising royal power, but at the same time it also limited and controlled the monarch's authority. Furthermore, the scope and speed of change in the preceding 25 years had left Elizabeth with a difficult legacy. Henry VIII's break with Rome had been swiftly followed by the establishment of a fully Protestant Church and then an equally swift return to Catholicism, all authorised by the monarch as Supreme Head of the Church in England. These rapid changes had created a great deal of discontent which the new Queen had to take into consideration when making decisions.

The purpose of this chapter is to look at the problems Elizabeth inherited in 1558 and the options she faced in dealing with them. Some of these problems reappeared throughout her reign and you will need to consider whether their recurrence means that Elizabeth failed to deal with them effectively in the first place.

A What problems did Elizabeth and England face in 1558? (pp. 27–28)

B What did the English people want Elizabeth to do? (p. 29)

C How might Elizabeth have dealt with her problems? (pp. 30–31)

D Review: What choices did Elizabeth face in 1558? (p. 32)

A What problems did Elizabeth and England face in 1558?

The state of England in 1558 is still a matter of debate among historians. Few now accept that Mary's 'barren' and 'sterile' reign had left the monarchy and country in a critical state. In fact, according to W. MacCaffrey (*Elizabeth 1*, 1993, p. 35), 'The throne which Elizabeth inherited was supported by a firm administrative and legal foundation.' Even so, her predecessors had still left her with problems that required immediate attention.

SOURCE 3.1 C. Hibbert, *The Virgin Queen*, 1990, p. 70

She had inherited an unhappy realm in which prices had risen faster than wages, the coinage had been debased, and one bad harvest had followed another. Foreign entanglements had proved disastrously expensive and religious animosities had led to social strife.

■ 3A Problems facing Elizabeth in 1558

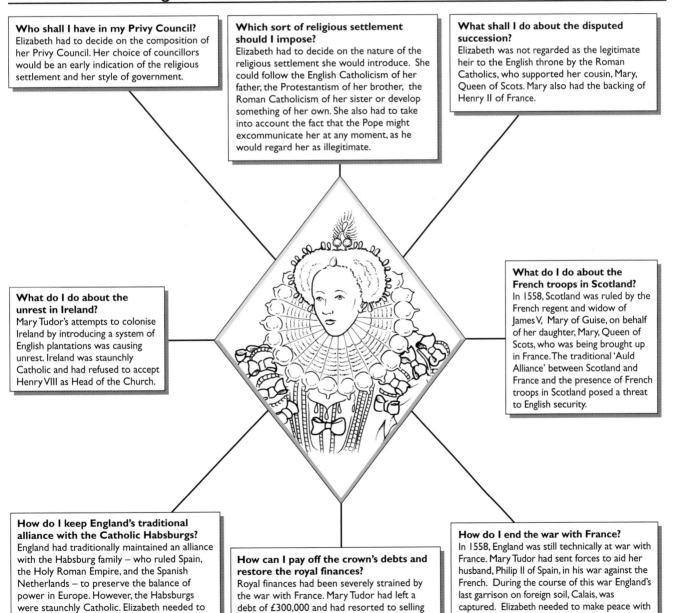

Who shall I have in my Privy Council?
Elizabeth had to decide on the composition of her Privy Council. Her choice of councillors would be an early indication of the religious settlement and her style of government.

Which sort of religious settlement should I impose?
Elizabeth had to decide on the nature of the religious settlement she would introduce. She could follow the English Catholicism of her father, the Protestantism of her brother, the Roman Catholicism of her sister or develop something of her own. She also had to take into account the fact that the Pope might excommunicate her at any moment, as he would regard her as illegitimate.

What shall I do about the disputed succession?
Elizabeth was not regarded as the legitimate heir to the English throne by the Roman Catholics, who supported her cousin, Mary, Queen of Scots. Mary also had the backing of Henry II of France.

What do I do about the unrest in Ireland?
Mary Tudor's attempts to colonise Ireland by introducing a system of English plantations was causing unrest. Ireland was staunchly Catholic and had refused to accept Henry VIII as Head of the Church.

What do I do about the French troops in Scotland?
In 1558, Scotland was ruled by the French regent and widow of James V, Mary of Guise, on behalf of her daughter, Mary, Queen of Scots, who was being brought up in France. The traditional 'Auld Alliance' between Scotland and France and the presence of French troops in Scotland posed a threat to English security.

How do I keep England's traditional alliance with the Catholic Habsburgs?
England had traditionally maintained an alliance with the Habsburg family – who ruled Spain, the Holy Roman Empire, and the Spanish Netherlands – to preserve the balance of power in Europe. However, the Habsburgs were staunchly Catholic. Elizabeth needed to work out how to keep the Habsburg alliance despite her own Protestantism.

How can I pay off the crown's debts and restore the royal finances?
Royal finances had been severely strained by the war with France. Mary Tudor had left a debt of £300,000 and had resorted to selling crown lands which only served to weaken the monarchy's finances in the long run.

How do I end the war with France?
In 1558, England was still technically at war with France. Mary Tudor had sent forces to aid her husband, Philip II of Spain, in his war against the French. During the course of this war England's last garrison on foreign soil, Calais, was captured. Elizabeth needed to make peace with France, but the permanent loss of Calais would be seen as a humiliation.

■ 3B Problems facing England in 1558

An inexperienced queen
The majority of English people welcomed the accession of Elizabeth. She was young and seemed to promise a new beginning after the setbacks of Mary's reign. Some, however, feared weak rule from an inexperienced woman. Stability in Tudor government seemed to require a strong, male monarch and an undisputed heir.

Threat from abroad
England was a weak country compared to France and Spain, both of whom were Catholic. Philip II of Spain had been married to Mary Tudor and intended to propose to Elizabeth. If England became Protestant, however, he might organise a Catholic crusade against it. The most pressing threat to security in 1558, however, came from Scotland which was under French control. Mary, Queen of Scots, declared that she, not Elizabeth, was the legitimate Queen of England. Her claim was also supported by some Catholics in England, raising the prospect of civil war.

Religious divisions
In 1558, England was a country divided by religion. The majority of people, including many of the gentry and nobility, were probably still Catholic. They believed that services should be in Latin and that churches should be highly decorated. Some believed that the Pope was the only true Head of the Catholic Church, although others had become used, since the reign of Henry VIII, to accepting the monarch as Head of the Church in England. Protestantism was strong in London, the south east, the universities, and among the politically-active classes, who believed that the monarch should be in charge of the country's religion, that services should be in English, and that churches should be plain. A third, much smaller group of extreme Protestants, known as the Marian Exiles, had fled to Protestant strongholds in Europe, such as Geneva, during Mary's reign, where they had been inspired by the teachings of John Calvin. They returned to England in 1558, expecting to be offered influential government posts and to oversee the establishment of a Calvinist or Puritan Church of England.

The loss of Calais
Many Englishmen saw the loss of Calais as a stain on the country's honour. Possession of Calais was symbolic of the time when English kings saw themselves also as Kings of France. If Elizabeth accepted its loss, England's status in Europe and, by implication, the prestige of the monarchy, might be reduced further.

A rise in prices and unemployment

In 1558, most people lived and worked in the countryside and made their livelihood from growing crops. The country's most important industry was the manufacture and export of woollen cloth. Both the population and prices had been rising since the beginning of the century. Some landlords had tried to increase their income by enclosing their land, leading to an increase in unemployment. In the early 1550s, trade with Antwerp, the main market for English cloth abroad, had collapsed, throwing thousands of spinners and weavers out of work. In the countryside tenants faced higher rents as landlords tried to keep rents in line with prices, while in the towns workers saw the value of their wages decrease.

Poverty and unemployment were increasing, especially among the lower classes. The problem of inflation was exacerbated by the bad harvests and flu epidemics (which killed up to 200,000 people) of Mary's reign. An atmosphere of gloom and pessimism made it hard to generate the wealth necessary for a prosperous economy, a situation which was made worse by repeated debasements of the coinage. Melting down coins and reminting them with a lower gold content benefited the crown financially, because it increased the amount of money in circulation, but it caused a loss of confidence in England's currency which harmed trade.

ACTIVITY

You are a member of the Privy Council. Draw up a list of Elizabeth's priorities in 1558. Explain which problems she should tackle first and why. Then suggest the most appropriate solutions.

B What did the English people want Elizabeth to do?

Although monarchs were not elected it was clear from the reigns of Edward VI and Mary Tudor that some degree of popular support, particularly among the politically-aware classes, was necessary for policies to succeed. In 1558, people's hopes and expectations for the new reign would have varied and would have been largely based on self-interest.

ACTIVITY

1 Look at Chart 3C. Draw up a list of expectations (a–x) and match up the appropriate characters (1–6) with each, giving reasons for your selections. Some characters will have more than one expectation.

2 In groups discuss the tactics Elizabeth could employ to gain as much support as possible for her decisions. In other words, which policies would be particularly popular and how could she 'sell' these to her people?

3 Look again at the Activity on page 28. Do you need to change your order of priorities to meet popular expectations?

■ 3C Expectations in 1558

1 Catholic noble — I live in the North of England and own a large estate. I feel responsible for supervising business in my region.

2 Protestant lawyer — I am based in London and am eager to make my way at Court by finding political patronage.

3 Prosperous farmer — I own large tracts of land in East Anglia.

4 Marian Exile — I am an extreme Protestant and spent Mary's reign in Geneva. I want a national Puritan Church, with no hint of Catholicism, to be established.

5 London merchant — My prosperity is based on the export of English woollen cloth to the Spanish Netherlands.

6 Town councillor — I am a member of the educated middle classes and I live in York.

I want Elizabeth to:

a) allow the amount of land under cultivation to be extended

b) establish a Calvinist-style Protestant Church in England

c) increase the powers of the great nobles

d) continue the Catholic religion under the authority of the Pope

e) expand overseas markets

f) allow food prices to rise with inflation

g) sack all Mary's councillors

h) increase JPs' powers to enforce law and order

i) marry a Catholic from a ruling European family

j) establish a national Church and expel the Pope

k) allow Parliament greater freedom of speech

l) marry a Protestant and produce a son

m) appoint new councillors who are Protestant and loyal to her

n) bring back pageantry and enjoyment to the capital

o) imprison the Catholic bishops and free all Protestants

p) ally with Protestant countries in Europe and aid Protestant rebellions against Catholic governments where possible

q) stabilise the currency and stop debasing the coinage

r) restrict the mobility of labour in the countryside

s) pass laws to stop beggars and vagrants moving around the country

t) increase crown patronage

u) increase spending on town walls/fortifications in case of an attack from Scotland

v) design measures to restrict the spread of the plague by isolating victims and supporting their families financially

w) restore the Anglo-Scottish alliance by negotiating with Mary of Guise

x) continue to demand the return of Calais from the French

How might Elizabeth have dealt with her problems?

ACTIVITY

Work in pairs and use what you already know about Elizabeth's background to decide which option she would have been most likely to choose to solve each of her problems in 1558. Give reasons for each choice, based on the likely advantages and disadvantages of each alternative. The answers are given on page 300.

You might think this kind of activity is more suitable for a magazine than a history textbook, but it's here for a reason. The best way to begin to develop a good understanding of Elizabeth's policies is to build up an outline of the issues initially and then, through further study, develop a deeper understanding of each issue. This kind of activity helps you develop that outline, so that when you read more deeply you recognise the issues, names and events and therefore find more complex accounts easier to follow.

1 When choosing her Privy Council Elizabeth will:
   a) introduce a new streamlined system of council and government departments to show she is going to establish a new style of monarchy.
   b) keep the existing council and governmental structures but select councillors on the basis of ability, even if this means including some from previous reigns because they would provide experience and stability.
   c) signal a break with the disasters of the previous reign by sacking all Mary's councillors and appointing her own friends to ensure support and loyalty.

2 In establishing the country's religion Elizabeth will:
   a) continue with the Roman Catholicism of Mary's reign. The majority of people in England are still Catholic and this option will enable England to remain friendly with Spain and the Pope.
   b) restore the Protestantism of Edward VI's reign. This will reflect her own religious preferences and win her the support of the politically powerful classes in London, but it might damage relations with Catholic Europe.
   c) follow her father's policy. She will break with Rome and become Head of the English Church, while retaining many of the beliefs and forms of worship of Catholicism. This will allow her to maintain the support of the majority of the English people, especially the nobility and gentry. It is also realistic given the fact that the Pope views her as illegitimate due to the circumstances of her parents' marriage.

3 In foreign policy, Elizabeth will:
   a) continue the war with France, to regain control of Calais whatever the cost.
   b) start peace negotiations with France and accept the loss of Calais as inevitable, even though public opinion is against this policy.
   c) use her friendship with Spain to mount a joint attack against France to regain Calais and to show other European rulers that she is a power to be reckoned with and not a feeble woman.

4 To deal with Scotland and strengthen English security Elizabeth will:
   a) support the Protestant nobles in Scotland and encourage them to drive the French out of Scotland.
   b) continue the war with France. Winning would enable Elizabeth to dictate her own terms and force the French to withdraw from Scotland.
   c) begin negotiations with the future Mary, Queen of Scots, and her representatives. She will promise to name Mary as her successor to the English throne in return for Mary's loyalty and support.

5 To establish the succession Elizabeth will:
   a) marry the most suitable English candidate quickly and hope to produce a male heir.
   b) declare her intention to remain single and name her closest relative, Mary, Queen of Scots, as her heir.
   c) play for time and wait to see if a suitable candidate emerges. In the meantime she will refuse to name a successor for fear it will encourage plots to replace her.

6 In 1560, the wife of Robert Dudley, Elizabeth's favourite, will die in mysterious circumstances. To stop the growing scandal about her relationship with Dudley Elizabeth will:
  a) refuse to marry him but keep him at court as her favourite and promote him whenever possible, even though this might cause jealousy.
  b) marry him. The rumours will soon be forgotten, particularly when she has children.
  c) send him from court in disgrace and refuse to have any more to do with him to distance herself from the scandal.

7 To increase trade Elizabeth will:
  a) subsidise the woollen industry and continue to rely on this as the basis of England's wealth.
  b) look for new overseas markets, even though this might cause war.
  c) begin to develop new industries such as shipbuilding and coal and iron production, at home, to make England more self-sufficient and to ensure a surplus of goods for export.

8 To cover the costs of the government Elizabeth will:
  a) continue to borrow money, although at a reduced level of interest, and make up the shortfall with taxation.
  b) debase the coinage and sell off crown assets, such as Church land.
  c) demand forced loans from her wealthier subjects in return for government offices and a position at court.

9 To gain the support of the aristocracy Elizabeth will:
  a) revive their feudal powers and give them control over their own counties, as they are the only ones strong enough to control their tenants.
  b) keep them occupied in London. She will create meaningless titles, such as Master of the Queen's Chocolate, so that her nobles are so busy squabbling over their status at court that they will not be a threat.
  c) allow them to exercise limited patronage and power in their regions, include some in her council and encourage others to come to court.

10 To enforce law and order Elizabeth will:
  a) introduce a nationwide system of paid officials who will report directly to the crown and who will be selected on the basis of ability.
  b) continue to use the gentry class as JPs. She will extend their powers and rely on their love of status as a guarantee of loyalty rather than pay them a salary.
  c) continue to use the gentry class as JPs. She will extend their powers and pay them a salary to ensure professionalism.

11 In her relations with Parliament Elizabeth will:
  a) control MPs by using a variety of tactics, ranging from dismissing the Commons and imprisoning MPs to playing for time and avoiding decisions.
  b) make it very clear at the start of the reign that she intends to reduce Parliament's role. She will begin by abolishing Parliament's power to raise taxes.
  c) recognise that Parliament's powers have grown considerably since her father's time and grant MPs freedom of speech within the House of Commons, a step that will boost her popularity.

12 To control the military forces Elizabeth will:
  a) make all tactical decisions herself, even though she lacks experience and is known to be cautious and indecisive.
  b) rely on her nobles who have the necessary experience.
  c) appoint a military supremo who will report directly to her. He will co-ordinate this whole area and present her with clear proposals for campaigns.

D Review: What choices did Elizabeth face in 1558?

Elizabeth faced a number of problems when she became Queen in 1558 and the choices she made initially would have important consequences. These consequences may have been short-term or long-term, positive or negative, calculated or accidental, but they would certainly have determined the future direction of the reign and Elizabeth's style of monarchy.

Yet governing was not simply a case of making decisions and agreeing on policy. If the monarchy was to function effectively, it was also important for it to have the support of the politically-active classes in the country. The effect government policies would have on people therefore had to be taken into account; but individual expectations of the new Queen were very varied and often conflicting. Perhaps more than any of her predecessors, Elizabeth was aware of the need to 'sell' her policies and her image as Queen to her subjects from the outset.

KEY POINTS FROM CHAPTER 3: What choices did Elizabeth face in 1558?

1 The main issues facing Elizabeth in 1558 were religion, marriage and the succession, foreign policy and the economy. They were to dominate policy throughout her reign.

2 The main problems facing the country in 1558 included loss of prestige in Europe, religious strife, competing nobles, inflation, and unrest in Ireland.

3 Popular expectation of Elizabeth was high in 1558. It would be hard for her to solve all the problems and meet these expectations.

4 The support of the politically-active classes was crucial to the success of government policy, but there was a lot of disagreement over which policies Elizabeth should follow.

TALKING POINT

Compare your own decisions in the Activity on pages 30–31 with the answers on page 300. What have you learned from the differences?

4

What sort of monarchy did Elizabeth create?

CHAPTER OVERVIEW

The reign of Elizabeth is still regarded as a Golden Age in English history, a time when 'Gloriana, the Faerie Queene' ruled her children with love and devotion, and presided over unparalleled achievements in the arts, overseas exploration and military exploits.

Elizabeth and her ministers were aware of the need to create a popular image for the Queen which would discourage the social and political unrest of the two previous reigns. In this chapter you will examine the extent to which propaganda helped to create this image and how historians have interpreted her reign in the light of this image. This chapter provides an introduction to one of the main questions in this book which asks you, by the end of your study of Elizabeth, to determine whether you think her style of monarchy was:

- a combination of a sound inheritance and luck
- deliberately created by Elizabeth and her ministers using propaganda
- created by historians
- a mixture of all three.

This chapter briefly introduces each of these interpretations.

A 'Accidental' monarchy? (p. 34)

B 'Manufactured' monarchy? (pp. 35–36)

C 'Rose-coloured' monarchy? (p. 36)

D Review: What sort of monarchy did Elizabeth create? (p. 37)

'Accidental' monarchy?

It is possible to attribute the successes of Elizabeth's reign and her style of monarchy to the institutions she inherited from her predecessors.

SOURCE 4.1   G. R. Elton, *England Under the Tudors*, 3rd edn, 1991, p. 193

That [Tudor rule] survived at all [between 1540 and 1558] was a tribute to the work of Henry VII, to the depth of king-worship and obedience to established authority which Henry VIII's terrifying personality had riveted upon ... England ... and also to the administrative reforms of Thomas Cromwell which up to a point made continued government possible even when the crown failed to play its part ... The years served a purpose: passions played themselves out in the clashing of extremes which, having had their turn, retained the less strength to trouble the government of Elizabeth.

In other words, the system was strong enough to survive the disastrous reigns of Edward and Mary, and merely needed a competent monarch and ministers to appear successful again.

The image of Elizabeth as Virgin Queen emerged equally accidentally.

SOURCE 4.2   W. MacCaffrey, *Elizabeth I*, 1993, p. 378

Without any effort on her own, she became the subject of an ever growing genre of celebratory poetry and prose. ... The proliferation of these images gave the Queen great delight ... they also added measurably to her political capital. The royal image which she inherited was of course that of divine right kingship.

SOURCE 4.3   Elizabeth I and the goddesses of women, wisdom, and beauty, painted by Hans Eworth in 1569

B 'Manufactured' monarchy?

Other historians have argued that the image of monarchy was deliberately created by Elizabeth and her councillors, to ensure that all the successes of the reign were perceived as being a direct result of Elizabeth's policies. This enhanced the Queen's status, disguised weaknesses and stifled opposition.

SOURCE 4.4   C. Haigh, *Elizabeth I*, 1988, p. 146

Elizabeth pursued a propaganda policy designed to maximise popular loyalty to herself, not just because she liked to be cheered, but because it was politically sensible. If she could attract the loyalty of ordinary people ... they would be on the lookout for any critics of the regime ... a loyal nation would be less likely to rebel in hard times ... so Elizabeth did not only have to present sophisticated and allusive images of female rule to her educated courtiers, she had to present a simpler, more basic message to ordinary people. Somehow, the townspeople and peasants of England had to be made to love her.

Christopher Haigh goes on to show how Elizabeth achieved this by making herself an accessible, public figure. In particular, her annual progresses around the country were carefully stage-managed public relations exercises (although she never visited the north of England). She also used every opportunity to hammer home her message through speeches, sermons, pageants and paintings. 'In prayers, ballads and speeches, the people of England were regularly informed of how lucky they were and how successfully Elizabeth had ruled them ... the English came to believe what they were told' (C. Haigh, *Elizabeth I*, 1988, pp. 154–55).

Although the use of propaganda was not new, Elizabeth went to greater lengths to manipulate it to her purpose. She used it to compensate for her gender and her single status, deliberately creating an image which declared her female but far above other women.

SOURCE 4.5   Elizabeth being carried in procession, *c.* 1600, in a painting attributed to Robert Peake. Royal progresses enabled Elizabeth to see and be seen by her subjects

SOURCE 4.6 C. Haigh, *Elizabeth I*, 1988, p. 20

She was not just a virgin of Mary-like significance; not just a wife but the wife of the realm; not just a mother but the mother of the English people and the English Church. Nor was she just a daughter; she was the daughter of Henry VIII.

TALKING POINT

What is propaganda? How well do you expect the propaganda of the Elizabethan era to compare with what advertisers and image-makers produce today?

SOURCE 4.7 Elizabeth I performing the Maundy Ceremonies, c. 1565, by Lievine Teerlink

C 'Rose-coloured' monarchy?

Very few historians have written critical accounts of Elizabeth's reign. From the seventeenth century onwards, particularly as the weaknesses of the Stuarts became clearer, historians looked back at Elizabeth's reign as a Golden Age. They wrote only in terms of a glowing achievement, which stood out particularly after the disasters of the previous reign.

More recently, historians have re-assessed the mid-sixteenth century, and the reign of Mary Tudor. As Mary's reputation as a ruler has improved so it has become harder to justify the simple contrast between Mary's failures and Elizabeth's successes. To some extent, therefore, Elizabeth's reputation was a product not just of her own reign but of historians' assessments of events before and after her reign.

It would seem that the obvious way to find the 'truth' would be to look at the contemporary evidence, but here too there is a problem: the chances of survival are far greater for documents which are supportive of Elizabeth's regime than for those which are critical of it.

SOURCE 4.8 R. Salter, *Elizabeth and Her Reign*, 1988, p. 2

Historians born in her own reign soon began to write the history of her reign in the light of Stuart history. Camden and Naunton particularly throw aspects of Elizabeth's policy into relief in such a way as to imply criticism of James I or Charles I. Much later, from the viewpoint of Victorian self-confidence, historians such as Pollard and Creighton see in Elizabeth's reign the birth of a nation. Some twentieth-century historians such as Rowse and Neale have continued to draw Elizabethan history along the same eulogistic road ... but from the sense of the comparison that could be drawn between sixteenth- and twentieth-century England as a nation under threat.

SOURCE 4.9 C. Haigh, *Elizabeth I*, 1988, p. 7 and p. 175

The monarchy of Elizabeth was founded upon illusion. She ruled by propagandist images which captivated her courtiers and seduced her suitors – images which have misled historians for four centuries ... it is almost impossible to write a balanced study of Elizabeth I.

TALKING POINTS

1 Why might historians writing in the 1940s and early 1950s present a very positive image of the first Elizabeth?
2 Modern society is full of propaganda and advertising. How might this affect historians' interpretations of Elizabeth?
3 Can historians ever really be objective, or are we all the products of the age in which we live?

D Review: What sort of monarchy did Elizabeth create?

You should now be aware of the continual need to ask yourself questions when considering the sort of monarchy Elizabeth created. When looking at statements made by Elizabeth and her ministers, bear in mind the fact that they were often written for public consumption, both at home and abroad. Similarly, when looking at the interpretations of historians, consider their reasons for romanticising or denigrating Elizabeth's reign. As Susan Doran writes ('Elizabeth I', *The Historian*, No. 54, 1997), 'It is undoubtedly true that the reality of Elizabeth's character and rule was far different from both the contemporary image and popular myth.'

It may well be that, as historians find more to praise in the reigns of Mary Tudor and James I, Elizabeth's status will decrease and our view of the Elizabethan period will be revised. As Christopher Haigh says (*Elizabeth I*, 1988, p. 181), 'On this as on many other aspects of Elizabethan political history there is still much to be done.'

ACTIVITY

Use Sources 4.1– 4.9 to answer the following questions.
1 Give three reasons to explain why it is difficult to achieve 'a balanced study of Elizabeth I'.
2 What reasons do Elton and MacCaffrey give to show that luck played a part in Elizabeth's success?
3 What were Elizabeth's motives when she created the propaganda machine which helped to elevate her status?
4 What methods of mass communication would Elizabeth and her government have been able to exploit?
5 Why have some historians seen Elizabeth's reign as a Golden Age?
6 Does lack of balance mean that it is impossible to know what Elizabeth's reign was really like?
7 Can you suggest which contemporary sources might be useful for investigating Elizabeth's reign?

KEY POINTS FROM CHAPTER 4: What sort of monarchy did Elizabeth create?

1 The degree to which Elizabeth's image was created by a Tudor propaganda machine is still debated by historians.
2 The image we have of Elizabeth and her reign has resulted from contemporary sources and their interpretation by historians, who are influenced by events going on around them when they are writing.

Introductory review

FOCUS ROUTE

Using all the material in Section 1, write an assessment of the problems Elizabeth faced in 1558, the policies she was likely to employ to solve them and your opinion on her potential for success.

ACTIVITY

1 What did you learn from your SWOT analysis (page 6)? Were there more strengths and opportunities in Elizabeth's position in 1558 than there were weaknesses and threats?
2 It is 1558. Rate Elizabeth's chances of having a stable and prosperous reign on a scale of 0–10 (0 = very unstable and poverty stricken, 10 = very stable and prosperous). Explain the reasons behind your choice.

TALKING POINT

Think about your preconceptions of Elizabeth. Do you see her as an English heroine, perhaps as a result of a film? How might this influence your study of her reign?

Coronation portrait of Elizabeth I by an unknown artist

Was Elizabeth in control of government?

In November 1558, the Spanish ambassador De Feria wrote of Elizabeth, 'I see her inclined to govern through men who are believed to be heretics . . . she is determined to be governed by no one.' Within a month, he reported to his master, Philip II of Spain, that the new Queen was 'incomparably more feared than her sister, and gives her orders and has her way as absolutely as her father did'.

From the start of her reign Elizabeth's intention to be in control of government had been made very clear during a sumptuous coronation which verged on the spectacular. Days of stage-managed tableaux and processions portrayed the Queen as an almost religious figure who was entitled to the respect and obedience of all her subjects, regardless of their status.

But that Elizabeth would be in control of government was by no means the foregone conclusion it sounds. Although the office of monarch carried with it considerable PREROGATIVE powers, the extent to which they were used successfully depended on the character of the person wearing the crown. There were plenty of examples from earlier reigns to show that if a monarch did not possess the necessary qualities of command their hopes of a long and successful reign were seldom realised. These powers also 'came with attached special conditions which circumscribed their use' (W. MacCaffrey, *Elizabeth I*, 1993, p. 34).

> **PREROGATIVE**
> A monarch's powers, as defined by common law, were based on their royal prerogative. This was derived from either their feudal rights or their personal concerns. A monarch therefore regarded these areas, which included marriage and succession, as not open for debate.

- In 1558, the English monarchy was based on a sound administrative and legal foundation, which had the **Privy Council** at its centre.
- Law was enforced through a medieval court system which had been added to by the introduction of the **Star Chamber and Chancery**.
- At local level, JPs and the **Assize Court** were the main instruments for maintaining law and order.
- A strong monarch and a supportive advisory council were essential to make this system of government work.

■ The monarch could not, however, be dictatorial. Even Henry VIII acknowledged the need to work with the existing system of government and under the constraints of the law.

■ Despite her powers, Elizabeth needed the co-operation of her nobles and gentry to ensure the success of her government. She didn't have a standing army to enable her to enforce her policies independently.

Section 2 will look at how far Elizabeth was in control of government. It will focus on the main institutions and personalities, as well as the areas of potential conflict and opposition and the strategies Elizabeth introduced to deal with them.

Elizabeth's coronation procession, 1559

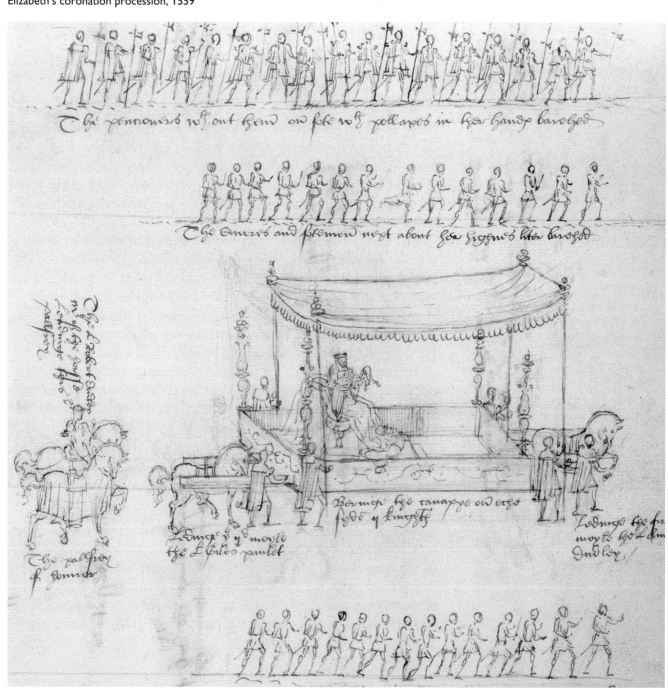

5

How did central government work?

CHAPTER OVERVIEW

The term 'government' refers to not only the institutions by which a country is run but also the people responsible for those institutions and the decisions they make. 'Good government' is, after all, more likely to refer to successful policies than to the presence of the Houses of Parliament.

Government operated on two levels. Central government – which included the Privy Council and the Exchequer – was based in London. At a local level a network of institutions, linked through the work of the Justices of the Peace, enforced central decisions and passed information back to the centre. Alongside the traditional institutions, the Queen had her own court which was the centre of power, ritual and celebration. A place at court was seen as essential for success, since political advancement depended upon a system of PATRONAGE which was ultimately controlled by the Queen. Banishment from court, on the other hand, was a disastrous disgrace.

The court was not always based in London. In order to charm and impress her subjects Elizabeth introduced 'progresses'. The whole court moved out of the capital for ten weeks each summer as a propaganda exercise which would enable Elizabeth to be seen by as many of her subjects as possible.

The final area of political influence was the Queen's household where appointments were given to trusted friends who were responsible for looking after Elizabeth on a daily basis.

Although the functions of the central institutions, the court and the royal household were separate and clearly defined, there was considerable overlap among the three. Many councillors were also courtiers. Some, like Robert Dudley through his position as Master of the Horse, were also members of the royal household. The success of the system depended upon Elizabeth's ability to maintain control over ambitious men, each backed by a group of supporters.

> **PATRONAGE**
> The rewarding of supporters with offices, titles and wealth.

■ 5A Patronage depended on a two-way traffic

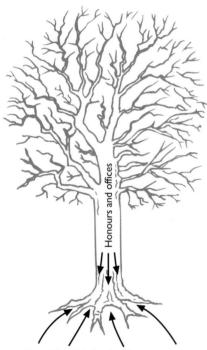

Honours and offices

Financial, political and military support

(Based on E.W. Ives, *Faction in Tudor England*, Historical Association, 1979)

SOURCE 5.1   C. Haigh, *Elizabeth I*, 1988, p. 87

Elizabeth attempted to control her councillors and her nobles by drawing them into a web of personal, even emotional relationships with her, in which she was by turns both Queen and coquette. ... Roughly one in five of the political heavyweights of England were thus under the regular influence of the Queen, subject to her tantrums and her temptings, but they were also well placed to exercise influence themselves.

This chapter will look at the different institutions of central government, the leading courtiers and councillors, and at how effectively Elizabeth kept control of the system, not least through her use of patronage.

A The Queen and her nobility

The hereditary nobles of England were men of great power and many had blood ties to the royal family. They had considerable influence in local and central government.

■ 5B The power network of the Duke of Norfolk

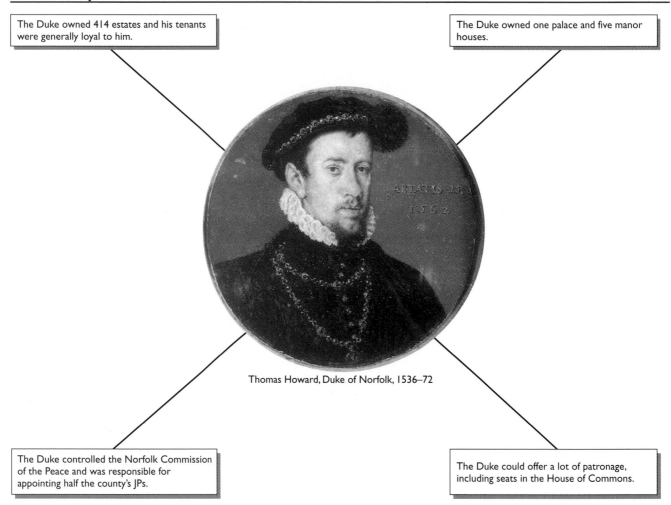

The Duke owned 414 estates and his tenants were generally loyal to him.

The Duke owned one palace and five manor houses.

Thomas Howard, Duke of Norfolk, 1536–72

The Duke controlled the Norfolk Commission of the Peace and was responsible for appointing half the county's JPs.

The Duke could offer a lot of patronage, including seats in the House of Commons.

Although the Duke of Norfolk was the most powerful of the nobles his situation was not unique. There were other families with vast wealth and influence throughout England: the Percy family in Northumberland and the Earls of Derby, Shrewsbury, Pembroke, Bedford, Westmorland and Cumberland. Elizabeth could not ignore such men, 'for nobles had come to be essential intermediaries; a county's representative at court and the court's representative at county level' (C. Haigh, *Elizabeth I*, 1988, p. 48).

Elizabeth's policy was to use the power of these men at a local level by appointing them to the post of Lord Lieutenant in their counties and to keep a careful eye on them by expecting them to spend some time at court. Lord lieutenants were gradually appointed and there was one in every shire by 1585.

This policy was not without its problems. At court nobles became involved in political debate, while direct access to Elizabeth gave them opportunity to push for personal advancement. And behind every great man at court there was an army of supporters stretching away to local level, each hoping that their fortune would rise along with their patron's. Yet Elizabeth, the source of honourable titles, offices, leases of crown lands, pensions, monopolies and grants, used her powers of patronage to ensure for herself not the support of a group or FACTION but the support of the entire noble class.

FACTION
A group of people which seeks personal and/or political objectives, such as political privileges, offices or the implementation of particular policies, and tries to deny such things to its rivals.

B The court

Sphere of influence
Centre of government and source of all political power.

Main functions
- It allowed the monarch to call leading subjects to counsel her, to arbitrate in their quarrels and to employ and reward their services and those of their dependents. Most Privy Councillors were also court or household officers.
- It displayed the power and magnificence of the monarch to impress foreign observers and reinforce obedience at home.

Frequency of meetings
Daily attendance upon the monarch.

■ 5C Life at court

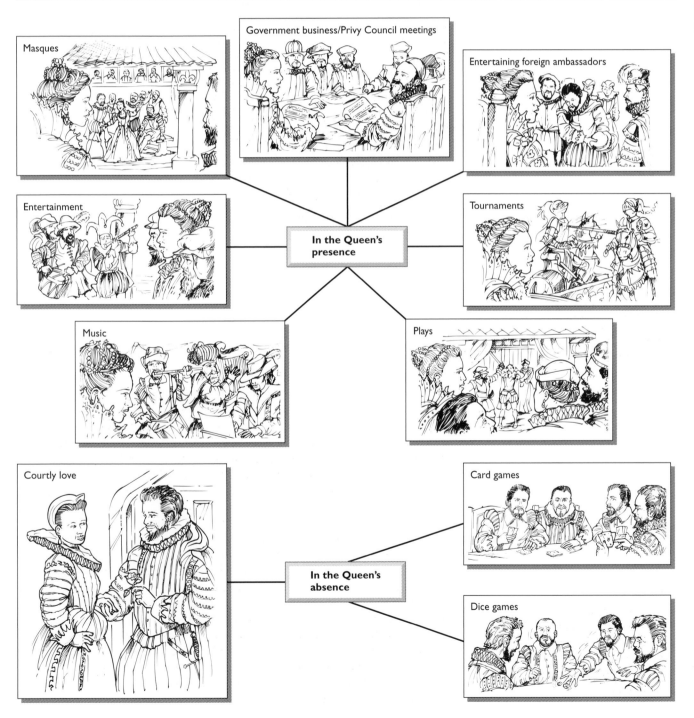

Masques

Government business/Privy Council meetings

Entertaining foreign ambassadors

Entertainment

In the Queen's presence

Tournaments

Music

Plays

Courtly love

In the Queen's absence

Card games

Dice games

Elizabeth's leading courtiers

FOCUS ROUTE

Copy and complete the following table, using the information given on pages 44–45 on the leading courtiers. Then, using the questions below as a starting point, make notes on life at court.

	Burghley	Hatton	Raleigh	Leicester	Essex	Walsingham	Robert Cecil
Origins							
Education							
Reasons for influence at court							
Offices							
Wealth/ patronage							
Allies/ enemies							
Downfall							

1 Which men's political advice did Elizabeth most trust?
2 Which men did Elizabeth promote because she enjoyed their company?
3 Why was Sir Walter Raleigh never made a councillor?
4 What did Elizabeth:
   a) respect in her courtiers?
   b) find it hard to forgive?
5 What do the careers of these men show about the importance of patronage?
6 What are the advantages and disadvantages of having the court as the centre of government?

DEVICE
The document that altered the line of succession so that Lady Jane Grey, not Mary Tudor, would follow Edward VI.

William Cecil, Lord Burghley
- **1520** Born in Lincolnshire to a gentry family. Educated at local grammar schools, then Cambridge University where he showed an enthusiasm for learning and an interest in moderate Protestantism
- **1541** Became a lawyer at Gray's Inn; married Mary Cheke who bore him a son before dying in 1543
- **1545** Married Mildred Cooke, the daughter of Anthony Cooke, a royal tutor and a Marian Exile. She bore him a son and two daughters
- **1547** Entered the service of the Duke of Somerset
- **1548** Promoted to Somerset's Secretary of State
- **1550** Survived Somerset's downfall and became a Privy Councillor under Northumberland. Appointed by Elizabeth to oversee her estates.
- **1553** Signed DEVICE then retired when Mary Tudor became Queen
- **1558** Made Elizabeth's Secretary of State
- **1561** Made Master of the Court of Wards
- **1571** Created Lord Burghley
- **1572** Made Lord Treasurer
- **1598** Died

Portrait of Lord Burghley by Marcus Gheeraerts the Younger, painted in 1585

Sir Christopher Hatton

- **1540** Born the son of a gentleman from Northamptonshire. Went to Oxford University and the Inner Temple without gaining any qualifications, but was gifted, industrious and loyal
- Elected MP for Northamptonshire. Attended court and acquired Elizabeth's friendship plus huge debts
- Appointed Gentleman of the Privy Chamber
- Appointed Captain of the Queen's Bodyguard
- **1557** Appointed Vice-chamberlain of the Household and a Privy Councillor
- **1587** Promoted to Lord Chancellor, despite his lack of legal training
- Rewarded by Elizabeth with lands, offices and the monopoly of the wine trade. Knighted and invested with the Order of the Garter
- Appointed Chancellor of Oxford University
- **1591** Died a bachelor at the age of 51

Sir Christopher Hatton, painted by Nicholas Hilliard

Sir Walter Raleigh

- **1552** Born to a gentry family in the West Country. Educated locally
- **1578** Given command of his first ship, *Falcon*. Served in France as a volunteer in the Protestant army and commanded a company in Ireland
- **1581** Returned to court, where his 'dashing and flamboyant' nature caught Elizabeth's attention. He became a close favourite, but was resented by Hatton
- **1585–88** Knighted by Elizabeth, made Captain of the Queen's Bodyguard and granted vast estates in England and Ireland plus the monopoly of playing cards
- Appointed Vice-Admiral of Devon and Cornwall. Queen invested in his privateering expeditions against Spain
- **1588** Named Virginia in Elizabeth's honour and introduced potatoes and tobacco to court
- **1595** Sent to the Tower for getting Elizabeth Throckmorton, one of the Queen's maids of honour, pregnant. Although eventually reinstated at court and entrusted with various diplomatic missions, his days as a trusted courtier were over

Sir Walter Raleigh painted in 1588. This portrait is attributed to 'H' (*detail*)

Robert Dudley, Earl of Leicester

- Fifth son of the late Duke of Northumberland
- **1555** Released from the Tower where he had been imprisoned for his part in his father's conspiracy to put Lady Jane Grey on the throne in 1553
- **1557** Fought against the French
- **1558** Appointed Master of the Horse by Elizabeth. Early rumours of a romantic attachment to Elizabeth despite his marriage to Amy Robsart
- **1560** Amy Robsart found dead in suspicious circumstances. Rumours grew that he and Elizabeth would marry
- **1562** Dudley given large estates and export licences followed by a seat on the council. Clashed frequently with Burghley
- **1564** Created Earl of Leicester
- **1567** Secretly married the Countess of Essex
- **1585** Appointed Lieutenant-General of the army in the Netherlands
- **1588** Died

Robert Dudley, Earl of Leicester, painted c. 1575 by an unknown artist (*detail*)

Robert Devereux, 2nd Earl of Essex

- **1567** Born. Inherited title aged ten. His mother married the Earl of Leicester on his father's death
- Very privileged childhood; grew up reckless, vain and extravagant
- **1587** Fully established as Elizabeth's favourite courtier. Made Master of the Horse and given the monopoly over sweet wines
- **1591** Married the daughter of Francis Walsingham and temporarily fell out of favour
- **1593** Commanded the force sent to assist Henry of Navarre
- **1593** Became a Privy Councillor
- **1597** Defeated Spanish navy at Cadiz
- **1598** Appointed Master of the Ordnance and Earl Marshal
- **1599** Appointed to command army being sent to Ireland. Disobeyed orders by attacking Munster and appointing his own favourites instead of marching against Tyrone in Ulster. Negotiated a truce with Tyrone and then returned to London, where he burst into the Queen's bedchamber. He was placed under house arrest and dismissed from all his offices
- **1601** Led an uprising to capture Elizabeth and force her to restore himself and his followers to their rightful offices. Arrested, tried and executed on 20 February

Robert Devereux, painted in 1597 by Marcus Gheeraerts the Younger (*detail*)

Sir Francis Walsingham

- **1532** Born to a lawyer from an old Norfolk family. Educated at Cambridge, then studied law
- A fervent Protestant, he spent Mary's reign on the continent gaining a knowledge of European affairs and languages
- **1558** Entered Parliament as MP for Lyme Regis; recommended to Sir William Cecil
- **1570** Appointed ambassador to Paris
- **1573** Promoted to Secretary of State with special responsibility for foreign affairs
- His bluntness and extreme religious convictions caused friction with Elizabeth, but she respected him and made him Chancellor of the Order of the Garter and Chancellor of the Duchy of Lancaster
- **1590** Died

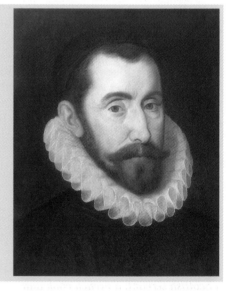

Portrait of Sir Francis Walsingham, painted by John de Critz the Elder (*detail*)

Robert Cecil

- **1563** Born, the younger son of Burghley. He was a sickly child who studied hard. He was educated at St John's College, Cambridge, at Gray's Inn and then at the Sorbonne, Paris
- Elected to Parliament as MP for Westminster
- Used by Elizabeth as her unofficial government spokesman in the Commons
- Carried out many of Walsingham's duties after his death, but early promotion prevented by Essex's dislike of him
- **1591** Appointed to the Privy Council
- **1596** Appointed as Elizabeth's Secretary of State after organising the Cadiz expedition, despite being challenged to a duel by Essex
- **1599** Appointed Master of the Court of Wards and given the right to receive duties on imported luxury materials such as satins and silks
- **1603** Supervised the arrangements for the succession of James VI of Scotland on Elizabeth's death
- **1612** Died

Portrait of Robert Cecil, 1st Earl of Salisbury, painted in 1602 by John de Critz the Elder (*detail*)

Reinventing the Earl of Leicester

Robert Dudley has traditionally been seen as the 'evil genius' of Elizabeth's court, an arrogant and wilful man whose first wife died in mysterious circumstances and whose command of English forces in the Netherlands was a military fiasco. However, his household account books have survived and they offer a revealing insight into his lifestyle. He emerges as a prominent patron of overseas exploration and trade, Puritanism, literature and science; a man whose household brimmed with talent.

SOURCE 5.2 A summary of the Earl of Leicester's accounts for 1558–85

December 1558
Received gift of Kew house from the Queen, with a household of 30 to 50 men. Many of his officers had been in the household of his parents, the Duke and Duchess of Northumberland.

April 1560
Granted an export licence for wool by the Queen, worth £3,000 a year. Loans taken out in the City from merchants. (December 1558–89 his expenditure totalled £2,100, including £350 spent on clothes and £109 on gambling.)

1563
Granted Kenilworth Castle and its landed estate. Kew sold and Paget Place near Temple Bar purchased.

1578
Wanstead House, near to Greenwich Palace, purchased. Personal household now numbered one hundred, many of whom went on to hold offices at court often as a result of Leicester's influence as Master of the Horse. His household was fairly cosmopolitan, and included a Scottish servant, a French cook and a French secretary.

1585
2s 6d given to the hospital, labourers on the highway, and three poor women at Highgate
12d given to 'three poore women at North Hall that were wedeng in the garden'
£2 given to the parson of Abingdon to distribute to the poor of the town
2s to a 'poor man at Kyllingworth that had his house burned'
£5 to the Puritan Thomas Cartwright whom Leicester had appointed Master of his hospital
£5 to Humphrey Fenn, the suspended Puritan minister of Coventry

SOURCE 5.3 Leicester remodelled the medieval Kenilworth Castle to create a luxurious palace; this engraving was made in 1575

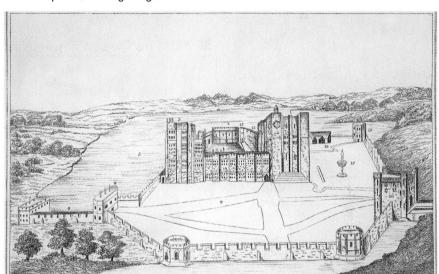

His accounts also show that Leicester was interested in health. He frequently made visits to the spa at Buxton and was a keen tennis player and hunter. He was not a great drinker, although he chose his wines carefully. His shopping list included oranges, lemons and other fruit; and instructions to his cook emphasised the importance of herbs and salads. Regular payments were made for flowers to be placed in his rooms.

When he died at the early age of 56, probably from overwork, he left debts of £86,203. Despite making economies, such as covering cushions with fabrics from his wife's old dresses, he never really lived within his income; an income which was based almost entirely on the Queen's generosity. Yet, this did not prevent Leicester himself from giving generously.

ACTIVITY

What can you learn from Source 5.2 about:

a) Leicester's personal interests and attitudes
b) how important a display of wealth was for a member of the nobility?

TALKING POINTS

1 Why is it difficult for historians to build an accurate picture of the Elizabethan court?
2 How can the discovery of a book of household accounts be useful?

C The Queen's household

Sphere of influence

Access to the Queen's suites (Privy Chamber) was the key to power and status. The Privy Chamber was largely staffed by women because Elizabeth was female; had she been a man, it would have been staffed by men. Many were the wives or daughters of leading politicians, such as Cecil, Knollys and Lord Clinton.

Main function

To attend the monarch and provide her with personal attendants and companions. Those entitled to 'bouge of court', the right to be fed at the monarch's expense, included all household officers and servants, and their servants.

■ 5D The Queen's household

SOURCE 5.4 A day in the life of the Privy Chamber

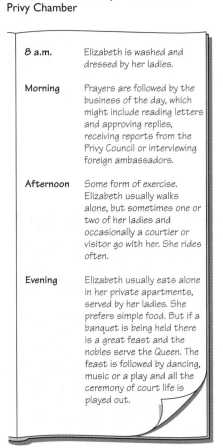

8 a.m.	Elizabeth is washed and dressed by her ladies.
Morning	Prayers are followed by the business of the day, which might include reading letters and approving replies, receiving reports from the Privy Council or interviewing foreign ambassadors.
Afternoon	Some form of exercise. Elizabeth usually walks alone, but sometimes one or two of her ladies and occasionally a courtier or visitor go with her. She rides often.
Evening	Elizabeth usually eats alone in her private apartments, served by her ladies. She prefers simple food. But if a banquet is being held there is a great feast and the nobles serve the Queen. The feast is followed by dancing, music or a play and all the ceremony of court life is played out.

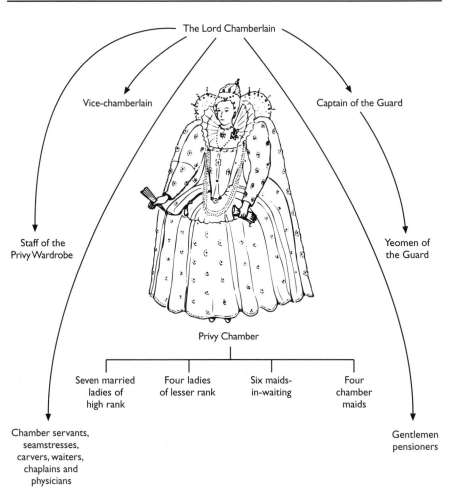

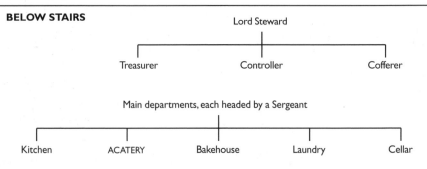

ACATERY
Store room for provisions

SOURCE 5.5   C. Hibbert, *The Virgin Queen*, 1990, p. 108

On feast days, when the Queen dined in public, visitors to court were permitted to see how well-rehearsed the ceremonial was. Escorted from Chapel by her guard in their black and red uniforms with her coat of arms embroidered in silver gilt on the back, she marched towards the Dining Hall behind Councillors bearing her sceptres and her sword of state. Attended by her Lord Chamberlain, the Master of the House, the Lord Chancellor and the Lord High Admiral, she sat down alone at her table; and then her ladies took their seats at another table, ready to watch her closely throughout the meal so that, as soon as she showed herself ready to rise, which she was likely to do even before the second course was served, they might rise themselves and make two deep curtseys. Grace was said by two bishops; and after this an attendant brought in a gold basin and a towel. The Queen ceremoniously removed her rings, handed them to the Lord Chamberlain, washed her hands, dried them, then put on the rings again. After the meal there was dancing; and, while this was in lively progress, the Queen called up to her, one after the other, those to whom she wished to talk. Having spoken to the last of them she stood up, raised a long white hand in valediction and was escorted from the hall back to her Privy Chamber. And here, late though it might be, as often as not she settled down to work.

Before embarking upon an evening of festivities, she would often have a rest about six o'clock; for, although her energy seemed never to flag in the hunting field or in the council chamber; or when appearing informally or in state before her people, she did weary of an evening at court when there was nothing of particular interest to engage her attention. In the privacy of her own chamber she amused herself with card games, chess or tables, a kind of backgammon, or by playing with her pets. She was said to have 'loved little dogs, singing birds, parrots and apes'.

SOURCE 5.6   Queen Elizabeth in her Privy Chamber

D Central institutions

ACTIVITY

The Privy Council, Parliament and the law courts each had clearly defined functions, yet, in practice, their daily workloads were often surprisingly similar. Ten of the following examples are taken from the proceedings of the council, four from the proceedings of Parliament, one from the Exchequer, one from Chancery, one from the Court of Requests, two from the household, one from the court and one from the Court of Star Chamber.

Read about these institutions on pages 50–53, then try to match the examples to the correct institution.

1 An order for the release of Thomas Watson, the former Bishop of Lincoln, in 1574
2 A summons leading to a large fine against the Earl of Hertford for marrying Lady Catherine Grey without the Queen's permission
3 A suit made to the Queen on behalf of the astrologer John Dee by the Countess of Warwick, 1592
4 A request from George Gilpin, to his patron Robert Dudley, for the speedy dispatch of a grant of land
5 A request to the Queen to marry Eric of Sweden
6 An order to the commissioners for supplies in Wiltshire, Dorset, Sussex and Hampshire to provide immediate help in supplying the Queen's navy
7 A petition from tenants against their landlord who was raising their rents unreasonably
8 A letter sent to the regent of Scotland promoting good relations between the two countries
9 An appeal by a married woman for a marriage settlement which would enable her to keep her own property
10 A discussion about the failure of individuals in Middlesex to contribute to a forced loan, 1597
11 A case of alleged depopulation caused by enclosures in the Midlands
12 An Act for the Queen's safety
13 An arrangement for the payment of troops who had been fighting in the Low Countries against the Spanish
14 A consideration of the case against Mary, Queen of Scots, resulting in a recommendation for her execution
15 An accusation of treason against Andreas van Mellor, a prisoner in the Tower, for plotting against the Queen
16 A legislative programme to deal with the Catholic threat, 1581
17 A request for a subsidy tax
18 A request from an Irish soldier for a daily allowance
19 A case between a Scottish merchant and a Norfolk gentleman over a shipwreck on the Norfolk coast
20 A proposal from the Queen to meet with the Catholic Mary, Queen of Scots, even though this would infuriate Protestants, 1562
21 A request from the University of Cambridge to keep its privileges.

Turn to page 300 for the answers.

The Privy Council

Sphere of influence
The chief administrative and executive body of the realm.

Main functions
- To advise the monarch on policy.
- To ensure orderly government and the security of the state. To this end it could use torture during its investigations and often diverted legal cases to other courts.
- To consider petitions from private individuals.

Frequency of meetings
A maximum of twenty members met three times a week at the start of the reign and daily by the 1590s.

Secretary of State
The Queen's principal adviser, the Secretary of State was expected to deal with any state matter or administrative problem that arose. William Cecil held the post from 1558 to 1573. Sir Francis Walsingham shared the post with William Davison from 1573 until Davison's dismissal in 1587 and then continued alone until 1590. Robert Cecil and his father shared the post from 1591 to 1596 when Robert Cecil took over officially. The principal secretary was in continual contact with the Queen and, as all her correspondence passed through him, he controlled written access to her.

Lord Chamberlain
The Lord Chamberlain ran the household, supervised appointments and controlled access to the Privy Chamber.

Vice-chamberlain
The Vice-chamberlain assisted the Lord Chamberlain.

Lord Treasurer
The Lord Treasurer was responsible for keeping England solvent. He administered ordinary revenues and kept government expenditure within limits. The post was held by the Marquis of Winchester until 1572, when Burghley took over.

Keeper of the Great Seal
This was an honorary office and gave the holder control over the physical means by which documents were legalised.

Comptroller of the Household
The Household accountant

Lord High Admiral
The Lord High Admiral commanded all naval personnel, adjudicated in disputes relating to matters at sea and appointed officers and assigned them their duties.

Chancellor of the Duchy of Lancaster
The Chancellor was responsible for administering the estates and revenues of the Duchy of Lancaster. In 1559 Sir Ambrose Cave's duties also included administering the Oath of Supremacy, raising a militia and adjudicating in cases of murder, burglary and other felonies.

■ Learning trouble spot

William Cecil was created Lord Burghley in 1571 and may be referred to by either name. If you are writing about Cecil/Burghley it is best to refer to him as Cecil before 1571 and Burghley after 1571.

Similarly, Robert Dudley was created Earl of Leicester in 1564.

VETO The Queen's right to reject an Act of Parliament	
BILL A draft copy of a proposed law	
KNIGHT A gentleman who represented a shire/county in Parliament	
BURGESS A Member of Parliament for a borough/town	
PEER A member of the nobility	

Parliament

Sphere of influence

Unlike Parliament today, it was not the most important element of government. It was controlled by the Queen through her power to imprison members, her use of the royal VETO, and her delaying of BILLS; and by the council who arranged the business of the House of Commons. The Queen alone could summon or dismiss Parliament when she saw fit.

Main functions

- To pass laws (legislation)
- To raise taxes

Frequency of meetings

Parliament did not meet regularly and when it did meet it was only for short periods. During Elizabeth's reign there were only thirteen sessions in 44 years.

Composition

About 462 men sat in the House of Commons. Two KNIGHTS from each county and two BURGESSES from each borough attended. They were usually elected through nomination by the crown or by a prominent nobleman or gentleman. Unlike today, therefore, members of the House of Commons were not democratically elected, there were no political parties and only the middle and upper classes were represented. The PEERS of the realm sat in the House of Lords, which was traditionally more important than the House of Commons.

SOURCE 5.7   A contemporary drawing of Elizabeth and her Parliament

■ 5F Elizabethan Parliaments

Parliament	Dates of sessions
1559	25 January–8 May
1563–67	12 January–10 April 1563 (I) 30 September 1566–2 January 1567 (II)
1571	2 April–29 May
1572–81	8 May–30 June 1572 (I) 8 February–15 March 1576 (II) 16 January–18 March 1581 (III)
1584–85	23 November 1584–29 March 1585
1586–87	29 October 1586–23 March 1587
1589	4 February–29 March
1593	19 February–10 April
1597–98	24 October 1597–9 February 1598
1601	27 October–19 December

Law courts

Sphere of influence
Variable.

Main function
To preserve law and order in England.

Frequency of meetings
Variable.

Composition
The highest officials were appointed by the crown, while lesser officials were appointed by their heads of department and usually came from the gentry class.

LAW OF EQUITY
It relied on principles of justice to correct or supplement COMMON or STATUTE LAW.

COMMON LAW
The unwritten law of England

STATUTE LAW
Written law based on Acts of Parliament

FEUDAL DUES
Payments traditionally made to the crown, for example when an heir came into his inheritance or a knight's daughter married

■ 5G The law courts

Chancery	The Court of Star Chamber	The Council of the North
Applied the LAW OF EQUITY, not the COMMON LAW or STATUTE LAW, and was therefore more flexible. It issued all legal documents.	This was the Queen's council sitting as a court. Most of its cases involved breaches of public order or powerful nobles who acted above the law.	Had wide administrative powers, and its main purpose was to enforce the policies of central government in the regions.
The Queen's Bench	**The Court of Common Pleas**	**The Court of Requests**
Criminal and civil cases were often referred here from lower courts.	Heard suits between subjects (civil suits)	Attracted less well-off parties as it dealt with tenants' rights as well as other civil suits
The Duchy of Lancaster	**The Court of Wards**	**The Exchequer**
Administered the revenue from its own lands	Was responsible for FEUDAL DUES	Dealt with revenue cases

■ Learning trouble spot

Central government is an area where the unwary student can lose marks in an essay by using incorrect terminology. An answer which talks about the 'Privy Council' when the question asks how Elizabeth controlled 'Parliament' is clearly inaccurate, even though it might be clear from the content that the student really is talking about Parliament. The roles and functions of leading political figures also adds to the complexities. So, remember:

1 • A courtier attended Elizabeth's court.
   • A councillor sat on Elizabeth's Privy Council.
   • An MP was elected to Parliament.

   If an individual had more than one role he was most likely a courtier and a councillor or an MP and a JP, although members of the council could sit in Parliament and usually did, in either the House of Commons or the House of Lords.

2 The word government is an umbrella term which covers all the institutions which ran the country as well as the monarch. You need to make it clear which arm of government you are referring to by using its specific title, although this is sometimes difficult because:

   • the council often acted as a 'clearing house' and was therefore the first port of call for petitions, requests, etc.
   • Tudor government was very personal. The nature of patronage meant that appeals were made to an individual rather than to an institution
   • the government was run by a small group of men, many of whom held more than one office. As a result there was often considerable overlap between different areas of government.

3 Essays about Elizabeth's government cover a long period of time. In most areas of government there was a high point, a successful period in the 1570s and 1580s when Elizabeth was at the peak of her powers and her councillors were politically experienced. In contrast, by the 1590s, Elizabeth was an old woman and most of her original councillors had died. It is therefore important to remember an obvious point: that in a reign lasting 45 years, things are bound to change.

SOURCE 5.8 Robert Naunton, a former servant of the Earl of Essex, writing in the 1630s

A principal note of her reign will be that she ruled much by faction and parties, which she herself both made, upheld and weakened, as her own great judgement advised.

SOURCE 5.9 E. W. Ives, *Faction in Tudor England*, 1979

Of course it took some years for the rules to be accepted or indeed for the Queen to transform instinctive caution and the dislike of commitment into a conscious policy. Cecil, Leicester and the other leaders spent the 1560s manoeuvring very much in the old style.

SOURCE 5.10 A. G. R. Smith, *The Government of Elizabethan England*, 1967, p. 111

The Essex–Cecil struggle was accompanied by, and indeed was partly the cause of, the decline in political morality which was a conspicuous feature of Elizabeth's last years.

Elizabeth has frequently been credited with maintaining a politically stable central government by creating a court where she exercised control by awarding offices and favours. In this way, she could control rival factions.

In recent years, historians have played down the impact of faction at least until the 1590s. There is general agreement that, until its decline in the 1590s, central government under Elizabeth was successful and that the Queen and her ministers provided firm direction. Elizabeth exploited the mystique of monarchy through her use of court rituals and progresses, and on a more mundane level kept in daily contact with the work of her councillors. That she was aided in government by statesmen of outstanding political abilities is also a testament to the fact that she selected the right men for the job.

This picture of a queen in firm control of government comes, however, from the high point of Elizabethan government during the 1570s and 1580s. It is hardly surprising that the picture was different at the beginning and the end of her reign.

By the 1590s Elizabeth was getting old. She was also deprived of many of her most prominent ministers and servants, and was facing new political, financial and social problems for which she had no new answers.

Faced with the twin disadvantages of her gender and the political ambitions of powerful nobles and councillors, it is difficult to see what choice Elizabeth had other than to ensure that as the mistress of faction she was able to maintain a balance of counsel and keep policy options open. For the first 30 years of her reign she successfully courted her politicians and entranced her people, making herself the guarantee of international safety and national stability.

ACTIVITY

This chapter should have helped you to understand that, although Elizabeth's government was composed of many institutions, the running of government was undertaken by a small group of individuals who had power and influence in more than one area. The key factor in determining an individual's influence was the extent to which he had access to the Queen.

In a group, choose one of the personalities described in this chapter. Work out the areas of government he had access to and outline his possible duties and responsibilities. Present your information to the rest of the class, then compile a chart showing the roles of all seven men using notes you have made from other groups' presentations.

KEY POINTS FROM CHAPTER 5: How did central government work?

1 The Tudor system of government was personal. It was based on the monarch. In order to enforce policy and maintain control Elizabeth was dependent on the noble and gentry classes. She kept these people loyal through the use of the court and a system of patronage.
2 In addition to the court and the royal household the main institutions of central government were the Privy Council, Parliament and the law courts. Although each had separate, clearly defined functions, their work overlapped.
3 The running of the government was undertaken by a small group of individuals, such as William Cecil and Robert Dudley, who held power or influence in more than one area. The key factor in determining an individual's influence was the extent to which he had access to the Queen.
4 Central government only worked when Elizabeth kept ambitious politicians in check. She did this well during the high point of her reign in the 1570s and 1580s. But in recent years, historians have increasingly criticised her use of patronage and faction to play off rival courtiers against one another during the 1590s.

6

Was Elizabeth in control of her Privy Council?

To a great extent the success of Elizabeth's government depended on the calibre of her senior advisers and on her ability to listen to all their views and select the most appropriate or reject them all. To be able to do this, while maintaining loyalty and ultimate authority was – and still is – a true test of political leadership.

SOURCE 6.1 W. MacCaffrey, *Elizabeth I*, 1993, p. 38

The first task and the first test of the new monarch was the choice of council. How effective this new body was depended on the monarch. It could be a finely tuned instrument of power or a hot bed of faction. Under Mary it had too often been the latter.

Elizabeth's predecessors used different methods to try to keep control of their ministers and their council. Henry VII selected men of ability, loyalty and experience rather than automatically choosing nobles from the traditional ruling classes. Henry VIII, who showed little interest in the day-to-day running of government, preferred to leave council business first to Thomas Wolsey and then to Thomas Cromwell. Under these two ministers, the Privy Council became more streamlined, efficient and business-like, but power politics proved to be more important than administrative success and Henry VIII sentenced both men to death. During the reign of Edward VI the council's efficiency declined and it became a playground for rival political factions, dominated first by the Duke of Somerset and then by the Duke of Northumberland. In 1553, Mary Tudor appointed a very large council. Some historians think this hampered the decision-making process. However, others argue that she relied on an inner council and her household servants and, although councillors often held different viewpoints, these differences of opinion did not hamper decision-making or the execution of policy. The work of William Paget in developing the efficiency of the Privy Council during Mary's reign meant that the institution passed on to Elizabeth was in good shape; it also highlighted the importance of selecting able ministers.

This chapter will assess the Privy Council through the following subsections:

A The composition and work of the council (p. 56)

B How important was William Cecil? (p. 57)

C How was the council divided? (pp. 58–61)

D Review: Was Elizabeth in control of her Privy Council? (p. 62)

A The composition and work of the council

ACTIVITY

What does Chart 6A tell you about Elizabeth's
a) desire for continuity from Mary's reign
b) desire for councillors that she could trust completely?

FOCUS ROUTE

Using the information in Chapter 5 and pages 56–62, make notes to answer the following questions.

1 Although Elizabeth's council numbered almost twenty, most business was conducted by a small professional inner ring. Which of her councillors were permanent members of this group?
2 What characteristics did this group share?
3 What were the three main functions of the council?
4 What did the council spend much of its time discussing?

■ 6A Elizabeth's council in 1558

Councillors who had served under Edward VI and Mary Tudor

Earl of Derby
Earl of Shrewsbury
• *High-ranking members of Mary's council, who were not expected to attend often*

Earl of Arundel
Earl of Pembroke
• *Powerful nobles and experienced politicians who had sat on Mary's council*

Lord Howard of Effingham
• *Elizabeth's great-uncle, who sat on Mary's council*

Lord Admiral Clinton
• *A member of Edward's council*

Marquis of Winchester
• *Lord Treasurer since 1550*

Sir William Cecil
• *Served the Duke of Somerset and the Duke of Northumberland as Secretary*

New councillors

Sir Richard Sackville
Sir Francis Knollys
• *Relatives of Anne Boleyn who held office under Edward*

Sir Nicolas Bacon
• *Attorney of the Court of Wards and Cecil's brother-in-law*

Earl of Bedford
• *The son of one of Henry VIII's courtiers*

Marquis of Northampton
• *Catherine Parr's brother*

Sir Edward Rogers
• *A member of Edward's Privy Chamber*

Sir Ambrose Cave
• *Connected to Cecil*

ACTIVITY

1 Which of the items in Source 6.2 could be classified as public matters and which as private matters?
2 Was discussing private matters a disadvantage? If so, why did the council continue to hear them?
3 At what times in the reign would the council have been faced with a completely different agenda than the one in Source 6.2?

SOURCE 6.2 The council agenda for 5 July 1574

Present
The Lord Treasurer, the Lord Chamberlain, the Lord Admiral, the Secretary, the Comptroller of the Household and the Earl of Leicester

Business
1 *Adjudicate on a private quarrel between Thomas Palmer and Thomas Stoughton*
2 *Arrange the journey of Count Swevingham, a Spanish agent, to the West Country*
3 *Decide on reprisals against Portugal for losses suffered by John Sambitores*
4 *Discuss a case involving the non-payment of marine insurance*
5 *Agree on orders to be sent to the commissioners for musters in Worcestershire*
6 *Make provision for the trial of two cases of murder*
7 *Order the preparation of 200 troops for service in Ireland*
8 *Consider two complaints brought by the French ambassador*
9 *Review the imprisonment of one Prestall, inmate of the Queen's Bench jail*
10 *Investigate the treatment of a Scottish refugee*
11 *Order the manning and provisioning of all the Queen's ships*
12 *Send warrants for payment of a master of the works and the Master Carpenter at Portsmouth*

FOCUS ROUTE

Use the information on Sir William Cecil in Chapters 5 and 6 to make notes about his contribution to Elizabethan government. These notes could take the form of a list of Cecil's qualities and achievements, with evidence to back up each one.

Cecil's great influence with Elizabeth was based on his fine intellect, his experience of managing people and his awareness of his own limitations. He recognised that it was his duty to speak his mind when he did not agree with the Queen, but he also knew that once he had given his opinion he had to enforce the Queen's decision whether or not he agreed with it. As might be expected, as the reign progressed Cecil developed strategies to persuade Elizabeth that his policies were best.

■ 6B Cecil's contribution to Elizabethan government

5 Contemporaries were in awe of Burghley's work rate. 'His labour and care ... were so incessant and his study so great as, in cases of necessity, he turned neither for meat, sleep or rest, till his business was brought to some end. This industry ... caused all his friends to pity him and his very servants to admire him' (A.G.R. Smith, *The Anonymous Life of William Cecil, Lord Burghley*, 1990, pp. 66–68).

4 After 1585, Burghley had to cope with the financial and administrative burden caused by the war with Spain, while struggling with his own declining health.

1 English intervention in Scotland in 1560 secured the success of the Scottish Reformation and the subsequent expulsion of French troops from Scotland. Cecil pushed this policy despite Elizabeth's reluctance to aid the Scottish rebels.

2 Spanish treasure ships on their way to pay Spanish soldiers in the Netherlands were seized while sheltering in ports along the coast of Devon and Cornwall in 1568. The seizure challenged the power of Spain and firmly established Cecil as Elizabeth's chief adviser. Cecil had argued that, as the money would not legally belong to the Spanish until it arrived in the Netherlands and therefore technically still belonged to the lenders (Genoese bankers), Elizabeth was free to 'borrow it'. Cecil was created Lord Burghley in 1571.

3 After his appointment as Lord Treasurer in 1572 historical opinion about his role is divided. MacCaffrey sees Burghley as 'the dynamo which kept the routine business of government running smoothly and effectively' (1993, p. 456); while Conyers Read (1960, p. 85) argues that, although he assumed responsibility for the national finances, he was primarily hereafter a councillor. What is clear, however, is that Burghley continued to undertake immense quantities of work and was responsible for the two main decisions of this period: the sending of English troops to help the Protestant rebels in the Netherlands in their battle with Spain, and the dispatching of Mary, Queen of Scots' death warrant.

■ 6C Cecil's achievements

drafting all Elizabeth's correspondence with foreign ambassadors and agents, particularly between 1558 and 1572, when he was principal adviser and executor for foreign affairs

continuing a prudent economic policy – cutting government expenditure, saving from ordinary revenues and selling crown lands – which ensured that England was able to meet the costs of war from the 1580s onwards and to end the reign with a comparatively small debt

creating an intelligence service at home and abroad

By the time of his death in 1598, Cecil had been instrumental in ...

managing the business of the House of Commons and the House of Lords through organisation and attention to detail

providing effective methods of administration for the Privy Council which, as the centre of government, concerned itself with everything that went on in the country

creating a propaganda system which ensured public acceptance of Elizabeth's political regime and her Religious Settlement

**Mary, Queen of Scots,
Queen of Scotland 1542–67**

- Mary inherited the Scottish throne in 1542, one week after the death of her father, James V. Mary, Queen of Scots, was sent to France in 1548 to be educated and married the heir to the French throne. A regency was established by her French mother, Mary of Guise, in 1554.
- Mary was widowed in 1560 at the age of eighteen. She returned to Scotland as Queen in 1561. If Elizabeth did not marry, Mary had a very strong claim to the English throne: her grandmother was Henry VIII's sister. Mary's desire to remarry therefore concerned Elizabeth and led to direct communication between the two queens. Elizabeth even offered Robert Dudley as a suitable candidate.
- Mary married Lord Henry Darnley in 1565. Darnley was also descended from Mary's Tudor grandmother, strengthening Mary's claim to the English throne. She was also regarded by some English Catholics as the natural Queen of England. The birth of a son only served to make Mary an even more credible successor.
- Darnley was murdered in 1567. Mary's subsequent marriage to the chief suspect, the Earl of Bothwell, turned Scotland against her. She was overthrown and imprisoned, but later escaped.
- Mary arrived in England in 1568, hoping that Elizabeth would help her regain her throne.

C How was the council divided?

■ 6D The issues which caused divisions in the council

1562 Elizabeth and the council disagree over her wish to meet Mary, Queen of Scots. Sir Nicholas Bacon says, 'It is very evident that no hope of good and great fear of ill is to be conceived by this interview, and therefore for my part I cannot allow it.' In the end Elizabeth does not go.

1567 The council splits over Elizabeth's decision to marry Catholic Archduke Charles of Austria. Elizabeth's councillors clearly see that it is their role to speak their minds when offering advice. But they also know that in the end Elizabeth will make her own decision. Leicester works desperately to prevent the match, while Norfolk, Sussex and Cecil are in favour of it. The division causes Elizabeth to hesitate and then reject Charles.

1569–70 The council meets frequently to discuss the dangers arising from the arrival of Mary, Queen of Scots, in England, the English Catholics and the threat from France and Spain. The council is divided between those, such as Cecil and Bacon, who want to establish alliances with foreign Protestants and those, such as Leicester and Arundel, who favour an agreement with Mary and France. Once again, Elizabeth shows that she is keen to hear advice from her council but that she is under no obligation to follow it.

1578 One of the main issues which divides the council is whether to give military aid to the Protestant rebels in the Netherlands in their fight against Spain. The split, with Leicester and Walsingham urging intervention and Burghley counselling against it, develops into a personal contest for political power as the council forms two distinct groups. 'We must all dutifully bear with her Majesty's offence for the time, not despairing, but howsoever she missliketh matters at one time yet, at another time she will alter her sharpness, especially when she is persuaded that we all mean truly for her and her surety' (Burghley to Walsingham). However, Leicester has to wait another seven years for Elizabeth's approval of military intervention, when it looks as if the whole of the Netherlands is about to fall into Spanish hands.

1579–81 Negotiations are held over the proposed marriage between Elizabeth and the French Duke of Alençon.
There is considerable public hostility towards this match and the campaign of hostile sermons is probably orchestrated by Leicester and Walsingham. The majority of councillors are opposed and in October 1579 report that they recommend neither for nor against the marriage. A furious Elizabeth threatens to create four new Catholic councillors and then asks the council for their advice again. Sussex, Burghley and Hundson (the Queen's cousin) again refuse to oppose the marriage, while the opposition led by Leicester continues to whip up public opinion. Despite exchanging betrothal rings in November 1581, Elizabeth eventually rejects Alençon, telling him that her people are against the marriage.

1586 The council pushes Elizabeth to call Parliament, so that it can sanction a death warrant for Mary, Queen of Scots. Burghley makes no secret of the fact that he is doing this to exert pressure on the Queen: 'We stick upon Parliament, which her Majesty disliketh, but which we do all persist.' Walsingham then claims to have heard about a plot to blow up Elizabeth with gunpowder under her bed to convince her that she is in danger while Mary lives. After Elizabeth has reluctantly signed the death warrant in 1587, the Secretary William Davison dispatches it without permission, for which he is sent to the Tower.

1590s A new generation of politicians has matured, led by Sir Robert Cecil and the Earl of Essex. Each commands a party of supporters at a local and a parliamentary level. Elizabeth is aware of Essex's huge ambitions and ensures that political vacancies go to Cecil and his followers. Essex demands that councillors make it clear whether they are for or against him. Lord Grey says, 'My Lord of Essex has forced me to declare myself either his only, or friend to Mr Secretary Cecil.' This polarises the council into two factions. Essex's execution, after his uprising in 1601, leaves the Cecil faction supreme.

FOCUS ROUTE

1 Construct a timeline showing the main problems facing the council and, where relevant, the opposing factions. Are there any common themes or recurring problems? If so, why would these so concern the council?
2 List the strategies Elizabeth used to deal with differences of opinion amongst her councillors and give examples of where she used them.
3 Make notes on how serious you think the divisions among the council were (try listing them in order of seriousness). Is there any way in which these divisions could have been an advantage to Elizabeth? Do these differences mean that Elizabeth was not in control?
4 Using your timeline, and what you know of the routine business of the council, write a paragraph for or against the view that personal rivalry undermined the daily running of central government.

■ 6E The tactics Elizabeth employed to control her council

Elizabeth participated in discussions to prevent the council agreeing on formal advice which she would later reject. She refused to deal with the council as a whole, only discussing policy with small groups.

Elizabeth kept accurate notes, which she used to question councillors closely and catch them out.

Elizabeth consulted with men outside the council, particularly foreign ambassadors.

Elizabeth promoted divisions among her councillors, encouraging them to compete for rewards.

Elizabeth displayed anger and even violence:
● exclusion from court (Leicester and Walsingham)
● house arrest (Arundel)
● imprisonment (Davison and Croft)
● execution (Norfolk and Essex).

Elizabeth displayed affection:
'God be thanked, her blasts be not the storms of other princes, though they be very sharp sometimes to those she loves best. Everyman must render to her their due, and the most bounden the most of all' (Leicester to Burghley, 1573).

FOCUS ROUTE

Use the following questions as a basis for your notes.

1 Why had Burghley and Leicester become rivals by the 1570s?
2 How far was government stability in the 1590s threatened by the power struggle between Robert Cecil and the Earl of Essex?

Case study 1: Rivalries at the start of the reign

William Cecil, Lord Burghley
Discreet and loyal, Cecil's promotion was based on merit and political ability. He was a cautious and devout man, and in foreign policy he was determined to assert English independence, maintain English security and above all avoid going to war unless national interest demanded it. He saw Dudley as a mere adventurer whose sole aim was to enrich his friends and gain power for himself.

Robert Dudley, Earl of Leicester
By 1560 Dudley was clearly established as Elizabeth's favourite at court. Tall and extremely handsome, gifted but unreliable and arrogant, his influence with the Queen caused dislike and distrust. Once it was obvious that Elizabeth did not intend to marry him, Dudley worked hard to prevent her marrying anyone else because this would lead to a decline in his influence. Eager to cast Elizabeth as the champion of international Protestantism, he constantly urged military intervention to support Protestant rebels in France and the Netherlands.

■ 6F Flashpoints in the 1560s and 1570s

1567
Elizabeth considered marrying Archduke Charles of Austria, but was worried about whether or not he would be able to restrict his Catholicism to private services. Leicester worked desperately to prevent the match. He played the Protestantism card against Norfolk, Cecil and Sussex who were in favour of the marriage. The Queen hesitated and finally rejected Charles. Cecil accused Leicester of exploiting religion for his own ends: 'If Protestants be but only Protestants! But if some have a second intent which they cloak with religion, and place be given to their counsel, God defend the Queen with his mighty hand!'

1579
Negotiations were held for a marriage between Elizabeth and the French Duke of Alençon. There were political advantages to gain from the marriage, such as influence over French policy in the Netherlands, but Alençon was Catholic. While Cecil declared it better than no marriage at all, Leicester whipped up public opinion against the marriage using sermons and pamphlets and the idea effectively died. 'Leicester stopped an Alençon marriage in 1579, just as Cecil had stopped a Dudley marriage in 1560 to 1561' (C. Haigh, *Elizabeth I*, 1988, p. 78).

1578
The question of whether to send support to the rebels in the Netherlands divided the council for seven years. Leicester and Walsingham joined against Burghley, as a personal contest for political power deepened with genuine policy divisions. These differences divided the Privy Council, with Leicester gaining most support. Elizabeth played for time for as long as possible and only agreed to send troops in 1585, when Spanish conquest of the Netherlands seemed likely. Burghley's group commanded the Queen's support, although Leicester's party was ultimately successful.

Case study 2: Divisions at the end of the reign

Robert Cecil
Robert Cecil was groomed to succeed his father in office, although his advancement was not rapid. His great organisational skills were eventually recognised, but Essex viewed him as his principal rival and his advancement was delayed. Cecil's impatience led him to exploit the patronage system as a means to gain prizes for himself and his followers and to reduce Essex's influence.

Robert Devereux, Earl of Essex
Devereux was charming and brilliant but also greedy and ambitious. He wanted to control royal patronage and appoint all his friends to court and government positions. Essex replaced his stepfather, Leicester, as the Queen's favourite despite the difference in their ages and was openly jealous of other men at court, especially Robert Cecil. He was aggressive in council meetings where his desire for military glory led him to promote dashing campaigns against the Spanish.

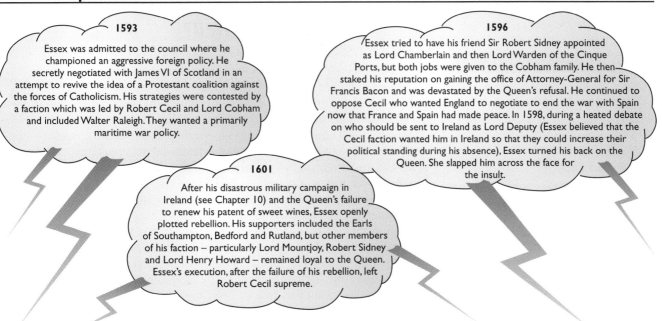

1593

Essex was admitted to the council where he championed an aggressive foreign policy. He secretly negotiated with James VI of Scotland in an attempt to revive the idea of a Protestant coalition against the forces of Catholicism. His strategies were contested by a faction which was led by Robert Cecil and Lord Cobham and included Walter Raleigh. They wanted a primarily maritime war policy.

1596

Essex tried to have his friend Sir Robert Sidney appointed as Lord Chamberlain and then Lord Warden of the Cinque Ports, but both jobs were given to the Cobham family. He then staked his reputation on gaining the office of Attorney-General for Sir Francis Bacon and was devastated by the Queen's refusal. He continued to oppose Cecil who wanted England to negotiate to end the war with Spain now that France and Spain had made peace. In 1598, during a heated debate on who should be sent to Ireland as Lord Deputy (Essex believed that the Cecil faction wanted him in Ireland so that they could increase their political standing during his absence), Essex turned his back on the Queen. She slapped him across the face for the insult.

1601

After his disastrous military campaign in Ireland (see Chapter 10) and the Queen's failure to renew his patent of sweet wines, Essex openly plotted rebellion. His supporters included the Earls of Southampton, Bedford and Rutland, but other members of his faction – particularly Lord Mountjoy, Robert Sidney and Lord Henry Howard – remained loyal to the Queen. Essex's execution, after the failure of his rebellion, left Robert Cecil supreme.

ACTIVITY

Prepare three press releases for the eve of Essex's Rebellion, explaining what happened to Elizabeth's government in the 1590s. One should be written by Robert Cecil, one by the Earl of Essex and one by an impartial court observer.

Did personal rivalries harm the work of government?

■ 6H Examples of successful government policy

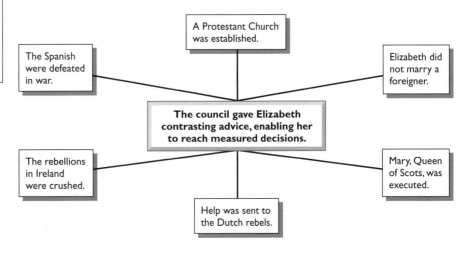

A Protestant Church was established.

The Spanish were defeated in war.

Elizabeth did not marry a foreigner.

The council gave Elizabeth contrasting advice, enabling her to reach measured decisions.

The rebellions in Ireland were crushed.

Mary, Queen of Scots, was executed.

Help was sent to the Dutch rebels.

■ 6I Examples of successful administrative practices

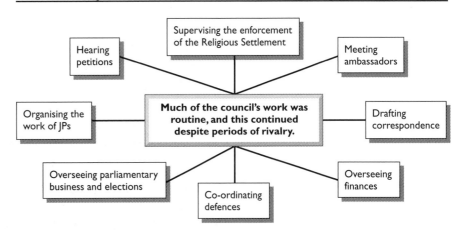

Supervising the enforcement of the Religious Settlement

Hearing petitions

Meeting ambassadors

Organising the work of JPs

Much of the council's work was routine, and this continued despite periods of rivalry.

Drafting correspondence

Overseeing parliamentary business and elections

Co-ordinating defences

Overseeing finances

Review: Was Elizabeth in control of her Privy Council?

Elizabeth's priority in 1558 had been to appoint a small Privy Council, made up of men selected on the basis of political competence and ability who were dependent upon her for reward. Although, at first, traditional nobles were included, their failure to attend frequently meant that government was carried out by a group of four or five professional administrators.

William Cecil emerged from this inner group as one of the greatest political statesmen of the sixteenth century, but even he did not enjoy unopposed access to the Queen. Giving an individual sole power over her would have reduced Elizabeth's control over policy and limited the effectiveness of patronage.

By appointing councillors with opposing views, such as Cecil and Dudley, Elizabeth was given a variety of advice which she was free to accept or reject. And whichever course of action she chose, she would be ensured of support from at least some of the council. As the reign progressed, the council became more involved in decision making although it never surrendered its administrative and judicial functions. The increasing urgency of foreign and religious issues meant that difficult decisions which aroused strong feelings had to be made. Both Elizabeth and her councillors therefore developed strategies to maintain control and bring the council round to their viewpoint.

It would be wrong, however, to highlight such strategies as a main feature of the working of the council. Despite all the personal differences and internal feuds, the council remained at the centre of government because it carried out the daily administrative tasks efficiently and Elizabeth valued its advice. Its success was due to the abilities of the men selected by the Queen, and above all to Cecil, who 'Was respected even by his enemies, who reputed him the most famous councillor of Christendom in his time – in matters of council nothing for the most part was done without him, for that nothing was thought well done whereof he was not the contriver and director' (J. Clapham, one of Burghley's clerks).

Despite the decline in her control over faction in her Privy Council, seen in the last decade of the reign, Elizabeth had clearly confounded her critics. She had shown that an unmarried female ruler could manage ambitious male politicians effectively and decide on policies which were in the national interest.

KEY POINTS FROM CHAPTER 6: Was Elizabeth in control of her Privy Council?

1 One of Elizabeth's first decisions was to choose the composition of her council. She opted for a balance between experience, retaining some of Edward's and Mary's councillors, and new blood, by appointing Boleyn relatives and men nominated by Cecil.

2 Within the council an inner group of professional administrators was responsible for day-to-day administration and for advising the Queen.

3 The most important member of the council was William Cecil, Lord Burghley, who advised the Queen throughout the reign, first as her personal secretary then as Lord Treasurer.

4 Although the council governed the country well, it was not always united. The greatest divisions were over the succession and foreign policy. Personal differences between William Cecil and Robert Dudley, and later between Robert Cecil and the Earl of Essex, led to domination by faction in the 1570s and the 1590s.

5 Elizabeth maintained firm control over her Privy Council by using her power of appointment and because, as Queen, ultimate decision making lay with her.

7

How effective was Parliament's opposition to Elizabethan government?

CHAPTER OVERVIEW

When Elizabeth became Queen in 1558, the English Parliament was emerging from a 25-year period during which it had taken responsibility for 'the highest matters of state, altered both religion and ecclesiastical organisation, encroached upon property rights in a drastic manner, and legislated on all aspects of the Commonweal' (M. Graves, *Elizabethan Parliaments, 1559–1601*, 1987, p. 17). The partnership between the monarch and Parliament, which was established in the 1530s, was recognised as representing the supreme authority in the country. And, Parliament was not simply the junior partner in the relationship. Its control over the granting of taxation gave it the opportunity to air its grievances and further its own interests, while a monarch desperate for money could do little but listen.

SOURCE 7.1 A. G. R. Smith, *The Government of Elizabethan England*, 1967, p. 33

In no fewer than eleven out of the thirteen sessions of Elizabeth's Parliament the government asked for money – in six out of the thirteen sessions it had important legislation to put before Parliament ... On only one occasion was Parliament specifically summoned to consider a major political issue: that was in 1586 when it was asked to discuss the position of Mary, Queen of Scots.

The growth in Parliament's importance did not, however, mean that it had become an integral part of government by 1558. It was, rather, a means by which extraordinary taxation and new laws were approved. It was the monarch who decided how often Parliament should meet and for how long, and policy making remained the monarch's prerogative. Despite its growing self-confidence, Parliament had not reached the stage where it could make the granting of taxes dependent on the withdrawal of an unpopular royal policy for example. This does not mean, however, that there was no debate or conflict during the parliamentary sessions. G. R. Elton claims that Tudor Parliaments 'were, as they always have been, areas for debate, argument, opposition and resistance to royal claims' (*The Parliament of England, 1559–1581*, 1986).

One of Parliament's functions was, after all, to provide a means of communication between the crown and members of the governing class, many of whom owed their seats to the patronage of the Queen or her councillors. In his classic work, *The Elizabethan House of Commons*, which was published in 1949, J. E. Neale argues that the gentry class that sat in the House of Commons regarded these meetings as their opportunity to discuss the great questions of the day. He also claims that an organised opposition, based around a group of PURITANS, emerged from these debates and increasingly challenged Elizabeth's control over Parliament.

The purpose of this chapter is to examine the nature, extent and effectiveness of parliamentary opposition to Elizabeth throughout her reign, and to see if Neale's case for an organised opposition is still viable.

> **PURITAN**
> An extreme English Protestant who regarded Elizabeth's Religious Settlement as incomplete and wanted to abolish the Popish ceremonies and hierarchy which remained.
>
> J. E. Neale refers to the small group of Marian Exiles who sat in the House of Commons as the 'Puritan Choir', on account of their volume.

A The organisation and role of Parliament (pp. 64–65)

B The extent of parliamentary opposition (pp. 66–71)

C Review: How effective was Parliament's opposition to Elizabethan government? (p. 72)

A The organisation and role of Parliament

■ 7A The organisation of Parliament

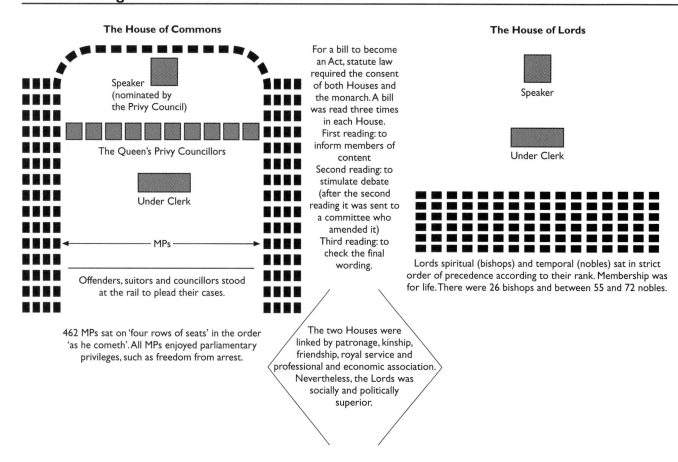

The House of Commons

Speaker (nominated by the Privy Council)

The Queen's Privy Councillors

Under Clerk

← MPs →

Offenders, suitors and councillors stood at the rail to plead their cases.

462 MPs sat on 'four rows of seats' in the order 'as he cometh'. All MPs enjoyed parliamentary privileges, such as freedom from arrest.

For a bill to become an Act, statute law required the consent of both Houses and the monarch. A bill was read three times in each House. First reading: to inform members of content Second reading: to stimulate debate (after the second reading it was sent to a committee who amended it) Third reading: to check the final wording.

The two Houses were linked by patronage, kinship, friendship, royal service and professional and economic association. Nevertheless, the Lords was socially and politically superior.

The House of Lords

Speaker

Under Clerk

Lords spiritual (bishops) and temporal (nobles) sat in strict order of precedence according to their rank. Membership was for life. There were 26 bishops and between 55 and 72 nobles.

■ 7B Early Tudor Parliaments

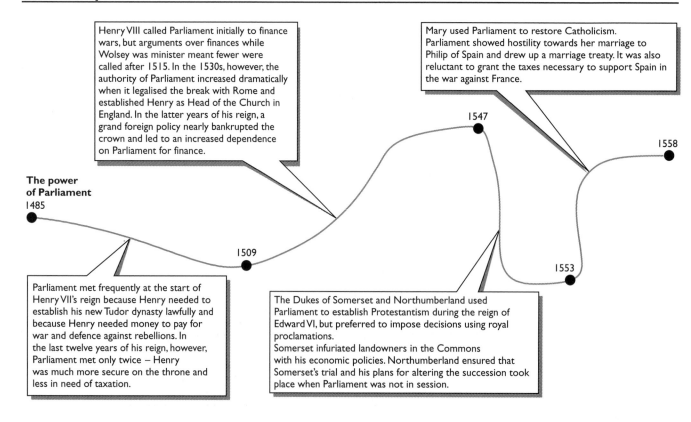

Henry VIII called Parliament initially to finance wars, but arguments over finances while Wolsey was minister meant fewer were called after 1515. In the 1530s, however, the authority of Parliament increased dramatically when it legalised the break with Rome and established Henry as Head of the Church in England. In the latter years of his reign, a grand foreign policy nearly bankrupted the crown and led to an increased dependence on Parliament for finance.

Mary used Parliament to restore Catholicism. Parliament showed hostility towards her marriage to Philip of Spain and drew up a marriage treaty. It was also reluctant to grant the taxes necessary to support Spain in the war against France.

1547

1558

The power of Parliament 1485

1509

1553

Parliament met frequently at the start of Henry VII's reign because Henry needed to establish his new Tudor dynasty lawfully and because Henry needed money to pay for war and defence against rebellions. In the last twelve years of his reign, however, Parliament met only twice – Henry was much more secure on the throne and less in need of taxation.

The Dukes of Somerset and Northumberland used Parliament to establish Protestantism during the reign of Edward VI, but preferred to impose decisions using royal proclamations. Somerset infuriated landowners in the Commons with his economic policies. Northumberland ensured that Somerset's trial and his plans for altering the succession took place when Parliament was not in session.

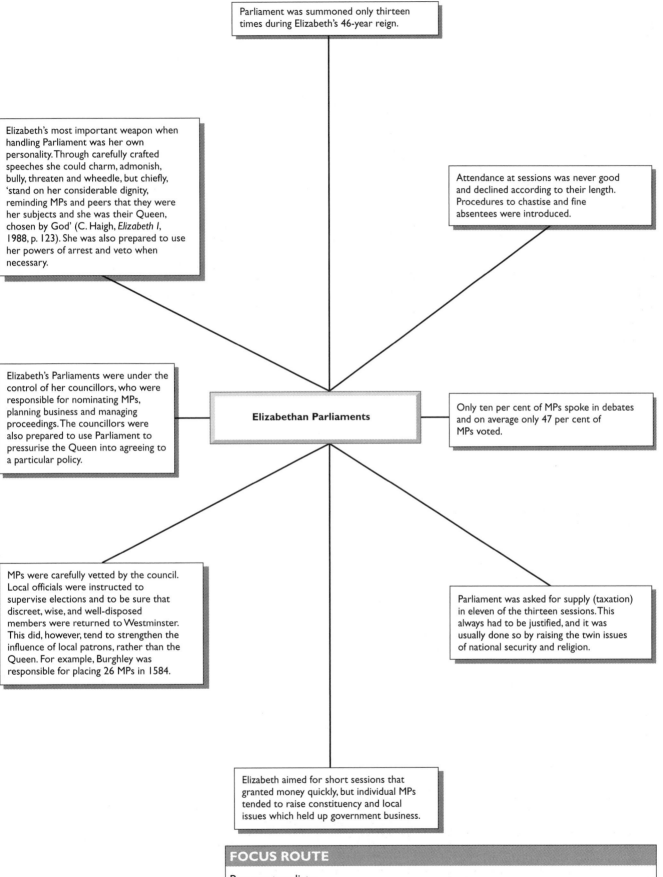

Parliament was summoned only thirteen times during Elizabeth's 46-year reign.

Elizabeth's most important weapon when handling Parliament was her own personality. Through carefully crafted speeches she could charm, admonish, bully, threaten and wheedle, but chiefly, 'stand on her considerable dignity, reminding MPs and peers that they were her subjects and she was their Queen, chosen by God' (C. Haigh, *Elizabeth I*, 1988, p. 123). She was also prepared to use her powers of arrest and veto when necessary.

Attendance at sessions was never good and declined according to their length. Procedures to chastise and fine absentees were introduced.

Elizabeth's Parliaments were under the control of her councillors, who were responsible for nominating MPs, planning business and managing proceedings. The councillors were also prepared to use Parliament to pressurise the Queen into agreeing to a particular policy.

Elizabethan Parliaments

Only ten per cent of MPs spoke in debates and on average only 47 per cent of MPs voted.

MPs were carefully vetted by the council. Local officials were instructed to supervise elections and to be sure that discreet, wise, and well-disposed members were returned to Westminster. This did, however, tend to strengthen the influence of local patrons, rather than the Queen. For example, Burghley was responsible for placing 26 MPs in 1584.

Parliament was asked for supply (taxation) in eleven of the thirteen sessions. This always had to be justified, and it was usually done so by raising the twin issues of national security and religion.

Elizabeth aimed for short sessions that granted money quickly, but individual MPs tended to raise constituency and local issues which held up government business.

FOCUS ROUTE

Prepare two lists:

- the main purposes of Parliament under the early Tudors
- the main purposes of Parliament under Elizabeth.

B The extent of parliamentary opposition

FOCUS ROUTE

Make notes on:

- J. E. Neale's view of the Elizabethan House of Commons
- how and why G. R. Elton challenged Neale's interpretation to produce the revisionist view
- where revisionist historians feel that opposition in the Commons originated from and why.

TALKING POINT

Why do historians' interpretations of historical events change? Is it ever possible to know 'the truth'?

■ **Learning trouble spot**

Although it is possible to write an essay on Elizabeth's control of Parliament without referring to the studies of J. E. Neale and G. R. Elton, this is an area where you will be expected to show an awareness of historical debate. For 30 years, students accepted Neale's interpretation. This view was revised by Elton and then, more recently, by Michael Graves, to form what is known as the revisionist interpretation.

The orthodox view

Neale's theory

The power of the House of Commons increased throughout Elizabeth's reign. The number of conflicts Elizabeth had with individual MPs and the problems which the Stuarts experienced with Parliament in the next century are evidence for this. The roots of the Civil War of the 1640s lay in Elizabeth's reign, when the Commons gained in self-confidence and developed a growing awareness of its powers. This was characterised by increasingly sophisticated methods of managing procedure.

These developments were due to the arrival at Westminster of a well-educated and articulate gentry class who now represented the boroughs as well as the shires, and to an orchestrated Puritan opposition group – the Puritan Choir – who deliberately planned confrontations to force the issue of parliamentary privilege (such as freedom of speech) versus the royal prerogative.

Has Neale got it right?

The Commons increased its powers in the 1530s (not in the latter half of the sixteenth century) when it gained equal status with the House of Lords as a result of its role in establishing the royal supremacy. However, its place in government was still dependent on the monarch who determined when a session was summoned and dissolved.

The techniques by which the Privy Council managed the Commons were well established by 1559. The council formulated policy, steered government bills through the House and cut down on time-consuming speeches. Elizabeth probably allowed the Commons less freedom of speech than her father, but this was not a major issue. The Commons itself ordered the imprisonment of Peter Wentworth, leader of the Puritan Choir, after he called for freedom of speech for the House of Commons over all issues in 1576. The thirteen parliamentary sessions averaged ten weeks each in length, and in this time 434 Acts, both public and private, were passed. Elizabeth asked for SUBSIDY in all but one of the thirteen sessions, and the subsidy bill almost always passed through all of its stages without trouble (the exceptions were in 1566 and 1571). Parliament was, therefore, principally a legislative, rather than a political, body.

SUBSIDY

A parliamentary tax, introduced in the 1530s, on land and goods. It was based on an individual's ability to pay.

The revisionist view

Elton's theory

Elton, writing in the 1980s, based his research on the legislative role of Parliament. By concentrating on law-making procedures and legislative output, he painted a different picture from Neale's, which concentrated exclusively on moments of conflict and confrontation. He demonstrated that Parliament mostly dealt with the routine administration required to vote subsidies, debate and pass public bills, and sort out private bills which were usually concerned with land ownership and local grievances. He did not deny that some sessions witnessed heated debates and even outright opposition, but claimed that this was part of the way Parliament normally functioned and did not prevent sessions from closing harmoniously, having passed the required legislation.

SOURCE 7.2 M. Graves, *Elizabethan Parliaments, 1559–1601*, 1987, p. 92

They [the revisionists] have convincingly rejected the notion that the Commons' political muscle and Commons centred opposition to royal government increased – and especially that organised opposition was a regular feature of the Elizabethan lower house ... they have also restored to a prominent place the House of Lords, whose institutional authority was augmented by the presence of so many patrons with kin and clients in the lower house.

Neale's theory was accepted for so long because it neatly explained what happened next. It showed that the origins of the Civil War could be found in the Commons-based opposition to royal authority which began in the reign of Elizabeth. It was then easy to trace the inevitable and upward progress of the Commons through from the seventeenth century to the twentieth century. Tudor Parliaments were therefore studied as part of a pre-conceived process and not in their own right. By focusing on the administrative and legal functions of Parliament, the revisionists have changed the emphasis. They believe that Parliament was keen to represent the local grievances of its members, but worked, above all, in harmony with the government. The danger now, however, in the light of revisionist views, is that the disputes will be seen only as political debates, which would be underestimating the force of feeling behind issues such as the succession and the Religious Settlement, and the consequent demands for reform.

> **PROROGUING**
> Discontinuing a session of Parliament without dissolving it, which meant it could be recalled later.
>
> **DISSOLVING**
> Dismissing Parliament, which meant new elections were necessary before the next meeting.

■ 7D How Elizabeth and her council controlled Parliament

Elizabeth controlled Parliament by ...

- isolating extremists through promises of moderate reform
- arranging business, especially at the committee stage
- making strong speeches to representatives from the Commons
- directly intervening to preserve the royal prerogative
- influencing the choice of speaker
- imprisoning awkward members
- summoning, PROROGUING and DISSOLVING sessions of Parliament
- managing Parliament's time
- influencing through her councillors the choice of MPs
- having her councillors present in Parliament

■ 7E Opposition in Parliament

Date and purpose of parliamentary session	Neale's interpretation of events	The revisionist interpretation of events	Elizabeth's strategies
25 Jan–8 May 1559 A bill was introduced by the Queen and Council to restore royal supremacy over the Church in England. Parliament initially refused to pass the bill.	Opposition came from Puritans in the House of Commons who wanted a more Calvinist Church.	There is 'no evidence for a cohesive pressure group in the Commons. Most resistance came from the Catholics in the Lords' (N. Jones, *Faith by Statute*, 1982).	Elizabeth imprisoned John White (Bishop of Winchester) and Thomas Watson (Bishop of Lincoln) after their public dispute with Protestants. All but one bishop refused to accept the Religious Settlement and were replaced in 1559. Elizabeth created an unusually small number of hereditary peers so that by 1603 the number in the House of Lords had fallen to 55. As a result of these measures, the House of Lords became increasingly small and under the Queen's control.
12 Jan–10 April 1563 30 Sept 1566–2 Jan 1567 Parliament was summoned to grant money to finance foreign policy towards Scotland and France. The Commons petitioned Elizabeth to marry and name a successor.	Opposition was organised by the Puritan Choir, who had developed well-organised tactics, such as planning their agenda and methods of opposition in advance. The group was led by Peter Wentworth, a university graduate who was skilled in public speaking. The Queen's response caused Wentworth to demand that the Commons enjoy freedom of speech.	The council, worried about her recent illness, orchestrated the campaign to request Elizabeth to marry and name her successor. The committee which drafted the petition was chaired by Sir Edward Rogers and included all eight Privy Councillors sitting in the Commons. And, in 1566, it was William Cecil who organised a joint delegation to the Queen and worded their request that she should name her successor.	Elizabeth reminded the Commons of her status as their monarch: 'I am your anointed Queen, I will never be by violence constrained to do anything.' She also forbade further discussion on the subject of her marriage and the succession, after promising that she would marry.
2 April–29 May 1571 Parliament met following the Northern Rebellion and Elizabeth's excommunication by the Pope. Unusually no money was requested, and Parliament was probably called as a result of pressure put on the Queen by the council.	The Puritan Choir gained new, radical leaders in the 1570s. These included Thomas Cartwright, John Field, Walter Travers and Thomas Wilcox. These men spearheaded a campaign to remove all elements of the 'Popish dunghill' from the English Church and came into continual conflict with the government over all religious matters. The campaign centred on a document called the *Admonition to Parliament*.	The council, fearing for the safety of the Queen after the Ridolfi Plot, pushed for the execution of the Catholic heir, Mary, Queen of Scots. Growing tension over the possible threats posed by Catholics was apparent. A campaign to exclude Mary from the English throne was led by two councillors, Knollys and Croft, their manager in the Commons, Thomas Norton, and Lord Bacon and Lord Burghley.	Elizabeth agreed to execute the Duke of Norfolk who had been implicated in the Ridolfi Plot. She refused to agree to the execution of Mary, Queen of Scots (using her veto), promised to consider excluding Mary from the succession (evading the issue), and then prorogued Parliament.

Date and purpose of parliamentary session	Neale's interpretation of events	The revisionist interpretation of events	Elizabeth's strategies
8 Feb–15 March 1576 The Queen requested money, even though the country was at peace.	Peter Wentworth demanded freedom of speech for the Commons on all subjects. In doing so he became the heroic figurehead of Parliament's struggle to gain liberties and privileges, a struggle which was realised during the Civil War.	Michael Graves, in *Elizabethan Parliaments, 1559–1601*, 1987, describes Peter Wentworth as, 'foolhardy, impetuous and politically inept' (p. 51). He argues that Wentworth 'did little to enhance the efficiency of the Commons and was little more than a parliamentary nuisance' (p. 51). Wentworth was sent to the Tower by the Commons for offensive remarks made against the Queen.	Elizabeth continued to impose her limited version of freedom of speech on the Commons, ensuring that it could discuss only matters of which she approved. Issues such as marriage, religion, foreign policy, etc. came under the sphere of prerogative and were not to be discussed. Despite his recklessness, Wentworth was not alone in his belief that these matters were of public importance and that Parliament was the best forum for discussion.
23 Nov 1584–29 March 1585 Parliament was called to provide for the Queen's safety, following the assassination of William, Prince of Orange, and the discovery of a plot by Mary, Queen of Scots, to kill Elizabeth.	The Puritans seized the opportunity to start the 'Bill and Book' campaign to replace both the Anglican Prayer Book and the Anglican system of Church government with a Calvinist model. 　Puritan opposition was becoming more organised: campaigns were characterised by pre-session planning where tactics were rehearsed and wide support within the Commons was exploited. The Puritans continued to demand unrestricted freedom of speech and make difficulties for the government.	Neale's views are based on supposition. Although Puritans in the Commons did want to demolish the Elizabethan Church, such campaigns were mounted by 'a handful of members, lacked general parliamentary sympathy or support, and were easily smothered by official action' (M. Graves, *Elizabethan Parliaments, 1559–1601*, 1987, p. 54). 　The House of Commons itself refused to hear Peter Turner's bill to change the Prayer Book and system of Church government. Parliament also passed an Act for the Queen's safety, an Act against all JESUIT PRIESTS, and a subsidy for maintaining the country's naval defences.	Elizabeth stopped Burghley's attempt to make the BOND OF ASSOCIATION statute law, although the first Act of Safety was similar. She also safeguarded the rights of Mary's son James, even if his mother were implicated in a plot against Elizabeth.
29 Oct 1586–23 March 1587 Elizabeth's councillors wanted Parliament to persuade Elizabeth to agree to the execution of Mary, Queen of Scots.	The debates emphasised the emerging threat of PRESBYTERIANISM, with Anthony Cope's re-introduction of Turner's 'Bill and Book' to abolish Church courts, the episcopacy, and the Queen's position as Head of the Church.	Any opposition was led by the councillors: Hatton and Knollys in the Commons, Burghley and Bromley in the Lords. Once again, the Privy Councillors in the Commons took the lead.	Elizabeth refused to commit herself, until Walsingham revealed the so-called Stafford Plot, which frightened her into signing Mary's death warrant. 　Although the Commons decided to hear Cope's bill, the Queen intervened to prevent it from proceeding. Wentworth, Cope, and three others were arrested for discussing the bill outside Parliament.

JESUIT PRIEST
A member of the religious order founded by the Spaniard Ignatius Loyola in 1540. The order was renowned for its self-discipline and its misssionary activities.

BOND OF ASSOCIATION
Drafted in 1584 by Burghley and Walsingham. The Association committed itself to protect Elizabeth by pledging that, in the event of Elizabeth's life being threatened, Mary, Queen of Scots, was to be executed (and any other who might benefit from Elizabeth's death, which could implicate James VI if he claimed the throne).

PRESBYTERIANISM
Presbyterian Churches are governed by elders of equal rank rather than a hierarchy of archbishops, bishops, etc.

Date and purpose of parliamentary session	Neale's interpretation of events	The revisionist interpretation of events	Elizabeth's strategies
24 Oct 1597–9 Feb 1598 **27 Oct–19 Dec 1601** Both Parliaments were called so that Elizabeth could request subsidies to finance the war against Spain. MPs, however, raised interests of their own.	This is an example of rebellion in the Commons by organised opposition, a response to the Queen's misuse of the royal prerogative. Grievances over the Queen's granting of monopolies (which raised consumer prices) caused considerable agitation. There was also general dissatisfaction over the heavy financial demands, which provoked a row in which the Commons claimed the right to initiate any votes for money. Parliament originally voted far less than the two subsidies requested.	This is an example of rising discontent, nothing more. It was 'a spontaneous response to a common grievance, voiced by the governing class through its representatives' (M. Graves, *Elizabethan Parliaments, 1559–1601*, 1987, p. 55).	The Queen ignored the complaints initially, but in 1601 she had to act in the face of public unrest. She promised to cancel some monopolies, suspend others, and to thoroughly investigate the situation. She preserved her prerogative and subsidies by conceding to Parliament's demands.

SOURCE 7.3   Peter Wentworth

There is a rumour which runneth about the house and this it is . . . take heed what you do, the Queen's majesty liketh not such a matter. Whosoever prepareth it she will be offended with him . . . upon this speech the house, out of a reverent regard of her Majesty's honour stopped his further proceeding . . . it was ordered by the house . . . that he should be presently committed to the serjeant's ward as prisoner.

SOURCE 7.4   Elizabeth

I know as well as I did before that I am mortal. I know also that I must discharge myself of that great burden God hath lain on me . . . by me you were delivered whilst you were hanging on the bough, ready to fall into the mud, yea to be drowned in the dung.

SOURCE 7.5   The Speaker of the House of Commons

It pleased her Majesty to command me to attend upon her yesterday . . . from whom I am to deliver unto you all her most gracious message . . . she said she never assented to grant anything that was evil in itself. And if in the abuse of her grant there be anything that is evil . . . she herself would take present order for reformation thereof.

SOURCE 7.6   Lord Keeper Bacon

. . . the Queen's most excellent majesty . . . having, as you know, summoned hither her high court of Parliament, hath commanded me to open and declare the chief causes and considerations that moveth her highness thereunto . . . the first is of well making of laws, for the according and uniting of these people of the realm into a uniform order of religion.

ACTIVITY

What do Sources 7.3–7.9 demonstrate about the relationship between Elizabeth and the MPs and councillors who sat in the Commons?

SOURCE 7.7   Anthony Cope

... offered to the house a bill and a book written ... her Majesty before this time had commanded the house not to meddle with this matter.

SOURCE 7.8   Burghley, writing to Walsingham

All that we laboured for and had with full consent brought to fashion – I mean a law to make the Scottish Queen unable and unworthy to wear the crown – was by her Majesty neither assented to nor rejected, but deferred with the feast of All Saints.

SOURCE 7.9   Elizabeth

I will marry as soon as I can conveniently, if God take him not away with whom I had to mind to marry, or myself, or some other great let happen ... but I shall do no otherwise than pleases me. Your bills can have no force without my assent and authority.

ACTIVITY

1 Divide into three groups and each choose one of the discussion points below. Produce a written answer, which should be presented to the whole class. Photocopies of each answer should be circulated.
   a) Elizabeth I faced powerful and increasing opposition from a hostile Parliament throughout her reign (traditional view).
   b) There was little real conflict in Elizabeth's Parliaments. They were mainly characterised by consent and co-operation (revisionist view).
   c) The main opposition to Elizabeth in Parliament came not from an organised Puritan group but from her own councillors (contemporary view).
2 Divide into nine groups and each group choose one parliamentary session to research. Produce a report for Radio Four's *Today in Parliament* programme, looking back over the debates, personalities, and achievements of that particular session, and highlighting Elizabeth's response to events. All quotations must be accurate and attributable.
3 Again in groups, brainstorm an essay plan for the question: Why were Elizabeth and her ministers able to manage Parliament successfully?

SOURCE 7.10 A. G. R. Smith, *The Government of Elizabethan England*, 1967, p. 40

The growing turmoil within Parliament was also partly due to the softening grip of the government on the House of Commons. The great councillors ... were dead or senile by 1593. It was during these years too that the committee system ... became a liability ... by the 1590s committees were ... beginning to take initiatives on questions of general policy. Above all, however, it was the government's financial situation in the 1590s which made it possible for the members of the Commons to make their voices heard in no uncertain terms.

Review: How effective was Parliament's opposition to Elizabethan government?

The history of Elizabethan Parliaments has undergone considerable revision in the past and the debate is continuing. At present, there is general agreement that, under the Tudors, Parliament's greatest period of evolution was in the 1530s, when the House of Commons legalised Henry VIII's break with Rome. This increase in responsibility was maintained in the reigns of Edward VI, Mary and Elizabeth, who all looked to Parliament to establish their religious settlements. However, this evolution is no longer seen as the beginning of the long process by which the House of Commons eventually emerged as constitutionally superior to the crown and the House of Lords.

Elizabeth was not a beleaguered monarch, desperately trying to hold on to the concept of the royal prerogative in the face of a united opposition claiming freedom of speech as parliamentary privilege. There is little doubt that the crown remained in overall control, not least because it determined when Parliament was called and for how long. This does not deny the existence of conflict. There were issues that individual MPs felt strongly about, but these tended to concern local affairs as much as the great matters of the day. Opposition to Elizabeth only became serious when it was engineered by her own councillors and united the Commons and the Lords in an attempt to influence policy. Yet, even here, the powers and strategies Elizabeth used ensured that such alliances seldom achieved their objectives; most MPs showing a marked reluctance to become involved. As with the council and the court, however, the success with which Elizabeth managed her Parliaments began to wane in the last decade of her reign.

FOCUS ROUTE

A lot of overlap existed between the main areas of central government. Use a table like the one below to help you make notes on the following:

* the key institutions of central government, in order of importance
* Elizabeth's choice of officials, including any common trends, and the possible implications of her choices
* potential areas of conflict
* the extent of the Queen's powers and the strategies she could employ to maintain control
* limitations on the Queen's powers.

Institution	Purpose	Main personalities	Potential areas of conflict	Elizabeth's role and her powers

KEY POINTS FROM CHAPTER 7: How effective was Parliament's opposition to Elizabethan government?

1 The Tudors needed Parliament to pass legislation and approve taxes.
2 The role and importance of Parliament changed during the Tudor period, notably in the 1530s under Henry VIII.
3 Elizabeth's control over Parliament is a source of controversy among historians. The original view, put forward by J. E. Neale, that she encountered well-organised opposition is no longer in favour.
4 Most historians now agree that Elizabeth's relationship with Parliament was harmonious and productive, with the possible exception of the 1590s.
5 The main areas of debate between Elizabeth and Parliament were religion, marriage and the succession, finance and the economy.
6 Elizabeth employed a range of strategies and traditional powers to maintain control over Parliament.

8

How did Elizabeth control the royal finances?

CHAPTER OVERVIEW

Throughout the Tudor period, monarchs were expected to govern the country out of their own sources of revenue. A monarch's ORDINARY REVENUE came from the rent or sale of crown lands, fines imposed by judges, customs duties on imports and feudal dues. Monarchs aimed to call Parliament to ask for EXTRAORDINARY REVENUE as little as possible. Henry VII was particularly prudent, building up the crown's revenue and, by avoiding unnecessary wars, leaving his successor a healthy treasury. From 1509 onwards, however, the monarchy found it increasingly difficult to make ends meet. In part, this was due to the policies of the rulers themselves, but other factors outside the crown's control also had an important effect. Throughout the sixteenth century, England experienced a rapid rise in prices. The crown had a fixed income and therefore found it increasingly difficult to meet rising costs. Policies to strengthen the crown's financial position were introduced by the Duke of Northumberland under Edward VI and also by Mary Tudor, and Elizabeth benefited from these.

This chapter will evaluate how effectively Elizabeth and her government managed its finances, and the extent to which its financial policies strengthened or threatened political stability.

ORDINARY REVENUE
The crown's regular and personal sources of income, which were paid directly into the Exchequer.

EXTRAORDINARY REVENUE
Occasional sums of money, to cover unexpected and expensive things such as warfare. It had to be granted by Parliament and usually came in the form of taxation.

A Finance under the early Tudors (pp. 74–75)

B How did Elizabeth manage her finances? (pp. 76–78)

C How successful were Elizabeth's financial policies? (pp. 79–81)

D Review: How did Elizabeth control the royal finances? (pp. 82–83)

FOCUS ROUTE

As you work through Chapter 8, keep the following questions in mind and return at the end to make detailed notes to answer each of them.

1 What were Elizabeth's main financial priorities?
2 What financial difficulties did she face in the early years of her reign?
3 Which financial policies did the Queen pursue between 1558 and 1585 and what were the results?
4 What events after 1585 threatened Elizabeth's financial stability? (You may wish to develop this answer after completing Section 5.)
5 Which strategies did Elizabeth resort to in the 1590s and what effect did they have on political stability and government control?
6 What criticisms have been levelled at Elizabeth's financial policies by historians?

FIRST FRUITS AND TENTHS
The first year's income from a newly appointed officer of the Church, and one-tenth of the yearly income from each parish, bishopric, etc.

TENTHS AND FIFTEENTHS
A basic parliamentary tax. It was, theoretically, a tenth of the value of moveable goods in urban areas and a fifteenth in rural areas.

A Finance under the early Tudors

■ 8A Sources of income and expenditure

	Ordinary	Extraordinary
Income	Crown lands, customs duties, feudal dues, profits of justice and, after 1534, FIRST FRUITS AND TENTHS	Subsidy taxes, TENTHS AND FIFTEENTHS, forced loans, local rates, ship money, loans
Expenditure	Running the government, including the court and the household	War

Henry VII, 1485–1509

Henry VII increased the size of the royal estates by confiscating land when its owners died so revenue from rents rose from £10,000 to £42,000 p.a. He increased the income arising from his position as feudal overlord, especially by exploiting wardship. Revenue from taxation and customs duties also increased. He ensured that all revenues were paid into the Chamber, rather than the Exchequer which was slower, and so was able personally to monitor its accounts. A sensible foreign policy even produced an annual income from France in the Treaty of Etaples, at the same time as avoiding the expense of prolonged warfare. Henry also increased the crown's solvency: by the end of the reign revenue was £100,000 p.a. compared to £65,000 in 1483.

Henry VIII, 1509–47

Cardinal Wolsey developed the subsidy tax and aimed to increase revenue from crown lands, but he failed to generate enough income to finance Henry VIII's wars. His demand for a non-parliamentary tax, the Amicable Grant, caused rebellion in 1525. The dissolution of the monasteries in the 1530s doubled the crown's income to £300,000 p.a., and Thomas Cromwell introduced new courts (government departments) to make the collection of money more efficient. Henry's wars in the 1540s required an expenditure of twice his annual ordinary revenue. Even taxation and forced loans could not provide the money needed. Henry therefore resorted to selling crown lands and debasing the coinage, which weakened the crown's finances in the long run as assets were sold off and trade affected.

Edward VI, 1547–53

Debasement of the coinage continued under the Duke of Somerset to fund foreign wars, making the rapid rise in prices worse. The financial policies of the Duke of Northumberland were more successful. He raised revenue in traditional ways, by selling crown lands and seizing Church property, but he was more efficient at collecting debts, reducing expenditure (withdrawing from foreign commitments brought a period of peace which allowed a degree of financial recovery) and accounting. For example, Thomas Gresham was appointed as an exchange manipulator to raise loans at lower interest rates.

Mary I, 1553–58

Mary amalgamated the revenue courts into a more efficient Exchequer, increased revenue from crown lands and negotiated favourable foreign loans. A new book of customs rates was introduced in 1558, which raised customs duties and extended the range of taxable goods, increasing yield from £29,000 to £83,000 in twelve months.

ACTIVITY

1 Which policies under the early Tudors had led to
   a) financial problems
   b) financial strength?
2 How had Elizabeth's immediate predecessors strengthened royal finances?

■ 8B The process of debasement

Unlike today where the value of a coin is arbitrary, in medieval times there was a direct correlation between the value of a coin and its precious metal content. A six gram gold coin was worth x amount because it was six grams of gold, not because the government had announced its value.

In the sixteenth century, monarchs, desperate to increase the amount of bullion in the treasury, melted down coins and re-minted them. A coin weighed the same as it had before but it contained less precious metal and more base metal. A gold coin was now not worth its weight in gold and people were unhappy.

B How did Elizabeth manage her finances?

FOCUS ROUTE

Copy and complete the table below by finding out what happened to each of these sources of revenue throughout Elizabeth's reign. Crown lands has been done for you as an example.

Source of revenue		What happened during Elizabeth's reign?
Ordinary	Crown lands	These were sold off throughout the reign, bringing £600,000 into the Exchequer but weakening the crown's financial base in the long term. Rents on existing lands were raised slightly and brought in about £100,000 p.a., but this was below the level of inflation.
	Customs duties	
	Profits of justice	
	Feudal dues	
	First fruits and tenths	
Extraordinary	Subsidy taxes	
	Forced loans	
	Local rates	
	Ship money	
	Loans	
	Tenths and fifteenths	

MONOPOLY RIGHTS

These were granted by the crown, and gave an individual exclusive rights over the sale or trade of a particular commodity.

WARDSHIP

The right of the crown to run the estates of an heir below the age of 21. The crown could grant this right to another individual.

Reducing costs

Elizabeth cut back government spending severely. Wherever possible the government used unpaid officials, such as JPs, or rewarded courtiers by giving them MONOPOLY RIGHTS or WARDSHIPS which did not involve financial outlay. There were few salaried officials in the sixteenth century, but salaries were kept low and did not keep pace with inflation. Elizabeth strictly monitored the costs of her household: no new royal palaces were built and annual maintenance costs were halved. Naval expenses were maintained at a minimum by remodelling old ships rather than building new ones. After 1573 a considerable sum was spent on the navy, but Elizabeth tried to avoid, for as long as possible, any overseas military commitments that would cripple royal finances.

■ 8C Management of royal revenue

ROYAL REVENUE

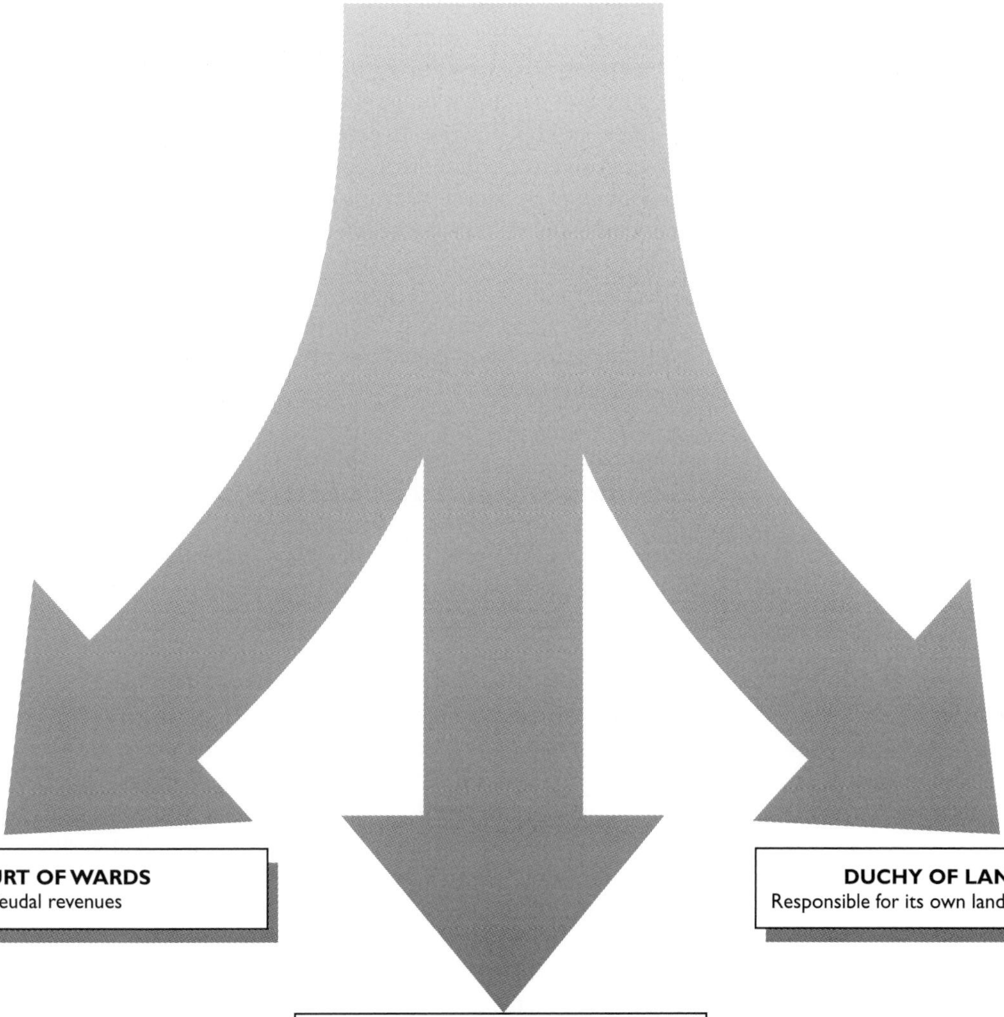

COURT OF WARDS
Supervised all feudal revenues

DUCHY OF LANCASTER
Responsible for its own lands

THE EXCHEQUER

All other revenues were paid directly into the Exchequer.

Since the Queen and the Privy Council took every decision on expenditure,no matter how small, they were in frequent contact with the Exchequer.

The volume of financial work increased greatly during the reign.

The Exchequer had about 79 staff on its payroll (although there were also a considerable number of privately appointed clerks), under the control of the Lord Treasurer.The crown was responsible for appointing the most important officers, who generally came from the gentry or merchant classes and from among the many Members of Parliament and Justices of the Peace.

The Exchequer building at Westminster was divided into departments and it was the heads of these departments who were the real financial experts of the day and who passed information directly to the council.

Improving financial administration

Appointing successful Lord Treasurers

Elizabeth inherited her first Lord Treasurer, William Paulet, Marquis of Winchester. Under his leadership the Exchequer continued to implement the financial reforms started during Mary's reign. These included modernising the Exchequer and making it more efficient, revaluing crown lands so rents and entry fines could be increased, and raising customs duties. Elizabeth wanted Winchester to ensure that the accounts were balanced, that expenditure did not exceed income. He therefore worked hard to call in debts owed to the crown, to raise income and to keep costs down. Winchester's replacement by William Cecil in 1572 saw no change in priorities. Like Winchester, Cecil vigorously pursued the same drive for economy, although not perhaps with the same degree of vision and creativity. As a result, by 1585 when war with Spain broke out, Elizabeth had been able to pay off Mary's debts of £300,000 and build up a reserve of £300,000.

Extending the sources of revenue

Elizabeth not only reduced expenditure, she also increased income; without this her ordinary revenue would not have kept pace with inflation. She did not do this by using strategies which made the problem of inflation worse, such as debasing the coinage. Her main policy was to sell crown lands, which raised over £600,000 and saw the last of the monastic properties seized by Henry VIII pass into private ownership. She also participated in JOINT STOCK TRADING COMPANIES and attempts to break the Spanish monopoly in the New World. The crown put up money to finance such ventures in return for a large percentage of the profits or treasure. The results, however, were extremely variable. The capture of the ship *Madre de Dios* in 1592 brought a profit of £77,000, but it was easy for the Spanish fleets to slip past the English in bad weather and Elizabeth's commanders did not always share their booty with her. In 1596 Lord Howard and the Earl of Essex handed over the plunder from the capture of Cadiz to their men. Elizabeth also increased ordinary revenue by collecting debts more vigorously, fining religious non-conformists, and by leaving ecclesiastical offices vacant in order to administer DIOCESES directly.

JOINT STOCK TRADING COMPANY
A business in which the owners raised capital by selling shares. Shareholders hoped to make a profit from their investment.

DIOCESE
A unit of Church administration, which is divided into parishes under the control of a bishop.

Increasing the demands for parliamentary taxation

The tradition that Tudor monarchs lived off their ordinary revenue and only asked Parliament for taxes during times of emergency finally disappeared during Elizabeth's reign. The distinction between ordinary and extraordinary revenue began to break down during the reign of Henry VIII, but by the second half of the sixteenth century taxation was increasingly seen as essential for the ordinary running of government. In the 1570s, Parliament was asked to approve subsidy taxes, even in peacetime, on the grounds that they were necessary for the country's defence. The outbreak of war with Spain led to unprecedented demands for taxation, even though Elizabeth's determination not to run up large debts influenced her military decisions. She preferred to send fleets into the Atlantic to attack Spanish silver ships coming from Mexico and Peru, rather than launch a massive campaign against the Spanish.

ACTIVITY

Modern Chancellors of the Exchequer deliver a budget statement in which they justify their financial policies. In the same spirit, draw up a speech for Elizabeth to give to the House of Commons before she asks for increased taxation. The year is 1584 and you should emphasise the steps that have already been taken to build up a surplus in the Exchequer.

Asking how successful Elizabeth's financial policies were might seem like a superfluous question. After all, in twenty years Elizabeth paid off her debts, ended the country's dependence on foreign loans, and had begun to build up a reserve. She was also able to finance wars against Spain and in Ireland without leaving a debt significantly larger than Mary's. And, not surprisingly, there is general praise for Elizabeth's record on expenditure. However, historians have criticised her for failing to undertake any reforms or initiatives that might have put the crown's finances on a more secure, long-term footing. In finance, as elsewhere, Elizabeth was cautious and conservative. She pursued short-term advantages at the expense of long-term gain and allowed vested interests and unfair practices to go unchallenged.

SOURCE 8.1   W. MacCaffrey, *Elizabeth I*, 1993, p. 385

She allowed the real revenue from customs and royal lands to fall, partly it would seem through administrative inertia, and partly perhaps in a conscious effort not to alienate merchants and royal tenants.

The main criticisms of Elizabeth's financial policies are as follows.

1: Ordinary revenue was allowed to stagnate

The government did not respond quickly enough to inflation and therefore, in real terms, income fell behind in a time of rising prices.

- Customs duties were not realigned to take account of inflation.
- Profits from feudal dues declined rather than increased, until Robert Cecil took over the Court of Wards in 1599.
- Crown land rents were raised only slightly and were obviously reduced in the long term by the sale of crown lands.
- Some revenue did not find its way into the Exchequer at all, as Elizabeth rewarded her favourites by allowing them to use the revenues from their offices. Winchester and Leicester alone owed nearly £70,000 to the crown, almost five times the annual income from feudal dues.
- Overall ordinary revenue did not keep pace with inflation and had to be supplemented by taxation.
- The crown's financial resources remained the same: no additions were made and existing resources were not exploited.

Some enterprising landowners were using inflation to their advantage (see pages 118–22), so Elizabeth could have done more.

2: Parliamentary taxation was not reformed

Although Tudor Parliaments had shown they were prepared to grant subsidy taxes, even in peacetime, requests always referred to national dangers or the need to defend the realm. Elizabeth was not prepared to state that extraordinary taxation was now necessary for the ordinary running of government. Nor was she prepared to fully tap the wealth of her subjects – taxes in England were lower than elsewhere in Europe. The subsidy tax was based on an individual's own assessment of his wealth and income and it was common practice for the rich to undervalue their assets. The value of each subsidy tax fell throughout the reign. The government made no attempt to improve tax collection, perhaps because it feared losing the support of the politically-active classes. It failed to institute an efficient record system, bring taxation in line with inflation, or impose it on all who were eligible to pay.

SOURCE 8.2 W. MacCaffrey, *Elizabeth I*, 1993, p. 389

Behind the Queen's obsession with a rigid economy stood a fundamental conception about the bounds of royal power. There was an underlying fear of taxpayer resistance ... the notion that there was a limit to taxpayers' liability, that their willingness to pay was inelastic, remained rigid in the royal [consciousness] as in the popular consciousness.

SOURCE 8.3 D. M. Palliser, *The Age of Elizabeth*, 1983, p. 128

Raleigh admitted in the Parliament of 1601 that 'a poor man pays as much as a rich' because 'our estates that be thirty pound or forty pound in the Queen's books, are not the hundred[th] part of our wealth'.

3: Cecil was not the right man for the job

Although William Cecil's considerable abilities as a statesman and an administrator are in no doubt, his success as Lord Treasurer is more mixed. He strictly followed Elizabeth's instructions to economise, reducing public expenditure and keeping a tight hold on government spending. Consequently, his outlook was basically conservative. He did not undertake any reforms, and opportunities to increase the crown's sources of ordinary income were missed. A. G. R. Smith, in *The Government of Elizabethan England*, points out that when Cecil's son Robert took over the Court of Wards in 1599 he raised the selling price of wardships to four times the annual value of the lands, a policy Burghley had never initiated.

SOURCE 8.4 A. G. R. Smith, *The Government of Elizabethan England*, 1967, p. 53

Burghley's stress on economy was a weakness as well as a strength. It narrowed his vision and was one factor in preventing him from attempting to achieve much-needed increases in the crown's ordinary revenue.

4: Measures in the 1590s threatened government control

As Elizabeth's wartime expenses mounted she relied increasingly on parliamentary taxation but, by the 1590s, subsidies plus the crown's ordinary revenues were not meeting her total annual costs. To make up the balance the crown resorted to unpopular measures which caused considerable political unrest. Chief among these were PURVEYANCE and monopolies. Although monopolies had long been used as a form of patronage, the number granted increased dramatically after 1597. It was felt that monopolies meant profits for the holder at the expense of the purchaser, because the price of goods such as iron, salt and oil increased. In the last Parliaments of her reign attacks on Elizabeth for granting monopolies were ferocious, causing her to back down and promise to investigate and restrict such grants.

PURVEYANCE
The right of the crown to purchase supplies or obtain transport for the royal household at prices below the current market value.

SOURCE 8.5 Mr Francis Moore speaking in a parliamentary debate on monopolies, 1601

I cannot utter with my tongue, or conceive with my heart, the great grievances that the town and country for which I serve suffer by some of these monopolies. It bringeth the general profit into a private hand, and the end of all is beggary and bondage to the subject.

5: The use of unpaid officials reduced their efficiency

For much of the reign it was accepted that officials worked for rewards – such as wardships, favourable leases on land, import and export licences, patents, constableships of castles, etc. – rather than regular salaries. In many ways this worked effectively: an individual, in order to achieve promotion and to increase his status by acquiring more rewards, tended to work hard to get noticed. Direct control by the monarch, however, was difficult. Office holders, many of whom held their positions for life, appointed their own staff and were responsible for distributing rewards to them. Elizabeth instituted oaths of loyalty, but there is little evidence that they made any difference; and, although she could dismiss Exchequer officials, she hardly ever did so. By the 1590s, the system had become increasingly corrupt. Inflation led people to search desperately for extra sources of income and, as the number of offices remained static, bribery was increasingly resorted to in order to gain an appointment.

SOURCE 8.6 D. M. Palliser, *The Age of Elizabeth*, 1983, p. 127

In some cases she granted leases of Crown loans in reversion [to pass on to heirs] to her servants to increase their income without raising their salaries. For she failed to pay her officials adequate salaries which kept pace with inflation, often tacitly allowing them to make up the differences with gifts, favours and bribes.

ACTIVITY

1 Use the information on pages 76–81 to complete the following table:

Area of royal finance	Achievements	Criticisms
Expenditure		
Administration		
Payment of officials		
Role of Lord Treasurer		
Ordinary revenue		
Parliamentary taxation		

2 a) Source 8.1 gives two reasons to explain why Elizabeth did not increase ordinary revenue. What are they?
   b) What reason is given in Source 8.2 to explain the Queen's reluctance to increase taxation?
   c) Using Sources 8.3 and 8.5, explain which classes benefited from the financial strategies used at the end of the reign and which lost out.
   d) Look at Source 8.6. How did Elizabeth maintain the loyalty of her officials despite their low salaries? Why do you think Elizabeth continued to use such measures if they contributed towards social unrest?
3 You are a foreign banker preparing to interview Elizabeth in 1601. Draw up an outline of her financial policies and compile a list of questions to ask her about her current financial situation.

TALKING POINTS

1 It is always easy to be wise in hindsight, but is it fair to criticise Elizabeth for not initiating more robust reforms when doing so might have lost her the support of the politically-active classes?
2 To what extent can a monarch be blamed for the repercussions of his or her actions if they occur as much as 40 years later? Can Elizabeth be blamed for the financial battle that took place between the Stuart kings and their Parliaments in the seventeeth century?

D Review: How did Elizabeth control the royal finances?

During Elizabeth's reign it became clear that the crown was no longer able to live off its ordinary revenue and only levy taxes in times of war. But, instead of recognising this fact and initiating measures more appropriate to the changing circumstances, Elizabeth tried to tinker with a system that had already passed its 'sell by date'. To some extent, however, the fault does not lie with Elizabeth alone. Whereas her male counterparts in France and Spain declared war first and worried about how to finance it later, all the indications show that Elizabeth was right to believe that her wealthiest subjects would not countenance any increase in the taxes they paid. Even her most loyal courtiers, such as Burghley and Leicester, saw the financial profits they made at the crown's expense as their due.

Elizabeth's financial policies were conservative and backward looking, and they were ultimately defeated by inflation and the difficulties involved in controlling officials. By the end of her reign, rents from crown lands had hardly increased at all while feudal revenue remained static at its 1541 level. Potential profit from customs duties was lost because Elizabeth used it to reward courtiers. Various government commissions also failed to increase duties in line with inflation. It was clear that the monarchy's financial foundation was inadequate. In the last years of her reign, Elizabeth increasingly resorted to 'bastard revenues' such as monopolies, forest laws and ship money which were seen by the propertied classes as a perversion of royal rights.

Most of the crown's debts were due to the length of the war against Spain. Despite the apparent popularity of the war and the eventual victory, the English were increasingly reluctant to support the war financially and not all the sums that Parliament granted were actually collected. At the end of the day, Elizabeth had few means of coercion available to her, and the health of her finances ultimately depended on what her subjects were prepared to pay.

ACTIVITY

Prepare an argument in support of one of the following statements:

a) Elizabeth is to be congratulated for implementing financial policies that enabled her to pay for eighteen years of warfare without significantly increasing the national debt or losing the support of the politically-active classes on whom she depended.

b) Elizabeth's only financial policy was to reduce expenditure. She failed to make reforms or attack corruption, and by selling off royal assets she left an under-resourced monarchy which was dependent on parliamentary taxation and heading towards disaster.

FOCUS ROUTE

Assess the contribution that Elizabeth's financial policies made to the breakdown of government control in the 1590s.

Causes of social and political unrest in the 1590s	Links to Elizabeth's financial policies
The long wars against Spain (Section 5), and in Ireland (Section 2)	
Bad harvests (Section 3)	
High prices (Section 3)	
Urban poverty (Section 3)	
Food riots (Section 2)	
Parliamentary taxation (Section 2)	
Purveyances and monopolies (Section 2)	
Faction at court: Essex and Cecil (Section 2)	

You may wish to come back to develop this exercise as you near the end of this book.

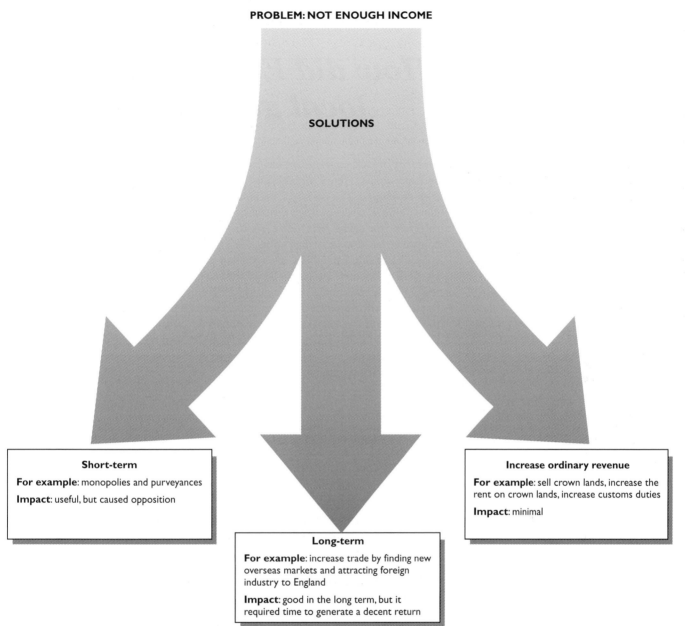

PROBLEM: NOT ENOUGH INCOME

SOLUTIONS

Short-term

For example: monopolies and purveyances

Impact: useful, but caused opposition

Long-term

For example: increase trade by finding new overseas markets and attracting foreign industry to England

Impact: good in the long term, but it required time to generate a decent return

Increase ordinary revenue

For example: sell crown lands, increase the rent on crown lands, increase customs duties

Impact: minimal

KEY POINTS FROM CHAPTER 8: How did Elizabeth control the royal finances?

1 The main sources of revenue came from crown lands, customs duties, profits from justice, feudal dues and taxation. These became increasingly inadequate because of inflation and the cost of a prolonged period of warfare.

2 Elizabeth tried to increase her income by economising, tightening control over the Exchequer, looking for alternative sources of revenue, and increasing parliamentary taxation.

3 The conservative nature of Elizabeth's financial policies has been criticised. She did not increase ordinary revenue, introduce stricter accountability, reassess who paid taxes, or reduce patronage.

9

How did Elizabeth control local government?

CHAPTER OVERVIEW

The area of local government has traditionally been seen as one of the successes of Tudor policy. Henry VII inherited a sound structure from the Yorkists which he then developed. The cornerstone of this system was the Justice of the Peace, an unpaid official who enforced central decisions and kept the peace in his locality in return for the status that such a position brought. The fact that there were comparatively few rebellions under the Tudors and that the Wars of the Roses appear to have subsided has strengthened the general impression of a loyal and law-abiding country. In fact, as David Palliser has recently shown, the situation in the provinces was not dissimilar to the situation at court: men of influence aimed to increase their political standing and power and rival groups formed factions in the struggle for supremacy. Powerful nobles or 'over-mighty subjects', whom historians once thought the policies of Henry VII had reduced, were still very much in existence in 1558, and exercising considerable influence, particularly in counties far from London.

Elizabeth needed to retain the goodwill of such powerful magnates, although, as we have seen, she tried to keep a close eye on them by summoning them regularly to court. Often, however, in the absence of such noblemen at court, faction at a local level increased as the gentry competed for position and status. Personal and local interests took precedence over royal interest, as shown by events in Norfolk after 1572. There was no guarantee that a law, once passed by Parliament, would be enforced throughout the country. The border regions of Wales and the North, in particular, had proved so difficult to govern that regional councils were set up by Henry VIII. Despite all these limitations, however, the crown did succeed. It was able to enforce legislation, develop the office of Lord Lieutenant, expand the duties of the JP and establish the parish as an administrative unit.

This chapter will focus on how central government overcame the considerable obstacles it faced in imposing its decisions throughout the country, and to what extent it was successful.

A What linked central and local government? (pp. 86–87)

B What did a Justice of the Peace do? (p. 88)

C What strategies did central government use to control local government? (p. 89)

D How effective was local government? (pp. 90–91)

E Review: How did Elizabeth control local government? (p. 92)

SOURCE 9.1 D. M. Palliser, *The Age of Elizabeth*, 1983, p. 352

In practice, each shire contained notables who exercised power and patronage because of their status, land holding, and wealth, whether or not they held government office or sat on the commission of the peace. And even those local leaders who did act as justices did not necessarily enforce government policies as they were ordered to.

SOURCE 9.2 D. M. Palliser, *The Age of Elizabeth*, 1983, p. 378

Success might come, when a determined government was united with merchants and gentlemen equally determined; but when interest groups conflicted, or short-term fluctuations altered attitudes, no consistent and successful policy was possible.

SOURCE 9.3 C. Haigh, *Elizabeth I*, 1988, p. 52

The Tudors had always faced a dilemma on the northern border: should they entrust office to powerful local lords, who would be effective governors, or should they use more controllable men, who might lack regional authority?

SOURCE 9.4 D. M. Palliser, *The Age of Elizabeth*, 1983, p. 378

Both the Queen and Cecil were aware that the powers of the government looked more impressive than the reality with its ramshackle and informal style ... and its lack of paid officials and law enforcers ...

ACTIVITY

Read Sources 9.1–9.4. What problems did Elizabeth have in ensuring effective local government?

TALKING POINT

To what extent has government been made easier by the huge advances in communication which characterised the late twentieth century? Has it also been made more difficult?

What linked central and local government?

Copy and complete the following table, comparing law enforcement in the 1590s and 2000s. Some parts have already been filled in to get you started.

		Administration: how the public is made aware of the law	Enforcement: who checks that people are obeying the law	Judiciary: who decides if the accused is guilty or innocent	Where would the trial be held?
Tax assessment	1590s				
	2000s	Civil service: the Inland Revenue			
Public house opening hours	1590s		Sheriffs and JPs		
	2000s				
Land ownership	1590s				
	2000s				
Keeping the peace	1590s				
	2000s		Police	Magistrate	
Divorce settlements	1590s				
	2000s				
Entitlement to benefits	1590s				
	2000s				
Tenancy rights	1590s				
	2000s				
Elections	1590s				
	2000s				
Acts of violence	1590s				
	2000s				Criminal court
Conscription	1590s				
	2000s				

ASSIZES

From the twelfth century onwards, paid judges were sent to counties to hear cases of theft, murder, treason, as well as some civil cases. The Tudors built on this system. Twice a year, judges visited 50 principal towns to hear cases referred to the Assizes by the Quarter Sessions. Each session lasted a few days.

1 Make notes on the functions of local government institutions and officials.
2 Explain why the links between central and local government were so important. For example, how did effective local government help Elizabeth to control the country?

Elizabeth and her Privy Council

Formal reports · Letters · Commands · Proclamations · Statute law · Quarter Sessions returns · Statistics · Census returns · Royal writs · Election results

Lord Lieutenant
- The post was created by the Tudors to institutionalise the role of leading magnates.
- It was originally a temporary position, to command the local militia during emergencies. But, by the 1580s, it had become a permanent administrative post.
- Lords Lieutenant were often Privy Councillors and might have had responsibility for more than one shire. Their absence at the centre led to the creation of the post of Deputy Lord Lieutenant.
- Their responsibilities were mainly military and involved assembling, inspecting and training the local militia. Their administrative duties included assessing and collecting loans, supervising recusants, and overseeing the enforcement of economic legislation.

Justice of the Peace
- The post was established in medieval times, but their numbers and work-load increased in the sixteenth century. This growth came as a result of pressure from the gentry who saw the office as a sign of prestige.
- The burden on JPs increased as a result of the social and economic legislation passed during the reign.
- Their powers included enforcing legislation, investigating breaches of the law, hearing cases and determining sentences. They also administered the Poor Law, controlled sheriffs and licensed ale houses.
- They were under the council's control and there was frequent communication between central and local government.

Sheriff
- Office declined in importance during Elizabeth's reign
- Presided over monthly meetings of the County Court
- Swore in juries, delivered prisoners to court and carried out sentences given by the Quarter Sessions
- Responsible for delivering all royal writs
- Presided over the County Court during elections, declaring the result and sending the returns to Chancery

Local officers
- Acted as constables, jurors and church wardens
- Elected MPs (if a freeholder worth over 40 shillings)
- Other functions included repairing roads, distributing poor relief and even organising vermin control

ASSIZES
- Held twice a year in principal towns by judges from Westminster
- Dealt with the most serious cases

Quarter Sessions
- Held every three months in principal towns by the resident JP
- Dealt with civil and criminal cases

Local courts
- Also known as Borough, Hundred and Manor Courts
- Dealt with everyday offences, such as disputes over land ownership and agricultural prices
- Disputes between tenants were particularly common cases

Ecclesiastical courts
- Case-load increased after the 1559 Religious Settlement
- Most cases dealt with matrimony, wills and disputes between neighbours
- Procedure was quicker, cheaper and more flexible than in the traditional law courts

The Council of the North and the Council of the Marches of Wales
- Enforced central government and enjoyed administrative and judicial powers
- Tried criminal cases and exercised civil jurisdiction
- Popular with suitors and petitioners as they tended to offer speedier justice than the traditional law courts
- The success of each depended on the abilities of its president

B What did a Justice of the Peace do?

Throughout Elizabeth's reign the theoretical workload of a JP increased considerably, largely as a result of the social and economic legislation passed by the government. This does not necessarily mean, however, that JPs worked harder. Historians have recently begun to question William Lombard's *Eirenarcha*, published in 1581, which, by listing all the duties of a JP, gives the impression that JPs carried on their shoulders the sole, unpaid responsibility for enforcing laws throughout the country.

While some JPs were doubtless loyal and conscientious, the evidence suggests that many saw their office as a social honour and did as little as possible to actively enforce royal policy. Indeed, on certain occasions they showed a marked reluctance to serve the government because their sympathy with local feeling prevented them from acting in the national interest. This was particularly true when they had to enforce recusancy laws against Catholics who did not attend church, impose assessments for taxation purposes, or do anything regarding the militia. The situation grew worse in times of poor harvests and high inflation, and the government therefore experienced real problems in trying to meet the demands of prolonged war during the social and economic distress of the 1590s. The Queen and Cecil were acutely aware of this and took measures to deal with it. When a task was particularly sensitive they employed special commissioners instead of local men. For example, they used committed Protestants to impose the anti-Catholic laws of the 1580s. At times the government was even forced to rely on informants, who passed on information which led to prosecution in return for a financial reward.

FOCUS ROUTE

1 Draw a spider diagram showing the duties and responsibilities of a JP. You may want to add to it after you have completed Section 3 on social and economic legislation.
2 Make notes on the main weaknesses in Elizabeth's system of local government.
3 List the advantages and disadvantages of using local men for local government.

SOURCE 9.5 D. M. Palliser, *The Age of Elizabeth*, 1983, p. 356

The main task of the Justices at Quarter Sessions was to hear cases brought before them by constables and juries and not to initiate action themselves; and they did not go out of their way to look for extra work. Of the 80 or so statutes concerned with economic or social offences which Lombard listed, very few were enforced.

SOURCE 9.6 P. Williams, *The Tudor Regime*, 1979, p. 152

Most of the statutes enumerated in the Eirenarcha *are either not mentioned in the printed Quarter Sessions records or appear in just one or two shires ... Tudor JPs were mainly concerned with the traditional offences of assault, forcible entry, disorderly conduct, riot, bastardy, alehouses, petty larceny, and unlawful gains.*

C **What strategies did central government use to control local government?**

■ 9B How central government controlled local government

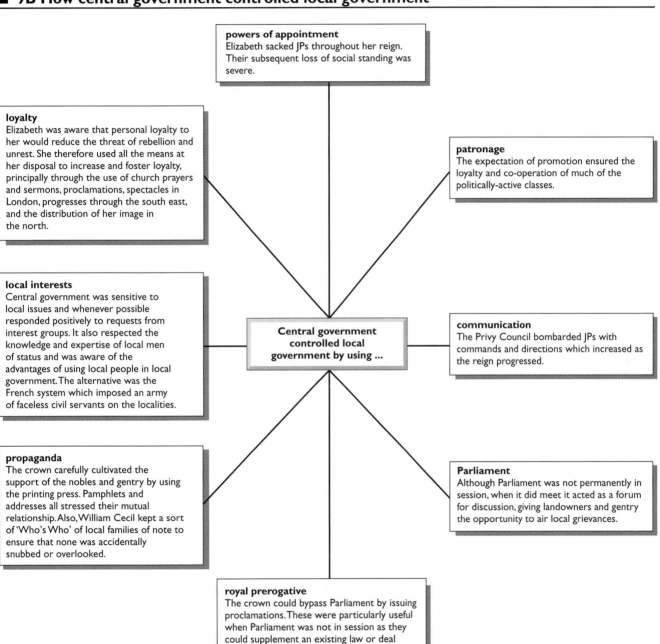

powers of appointment
Elizabeth sacked JPs throughout her reign. Their subsequent loss of social standing was severe.

loyalty
Elizabeth was aware that personal loyalty to her would reduce the threat of rebellion and unrest. She therefore used all the means at her disposal to increase and foster loyalty, principally through the use of church prayers and sermons, proclamations, spectacles in London, progresses through the south east, and the distribution of her image in the north.

patronage
The expectation of promotion ensured the loyalty and co-operation of much of the politically-active classes.

local interests
Central government was sensitive to local issues and whenever possible responded positively to requests from interest groups. It also respected the knowledge and expertise of local men of status and was aware of the advantages of using local people in local government. The alternative was the French system which imposed an army of faceless civil servants on the localities.

Central government controlled local government by using ...

communication
The Privy Council bombarded JPs with commands and directions which increased as the reign progressed.

propaganda
The crown carefully cultivated the support of the nobles and gentry by using the printing press. Pamphlets and addresses all stressed their mutual relationship. Also, William Cecil kept a sort of 'Who's Who' of local families of note to ensure that none was accidentally snubbed or overlooked.

Parliament
Although Parliament was not permanently in session, when it did meet it acted as a forum for discussion, giving landowners and gentry the opportunity to air local grievances.

royal prerogative
The crown could bypass Parliament by issuing proclamations. These were particularly useful when Parliament was not in session as they could supplement an existing law or deal with a specific local problem.

D How effective was local government?

FOCUS ROUTE

1 Draw a timeline detailing the main disturbances of Elizabeth's reign.
2 Using Chart 9C and Sources 9.7–9.12, make notes on:

- the main causes of unrest, 1558–1603
- the seriousness of this opposition
- the effectiveness of central government
- the effectiveness of local government.

Elizabeth's reign saw one major rebellion in the north in 1569–70 and many armed riots. The latter were expressions of local anger, the former a national uprising which challenged the stability of the government.

■ 9C Elizabethan disturbances

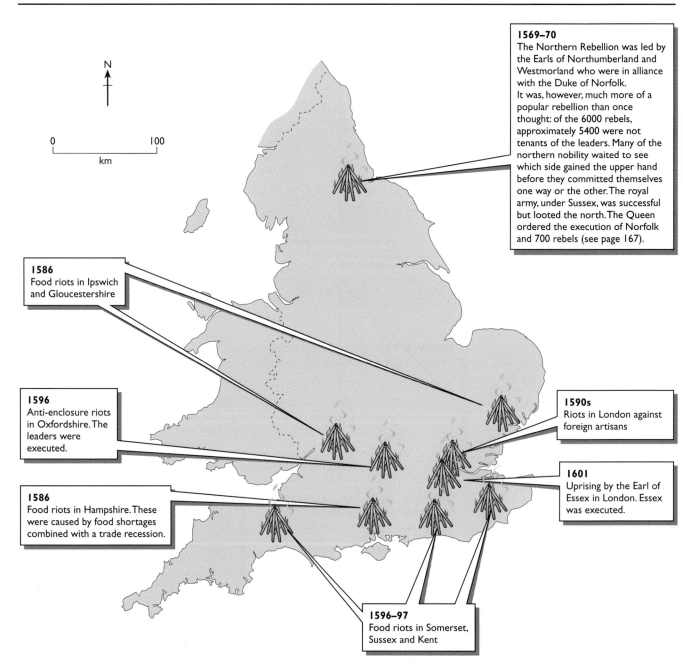

1569–70
The Northern Rebellion was led by the Earls of Northumberland and Westmorland who were in alliance with the Duke of Norfolk.
It was, however, much more of a popular rebellion than once thought: of the 6000 rebels, approximately 5400 were not tenants of the leaders. Many of the northern nobility waited to see which side gained the upper hand before they committed themselves one way or the other. The royal army, under Sussex, was successful but looted the north. The Queen ordered the execution of Norfolk and 700 rebels (see page 167).

1586
Food riots in Ipswich and Gloucestershire

1596
Anti-enclosure riots in Oxfordshire. The leaders were executed.

1586
Food riots in Hampshire. These were caused by food shortages combined with a trade recession.

1590s
Riots in London against foreign artisans

1601
Uprising by the Earl of Essex in London. Essex was executed.

1596–97
Food riots in Somerset, Sussex and Kent

TALKING POINT

Does the occurrence of riots and arrests mean that law and order was breaking down?

SOURCE 9.7   W. Rye, *England as seen by foreigners in the days of Elizabeth I and James I*

One dare not oppose them else the street boys and apprentices collect together in immense crowds and strike to the right and left of them.

SOURCE 9.8   J. Hooker, *Description of the city of Exeter, Devon and Cornwall, 1558*

Forasmuch as Richard Gyfforde, butcher, and John Howell, cordwainer, men of good reputation . . . have very unseemly, disorderly and indecently misdemeaned themselves . . . in fighting and brawling that the said Richard Gyfforde shall abide in prison at the will and pleasure of the mayor and corporation.

SOURCE 9.9   Edward Hext, a Somerset JP, writing to Lord Burghley, 1597

Having long observed the rapines and thefts committed within this county where I serve, and finding they multiply daily . . . The inhabitants made complaint at our last Easter sessions, whereupon precepts were made to the constables of the Hundred, but few apprehended, for they have intelligence of all things intended against them.

SOURCE 9.10   To the mayor and justices of Norfolk; from the Calendar of the manuscripts of the Marquis of Salisbury, Vol.13

For seven years the rich have fed on our flesh. Bribes make you Justices blind . . . what are these edicts and proclamations . . . but a scabbard without a sword, for neither are those murdering maltsters nor the bloody corn buyers stayed.

SOURCE 9.11   From *Acts of the Privy Council, 1596–97*

Her Majesty being informed that there are certain ill-disposed persons in that county of Oxfordshire . . . that purpose to gather together in some numbers under pretence to pull down enclosures and that they to execute their further malicious purposes have an intent to seize upon the armour and horses of Sir Henry Lee . . . for the speedy preventing of such attempts . . . we have thought good to relieve you, being her Majesty's lieutenant of that county, to call unto you some Justices of the Peace . . . to take present order to apprehend the ringleaders . . . and to send the principalest of them up hither.

SOURCE 9.12   From the memoirs of Robert Carey, warden of the Midale March on the Scottish borders, 1598

The thieves hearing of my being settled there, continued still their wonted course in spoiling the country, not caring much for me, nor my authority . . . afore that summer was ended they were somewhat more fearful of me . . . I took not so few as sixteen or seventeen . . . of notorious offenders, that ended their days by hanging or beheading.

ACTIVITY

1 **a)** Who or what do the writers in Sources 9.7 and 9.8 blame for the local disorders?
   b) In Source 9.9 why does Hext claim it is so hard for JPs to maintain law and order?
   c) What reasons are given in Source 9.10 to explain the popular unrest?
   d) What does Source 9.11 demonstrate about the communication between local and central government?
   e) Look at Sources 9.11 and 9.12. What methods could central government use to enforce control in local areas?
2 Have the authors of all of these sources assessed the seriousness of these disturbances?

E Review: How did Elizabeth control local government?

Recent interpretations of local government have shown that – as with central government – it was dominated by a group of powerful and ambitious men whom Elizabeth had to keep on her side by using a variety of strategies. The old picture of a loyal gentry class eagerly enforcing an ever-increasing number of government statutes in return for the social prestige of the office has been revised. Powerful men, with their networks of clients and tenants, competed for political power both at court and in localities and, in doing so, tended to serve the royal interest unless or until it clashed with their own. Faced with the necessity of basing government on the consent and co-operation of the political classes, the Queen used her prerogative powers, particularly patronage, and created, a 'propaganda policy designed to maximise popular loyalty to herself' (C. Haigh, *Elizabeth I*, 1988, p. 146).

The nobles, faced with rising inflation, came to see the financial benefits of office-holding as a necessary way of supplementing their incomes, while the more financially robust gentry class gained from office-holding a social standing that birth had not given them. For most of the reign, therefore, the system of local government worked well enough because it represented the interests of the politically-active classes. As elsewhere, however, it began to break down in the 1590s when central government continued to press for taxation to finance war, against the background of real social and economic distress. The decline of authority at the centre was mirrored at local level when, during the 1590s, the political conflict between Robert Cecil and the Earl of Essex was played out in the country at large as each tried to build up support through the distribution of local offices to his own followers. Yet, the breakdown of the system in the Queen's declining years need not detract from its success for much of the reign. Despite recent changes in emphasis, the verdict of A. G. R. Smith still holds: 'the majority of the governing classes throughout the country were in broad agreement with most of the Queen's policies during her reign. That is one important reason why Elizabeth's government was in the main successful' (*The Government of Elizabethan England*, 1967, p. 99). The fact that local magnates still exercised considerable local and feudal powers and that JPs were often unwilling to carry out their duties makes the work of Elizabeth and her councillors more, not less, impressive.

ACTIVITY

Using the evidence in this chapter, prepare an answer to the essay question: How successfully did local and central government work together in the period 1558–1603 to maintain law and order.

KEY POINTS FROM CHAPTER 9: How did Elizabeth control local government?

1 The influence of the nobility at local level was a major consideration. The Queen needed to control powerful local families.

2 The links between central and local government – the institutions and officials – formed a framework that enabled Elizabeth to enforce policy and maintain law and order.

3 The problems of law enforcement and a re-evaluation of the role of the Justice of the Peace have led historians to believe that JPs were less acquiescent than was once believed.

4 The strategies which central government used to control the localities varied, but the most important were the use of the royal prerogative and propaganda.

5 A study of the effectiveness of local government requires an examination of instances of unrest and reactions to it. Most of these occurred in the 1590s and were motivated by economic grievances.

Was Ireland governed successfully?

CHAPTER OVERVIEW

TALKING POINT

Does history really teach us to learn from the past? If so, why have politicians failed for so long to learn from earlier mistakes made over the government of Ireland?

In central and local government Elizabeth controlled men, events, and ultimately policies. By employing a variety of strategies she was able to ensure support for her decisions, or at the least prevent any united long-term opposition, and it is possible, with some qualifications, to paint a picture of success. When it came to dealing with Ireland, however, Elizabeth's sureness of touch deserted her.

Ireland was not considered an immediate problem by the Tudors and, except for times when it threatened national stability, policy towards it tended to be somewhat laissez-faire. This was mainly due to the fact that the Tudors lacked long-term goals in Ireland and, because of the costs involved in developing a consistent policy, tended to opt for short-term expedients. The very nature of Ireland in the sixteenth century caused English politicians and decision makers to think twice before committing themselves. Despite the work of the early Tudors, Ireland in 1558 was a land where, 'The descendants of the Anglo-Norman Earls of Desmond, Ormond and Kildare held sway over a society in which English influence only slightly diluted the older culture while in most of the rest of the island the ancient Gaelic society remained untouched by the alien conqueror' (W. MacCaffrey, *Elizabeth I*, 1993, p. 417).

The English conquest of Ireland began in the twelfth century but had not been sustained. Although the King of England was, until 1540, also Lord of Ireland, real English influence was restricted to an 80-km area around Dublin known as the Pale. The rest of Ireland was controlled by powerful feudal magnates, a scene not dissimilar to the situation in the English regions. Any similarities, however, end there. Gaelic society was very different from the Anglo-Norman feudal system. It had a different system of land ownership, property rights, personal dependence on the crown, military obligations, language, fashion and, after 1558, religion.

If the English were to assert effective control over Ireland they would need to abolish the power of the great earldoms and change the country's social structure. There were many ways in which this could be done, ranging from a gradual extension of English administrative control to outright conquest. During her reign, Elizabeth's deputies tried elements of all of the available options, yet Elizabeth herself remained indifferent.

Concerns in Ireland did not receive the urgent attention which characterised Elizabeth's dealings with mainstream issues. She saw Ireland as a drain on resources and the constraints of geography and communication pushed it to the back of her mind; until, that is, her failure to act decisively pushed England into a bloody and expensive conquest of the country in the 1590s.

The purpose of this chapter is to examine the methods employed by Elizabeth and her deputies to govern Ireland and, by analysing the threat to stability posed by the unrest and rebellions, evaluate their effectiveness.

A What was Elizabeth's Irish inheritance? (pp. 94–95)

B What policies did Elizabeth and her deputies pursue in Ireland? (pp. 96–99)

C Review: Was Ireland governed successfully? (p. 100)

SOURCE 10.1 W. MacCaffrey, *Elizabeth I*, 1993, p. 420

Events in Ireland reached her through a kind of sound barrier, muted by distance and the lapse of time . . . among her chief officers of state, the Irish deputy was the one most rarely in face-to-face contact. Information reached her through his letters but was also filtered through many sources, members of the Dublin council, and interested parties in her own court and council . . . but her Irish subjects were hard put to get a hearing at court.

LORD DEPUTY LIEUTENANT
The Lord Deputy Lieutenant ruled Ireland in the name of the King or Queen of England. Appointed by the monarch, he could be Anglo-Norman, Irish or English.

A What was Elizabeth's Irish inheritance?

■ 10A Milestones in the Tudor government of Ireland

FOCUS ROUTE

Make notes on:

- the priorities of the early Tudors in Ireland
- the legacy Elizabeth inherited in 1558.

1485
Henry VII inherited an Ireland under the control of the Yorkist LORD DEPUTY LIEUTENANT, the eighth Earl of Kildare.

1487–91
Two claimants to Henry VII's throne, Lambert Simnel and Perkin Warbeck, landed in Ireland where they received limited support. Henry VII dismissed Kildare.

1494
The new deputy introduced Poynings Law, which greatly increased English control over Ireland's administration and institutions.

1497
Kildare was reinstated when Poynings Law proved too expensive for England. He served Henry loyally for the rest of Henry's reign.

1513
Henry VIII continued his father's policies. The ninth Earl of Kildare replaced his father as Lord Deputy Lieutenant.

1520
Henry VIII appointed the English noble Thomas Howard, Earl of Surrey, as Lord Deputy Lieutenant. Although instructed to rule through diplomacy, Surrey believed Ireland could only be controlled through conquest. He was recalled in 1523 and replaced by eight governors in rapid succession, the majority of whom were Anglo-Irish nobles.

■ 10B Ireland in 1558

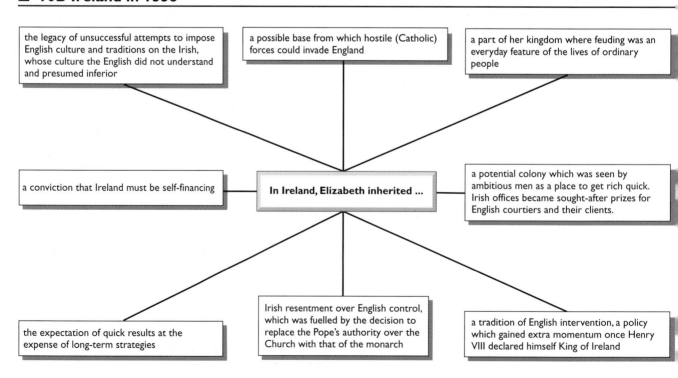

the legacy of unsuccessful attempts to impose English culture and traditions on the Irish, whose culture the English did not understand and presumed inferior

a possible base from which hostile (Catholic) forces could invade England

a part of her kingdom where feuding was an everyday feature of the lives of ordinary people

a conviction that Ireland must be self-financing

In Ireland, Elizabeth inherited ...

a potential colony which was seen by ambitious men as a place to get rich quick. Irish offices became sought-after prizes for English courtiers and their clients.

the expectation of quick results at the expense of long-term strategies

Irish resentment over English control, which was fuelled by the decision to replace the Pope's authority over the Church with that of the monarch

a tradition of English intervention, a policy which gained extra momentum once Henry VIII declared himself King of Ireland

ACTIVITY

It is 1558. You are one of Elizabeth's councillors. Choose one of the options available to her to keep control over Ireland. Put forward an argument to convince her of the merits of this policy. You should include counter arguments for the objections you know she is bound to make.

1541
Henry VIII altered Ireland's constitution when he declared it a kingdom and himself its king. All the Irish, not just those already under English control in the Pale, were now his subjects. The new deputy, Sir Anthony St Leger, then embarked on a scheme whereby Irish lords surrendered their lands and regained them as feudal subjects of the crown with a title recognised under English law. In return for their land, Irish lords had to obey the King's officers, do military service, pay taxes, learn English, adopt English customs, and reject the Pope. Although progress was slow, the initiative was beginning to make real headway when it was suspended in 1543 because of Henry's war with France and Scotland. After this, policy became increasingly aggressive and increasingly purposeless.

1536
Lord Leonard Grey was appointed as deputy, to carry out Cromwell's new policy. Dublin was to extend its control to the Pale, but beyond it the powers of the Irish lords were not to be challenged. Grey was to negotiate peace with the Irish lords, but the frontier would still be garrisoned. Ireland was expected to finance itself. Grey's arrogance united all the Irish lords against English rule and Protestantism.

1534
Thomas Cromwell returned to the policy of appointing London bureaucrats to the post of Lord Deputy Lieutenant, rather than using local magnates. A rebellion by the tenth Earl of Kildare was defeated by Sir William Skeffington and Kildare was executed at Tyburn in 1537.

1547–49
The Duke of Somerset reinforced the English army in Ireland by establishing garrisons in frontier areas, and began the first steps towards colonisation by introducing English settlers into the counties of Leix and Offaly.

1553
Mary Tudor continued Somerset's policies and created two new shires.

■ 10C Leading Irishmen in Elizabeth's reign

The Anglo-Norman Irish nobles

- Fourteenth Earl of Desmond, Gerald Fitzmaurice Fitzgerald (1533–83). He governed Munster and opposed English rule.
- Eleventh Earl of Kildare, Gerald Fitzgerald (1525–85). He was regarded by the Irish as the natural ruler of the Pale and therefore the automatic choice for Lord Deputy.
- Eleventh Earl of Ormonde, Thomas Butler (1531–1614). He governed Leinster. He was related to Elizabeth and remained loyal to her, the one Irishman who felt at home at court.
- Second Earl of Tyrone, Hugh O'Neill (1550–1616). With the O'Donnells, he governed Ulster and led the main thrust of Irish resistance against English rule.

The Gaelic chieftains

- O'Neill of Tyrone: Shane (clan chief 1559–67) and Hugh (1595–1603)
- O'Donnell of Tyrconnel: Hugh (1566–92) and Hugh Roe (1592–1601)

As an Anglicised Irishman, Hugh O'Neill appears in both lists.

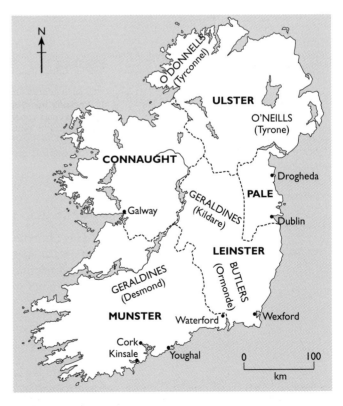

SOURCE 10.2 A map of the Irish provinces and their leading families in 1500

What policies did Elizabeth and her deputies pursue in Ireland?

FOCUS ROUTE

As you read pages 94–98, make detailed notes on:

• why Elizabeth could not ignore Ireland
• Elizabeth's aims in Ireland
• the policies that Elizabeth's deputies enforced
• the four rebellions against English rule.

Shane O'Neill's rebellion in Ulster, 1559–66

The Earl of Sussex

Elizabeth ordered Sussex to maintain control in Ireland, reduce expenditure and enforce the 1559 Religious Settlement. He therefore continued attempts to colonise Ireland by establishing plantations, as well as increasing English forces in Ireland. His period in office is seen as unsuccessful because he was unable to defeat Shane O'Neill's rebellion in Ulster, largely through lack of quick support from Elizabeth.

Sir Henry Sidney

Sidney was sent to quash O'Neill's rebellion in 1565 after Sussex's failure to do so. He marched through Ulster and, with the help of rival clans, destroyed O'Neill's power. O'Neill was murdered by the clans he took refuge with. Sidney then continued Sussex's policy of strategic colonisation. He later proposed setting up regional councils along the lines of the Council of the North. His nominee for the presidency of the Munster Council caused uprisings in Leinster. The Queen refused to send further funds and replaced Sidney in 1567.

SOURCE 10.3   S. Ellis, *Tudor Ireland*, 1985, p. 255

Ten years campaigning in Ulster had done little to advance royal influence there, but Shane's fortuitous assassination removed a serious international embarrassment to the government and left Elizabeth well placed to exploit the ensuing alterations in the balance of power. While the Privy Council debated how best to exploit the opportunity however, the chance was missed.

SOURCE 10.4   S. Ellis, *Tudor Ireland*, 1985, p. 246

By 1564 the trend of government policy since 1547 had largely confirmed Gaelic chieftains in their view that St Leger's initiatives were a flash in the pan and that, whatever her ministers said or did, Elizabeth's aim was the traditional English one of military conquest and expropriation of Gaelic land.

SOURCE 10.5   W. MacCaffrey, *Elizabeth I*, 1993, p. 423

Once again the key Irish appointment was determined by the twists and turns of English politics . . . dismayed by the heavy cost and lack of success in the introduction of the presidencies, the Queen now listened to proposals for experiments in which the cost could be shifted to private shoulders – colonisation.

The Fitzgerald Rebellion in Munster, 1569–72

Sir Henry Sidney

Sidney was recalled to Ireland to put down the Fitzgerald Rebellion in Munster. Although initially a private war between the Earl of Desmond and the Earl of Ormonde, Elizabeth became worried when Desmond's cousin, James Fitzmaurice Fitzgerald, appealed for Catholic and foreign aid. The rebellion was quickly subdued but the foreign support, backed by the Papacy, triggered off increasing discontent against colonisation schemes in Munster.

SOURCE 10.6 S. Ellis, *Tudor Ireland*, 1985, p. 260

Very probably however, the revolts of 1569–70 were an Irish manifestation of the court intrigues which culminated in the northern rising of 1569–70. Two northern rebels later joined Fitzmaurice ... despite the Papal Bull of 1570 excommunicating Elizabeth, another decade was to elapse before Irish dissidents would generally identify political and religious grievances and actively support the developing COUNTER REFORMATION *movement.*

> **COUNTER REFORMATION**
> A movement led by the Catholic Church to stop the popularity and expansion of Protestantism.

In the wake of the rebellion, two privately based attempts at colonisation failed, and the Queen recalled Sidney after the introduction of a new land tax in Munster and Connaught failed to stop expenditure in Ireland soaring. There was an increasing conviction that military conquest was the only option.

The Fitzgerald Rebellion in Munster, 1579–83

Lord Arthur Grey

In 1580, Grey was sent, with an army of 6500 men, to put down a rebellion led by James Fitzmaurice Fitzgerald and backed by the Pope. The rebels were joined by the Earl of Desmond and the rebellion spread to Munster, Leinster, Ulster and Connaught. Grey put down the conspiracy savagely: the garrison at Smerwick – composed mainly of reinforcements sent from Spain – was massacred after surrendering, there were widespread executions, the harvest was burned and cattle were slaughtered. Grey was recalled by Elizabeth because his methods had alienated traditional government supporters in the Pale. Nevertheless, he had paved the way for the successful colonisation of Desmond's lands in Munster and Connaught.

SOURCE 10.7 S. Ellis, *Tudor Ireland*, 1985, p. 297

With the Munster plantation and the consolidation of presidential control in North Connaught, it seemed that Tudor rule might be extended throughout Ireland without further serious trouble. By 1590, English local administration operated everywhere outside Ulster and a system of garrisons had been created to contain and localise disturbances.

Source 10.8 Hugh O'Neill, Earl of Tyrone, desires a parley with Lord Mountjoy at Kinsale in 1601

Dolose agunt filij iniquitatis

■ 10D A timeline of events

1594 Tyrone, having announced he was willing to fight to the death, begins to build up his forces and harry the English army.

1595 Tyrone seizes the English fort on the Blackwater, captures Enniskillen Castle and defeats the English at Clontribet.

1596 Elizabeth pardons Tyrone, giving him time to extend his power base.

1597 Tyrone defeats the English garrison at the Battle of the Yellow Ford.

1599 The Earl of Essex is sent to Ireland as deputy with an army of 17,000 men. But he is reluctant to take command, convinced that his enemies at court will capitalise on his absence. Essex fails, marching into Ulster instead of confronting Tyrone and then agreeing to a truce. His unauthorised flight back to London marks the beginning of his fall from grace.

1600 Charles Blount, Lord Mountjoy, veteran of campaigns in the Netherlands and Brittany, is sent to Ireland with a large army and the full backing of the Queen and her council.

1601 Spanish forces land at Kinsale to join with Tyrone. Mountjoy implements a three-pronged attack from Armagh, Lough Foyle and Tyrconnel.

1602 Tyrone is defeated in battle.

1603 Tyrone's negotiated surrender comes six days after Elizabeth's death.

Tyrone's rebellion in Ulster, 1594–1603

The causes of Tyrone's rebellion are as follows.

- War with Spain meant that expenditure on Ireland had to be kept low, while the country had to be secured in case the Spanish used it as a base for an invasion of England.
- Ireland was increasingly neglected by Elizabeth and her council. The 60-year-old deputy, Fitzwilliam, could not control the bitter disputes between factions in Dublin.
- Clan warfare increased with accusations of cattle raiding, summary executions, etc.
- Irish chieftains saw their whole system under threat. Trust in the English deputies plummeted.
- The greatest Gaelic leader, Hugh O'Neill, Earl of Tyrone, came to power in Ulster.
- Tyrone was in contact with Spain from 1590 and began to train an army. The council, however, was divided about its strategies: Elizabeth wanted peace almost at any cost.

SOURCE 10.9 Charles Blount, Lord Mountjoy

Historians' criticisms of Elizabeth's Irish policy

SOURCE 10.10 W. MacCaffrey, *Elizabeth I*, 1993, p. 432

With Tyrone's capitulation, Elizabeth finished the task set by her father 80 years earlier, the completion of the English conquest of Ireland . . . it was achieved in agony and pain through the misery and deaths of countless of the Queen's subjects . . . it evoked on both sides a venomous outpouring of hatred which would permanently poison relations between the two islands.

SOURCE 10.11 W. MacCaffrey, *Elizabeth I*, 1993, p. 433

To these problems (geographic distance, money, greater urgency of other problems, and a lack of consistent long-term goals), Elizabeth contributed nothing. So far as possible she avoided them, invariably resorting to the cheapest remedy which would buy a short-term solution . . . when men of larger vision, such as Sydney and Perrot, pressed for programmatic strategies aimed at structural adaptation, she was incapable of balancing short-term costs against long-term advantage.

SOURCE 10.12 S. Ellis, *Tudor Ireland*, 1985, p. 315

Undoubtedly, the planning, preparation and execution of Mountjoy's campaign was an extraordinary feat of government. Yet it placed an enormous strain on the English economy and the crown's limited financial resources – the cost of victory was unexpectedly high. Large parts of Ireland had been devastated, crops burned, cattle slaughtered, or buildings razed. Ulster was almost a wilderness, Munster west of Cork almost uninhabited, trade disrupted, the coinage debased, towns ruined or declining, and the population decimated by famine.

SOURCE 10.13 S. Ellis, *Tudor Ireland*, 1985, p. 318

Elizabeth's rule by faction, parsimony, and an irresolute conduct of government, proved particularly disastrous in Ireland and certainly strengthens the revisionist interpretation beginning to emerge of a queen who made serious mistakes as well as enjoying spectacular successes.

ACTIVITY

Divide into two groups and each choose one of the following statements. Prepare a spider diagram to present to the rest of the class.

- Elizabeth made serious mistakes in her policies towards Ireland.
- Elizabeth did the best she could in Ireland, in view of the problems she faced there and elsewhere.

■ Learning trouble spot

To what extent did English policy achieve its aims in Ireland between 1559 and 1603? Faced with a question like this, students often struggle with the complexity of events and resort, in panic, to a narrative account of the four rebellions. The Focus routes and Activities in this chapter have been designed to help you to avoid this. If you have worked through them you should be able to construct an answer based around the following key points:

- the legacy Elizabeth inherited in Ireland and her aims there
- the different strategies her Lord Deputy Lieutenants used to enforce control
- the effectiveness of the strategies used, including the seriousness of the four rebellions
- an evaluation of the extent to which Elizabeth achieved her aims, some comment on their validity and historians' criticism of her lack of vision.

Now, have a go at writing the essay for yourself.

FOCUS ROUTE

The government used the following strategies in its attempts to control Ireland:

- regional councils
- colonisation
- negotiation with Irish chiefs
- military conquest.

Construct a table, like the one below, giving examples of where each strategy was used with some analysis of its result. Regional councils has been done for you.

Strategy	Example	Result
Setting up regional councils	Attempted in Munster by Sir Henry Sidney, 1566–67	Failed. There was tension over the choice of president and Elizabeth withdrew her support, fearing more financial commitment. Government in Ireland continued to rely on the Lord Deputy Lieutenant enforcing English policies and maintaining good relations with the Irish nobles and chiefs. An opportunity lost?

C Review: Was Ireland governed successfully?

Elizabeth faced far greater problems in Ireland than in any other territories under her control. Much of this was due to the situation she inherited in 1558: a country only partly under English rule, with a mixture of Gaelic and Anglo-Norman cultures, which had been subjected to half a century of changing initiatives and styles of government from London. She could not simply preserve the status quo because, within a year, the first of four major rebellions broke out. In addition, as the reign progressed, religion became an increasingly significant factor in her dealings with Ireland as Roman Catholicism grew in strength, partly as a result of missionary work and partly as a reaction against the Protestant English. There were even times when the Papacy and Spain intervened on behalf of the Irish.

Given the volatile situation, Elizabeth perhaps should not be blamed for the failure of her policies. Yet it is possible to see a similar scenario in England when looking at the powers and religious convictions of the mighty feudal magnates in the north, and the government successfully resolved those problems. In Ireland however, there were clearly periods when government control virtually broke down. The usual explanation for this has been that, 'Geographical, cultural and social differences within Ireland and between Ireland and England created conditions which were so extraordinary by English standards as to constitute an intractable problem of government' (S. Ellis, *Tudor Ireland*, 1985, p. 316). More recently historians have begun to see the whole direction of England's policy towards Ireland as an error. The individual policies themselves were all workable but none of them was given the chance to succeed, because, until the 1590s, Elizabeth hoped to govern Ireland on the cheap and avoid any long-term drain on resources. As a result, 'The demands made of successive governors greatly outstripped the resources available to them to perform their duties ... policies failed in Ireland because they were not given the chance to succeed' (S. Ellis, *Tudor Ireland*, 1985, p. 316). Until her decision to appoint Mountjoy and equip him with an army of realistic proportions, Elizabeth failed to support the reforms of her able deputies, such as Sidney, and appointed men, such as Sussex, Grey and Essex, who were a mistake.

The result of Elizabeth's inconsistently applied goals in Ireland was not completion of the Tudor conquest of Ireland, but another stage in the country's unhappy relationship with England. Protestantism was not established uniformly. The Gaelic and the old Anglo-Irish families remained loyal to Catholicism. The cost of defeating the last rebellion led to social and economic distress in England, which in turn led to unrest in Parliament and a modest decline in Elizabeth's popularity. It therefore seems difficult to disagree with Stephen Ellis' conclusion that, 'The Tudor achievement in Ireland remains distinctly unimpressive' (*Tudor Ireland*, 1985, p. 315).

KEY POINTS FROM CHAPTER 10: Was Ireland governed successfully?

1 Ireland was important to the Tudors. For strategic reasons it needed to be, at the very least, not hostile to England.

2 The possibility of Ireland being used as a base for a foreign invasion increased in the 1540s, when England turned to Protestantism.

3 The earlier Tudors used a variety of policies to bring Ireland under their control.

4 Elizabeth inherited her problems in Ireland. Although she varied her strategies and Lord Deputy Lieutenants she did not commit to any long enough to ensure success, usually because of their expense.

5 There were four rebellions against English rule in Elizabeth's reign. The last one, led by the Earl of Tyrone, was particularly bloody.

Review: Was Elizabeth in control of government?

This section set out to answer the question: was Elizabeth in control of government? The answer must be a resounding yes. The system she inherited was hierarchical and based on the power of the monarch, who:

- decided who to appoint to her Privy Council
- chose when to summon or dismiss Parliament
- ensured loyalty and support through a system of patronage based on titles, office holding, and attendance at court
- ensured the rise of members of the gentry class, in London and in the provinces, through their appointment as JPs
- directly or indirectly controlled all appointments and dismissals
- had the final say in all policy decisions including signing bills.

If we change the emphasis of the question, however, and ask, 'Did Elizabeth successfully control government?', then despite an overall yes some qualifications arise.

- Although Elizabeth successfully selected extremely capable men as her ministers, their ability and commitment meant that they were never prepared to be 'yes men'. The Queen had to devise strategies to ensure that her policies were accepted, while members of the council were equally adept at implementing strategies of their own to promote different policies.
- Although Elizabeth did not encounter an organised opposition party in the House of Commons, she did experience opposition over specific areas (religion in the House of Lords and monopolies in the House of Commons). She was also unhappy at the extent to which Parliament wanted to discuss areas such as religion, foreign policy and the succession, which she felt came under the royal prerogative and should not therefore be raised by her subjects.
- Although Elizabeth successfully used the gentry class as unpaid JPs to enforce the law at local level, many of them did not impose central decisions when they ran counter to the interests of their local community.
- Although Elizabeth successfully defeated rebellions in Ireland, she had no long-term aims for the country. This lack, combined with her failure to support her more able deputies, both caused these rebellions and prevented a long-term solution being found for the problems in Ireland.
- Although Elizabeth successfully managed the country's financial resources, showing prudence and thriftiness, she missed opportunities to expand the crown's resources in line with inflation and to raise taxation and improve its collection.
- In all areas of government there were times when Elizabeth was not in control, particularly in the 1590s. The episode with the Earl of Essex is one example.

At this point, it would be timely to raise two points made in Section 1.

- Despite the considerable powers of the monarch, the English system of government depended on the support of the politically-active classes. To this extent, whatever their power on paper, in reality a monarch's power was limited by their need to work with councillors, JPs and MPs to run the country on a day-to-day basis.

• At the start of her reign, Elizabeth was handicapped by uncertainties over the succession. She was also faced with very serious problems and high popular expectations as a result of the previous two reigns. In 1558, she was a young, inexperienced female, who was expected to make immediate decisions and surround herself with ambitious, dominating men. The methods she chose to deal with the situation were to characterise the way she ran her government for the next 40 years. They can be interpreted as clever, pragmatic and assertive, or nervous, indecisive and muddled.

You should review Section 2 once you have studied Elizabeth's domestic and foreign policies, so that you can assess whether events aided or threatened the successful working of government and therefore England's security.

ACTIVITY

1 Find out what happened in the years 1559, 1567, 1569, 1570, 1572, 1578, 1584, 1586 and in the 1590s and then fill in a table like the one below to highlight the problems Elizabeth and her government faced.

Date	Privy Council	Parliament	Local government	Ireland
1559				
1567				

2 Which were the most difficult years for Elizabethan government? Why?
3 How well did Elizabethan government deal with the difficulties it faced?
4 Prepare an answer for the following questions:
  a) What were the functions of the Privy Council and of Parliament and why did these sometimes overlap? (5)
  b) Which major issues caused the most difficulties for Elizabeth and her government and how successfully were they resolved? (5)
  c) How effectively did central government communicate with areas outside of London?
  d) In what ways, and why, did government operate less successfully in the 1590s? (10)

What two leading historians have said about Elizabeth's government

SOURCE 11.1 C. Haigh, *Elizabeth I*, 1988, p. 169

The Protestant enthusiasts of the early seventeenth century produced a picture of Elizabeth I which has proved attractive and influential. Like the approved pattern-portraits in her reign, the Protestant picture has been replicated many times in different clothes and against different backgrounds. The imperialistic historians of the late nineteenth century and the romantic English nationalists of the mid-twentieth both saw her as a sympathetic manager of the urgent aspirations of an energetic Protestant England – a midwife for the future. But Elizabeth had little enthusiasm for the growth of popular Protestantism, of parliamentary oversight, of continental alliances, and of maritime challenges to Spain. She did not lead advances from the front, she restrained them from behind: her reign was a constant struggle to avoid policies and contain forces which she disliked. Elizabeth was not a wise and powerful statesperson, implementing the constructive policies she knew her nation needed: she was a nervous politician struggling for survival.

SOURCE 11.2 C. Haigh, *Elizabeth I*, 1988, p. 172

Elizabeth brought real dramatic talent to the role of Virgin Queen and mother, and freed herself from some of the restrictions of her sex. But the production in which she starred ran for forty-five years, she had no understudy, and she had to appear in every show: it was a constant strain. Her performances were not flawless: she disliked her part in the early years, when she hoped to marry Dudley; she was bored with it in 1579, when she thought of marrying Alençon; and she could not quite carry it off in her last decade. She fluffed her lines on important occasions – in her dealings with the Duke of Norfolk and the northern earls in 1569, and with Essex and his allies from 1596. She often alienated her Protestant fans by not wearing their costumes, in 1561, in 1565, in 1575, in 1579, and in 1584. She lost confidence in her interpretation of the part in 1585, and allowed her leading man to persuade her into a more aggressive version for foreign audiences. Her relationship with supporting actresses was always poor, she worked uneasily with newcomers, and as an old trouper she was upstaged by the fiery talent of Essex. But hers was an award-winning performance, and what was missing in dramatic conception was more than made up for in sheer professional skill.

The metaphor of drama is an appropriate one for Elizabeth's reign, for her power was an illusion – and an illusion was her power. Like Henry IV of France, she projected an image of herself which brought stability and prestige to her country. By constant attention to the details of her total performance, she kept the rest of the cast on their toes and kept her own part as queen.

SOURCE 11.3 S. Doran, 'Elizabeth I', *The Historian*, No. 54, 1997

. . . over the last decade historians have tended to adopt a more critical line. Perhaps the most extreme case is Dr Christopher Haigh's 1988 political profile of the Queen, which in seeking to destroy Elizabeth the icon produced a harsh interpretation of Elizabeth the woman: Haigh's Elizabeth was bossy rather than imperious, selfish rather than self-sacrificing, a vain, evil-tempered, and even at times silly creature. Her abilities were slight and her achievements negligible: 'Queen Elizabeth', he wrote, 'did not attempt to solve problems, she simply avoided them – and then survived long enough for some to go away.'

Haigh's profile of the Queen, however, is no less one-sided than the laudatory biographies and studies it attacks; it also shares one of their other shortcomings: it is unashamedly sexist. Whereas Professor Neale unconsciously absorbed the gender stereotyping of his own day, Dr Haigh appears to take delight in the use of politically incorrect language and analogies: his Elizabeth is labelled as 'something of a fish-wife', 'a spinster aunt' to her nobles, 'a nagging wife' to her councillors, and 'a nanny' to her MPs. Haigh's piece is often provocative, certainly amusing, but not particularly helpful. Furthermore, a less self-conscious stereotyping creeps into Haigh's more conventional interpretations of Elizabeth's character. Thus he accepts uncritically contemporary descriptions of the Queen as 'vain' and 'vacillating', even though they conform so well to sixteenth-century expectations of the 'weaker' sex that they are somewhat suspect as character traits. At times he also seems to be taken in by Elizabeth's love of theatricality. Always on public display, she deliberately played a part for public consumption and it is disputable whether or not her behaviour on any single occasion was spontaneous or contrived. Was she as evil-tempered, for example, as Dr Haigh declared, or were at least some of her public rages an instrument of political management?

SOURCE 11.4 S. Doran, 'Elizabeth I', *The Historian*, No. 54, 1997

Clearly then, Elizabeth's political aims and style of government were more complex than her image-makers and admirers have admitted. In addition, her popularity and solidarity with her subjects can no longer be taken for granted, especially during the last decade of her reign. Nonetheless, her achievements as a ruler should not be underestimated. Despite enormous difficulties and several major crises, she survived as monarch with her Protestant religious settlement intact, while her realm was preserved from successful invasion and the civil wars, which afflicted her neighbours, Scotland, France, and the Netherlands. Fifteen years of warfare created stresses certainly, but not the financial collapse or large-scale political unrest which often came in the wake of war. This stability and security owed much to Elizabeth's firm but flexible leadership, and her conservative and relatively cautious policies. What more could be expected of a sixteenth-century ruler?

ACTIVITY

1 Read Source 11.1.
   a) Why has the image of Elizabeth produced by Protestants lasted for so long?
   b) Why does Christopher Haigh question this image?
2 Read Source 11.2.
   a) What does Christopher Haigh think Elizabeth was?
   b) What does he consider are examples of Elizabeth being less in control than she would have wished?
3 Read Source 11.3.
   a) Why does Susan Doran criticise Christopher Haigh's interpretation of Elizabeth?
   b) Why does Susan Doran think that Christopher Haigh is wrong about Elizabeth?
4 Read Source 11.4.
   a) What does Susan Doran think Elizabeth's strength as a ruler was due to?
   b) Are there any direct contradictions between Susan Doran's conclusions and those of Christopher Haigh?

TALKING POINT

How can two such eminent historians, who have presumably researched much of the same material, come to such different conclusions about Elizabeth I?

■ Learning trouble spot

Although students tend to want answers rather than interpretation, history is always changing, especially in areas where the original sources are vague or – in the case of Elizabeth's government – have deliberately been written to show events in a positive light and to paper over any cracks. You are not expected to come up with any definitive answers, but to show that you understand that history is about debate and that historians constantly reassess the past in the context of their own age and sympathies.

As Sources 11.1–11.4 show, it is possible to come to two very different conclusions about the extent to which Elizabeth was in control throughout her reign. You have to show the examiner that you have thought about this, have your own opinions and can support them by referring to the facts.

TALKING POINT

The bigger picture! Look back at page 5 and you'll see that this book has an overarching theme: the investigation into whether Elizabeth's reign was a Golden Age.

Has your work on Section 2 modified the views you had of Elizabeth before you began this study? How do you think Elizabeth's role in government affects her reputation for creating a cultural Golden Age?

Did Elizabeth's government bring prosperity to her people?

The format of Section 3 will be slightly different for several reasons.

- Social and economic history in the sixteenth century will probably be an area of study that is entirely new to you.
- The terms we use today, to describe prosperity for example, often have very different meanings in a pre-industrial society.
- Specific terms will be new to you, but they are important if you are to make sense of what was happening, to whom, and why.
- This is an area of considerable controversy and there are fewer certainties than usual. This is because complete records of the lives of ordinary people have not survived in the same way that a government Act has, for example. Historians have had to try to build up an accurate picture of society from a variety of different and often incomplete sources.
- It is easy to use generalisations, such as 'the people'. You need to know who the people were and, more importantly, that despite general economic trends different things happened to different people at different times and for different reasons.

Although the section will be divided into chapters, the main social and economic changes which took place during the period will run through each of them. The focus of the whole section will therefore be on:

- the main sources of wealth
- whether wealth increased or decreased during the period and why
- the resulting social changes
- the government's response.

As a whole, Section 3 aims to assess the effectiveness of government policies in terms of how successfully, or otherwise, they promoted not only prosperity but also national stability.

12

What was Elizabethan England like?

CHAPTER OVERVIEW   It is impossible to study government policies in a vacuum which ignores what is going on in the country at large. Social and economic changes influence what a government can and must do, just as much as government policies themselves can change society and the economy. We live in an age where politicians and economists think they can control market forces and so, for example, reduce unemployment and increase trade. In the sixteenth century, however, there was very little understanding of the causes of social and economic change. The lack of records and statistics, combined with poor levels of communication, meant that contemporaries themselves were often unaware of how their lives were changing, or if changes they were experiencing were peculiar to themselves or happening nationwide. Government policy tended to be conservative and reactive; it dealt with social and economic change only when it perceived there was a problem, and only then if that problem threatened economic, social, or indeed national stability.

Despite the difficulty of collecting reliable information, historians have been able to identify major social and economic trends, although inevitably there is much controversy over their causes and effects. These trends tend to be long term, so, although Section 3 focuses on the reign of Elizabeth, events sometimes need to be set against the context of changes between 1500 and 1558.

A What evidence do we have? (pp. 108–109)

B What was the population of Elizabethan England? (p. 110)

C What do statistics tell us? (p. 111)

D Who lived in Elizabethan England? (pp. 112–13)

E Review: What was Elizabethan England like? (p. 114)

ARISTOCRACY	Titled members of society
CAPITALISM	An economic system where the means of production are privately owned and a maximum profit is the main goal
COMMONWEALTH/ COMMONWEAL	The community of England and what is in its best interests, 'for the good of all'
ENCLOSURE	A process of hedging and ditching whereby open land was closed off
ENTRY FINES	The fee paid by a tenant to a landlord to renew the lease on a property
HOUSEHOLD	A domestic unit of residence comprising parents, dependent children, relatives and servants
INFLATION	An increase in prices. In the sixteenth century the effect was usually rising food prices.
INVENTORY	A list of someone's belongings, including their house and its contents, which was usually drawn up after they died
PARISH	An administrative area served by a single church and under the spiritual jurisdiction of an ordained minister
RENT	From the beginning of the sixteenth century leases tended to ask for some part of the rent to be paid in produce rather than money.
STAPLE TOWNS	Towns in which merchants had been given a licence to trade in specific goods
SUBSIDY	A parliamentary tax, introduced in the 1530s on land and goods. It was based on an individual's ability to pay.
TENTHS AND FIFTEENTHS	A basic parliamentary tax. It was, theoretically, a tenth of the value of moveable goods in urban areas and a fifteenth in rural areas.
TILLAGE	Land which has been ploughed

A What evidence do we have?

■ 12B Sources of information

Trade
Registers of customs duties were kept by ports. They give us some idea of the volume and nature of trade.

Central government
Government legislation often set out problems as perceived by the Queen and her council. Debates in Parliament show the concerns of the land-owning classes.

Towns
Town rolls are records of the number of registered freemen. In some towns, such as Hull and Worcester, they also list the main occupations pursued in the town.

Individuals
Some evidence, written by individuals complaining about specific issues, survives. This can be in the form of letters, diaries, leaflets or petitions to Parliament. Some of these documents, letters from JPs to the council, for example, are more formal.

SOME SOURCES OF INFORMATION

Crime and punishment
Court books, Quarter Sessions records, and details from houses of correction often include valuable insights into the links between crime and poverty, while also giving details of government legislation.

Personal belongings
Some personal information – in the form of accounts, inventories and paintings – has survived.

Taxation
Annual assessment returns were used for taxation and military purposes. They first started in 1522, and provide a valuation of lands and personal wealth as well as details of land ownership.

Parish registers
Parish registers recorded births, marriages and deaths. They started in 1538. Some clergy were more conscientious than others in keeping them up to date. Many have been lost.

SOURCE 12.1 A family group: Lord Cobham and family

SOURCE 12.2 Some towns, notably Norwich and Ipswich, ordered censuses to be taken of the poor. The conditions of the poor is also a feature of the accounts left by church wardens and overseers of the poor. This is part of the Norwich Census

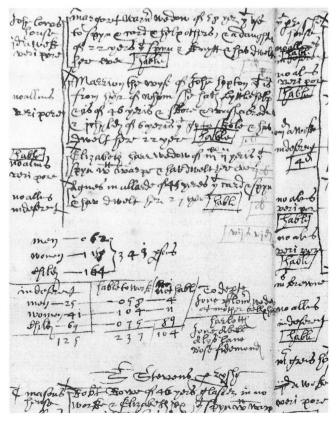

TALKING POINT

Is it possible to build up a complete picture of Tudor economy and society, when we lack complete records and contemporaries themselves had only a muddled understanding of the reasons behind their circumstances?

ACTIVITY

1 a) Given the sources of information referred to in Chart 12B, which areas of Elizabethan life are we likely to make the most accurate judgements about?
   b) Which areas do we have least information about?
   c) What can we learn from each kind of source?
2 What can you learn from Sources 12.1 and 12.2 about Elizabethan life and why do you need to use these sources carefully?

B What was the population of Elizabethan England?

SOURCE 12.3 Population, 1500–1600

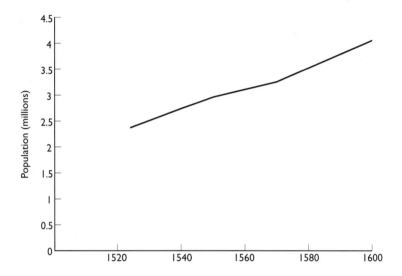

SOURCE 12.4 The growth of the urban population

Town	c. 1520	c. 1600
Metropolitan London	60,000	200,000
Norwich	8,000	15,000
Bristol	10,000	12,000
York	8,000	11,500
Exeter	8,000	9,000
Newcastle upon Tyne	–	9,000
King's Lynn	4,500	8,000
Salisbury	8,000	7,000
Plymouth	–	7,000–8,000
Cambridge	2,600	6,500
Oxford	5,000	6,500
Ipswich	3,100	5,000
Canterbury	3,000	5,000
Colchester	3,000–4,000	5,000
Yarmouth	4,000	8,000
Shrewsbury	2,900	6,000
Worcester	–	5,000
Chester	–	5,000

■ 12C Family life in the sixteenth century

The average family had four or five members.

Bubonic plague and pneumonic plague were the main killers in Tudor England.

Poor harvests endangered life and were often combined with sweating sickness or influenza.

Life expectancy was about 35 years.

Infant mortality was high: approximately 134 of every 1000 babies born died in infancy.

A couple married when they were able to set up home, usually around 26 years of age.

Illegitimacy rates were low. Only 2.8 per cent of recorded live births occurred out of wedlock.

■ 12D Wealth and poverty in the sixteenth century

WEALTH

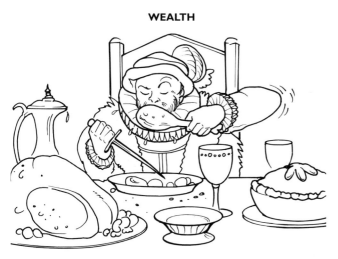

POVERTY

- There were close links between wealth and social status.
- Fourteen per cent of the national income belonged to 1.2 per cent of families.
- 'Great landlords' owned 17 per cent of all the cultivated land.
- The south east was the most prosperous part of the country.
- London was the wealthiest urban centre.
- All but two of the 25 richest towns were in the south.
- Taxes based on goods show that the richest 23 per cent of the population owned 55 per cent of the taxable wealth.
- Wealth depended on land ownership, although it could be supplemented by government office or profits from commerce or industry.
- Lawyers and merchants had the greatest opportunities to build up profits, which they often used to buy land.
- An increase in prosperity resulted in building on an unprecedented scale.

- Half the families in sixteenth-century England could be classified as 'labouring poor'. This group received only 20 per cent of the national income. They earned little, rented their property, and had few savings to help them through the bad times.
- The north west was the poorest part of the country.
- Food and drink accounted for 80 per cent of the expenditure of the poor.
- Recent research suggests that 10 per cent of people in the countryside, and 20 per cent of people in towns, lived in absolute poverty.
- Poverty increased during times of crisis caused by warfare, inflation, plague, famine, etc.
- The popular perception was that poverty was on the increase. This led to a growth in government legislation which culminated in the Elizabethan Poor Laws.
- Exact statistics for the poor, with the exception of beggars, are hard to come by because, unlike the rich, they generally did not leave wills and inventories behind.

D Who lived in Elizabethan England?

■ 12E The social structure in the countryside

Monarch
The greatest
landowner

**The peerage (spiritual
and temporal lords)**
The wealthiest lords were worth
up to £6000 per annum.

The gentry
The gentry – which included knights and squires
– usually owned more land than they could farm
themselves, and in medieval times they would have been
called 'lords of the manor'. Their wealth ranged from £10
to £200 per annum. The gentry mixed socially with members
of the peerage and worked with them in local politics. The
wealthier gentry had more money than the poorer peers.

Yeomen
Yeomen were freeholders or else leaseholders with long leases.
Freeholders could vote in elections and many yeomen had servants and
sometimes sub-tenants. They made a substantial income from farming their land.

Tenant farmers
Tenant farmers farmed between ten and 30 acres of land which they held on lease, and were of
three kinds: tenants-at-will, customary tenants and copyholders (see Chart 12F).

Cottagers
Cottagers had small gardens to farm, and supplemented their income
with some form of cottage industry such as spinning.

Landless labourers
Landless labourers were seasonal workers, who were hired in return for wages.

ACTIVITY

1 a) Which of the social groups
   featured in Chart 12E would have
   been landowners?
  b) Which would have rented land as
   a tenant?
2 Is it possible to work out tenants'
   social standing from the type of lease
   they held?
3 What effect would population
   growth and an increase in prices have
   had on landowners and their tenants?
4 Why were tenants-at-will so
   vulnerable?
5 What effects might increases in rents
   and entry fines have had on:

   • people renting the land?
   • the Tudor economy in general?

■ 12F The system of land ownership

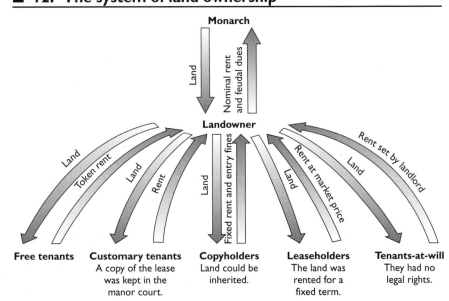

Monarch

Land

Nominal rent
and feudal dues

Landowner

Land — Token rent — Land — Rent — Land — Fixed rent and entry fines — Land — Rent at market price — Land — Rent set by landlord

Free tenants

Customary tenants
A copy of the lease
was kept in the
manor court.

Copyholders
Land could be
inherited.

Leaseholders
The land was
rented for a
fixed term.

Tenants-at-will
They had no
legal rights.

■ 12G The social structure in towns

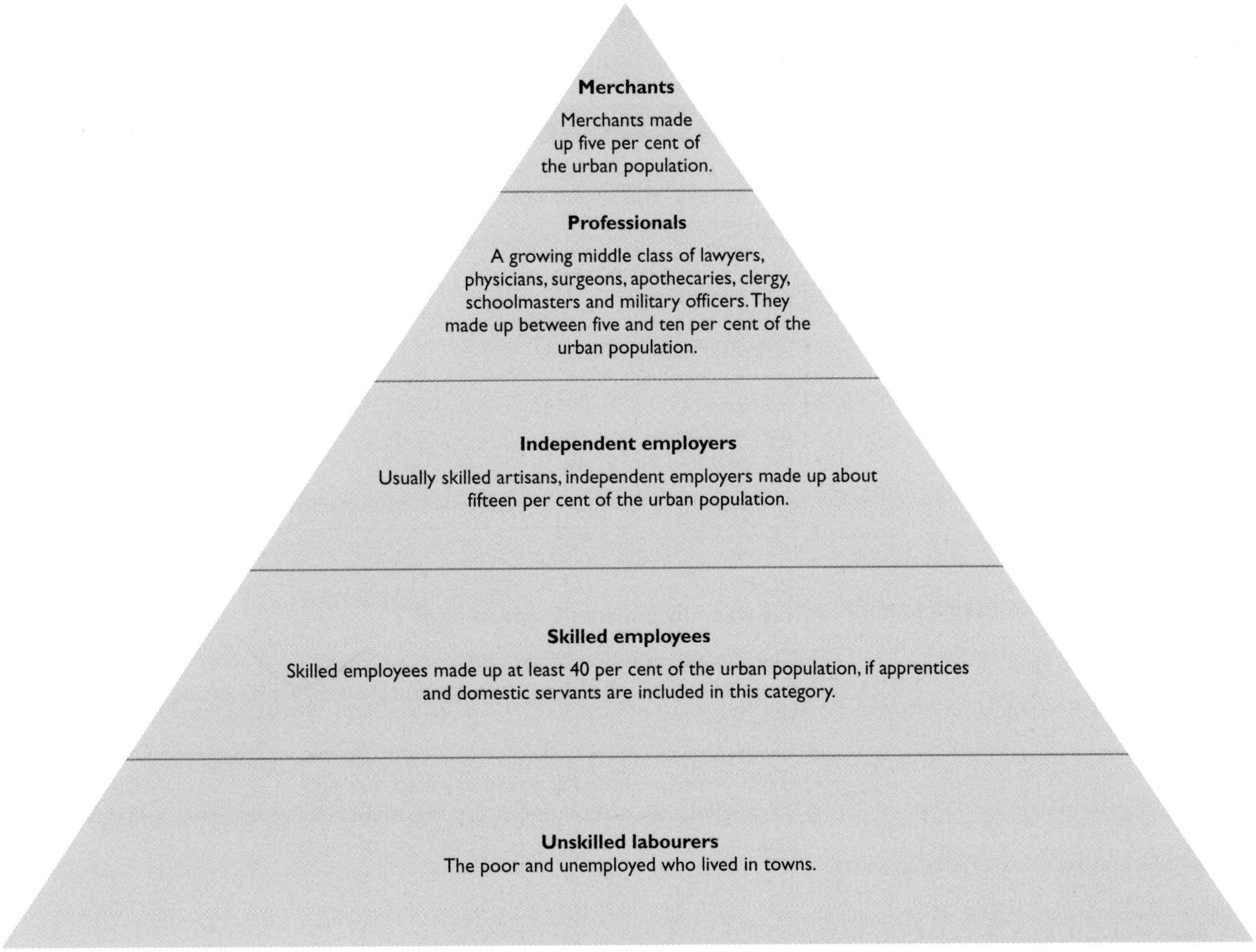
Merchants
Merchants made up five per cent of the urban population.
Professionals
A growing middle class of lawyers, physicians, surgeons, apothecaries, clergy, schoolmasters and military officers. They made up between five and ten per cent of the urban population.
Independent employers
Usually skilled artisans, independent employers made up about fifteen per cent of the urban population.
Skilled employees
Skilled employees made up at least 40 per cent of the urban population, if apprentices and domestic servants are included in this category.
Unskilled labourers
The poor and unemployed who lived in towns.

ACTIVITY

1 Would an increase in population have automatically brought economic prosperity to towns?

2 **a)** Which groups would have done well as the price of goods rose but wages remained largely the same?

b) Which would have done badly?

3 What problems might you have found in the towns that you would have been less likely to find in the countryside?

■ Learning trouble spot

Students often refer to the bulk of the English people, those outside the sphere of government and the nobility, as 'the peasants'. The diagrams on these pages are an attempt to show how unhelpful a term this is. There were recognised class structures in towns and in the countryside. Even if 'peasant' is used to refer to all those people who made a living from the land, it still hides the vast differences that exist between the gentry – who owned and rented out large estates – and their tenants. Wherever possible, therefore, it is better to be as specific as possible or, if talking generally, to refer to the rural or urban populations or the people/commonwealth.

TALKING POINT

What image does the word 'peasant' create in your mind? Why might this be unhelpful for understanding how ordinary people lived in sixteenth-century England?

Review: What was Elizabethan England like?

This chapter has equipped you to find your way through Chapters 13 and 14.

ACTIVITY

You have been asked to produce a report for Elizabeth on the economic state of the nation in 1558. You should work in groups and organise your findings under the following headings:

- records and sources
- population growth
- the social structure of the country
- agriculture and enclosures
- growth of towns
- industry
- overseas trade
- the wealth of the crown.

You may wish to do this activity after you have studied Chapters 13 and 14.

KEY POINTS FROM CHAPTER 12: What was Elizabethan England like?

1 The Tudor era saw extensive economic changes.
2 Many of the changes, such as population growth, were outside government control.
3 Ownership of land was the key to wealth. People who acquired wealth through trade or the professions would use it to buy land.
4 Throughout the sixteenth century, the number of gentry grew and this group acquired an increasingly large proportion of the land.

Were people in the countryside prospering?

CHAPTER OVERVIEW

The rise in prices affected all of English society throughout the sixteenth century. A rapid increase in the price of wheat and other consumables meant that people in the countryside had to resort to bartering to acquire food. Those living on fixed incomes, landlords in particular, began to look for ways of using inflation to their own advantage. Clearly anyone with surplus yield to sell would be able to make a nice profit to supplement their regular income.

There is still considerable debate among historians and economists as to the reasons behind the inflation of the sixteenth century. Contemporaries and historians in the first half of the twentieth century tended to blame repeated government debasements which led to a disastrous fall in the exchange rate, which was based on the cloth market in Antwerp. After 1945, the main cause was believed to be the influx of silver bullion from the New World into Europe which, by increasing the amount of money in circulation, forced up prices. More recently, historians such as Professor D.C. Coleman (*The Economy of England 1450–1750*, 1977) and Professor R.B. Outhwaite (*Inflation in Tudor and Early Stuart England*, 1982) have acknowledged that debasement and silver bullion did accelerate the increase in prices, but have shown that the real cause of inflation was an imbalance between supply and demand as an increasing population threatened to outstrip the country's resources.

By the end of the sixteenth century the price of cereals had increased six or seven times and the effect on the countryside was considerable. This chapter will examine the methods that people living off the land employed to cope with the problem and what policies the government pursued to help them.

A What were the main sources of income for people living in the countryside? (p. 116)

B Who were the winners and losers in the countryside? (pp. 117–118)

C What were the main changes that took place in the countryside? (pp. 119–22)

D What did the government do? (pp. 123–24)

E What was life like for country folk during Elizabeth's reign? (pp. 125–26)

F Review: Were people in the countryside prospering? (p. 127)

FOCUS ROUTE

Using the information in this chapter, make detailed notes to answer the following questions.

1 Is it possible to reach a definite conclusion as to whether country folk prospered during Elizabeth's reign?
2 Which factors were necessary to ensure that an individual's wealth increased?
3 How far were these factors due to a consistent economic policy pursued by the government?
4 Which group/s of people saw their standard of living:
   a) increase
   b) decline
   during this period? Why?

A # What were the main sources of income for people living in the countryside?

Income in the countryside was based on rent from land and on the profits to be made from the sale of agricultural produce, largely wheat but also milk, cheese and meat. Also, unskilled labourers were paid to work on other people's land; blacksmiths, carpenters, millers, etc. earned a living providing a vital service, and some people were paid to work as domestic servants. Almost equally important in terms of employment opportunities was the woollen industry: income could be derived from skilled tasks such as spinning and weaving. Other industries such as tin and coal mining remained largely undeveloped in the sixteenth century.

Throughout the sixteenth century inflation led to rising prices, rents and wages. In general, however, wages in the countryside failed to keep pace with prices.

SOURCE 13.1 Price increases

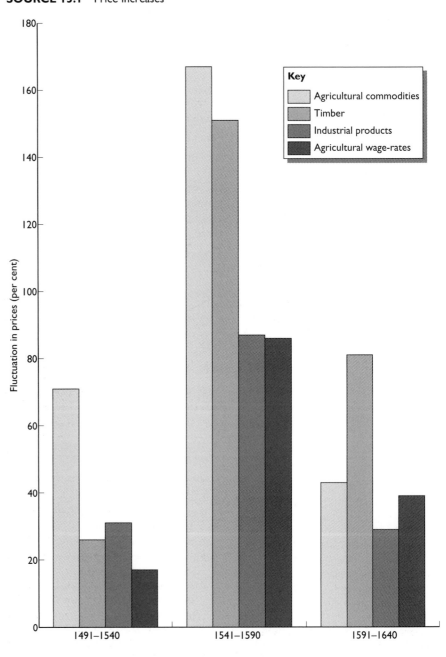

■ 13A The opinions of historians and economists

Sixteenth-century commentators, such as John Hales, believed that labourers, who were dependent on wages, and landowners, who were unable to increase their rents because their tenant had a fixed lease, were the ones who lost out because of the price rises.

Nineteenth-century historians, such as Tharold Rogers, thought that the increase in prices changed the traditional structure of society. It created great opportunities for individuals to make money through capitalist ventures, but contributed to an even greater disparity between incomes.

Marxist historians believe capitalism began to emerge in sixteenth-century England, when manufacturing and farming for profit increased and peasants were driven from their land by force.

Early twentieth-century historians, such as R.H. Tawney in 'The Rise of the Gentry' (1941), believed the gentry as a whole benefited during this period at the expense of the crown and the traditional aristocracy. This view was supported by Lawrence Stone, in *The Crisis of the Aristocracy* (1965), who claimed that 28 per cent of the nobility had to sell their manors.

Tawney's views sparked a heated academic debate. Professor H.R. Trevor Roper (in a series of articles culminating in 'The Gentry, 1540–1640', *Economic History Review*, 1953) concluded that the fortunes of the gentry both rose and fell. More recently, David Palliser, in *The Age of Elizabeth* (1983), has shown that all landowners faced similar problems, the differences in their success lying in their ability and determination to deal with these problems.

ACTIVITY

1 Which people did John Hales feel suffered most from the price rises? Why?
2 Why did nineteenth-century historians such as Tharold Rogers argue that neither the landless labourers nor the large landowners did well during the price rises? Who does this leave that might have benefited from rising inflation?
3 Why do Marxist historians see the growth of capitalism as an undesirable development? Does this surprise you?
4 What do early twentieth-century historians such as Tawney base their argument on?
5 Why has this been challenged?
6 Does Palliser believe that entire social groups benefited or declined? How does he explain what happened to individuals?
7 Look at Charts 12E and 12F which show the social structure in the countryside and the system of land ownership. For each social group, work out how they could supplement their income during the rise in prices and whether, on balance, they benefited or lost out.
   When you have finished, look ahead to Chart 13B and see if you were correct.

What effects did the price rises have on different social groups?

FOCUS ROUTE

Using the information on pages 115–18, construct a chart to show the effects of the price rises on different social groups.

■ Learning trouble spot

Students tend to generalise about what happened to entire social groups as a result of inflation, much in the same way that Tawney wrote of the rise of the entire gentry class. The options available to members of the same social group to deal with inflation were broadly similar, but the decisions an individual made depended on their own circumstances. One landlord might have been able to raise rents, while another, because of the nature of his lease agreements, might have been unable to do so. Similarly, one evicted copyholder might have found employment locally, while another might have decided to move to the nearest town and fallen into deeper poverty. It is therefore important to stress in your written work that within each social group some individuals prospered while others suffered, although as a general rule landowners were in a far stronger position than wage earners.

■ 13B Strategies for dealing with rising prices

Landowners could:
- increase the prices of their farm produce
- keep their expenditure from rising by maintaining expenses and wages at fixed levels wherever possible
- increase annual rents
- increase entry fines
- take rent in the form of produce rather than cash
- buy more land
- farm their existing land themselves rather than let it to tenants
- enclose their land.

Yeomen could:
- use their land to grow enough food to feed their families
- sell any surplus food at a high price
- save or invest their profits in farm buildings.

Freeholders could:
- sell their surplus produce at a profit while their rents remained the same.

Customary tenants, **copyholders** and **leaseholders** could:
- sell their surplus produce at a profit, but they might face an increase in their rents and entry fines.

Tenants-at-will could:
- feed their families and sell any surplus produce, but they could be evicted without notice and generally faced rent increases with which their incomes could not keep up.

Landless labourers (as well as tenant farmers) could:
- supplement their regular wages through, for example, spinning and weaving
- use the common rights over moorland and woodland to, for example, dig for coal and sell it
- live off the common land by eating the hares, fish, pigeons, etc. that they caught
- keep hens, geese, or even a cow, on common land
- ask for part of their wages to be paid in food and drink
- turn to the parish for poor relief.

C What were the main changes that took place in the countryside?

Enclosure

FOCUS ROUTE

To increase food production landlords enclosed land. Read pages 119–21, then make detailed notes on:

- the advantages and disadvantages of enclosure
- why enclosure was so reviled by contemporaries
- the effects of enclosure on different social groups.

■ Learning trouble spot

Students often make the same mistake as sixteenth-century observers and use the term **enclosure** to describe a nationwide movement which benefited greedy landowners. In fact, the amount of land enclosed in the sixteenth century was small and spread unevenly across the country. Enclosure itself often proved advantageous if, for example, wasteland was enclosed and farmed with general consent. What contemporaries, including the government, objected to was the enforced enclosure of common land without local agreement, the merging of several small farms and the eviction of tenants, and the conversion of arable land to pasture. These were likely to lead to depopulation.

SOURCE 13.2 A map showing the extent of enclosure in England, c. 1600

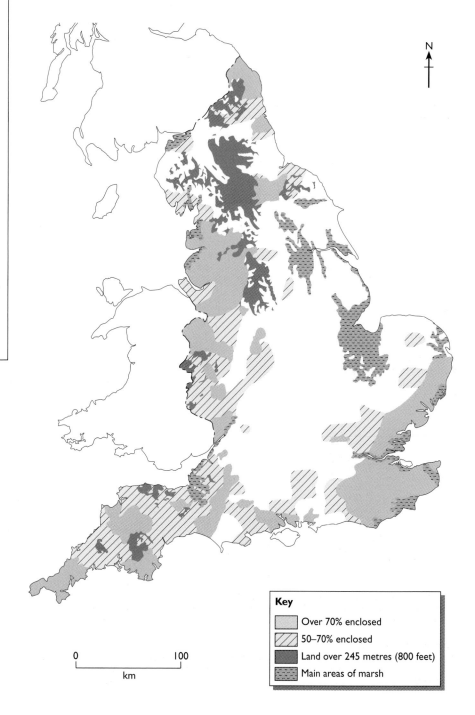

N

Key

	Over 70% enclosed
	50–70% enclosed
	Land over 245 metres (800 feet)
	Main areas of marsh

0   100

km

SOURCE 13.3 The village of Waltham, in Essex, before and after enclosure

The open-field system

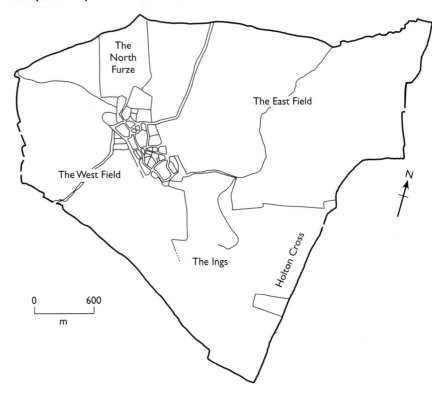

The North Furze

The East Field

The West Field

The Ings

Holton Cross

0   600

m

After enclosure

Luck and Joseph Anningson Esqs.

Mr Brackenbury

Revd Mr Jackson

In lieu of out rents

Manor

L and J Anningson Esqs.

Revd Mr Jackson

Glebe

Mr Parkinson

Glebe

Mr Thomas Hewson

Revd Mr Best

Mr Raistrick

Johnson

Revd Mr Beatniffe

Mr John Colebeck

Langley

Glebe

Mr Bonsor

Mr John Colebeck

Mr Bonsor

Mr Whelpdale

W. Drant

Hobart

The Rector of Waltham

Mr Thompson

0   600

m

Fact file

Before enclosure the three, huge, open fields would be divided into manageable strips (marked by ditches or paths) which were owned or rented by the villagers.

After enclosure the open fields, including the common land, were parcelled into units or farms (with boundary fences or hedges) and sold.

Why did landlords enclose their land?

- There was an increase in the demand for food, particularly from urban areas. Landlords could only practise intensive farming methods where land was enclosed.
- Pasture farming had lower overheads than arable farming, where landlords had to meet the costs of labourers' wages, etc.
- The rising demand for woollen cloth, both at home and abroad, meant that landowners who converted to sheep farming found a ready market for their produce.
- The Black Death in the fourteenth century had left some areas depopulated and others with a small labour force.

Why was enclosure disliked?

- Fencing or hedging common land meant people lost their common rights, to graze their livestock there.
- Tenants-at-will and copyholders had no legal claim to land they rented and therefore faced either summary eviction or an increase in rent for a new lease which most would be unable to afford.
- Those evicted looked for alternative employment in their villages but if it was not forthcoming many had to move to the towns to look for work. Contemporaries and the government were alarmed by the growth in the numbers of urban poor.
- Although some enclosures took place with the consent of all concerned, enclosure as a whole received a bad press when areas became depopulated. Complainants also associated enclosure with RACK RENTING. The greatest criticisms came during times of general economic pressure, such as the series of disastrous harvests in 1594–97. Contemporaries blamed enclosures for all social ills, particularly unemployment, vagrancy and a decline in law and order.

RACK RENTING
A form of tenure where the rent was not fixed. In theory this allowed for flexibility because rents could be adjusted up or down depending on the economic climate. In practice, however, many landlords kept rent at a maximum.

SOURCE 13.4 Thomas Trusser, *Five Hundred Points of Good Husbandry*, 1557

More plenty of mutton and beef,
Corn, butter, and cheese of the best,
More wealth anywhere, to be brief,
More people, more handsome and prest [willing],
Where find ye? (Go search any coast),
Than there, where enclosure is most.

SOURCE 13.5 Sir Thomas More, *Utopia*, 1516

Therefore, [so] that one covetous and insatiable cormorant [reference to landlords] and very plague of his native country may compass about and enclose many thousand acres of ground together within one pale of hedge, the husbandmen be thrust out of their own ... or by wrongs and injustices they be so wearied that they be compelled to sell all. ... All their household stuff ... they be constrained to sell it for a thing of nought. And when they have wandered abroad till that be spent, what can they else do but steal – or else go about a-begging.

Fact file
- Between 1500 and 1600 the amount of land enclosed increased by only two per cent.
- By the end of Elizabeth's reign the total area enclosed, even in the worst affected regions, was less than nine per cent.
- There was no wholesale depopulation of villages after 1520.
- After 1550, enclosures were carried out to increase the efficiency of arable farming. The increase in population meant corn was more profitable than wool.
- The effects of enclosures on individuals varied according to the region and to the type of lease a person held.
- The increasing number of vagrants was made up of wage earners, younger sons, and villagers who had relied heavily on common land to survive.
- Larger, more efficient farms ensured that grain production kept pace with the rising population.

ACTIVITY

Prepare the arguments for and against enclosure, and role play a village meeting where the local landowner is trying to convince the villagers of the benefits of enclosure.

FOCUS ROUTE

Make notes to answer the following questions.

1 What were the main agricultural developments in the sixteenth century?
2 How successful were these innovations?

What developments took place in agriculture in the sixteenth century?

SOURCE 13.6 C. E. Challis, *Economic History Review*, XXXIX, 1986, p. 296

If population doubled between 1540 and 1660, while at the same time subsistence crises disappeared and argiculture prices levelled out ... something remarkable must have happened to agriculture output overall.

■ 13C Agricultural innovation

FALLOW FIELD
A field which was left unploughed or unsown for twelve months to allow the soil to recover its goodness. In an open-field village with three fields, crop rotation was practised: one field was left fallow, the other two grew crops.

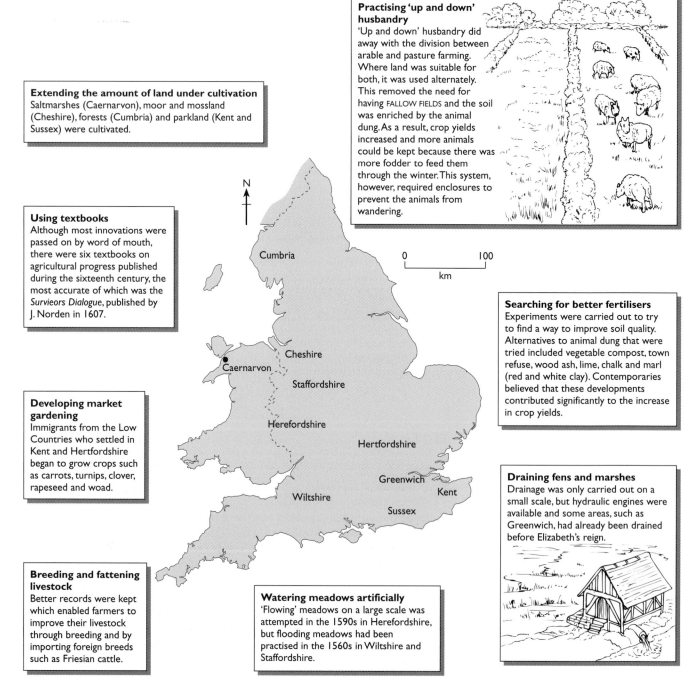

Extending the amount of land under cultivation
Saltmarshes (Caernarvon), moor and mossland (Cheshire), forests (Cumbria) and parkland (Kent and Sussex) were cultivated.

Practising 'up and down' husbandry
'Up and down' husbandry did away with the division between arable and pasture farming. Where land was suitable for both, it was used alternately. This removed the need for having FALLOW FIELDS and the soil was enriched by the animal dung. As a result, crop yields increased and more animals could be kept because there was more fodder to feed them through the winter. This system, however, required enclosures to prevent the animals from wandering.

Using textbooks
Although most innovations were passed on by word of mouth, there were six textbooks on agricultural progress published during the sixteenth century, the most accurate of which was the *Survieors Dialogue*, published by J. Norden in 1607.

Searching for better fertilisers
Experiments were carried out to try to find a way to improve soil quality. Alternatives to animal dung that were tried included vegetable compost, town refuse, wood ash, lime, chalk and marl (red and white clay). Contemporaries believed that these developments contributed significantly to the increase in crop yields.

Developing market gardening
Immigrants from the Low Countries who settled in Kent and Hertfordshire began to grow crops such as carrots, turnips, clover, rapeseed and woad.

Draining fens and marshes
Drainage was only carried out on a small scale, but hydraulic engines were available and some areas, such as Greenwich, had already been drained before Elizabeth's reign.

Breeding and fattening livestock
Better records were kept which enabled farmers to improve their livestock through breeding and by importing foreign breeds such as Friesian cattle.

Watering meadows artificially
'Flowing' meadows on a large scale was attempted in the 1590s in Herefordshire, but flooding meadows had been practised in the 1560s in Wiltshire and Staffordshire.

Cumbria

Cheshire
Caernarvon
Staffordshire
Herefordshire
Hertfordshire
Greenwich
Kent
Wiltshire
Sussex

N

0   100
km

■ 13D The government's responsibilities towards the economy

FOCUS ROUTE

Government intervention in the economy increased throughout the Tudor period. Read pages 123–24 and make notes on:

* the motives behind government intervention
* the legislation passed and what it was intended to do
* the likely effects of this legislation, including its impact on the wealth of different social groups.

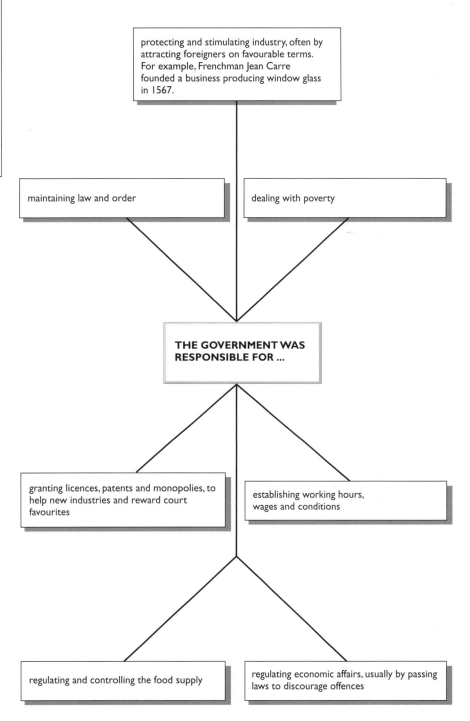

protecting and stimulating industry, often by attracting foreigners on favourable terms. For example, Frenchman Jean Carre founded a business producing window glass in 1567.

maintaining law and order

dealing with poverty

THE GOVERNMENT WAS RESPONSIBLE FOR ...

granting licences, patents and monopolies, to help new industries and reward court favourites

establishing working hours, wages and conditions

regulating and controlling the food supply

regulating economic affairs, usually by passing laws to discourage offences

■ Learning trouble spot

Using the phrase 'the government was responsible for' in relation to the sixteenth-century economy is misleading. By the nineteenth century the government had accepted that it had a responsibility to intervene in the economy and that it could have some effect on economic forces. In the sixteenth century, however, the government had no economic policy as such. It intervened only if the economy was adversely affecting its plans and priorities: trade wasn't bringing in enough revenue, high prices were affecting social stability, etc.

Date	Act	Details	Significance
1563	Act for Maintaining Tillage	All land which had been under tillage for four years since 1528 must remain under tillage. No land currently under tillage could be converted to pasture. This Act was against depopulation.	The government's dislike of enclosure was based on the fear not only of social unrest but also that the number of tenants available for military service might decline.
1563	Statute of Artificers	This was an attempt to regulate both industry and agriculture. It fixed maximum but not minimum wage rates. The standard wage rate was to be assessed by JPs and to be kept in line with prices.	A landmark in economic legislation, it recognised the right to work and focused on young, single, full-time labourers. All able unemployed persons were obliged to seek work in either farming or domestic service. Employers were to provide their employees with training and annual contracts were to be issued. However, the Act did not live up to its expectations because it failed to take into account the increasing level of unemployment caused by inflation. Instead, by fixing a maximum wage, it held down wages at a time when the number of people looking for waged employment rose. It therefore indirectly contributed to the growth of poverty.
1563	Act for the Maintenance of the Navy	This Act included a clause which raised the price limit on the amount of grain that could be exported to ten shillings a quarter.	A series of good harvests enabled the government to concentrate on expanding the food supply.
1592–93	Statute Regarding the Export of Corn	A price limit was set on corn at twenty shillings a quarter. Export of corn was permitted when the price fell below this.	During good years, farmers were allowed to export surplus corn. This is an indication that corn was in sufficient supply even for the growing population.
1592–93		The 1563 Act for Maintaining Tillage, preventing the conversion of tilled land to pasture, was repealed.	This followed a series of good harvests between 1587 and 1593 when there was a surplus of grain.
1598	Statute Against Conversions to Pasture Statute Against the Engrossing of Farms	These Acts were designed to prevent further conversion of tillage into pasture.	The Parliament of 1598 was panicked into these measures by a spate of enclosures between 1591 and 1597. In some areas, such as Staffordshire in 1592–94, enclosures caused real distress. There were four disastrous harvests between 1594 and 1597 which led to revolts against enclosure and high prices in Oxfordshire in 1596. The number of Acts passed against enclosures and depopulation during the Tudor period shows the difficulty of government in balancing its need for the profits that could be made from the cloth industry with the demands of an increasing population.

ACTIVITY

In a group, brainstorm an answer to the following examination question. Display your answer as a chart.

a) What were the main changes that took place in the countryside in Elizabeth's reign? (12)

b) Why, and with what effect, did the government intervene in the agricultural economy between 1558 and 1603? (8)

FOCUS ROUTE

From Sources 13.7–13.16 draw some conclusions about the living standards of people in the countryside during Elizabeth's reign.

E What was life like for country folk during Elizabeth's reign?

SOURCE 13.7 W. Harrison, *The Description of England*, 1577

Yet now, a typical farmer or husbandman had a good reserve of cash, beside a faire garnish of pewter on his cupbord ... three or four feather beds, so manie coverlids and carpets of tapestrie, a silver salt, a bowle for wine ... and a dozzen of spoons to finish up the sute.

SOURCE 13.8 A restored Elizabethan yeoman's house

SOURCE 13.9 William Smith describing Cheshire in 1585

In building and furniture of their houses (till of late yeares) they used the old maner of the Saxons. For they had their fyre in the middest of the house against a hob of clay, and their oxen also under the same rouff. But within these forty yeares it is altogether altered, so that they have builded chimnies and furnished other parts of their houses accordingly.

SOURCE 13.10 William Camden, 1574

For now more houses of noble men and private citizens – remarkable for their elegance, size and splendour – began to arise throughout England than in any previous age.

SOURCE 13.11 Montacute House, Somerset, built 1588–1601

SOURCE 13.12 The inventory of John Lawson of Chester, who died in 1580. He was comfortably, but not conspicuously, well off

July 21, 1580. In the hall. *One irone chymney* [fireplace], *with all the appertenances to it belonging, 6s. 8d. A drawing table with a carpet, a forme, and iii buffett stooles 13s. 4d. One counter* [table], *i carpett, i forme, ii chayres, with a little chayre, and i salte kytt* [box] *for salte 13s 4d. One almerie* [cupboard], *with a Danske chiste, and i payre of tables 18s. xi qwyshinges* [cushions] *4s. One raper* [dagger] *with a hanger 5s. In the chamber. One trussyng* [bundle of straw], *i leather bead, i bolster, i pillowe, ii hanginges, i coverlett, and ii blankettes 13s. One table, iii bolsters, and viii coodes* [pillows] *10s. Two old chystes 2s. One chyste covered with leather, wherin iii payer of shettes is lying, 14s. v payer of straking shettes 13s 4d. iii payer of harden shettes* [types of linen sheets made from different parts of the flax plant] *6s. ii payer of course shettes for servantes beddes 3s 4d. xiiii pillowberes 13s. 4d. ix table cloths, whereof one is of dyaper* [linen], *with two course tabel clothes 20s. iiii lynnen towelles, iiii straking towelles, and i harden towell 6s. 8d. Two dozen and a hallfe of table napthkens 6s. 8d. The painted clothes hanginges about the chamber, with a capcase 2s. 6d. In the parler One stand bedd with i feather bedd, i payer of blanketts of wollen, ii happynges* [coverlets], *i coveringe, i bolster, i pillowe, with hangings of wollen 22s. v coverlettes, ii happings and iii payer of wollen blankettes 13s. 4d. One long settell bedd, i chyste, i coffer, i other little chyste, and i forme 13s. 4d. One peace of lynnen 10s. The inner chamber. One servantes bedde, ii happings, i payer of shettes and i bolster 5s. One almerie 5s. xviii peace of putter* [pewter] *vessell, as plateres and dyshes, i basinge, iiii sawseres, i chamber pott, i quart pott, ii bountinge potts* [a type of short, wide pot], *i pynte poot and ii salt salleres 20s. The ketchinge vessel, viz., ii brase pootes, i posnett* [a metal pot with feet], *i yetlinge* [a cast iron pot], *v panes* [pans], *i morter with a pestell, i ladell, i grayt, i gyrdeiron, i fleshe knyfe, ii rackes, i payer of gybcrockes* [pot hooks], *and ii spettes* [spits] *20s. In the butrye and ketchen 10s. One greate arke for corne or bread 6s. 8d. iiii sylver sponnes 12s. The brewe vessell with a tappe stone 6s. 8d. One almerie 6s. 8d. Apperell geven by legacie to the value of 20l. Apparell not geven 30s. Two cappes, i sworde with a buckler, and a stafe with a sworde in it 30s. One steyle cape with a cover 5s. iiii shyrtes 20s...*

SOURCE 13.13 D. M. Palliser, *The Age of Elizabeth*, 1983, p. 133

The very poor ... in the countryside built themselves one roomed hovels ... mean beyond imagination, without windows, only one storey.

SOURCE 13.14 W. Harrison, *The Description of England*, 1577

Poore neighbours are inforced to content themselves with rie, or barleie, yea, and in time of dearth, with bread made ... of peason, beans or otes.

SOURCE 13.15 D. M. Palliser, *The Age of Elizabeth*, 1983, p. 110

Humphrey Gibbons, a labourer arrested at New Romney in 1596, claimed to have farmed six or seven acres until the terrible harvest of that year proved his undoing.

SOURCE 13.16 Hardwick Hall, Derbyshire, built 1591–97

Review: Were people in the countryside prospering?

ACTIVITY

The crown owns the greatest amount of land in the country and, as a major landowner dependent on a fixed income, is suffering from the increase in prices. Work in pairs.

a) One of you is the author of a new textbook on agricultural changes. You have been asked to draw up a list of recommendations to try to improve royal income.

b) The other should draft a reply which focuses on the likely political and social effects of these suggestions and explains:

- why the Queen cannot carry them all out
- the ways in which she will try to increase her income, and reduce her expenditure
- what effects they will have on the prosperity of country people.

This is clearly an area where, despite gaps in the available source material, historians have dealt in large headings:

- The Rise of the Gentry
- The Agricultural Revolution
- The Birth of Capitalism
- The Crisis of the Aristocracy.

Contemporaries, too, on the basis of their own limited experiences, generalised over what was happening nationally. They talked about the evils of enclosure and the increase in poverty and vagrancy, often linking the three and predicting a breakdown in law and order.

Historians today, such as David Palliser, try to focus on the causes of social and economic change and on the extent to which an individual's ability to prosper depended on factors unique to his own set of circumstances. In other words, even within the same social group in the same rural area, some individuals saw their wealth increase and some saw their wealth decline. Nevertheless, it is still possible to determine general features for this period which are summarised in the key points below.

KEY POINTS FROM CHAPTER 13: Were people in the countryside prospering?

1 Prices, particularly of grain, rose throughout the period and this is now thought to be the result of an increase in population.

2 Those who did well out of inflation owned their land and were able to enclose land and use the new intensive farming methods to increase productivity.

3 People whose tenancy agreements gave them no legal right to the land they farmed and those who were dependent on wages suffered a decline in their standard of living during this period.

4 The most controversial development in the countryside in the sixteenth century was the enclosure of arable land. The amount of land actually enclosed, however, was limited.

5 The government had definite aims and responsibilities in social and economic affairs, but did not have a coherent policy and tended to react to problems or issues as they arose.

6 Although it is difficult to come to firm conclusions about wealth and poverty, contemporaries agreed that this was a period of increasing prosperity (increase in house building, social mobility, and standards of living) and increasing poverty and vagrancy (the need to provide poor relief). Such extreme views have led some historians to talk of a polarisation of wealth and poverty in Elizabeth's reign. Others have argued that in the countryside, although not in towns, the majority took advantage of the rise in agricultural prices, resulting in an overall rise in the standard of living.

Were people in towns prospering?

CHAPTER OVERVIEW

Most towns grew up because they had an economic function – they were a centre for the processing and manufacture of a raw material, or their geographical location encouraged the growth of trade. Often both these features were present.

By the sixteenth century, the largest towns had been given royal charters on the understanding that they would administer criminal and civil jurisdiction on behalf of the crown at a local level. To do this they were strictly governed by a network of officials. The mayor and his closest advisers, usually aldermen, sat at the top of this hierarchy. There were also paid officials, including the town clerk, the coroner, constables, clerks and gaolers. Although in decline by the beginning of Elizabeth's reign, membership of a GUILD still ensured social status and advancement within the urban OLIGARCHIES.

Most towns were very small by today's standards, with populations sometimes as low as 250. The majority were market towns, which were responsible for meeting the need of the surrounding countryside – through fairs, markets and shops – and were the centre for specialist crafts and trades.

As in the countryside, whether individuals prospered or not depended a great deal on the town they lived in, their social class, and their means of income. The traditional view, that urban growth suffered irreversible decline throughout the sixteenth century, is no longer accepted. It is increasingly clear that, even as early as 1558, economic recovery in some towns was taking place. However, it is equally clear that towns, and not the countryside, bore the brunt of the rise in poverty caused by inflation and the increase in population. Towns therefore experienced periods of such intense poverty that local authorities and the government were forced to implement a system of poor relief.

About ten per cent of the English population lived in towns. Only the capital, London, was big enough to compare favourably with European cities. This section will therefore focus on London. It will examine wealth and employment in towns, the main changes that took place and government intervention and legislation.

> **GUILD**
> A medieval organisation. A group of craftsmen who joined together to administer their craft in a particular town, training apprentices and ensuring the quality of their product.
>
> **OLIGARCHY**
> A small group who, although a minority, maintain a high level of political influence.

A What were the main sources of income for people living in towns? (p. 129)

B Who were the winners and losers in the towns? (pp. 130–33)

C What were the main changes that took place in towns? (pp. 134–37)

D What did the government do? (pp. 138–39)

E What was life like for townspeople during Elizabeth's reign? (pp. 140–41)

F Review: Were people in towns prospering? (pp. 142–43)

A What were the main sources of income for people living in towns?

■ 14A The leading occupations in six English towns

Chester 1558–1603		Leicester 1559–1603		Norwich 1569		Nottingham 1580–1620		Worcester 1540–49		York 1550–1600	
Shoemakers	120	Tailors	67	Worsted weavers	166	Butchers	115	Weavers	77	Tailors	309
Glovers	76	Tanners	63	Grocers	150	Cordwainers	83	Clothiers	45	Merchants	301
Tailors	76	Butchers	63	Tailors	146	Glovers	81	Mercers	28	Bakers	153
Tanners	73	Shoemakers	53	Cordwainers	59	Tanners	62	Walkers	26	Cordwainers	143
Ironmongers	68	Glovers	43	Mercers	48	Tailors	42	Drapers	16	Butchers	128
Merchants	65	Bakers	37	Dornix weavers	35	Bakers	41	Brewers	16	Tanners	127
Bakers	57	Mercers	36	Hatters	35	Blacksmiths	34	Shoemakers	15	Innholders	109
Drapers	55	Weavers	30	Tanners	34	Joiners	17	Tailors	14	Glovers	98
Weavers	55	Chandlers	20	Bakers	32	Mercers	17	Butchers	12	Carpenters	83
Butchers	52	Smiths	20	Carpenters	31	Ropers	17	Tanners	11	Drapers	78
Shearmen	51			Butchers	29	Fishmongers	14	Barbers	11	Tilers	71
Mercers	47			Masons	26	Yeomen	14	Smiths	11	Joiners	60

Note: Figures are of the numbers of freemen or craftsmen attributed to each occupation

(Data taken from D. M. Palliser, *The Age of Elizabeth*, 1983, p. 284)

■ 14B The social groups in towns and their incomes

Merchants lived off the profits from trade, and in towns with a thriving port, such as London or Hull, they were able to amass large fortunes to rival the gentry. Most mayors were merchants.

Like merchants, **professionals** had the opportunity to make large profits. Both merchants and lawyers often bought up landed estates. Some lawyers went on to have successful political careers at court.

Independent employers often worked from home. Their small businesses usually incorporated all the stages of production, from buying the raw material to selling the finished product, and they traditionally included shoemakers, sailors and bakers. The prices of the goods they produced rose, but not as quickly as the price of grain. In addition to those who produced goods, this group also included retailers and people supplying services.

Skilled employees were taken on by successful employers whose businesses were growing. They usually learnt their craft through a seven-year apprenticeship. If they had the resources they could go on to set up as master craftsmen themselves, but many became journeymen and worked for a master at a daily rate of pay.

Around 40 per cent of the urban population were **unskilled labourers**. Members of this group were in a precarious position because they could easily become destitute as a result of poor harvests, a trading slump or personal illness. They were employed in a variety of trades, including the textile, building, leather, clothing, food, drink and metal trades.

The **urban poor** were a destitute group which included the unemployed, tenants evicted from their homes in the countryside, former soldiers and sailors, and ex-monastic servants. They formed two distinct groups: those who were prepared to work and those who were not. The latter included beggars, thieves and murderers, who were dependent on the authorities or the profits from crime.

ACTIVITY

Predict which groups of people living in towns were in a position to prosper during Elizabeth's reign, and which were not. Why did you make these choices?

Read the rest of this chapter and see if your predictions are correct.

B Who were the winners and losers in the towns?

ACTIVITY

1 Read Source 14.1. How did the trading opportunities for merchants expand in the sixteenth century?
2 Read Source 14.2. What was one obvious result of expanding trading opportunities?
3 Read Sources 14.3 and 14.4. Why would it be wrong to conclude that the wealth of all merchants increased during this period?
4 Read Source 14.5. What evidence is there that lawyers prospered during Elizabeth's reign?

SOURCE 14.1 S. M. Jack, *Towns in Tudor and Stuart Britain*, 1996, p. 63

In 1500, British merchants lacked the skills which made the Italians so effective. Businesses were small and transitory, risks were if possible avoided and there was comparatively little specialisation, even merchant adventurers dealing in a range of imported goods. The closure of the traditional markets, like Antwerp, pushed reluctant English merchants into a more entrepreneurial attitude. In the 1560s they started interloping in the prohibited Spanish and Portuguese American markets; in the 1570s they pushed into the Mediterranean; in the 1580s they began hesitantly to consider colonisation and in the 1590s and 1600s they traded directly to the East.

The merchants who did best were those London merchants who started with adequate capital, but when a lucky 'adventure' (trading voyage) could offer a profit of 400 per cent many poorer people became involved.

As trading patterns became more complex, the bigger merchants specialised in particular commodities and markets, profiting from both insider knowledge and a large market share.

SOURCE 14.2 S. M. Jack, *Towns in Tudor and Stuart Britain*, 1996, p. 65

Londoners were wealthier than their provincial counterparts, although merchants from Bristol, Exeter and Norwich impressed even Londoners with their state.

SOURCE 14.4 D. M. Palliser, *The Age of Elizabeth*, 1983, p. 180

A rising merchant class has often been seen as a consequence of the inflationary process; but trade remained a very uncertain means of profit compared to land, for the former might yield a very high return or might fail altogether. John Isham, who had made high profits during the debasement period and after as a London mercer, retired to his Northamptonshire estates in the 1570s after a discouraging period of trading.

SOURCE 14.3 S. M. Jack, *Towns in Tudor and Stuart Britain*, 1996, p. 47

Mere evidence of trading and manufacturing activity does not give an accurate indication of wealth. The merchant juggling the greatest amount of business may already be effectively bankrupt.

SOURCE 14.5 D. M. Palliser, *The Age of Elizabeth*, 1983, p. 123

Lawyers, like merchants, had the opportunity to make money rapidly if they were sufficiently fortunate or ruthless. 'Now all the wealth of the land dooth flow unto our common lawiers', lamented Harrison in 1587, 'of whome, some one having practised little above thirteene or fourteene yeares is able to buie a purchase of so manie 1000 pounds.' Sir Nicholas Bacon and Sir Edward Coke both made fortunes from the law with which they were able to buy large estates.

SOURCE 14.6 Wage rates and their purchasing power, 1540–1609 (1450–99 = 100)

Decade	Money wage rate	'Cost of living'	Agricultural labourer: purchasing power of wage rate	Building craftsman: purchasing power of wage rate	London building worker: purchasing power of wage rate
1540–49	118	167	71	70	76
1550–59	160	271	59	51	72
1560–69	177	269	66	62	82
1570–79	207	298	69	64	81
1580–89	203	354	57	57	78
1590–99	219	443	49	47	69
1600–09	219	439	50	46	72

(Data taken from D. M. Palliser, *The Age of Elizabeth*, 1983, p. 183)

SOURCE 14.7 D. M. Palliser, *The Age of Elizabeth*, 1983, p. 182

Most building craftsmen were self-employed, and few were totally dependent on wages for the support of their families.

SOURCE 14.8 D. M. Palliser, *The Age of Elizabeth*, 1983, p. 184

Even urban craftsmen had their common lands on which they could keep a cow.

SOURCE 14.9 Wage rates, 1561, from the records of the Justices of the Peace of Buckinghamshire

The Queen Majesty's Justices of Peace ... assembling themselves for the reformation of wages ... set forth the rates and orders for the same severally as hereafter followeth ...

Artificers from Easter to Michaelmas (29 September)		
	With meat and drink	**Without meat and drink**
The master carpenter and sawyer	vi d.	ix d.
Other men	iii d.	vii d.
Bricklayers, tylers and thatchers	v d.	viii d.
Other men	iii d.	vi d.
Artificers from Michaelmas to Easter		
	With meat and drink	**Without meat and drink**
The master carpenter and sawyer	iiii d.	vii d.
Other men	iii d.	vi d.
Bricklayers, tylers and thatchers	iii d.	vi d.
Other men	ii d.	v d.

SOURCE 14.10 The Statute of Artificers, 1563

Be it further enacted by the authority aforesaid that after the first day of May next coming it shall not be lawful to any person or persons, other that such as now do lawfully use or exercise any art, mystery or manual occupation, to set up, occupy, use or exercise any craft ... except he shall have been brought up therein seven years at the least as apprentice, in manner and form abovesaid, nor to set any person on work in such ... occupation, being not a workman at this day, except he shall have been apprentice as is aforesaid, or else, having served as an apprentice ... will become a journeyman or be hired by the year: Upon pain that every person willingly offending or doing the contrary shall forfeit and lose for every default 40s. for every month.

SOURCE 14.11 Edward Hext, a Somerset JP, writing to Burghley, September 1596

...there are in the towne of Sheffielde 2207 people; of which there are 725 which are not able to live without the charity of their neighbours. These are all begging poore. 100 housholders which relieve others. These (though the best sorte) are but poor artificers; among them is not one which can keepe a teame on his own land, and not above tenn who have grounds of their own that will keepe a cow.

SOURCE 14.12 J. Pound, *Poverty and Vagrancy in Tudor England*, 1978, p. 25

Above the level of the absolutely poverty stricken in the city were those who possessed sufficient goods to have them recorded in an inventory, albeit one whose total value was less than £10. Sixty per cent of these individuals lived in houses which had between three and five rooms; only one quarter lived in those with two or less. A few had animals, such as cows, pigs, horses or chickens...

SOURCE 14.13 The inventory for Thomas Herries, 1599

A true and perfect inventory of all and singuler the goods and chattels of Thomas Herries late deceased in the parishe of St Gregoryes in Norwich prysed by us William Rogers and Gregorye Wesbye the xvth daye of October in the yeare of oure Lord God 1599.

In primis:	one borded bedsted	3s 4d
Item:	one mattresse and one under cloathe	1s 6d
Item:	one flocke bed	2s 6d
Item:	one bolster	2s 0d
Item:	one downe piliowe and an old cushaigne	1s 6d
Item:	two leather pillowes filled with feathers	3s 4d
Item:	one payer of shetes	2s 0d
Item:	one bed blanket	1s 8d
Item:	one old cofer	2s 0d
Item:	one drye barrell	3d
Item:	2 salt boxes	1s 0d
Item:	one hake, a fyer pann, a payer of tonges and a rostinge yron	1s 6d
Item:	one litle ketle, a sawer and 3 pewter spoones	2s 6d
Item:	3 little boles	1s 0d
Item:	one ketle, one potspone, 28 trenyens	1s 0d
Item:	2 woodinge platters and 5 dishes and twoo erthen Potts	8d
Item:	a stone pott and 5 galley pottes	4d
Item:	a hamper and certen old washe	6d
Item:	4 frayles and 2 stooles	6d
Item:	a little table and 4 stoles	3s 0d
Item:	3 chiselles, 2 hamers and a perser	8d
Item:	3 old cushings	6d
Item:	2 payers of hand cuffes and one dozen of hand kerchers and an old pillowbere	2s 6d
Item:	2 old shirtes	1s 8d
Item:	one old forme and 2 old cappes	1s 0d
Total:		£1 18s 5d

ACTIVITY

5 What does the table in Source 14.6 suggest happened to the purchasing power of craftsmen?

6 Read Sources 14.7 and 14.8. Why might the effects of the price rise on craftsmen not be as severe as was once thought?

7 Look at Source 14.9. What prevented craftsmen from earning wages which kept pace with inflation?

8 Read Source 14.10. What made it so hard for people to set up in business for themselves?

9 a) Why do Sources 14.11–14.13 make it hard to reach firm conclusions about the prosperity of craftsmen and labourers? What would this depend on?

   b) What factors influenced the prosperity of craftsmen and labourers?

ACTIVITY

10 Study Source 14.14.
   a) What were the main causes of families becoming poor?
   b) How did families try to bring in money during periods of hardship?
   c) Which group of people would have been even poorer than those depicted here?

SOURCE 14.14 An extract from the Norwich Census of the Poor, 1570

ST STEVENS P(A)RRYSHE (AND WARD)

Robert Rowe of 46 yers, glasier, in no worke, & Elizabeth, his wyfe, that spyn white warp; & 5 children, 2 sons, the eldest 16 yeris that kepe children, & the rest the daughters spyn, & hav dwelt here ever. (hable) – Thomas Masons house. No allms. Indeferent.

Agnes Nicols, wedow, of 40 yere, that sowe & have dwelt here ever. (hable) – Thomas Browns house. No alms. Indeferent.

John Hubberd of 38 yere, bocher & occupi slawteri, & Margaret, his wyfe, of 30 yer that sell souce etc., & 2 yonge children, & hav dwelt here ever. (hable) No alms. Veri pore.

Ane Bucke, wedow, of 46 yeris, a souster & teacher of children, & 2 children of 9 & 5 yer & work lace, & have dwelt here ever (hable) No alms. Veri pore.

Richard Gugle of 30 yer, glaser, that work not, & Dorethe, his wyf, of that age that spyn white warp, & a yonge child, & dwelt her ever. (hable) – His owne house. Indeferent.

Margaret Turn(er), wedow, of 50 yer, that spyn & help others, & hav dwelt her 12 year (hable) – Ro. Carters house. Indeferent.

Johane Bongey, wedowe, of 60 yere, that spyn white warp & have dwelt here ever. No allms. Veri pore.

& Elizabeth Norton of 40 yere that spyn & help other (hable) (At Osmondes) Veri pore.

Wylliam Carter (at Carters) of 22 yer that is dyseased of a sore legge, & withoute comforte, & hath dwelt here ever (hable) No alms. Veri pore.

Thomas Pele of 50 yere, a cobler in worke, & Margaret, his wyfe, that spyn white warp; & 3 children, theldest 16 yere & spin, & thother 2, 12 & 6 yere, & go to skole & hav dwelt her 9 yere & cam oute of Yorkshire. (hable) – The paryshe house. No alms. Veri pore.

Robert Galiarde of 60 yer, laborer in no worke, & Margaret, his wyfe, of that age, that spyn white warpe (hable) – The parryshe house. No alms. Indeferent.

& Elizabeth Gray, wydow, of 36 yers, that spyn also, & hath a son of 4 yers, & hav dwelt here 5 yers, & cam from Wrouxham (hable). No alms. Veri pore.

[St Steven's had a further 39 families recorded.]

SOURCE 14.15 William Fleetwood, Recorder of London

Among our travels this one matter tumbled out of the way, that one Wotton, a gentleman-born and sometime a merchant-man of good credit, who falling by time into decay kept an ale-house at Smart's Quay near Billingsgate, and after that, for some misdemeanour being put down, he reared up a new kind of life, and in the same house he procured all the cutpurses about this city to repair to his said house. There was a school-house set up to learn young boys to cut purses.

ACTIVITY

11 What does Source 14.15 show was the greatest concern of both town authorities and the government about the increase in the number of urban poor?
12 What conclusions, if any, can be drawn from Sources 14.1–14.15 about wealth and poverty in sixteenth-century towns?

TALKING POINT

Contemporary evidence is insubstantial and historians disagree about the prosperity of townspeople, so is there really any point in learning about ordinary people? Do we need to study social history?

C What were the main changes that took place in towns?

The growth of London

Population growth
The population of London grew from 120,000 in 1550 to 200,000 in 1600. This growth was a result of:
- expansion in trade, particularly to the New World
- an increase in the number of government officials and lawyers, many of whom bought houses in London and became long-term residents. Although the Universities of Oxford and Cambridge were the centres of learning, aspiring lawyers attended the Inns of Court; London had good schools and, after 1597, a college of higher education.
- a continual influx of people from the countryside and towns attending the court and Parliament, carrying out legal transactions and generally advancing their own interests
- the increasing number of unemployed and poor who flocked to the capital in the hope of gaining employment, poor relief or charity.

Government
The royal court, the law courts and Parliament brought a vast army of courtiers, professionals and gentry, along with their retinues, into London.

Trade, commerce and banking
London was England's commercial capital and its greatest port.

Employment
Apart from traders, fortunes could be made by builders, cloth-finishers, distillers and dress makers.

Culture and learning
The desire for leisure pursuits led to a growth in theatres, music rooms, art galleries, and museums, alongside the more common spectacles of bull- and bear-baiting and cock-fighting.

Religion
London was home to England's largest cathedral, the largest group of urban religious houses and over 100 parish churches. The Archbishop of Canterbury administered the Church of England from Lambeth Palace.

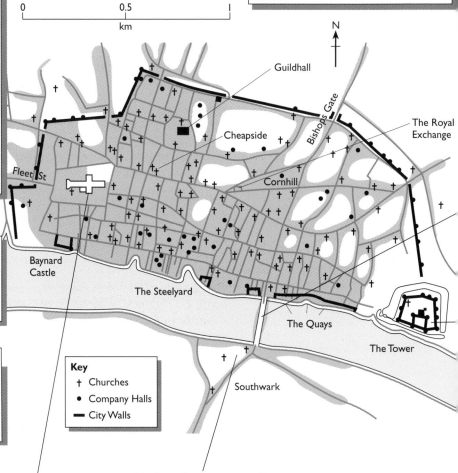

Key
- † Churches
- • Company Halls
- ▬ City Walls

St Paul's Cathedral

The Bear Garden and the Globe

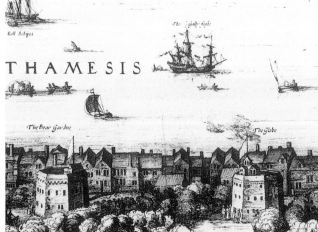

FOCUS ROUTE

Make detailed notes to answer the following questions.

1 Why did London grow in importance during this period?
2 To what extent was London's growth at the expense of other towns?
3 What evidence is there that towns declined during Elizabeth's reign?
4 How far was a town's wealth due to its ability to change its economic function?

London Bridge

The Tower of London

The four drawings (right and above right; and on page 134) are details from a panorama of London by Cornelius Visscher

Westminster (to the west of the map area): a print by Wenceslaus Hollar

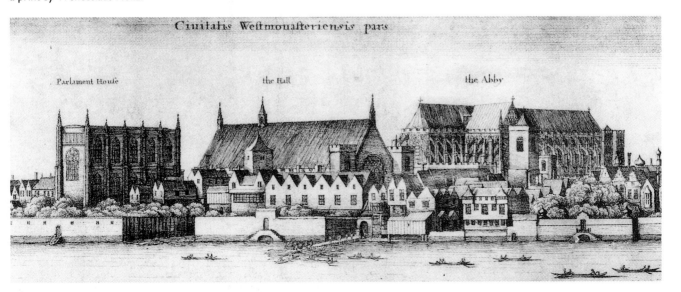

1 Make detailed notes on the importance of London in the commercial life of Elizabethan England.
2 Investigate the prosperity or otherwise of the leading provincial cities and towns during this period.

The effects of London's growing population

- There was intense pressure on space. The growth of the docks around London Bridge led the rich to move into segregated areas such as the West End. Houses, usually constructed of timber, were built close together.
- The poor tended to congregate in the suburbs, usually in the north and east.
- Certain areas became identified with specialist trades or crafts, and therefore attracted labourers and immigrants. (For example, Islington was the centre of brick and tile making.)
- Many vacant plots of land were built on, and former mansions or religious properties were altered, to provide tenements for the poor. The rents for such properties rose throughout Elizabeth's reign as demand continued to outstrip supply.
- There was an increase in pressure on public services, such as water supplies and cleansing. In 1571, London was described as a 'stinking city, the filthiest of the world'. In addition, the overcrowded and insanitary conditions were more likely to increase the impact of the plague, famine and fire.
- The government, which saw the potential for disorder and social unrest in this expanding population, tried to limit it by issuing proclamations preventing further house building and ordering lodgers who had arrived within the last seven years to leave.

SOURCE 14.16 Extracts from the burial register of the London parish of St Botolph's without Aldgate, 1593–98

Edward Ellis, a vagrant who died in the street.

A young man not known who died in a hay-loft.

A cripple that died in the street before John Awsten's door.

A poor woman, being vagrant, whose name was not known, she died in the street under the seat before Mr. Christian Shipman's house called the Crown ... in the High Street.

A maid, a vagrant, unknown, who died in the street near the Postern [gate].

Margaret, a deaf woman, who died in the street.

ACTIVITY

Produce a travel brochure explaining London's importance in Elizabethan England.

Did the growth of London cause the decline of other towns?

SOURCE 14.17 *Discourse of Corporations*, published in the sixteenth century

London hath eaten up all the rest of the townes and havens of England.

TALKING POINT

Is there any value in studying the development of just one town, even when it is the capital? Is knowledge about the growth of London necessary to an understanding of the economic situation during Elizabeth's reign?

ACTIVITY

In groups prepare a presentation about the development of an industry or an area (which should include at least one major town). Use the information in this chapter as a starting point and make sure that, as a class, you cover a variety of industries and regions in order to build up a national picture.

■ 14C Did the growth of London cause the decline of other towns?

137

YES

- The only industry of any note in England was the textile industry. During the sixteenth century the demand for English cloth grew, because of the increase in population and its popularity abroad. Innovations in cloth making, which resulted in the production of lighter draperies, led to the decay of some of the traditional cloth-making areas such as Winchester, but encouraged the growth of new towns like Halifax. However, the Merchant Adventurers had a monopoly on cloth export and shipped it, in protected convoys, from London. In the 1590s, 93 per cent of cloth exports went through London.

- The export of cloth rose by 125 per cent between 1510 and 1550. Most historians agree that, with the exception of London, most towns were in decline during this period. If there was an increase in prosperity, therefore, it was not shared by most towns.

- Smaller ports, such as Kings Lynn and Rye, continually complained that they were losing overseas trade, particularly in times of economic depression. Contemporaries recorded provincial jealousy of London, with its trading companies and established overseas trading routes. Overseas trade was 'decayed in many port townes and flourisheth only or chiefly at London,' while, 'it is no marvaile if they [retailers and craftsmen] abandon countrie townes and resort to London' (J. Stow, *A Survey of London*, 1598).

- London was the cultural and political centre of the nation. The upper groups in society might build homes in the country and employ writers and musicians there for short periods but, in an age of patronage, it was the capital, with its theatres and printing presses, that attracted resident writers and became the centre of the literary world. The arrival, for 'the season', of the peerage and the gentry, with their household retinues, poured money into London, providing profits particularly for those engaged in the food or clothing trades.

- London was four times bigger than the next largest town and its merchants were far wealthier than any others in the kingdom. Ambitious entrepreneurs, particularly if they had capital, did not stay to build up their fortunes in, for example, Exeter but moved to London, where there were greater opportunities and credit and financial backing were more readily available.

- The growth of credit and banking and its unique trading position gave London a series of advantages with which provincial towns could not compete. London could:
  - weather slumps in the cloth trade by developing new trade routes to the Americas and the East Indies
  - develop large-scale brewing to meet visitors' demands, which led to an explosion in the catering and leisure sector
  - exploit the growing number of poor looking for work, by paying low wages
  - use its dominance of the cloth export trade to build up associated industries such as clothing manufacture
  - promote shipbuilding in towns along the Thames
  - capitalise on its expansion by building houses and new purpose-built warehouses.

NO

- Some towns benefited directly from London's growth. Newcastle provided the capital with coal and Manchester sent all its cloth there.

- Many ports, which might have expected to lose trade to London, flourished during this period, particularly Exeter, Bristol, Newcastle, Chester and Great Yarmouth.

- Towns which declined usually did so for a variety of reasons; the growth of London was one factor among many. Coventry's decline was due to its distance from a good road network and navigable waterways at a time when neighbouring towns with better infrastructures, such as Birmingham, were developing as a result of their specialisation in the metal industry.

- To grow, towns had to offer a broad spectrum of trades and services or specialise in a single economic activity. Nantwich grew up as the centre of the salt industry, Woolwich as a supplier for the royal navy, while Lincoln, which lacked a specialised trade, declined.

- Many of the older towns were weakened at the beginning of the century by the heavy cost of maintaining civic offices and ceremonies, coupled with the often restrictive practices of guilds and town corporations. Norwich, York and Winchester all declined as the cloth industry moved into rural areas or free-trade towns such as Leeds.

- Decline was not always irreversible, as it would be if it were directly caused by the growth of London. The fortunes of Reading and Colchester revived, Worcester rebuilt its cloth industry and Norwich attracted foreign immigrants to restore its cloth industry.

- Far from threatening the growth of other towns, increased centralisation from London actually benefited some. For example, York regained its status: from 1561 it not only had county and ecclesiastical courts, but was also the seat of the Council of the North.

D # What did the government do?

FOCUS ROUTE

Make notes on how the government:

- protected, regulated and stimulated crafts and industries
- attempted to maintain law and order by dealing with the growing numbers of urban poor.

■ 14D Important social legislation passed during Elizabeth's reign

Date	Act	Details	Significance
1563	Statute of Artificers	Seven-year apprenticeships were made compulsory in all urban crafts. A regulated number of apprentices was permitted per master and journeyman. Maximum wage rates were fixed.	The main objective was to maintain high standards of craftsmanship and to tie industrial activity to the guild system. Trying to create employment and tie a man to one trade also showed the government's preoccupation with the notion that unemployment meant vagrancy, which in turn meant social unrest.
1572	Vagabonds Act	Severe penalties were to be enacted against vagrants. JPs were to keep a register of the poor in their parish and raise a poor rate to provide a shelter for the elderly and the sick.	The government's fear of the vagrant class was clearly illustrated by this Act, which allowed whipping, boring through the ear, and finally the death penalty for a third offence. On the positive side the wording of this, and the 1576 Act for the Relief of the Poor, showed some government awareness that the plight of the poor was not always their own fault. A move had been made toward the government's accepting some responsibility to help people: to find work for the unemployed, or, where this was not possible, to provide poor relief financed by contributions from those in work.
1576	Act for the Relief of the Poor	The able-bodied poor were to be directed by JPs to find work. Those refusing to do so would be sent to a house of correction.	See above.
1598	Act for the Relief of the Poor	Four overseers were to be appointed to supervise the administration of poor relief. They were to secure apprenticeships for children, provide employment or materials for adults and build hospitals for the old and sick. Finance was to be raised through a compulsory poor rate paid by the inhabitants of each parish.	This Act was passed against a background of rising population, war with Spain leading to high taxation and disruption to trade, increasing urban poverty, and a series of disastrous harvests which pushed up the price of corn by 80 per cent. Riots broke out in London, Oxfordshire and Norfolk. It was to remain in force until 1834 and was based on the earlier Acts of the 1570s and on the experiments to cope with poverty carried out by towns such as Norwich. The degree to which the Act worked is difficult to assess. Certainly nothing had been done to investigate or remove the actual causes of poverty: the 1598 Acts against the further conversion of tillage to pasture were a cynical exercise by a landowning class who had little intention of enforcing them, even assuming that enclosures were the main cause of poverty.
1598	Act for the Punishment of Rogues	JPs were to establish houses of correction for rogues and vagabonds. Rogues were to be whipped before being returned to their own parishes.	This Act enabled the authorities to contain poverty and vagrancy and therefore to try to reduce the likelihood of social unrest which threatened political stability.

SOURCE 14.18 A vagabond being flogged as a punishment for begging

What was poor relief?

In medieval times, society's poor and destitute were looked after by the Church. Wealthy benefactors left bequests in their wills to be used for charitable purposes and the Church gave the poor shelter in almshouses or monasteries.

Henry VIII's dissolution of the monasteries caused some distress because people feared the loss of what was basically a social service; although, as W. G. Hoskins has shown in *The Age of Plunder* (1979), the amount monasteries gave in hospitality and charity varied considerably, and in some areas was only around two or three per cent of an institution's total income. The apparent increase in poverty during the sixteenth century was no doubt due to a combination of factors, most of which can be traced back to the rise in population and its subsequent effects.

For much of the century, Tudor governments continued to see the poor in the same way. The 'impotent poor' – those unable to work due to age, handicap or other infirmity – needed support which would be provided by the community in which they lived. The 'able-bodied poor' – those thought capable of work – were to be encouraged or forced to work, to prevent them from becoming vagrants or beggars. By the end of the century, however, government attitudes had undergone a fundamental change. The sheer number of urban poor meant that there was neither enough charitable support nor enough employment opportunities for them all. The government began to recognise that not all able-bodied poor were idle, that some who wanted to work were unable to do so. The poor laws of Elizabeth's reign, which culminated in the 1598 Act for the Relief of the Poor, incorporated the following principles, which were to remain the basis of poor relief until the Victorian age.

- The administration of poor relief was based on the parish and was the responsibility of JPs or Overseers of the Poor, and churchwardens.
- The impotent poor were looked after, if necessary, in purpose-built premises.
- The able-bodied poor were provided with materials and given the opportunity to work, at spinning and weaving for example.
- Able-bodied poor who refused to work were punished and confined.
- The cost of the system was met by a poor rate, paid by people in work.

Although the Act was motivated by the government's fear of social unrest in the 1590s and focused far more on punishing vagrancy than on providing for the needy, it nevertheless reflected a considerable shift in the attitudes of those in government. At the very least, they now recognised that they did have some responsibility to look after the poor. It would, however, be misleading to attribute responsibility for poor relief solely to the government. Richer members of society were still expected to provide charity for the poor and, although there is controversy as to the extent to which charity declined during Elizabeth's reign, charitable organisations were set up which supplemented the aid provided by the government.

E What was life like for townspeople during Elizabeth's reign?

FOCUS ROUTE

Make detailed notes to answer the following questions.

1 Why did towns decline in the first half of the sixteenth century?
2 How important a contribution did each of the following make to this decline:
   a) people moving from the countryside to the towns
   b) the religious and foreign policies of Henry VIII and the Duke of Somerset
   c) natural disasters?
3 Was this decline reversed during Elizabeth's reign?
4 What are the difficulties in interpreting statistical and contemporary evidence about townspeople?

■ Learning trouble spot

There are many pitfalls to be avoided when answering questions on the change and development of towns during Elizabeth's reign.

- A generalisation is likely to be inaccurate and is anyway unhelpful. What was true of London was not necessarily true of all towns. Factors which caused the fortunes of a town to rise or fall were usually peculiar to its own situation.
- Not all decline was irreversible. Some towns which had declined at the beginning of the sixteenth century were enjoying an economic revival by the end of the century.
- Although the government did not pass legislation specifically directed at towns, government policies had a direct effect on their prosperity. It is therefore necessary to set the rise and fall of towns' fortunes against the political and economic climate of the day.

■ 14E Why did towns decline in the first half of the sixteenth century?

The dissolution of the monasteries and the Reformation in the 1530s and 1540s had drastic effects on cathedral towns and towns with religious houses. Property was often bought up by speculators and the decline in visitors depressed trade.

The number of people living in towns dropped. By 1540, almost all the towns in England had fewer people living in them than they did in medieval times.

By 1550, many industries were based in the countryside or in small market villages.

Living in towns became increasingly expensive, as wealthier citizens had to meet the costs of rates and taxes. Many moved to surrounding villages.

Debasement of the coinage reduced confidence in England's currency and therefore affected trade. This problem was exacerbated by the depression in the cloth industry which led to a decline in the quantity of wool exported to Antwerp.

The cloth industry moved its location from some of the older urban centres to the smaller, free-trade towns in order, it has been argued by some historians, to escape from the restrictive practices of the guilds and the town corporations.

A series of disastrous harvests in the middle of the century were followed by severe epidemics in which, it is estimated, between 5 and 25 per cent of the population died.

The debasement of the coinage, the selling off of crown lands and the levying of high taxes to finance the aggressive foreign policies of Henry VIII and the Duke of Somerset harmed the economy which made it difficult for towns to prosper.

■ 14F Did the climate in which towns declined in the first half of the sixteenth century continue in Elizabeth's reign?

Elizabeth's Religious Settlement heralded a new era of peace and prosperity in England. Religious wars in France and the Netherlands brought many skilled refugees to England who established new industries such as glass and paper making.

The Duke of Northumberland and Mary stopped debasement, initiated financial reforms and renegotiated loans on favourable terms. Elizabeth also showed her determination to bring about economic and social stability, by increasing customs revenues, regulating labour, wages and apprenticeships, and keeping the level of foreign borrowing down.

England enjoyed peace from 1564 to 1585.

The population began to rise. Although this may have increased urban poverty, the government responded by introducing a system of poor relief.

Throughout the 1560s, trade routes were extended into the Baltic and to the coast of West Africa. Foreigners, such as the Hanseatic League, lost their privileged status to transport English exports. The growing conflict with Spain in the 1580s led the government to look for alternatives to a cloth industry based on Antwerp. New outlets for English cloth were established in Germany and trade was also extended to Russia, Turkey, the New World and the East Indies.

Using statistics to reach accurate conclusions about townspeople is particularly difficult. You need therefore to make the following points in written answers on this topic.

- There is considerable disagreement among historians on the living standards of urban wage earners. Tables of statistics drawn up by E. H. Phelps-Brown and S. V. Hopkins (*A Perspective of Wages and Prices*, 1981) show the purchasing power of wages falling to 43 per cent. However, according to D.M. Palliser in *The Age of Elizabeth* Rappaport's figures for London show a decline of only half that figure.

- Wage rates themselves do not give us the whole picture. We also need to know the number of days worked, the number of families totally dependent on one wage, and so on. Similarly the increase in grain prices does not automatically mean that the living standards of wage earners fell. They may, for example, have changed their diet to include more vegetables.

- The few contemporary statistics surviving from Elizabeth's reign cannot give us the whole picture. Tax assessment returns show the number of people earning enough to pay tax but not the number of people who were not; nor do they show the proportion of wage earners to urban poor in a particular town.

- The main concern of the government, town authorities and people themselves was social unrest arising from urban poverty. Consequently, there is a lot of evidence about fear of beggars and vagrants but very few reliable statistics. This can give a distorted picture of town life.

What does the evidence show us about the prosperity of townspeople?

SOURCE 14.19 The main towns

D.M. Palliser, *The Age of Elizabeth*, 1983, p. 134

At a more prosperous level, a common bequest in the wills of urban craftsmen and their wives was of 'my workday gown' and 'my holyday gown'.

A. Raine, *York Civic Records*, Vol. 5, 1939–53

[In York poor men and women] were fayne to sell their pott or their panne and other implements, some laied their apparrell to pledge to pay with their taxe; and of certayne vacant howses ... the collectours had nothing to distrayne but toke of the doores and wyndowes to make up stake with.

W. Camden, *Britannia*, 1586

[Newcastle is] now in a most flourishing state of wealth and commerce.

Some enlightened and prosperous towns began to provide public services: lighting (lanterns in Hereford); cobbled streets; the collection of refuse; orders for keeping the streets clean; piped water (Chester); provision for dealing with the plague.

W. Camden, *Britannia*, 1586

[Plymouth, which] in the last age from a smaller fisher village ... grew up to a large town, ... is not inferiour to a city in number of inhabitants.

D.M. Palliser, *The Age of Elizabeth*, 1983, p. 242

The main streets may have become a little less muddy and dirty, but the poorer quarters remained squalid; at Bristol the merchants' homes largely escaped the epidemic of 1603, but the cottages in the narrow alleys behind them were severely hit.

As in the countryside, prosperous townsmen invested their wealth in buildings. Even towns such as Southampton, which was in overall decline, experienced the replacement of some of the older housing as the next generation sought to better themselves.

Map of England showing towns: Newcastle, York, Chester, Hereford, Bristol, Southampton, Plymouth. Scale 0–100 km. North arrow.

F Review: Were people in towns prospering?

During the first half of the sixteenth century most towns experienced a period of decline. The conditions of Elizabeth's reign – a stable government and Church, long periods of peace, relatively low taxation and the expansion of overseas trade – meant that some towns were able to stop or even reverse that decline, although for a small number it was too late. The economic changes of Elizabeth's reign – the regulation of employment and wages, the growth and specialisation of new industries and the discovery of new markets overseas – created opportunities for individuals and for towns.

This was, however, a period of considerable transition and many of the positive economic effects were not obvious until the seventeenth century. The growing population, for instance, was not seen as a potential new labour force, as it was in the eighteenth century, but as a threat to stability. Moreover, as evicted tenants from the countryside drifted into towns, pressure on resources and fear of vagrancy increased. It was during this period that the term 'labouring poor' began to be used to describe those people drifting in and out of work in the towns. In addition, the rapid rise in the price of agricultural produce, combined with a slow increase in wage rates and the price of industrial goods, meant that it was difficult for urban craftsmen to maintain their standard of living. Contemporaries, therefore, were in little doubt that the standard of living of the majority of the population was falling.

As in the countryside, however, some towns and some individuals did prosper. Merchants, lawyers, employers in the textile or metal industries, and employers providing a service to the town and surrounding countryside, were self-employed and dependent on profits rather than on wages. In a thriving city there was the potential for them to do well. Apprenticeships had become contractual and tightly regulated, providing opportunities for advancement. More new houses were built and people invested in better furnishings and pewter plate. The number of theatres in London grew, as did public services and leisure activities in provincial towns. Above all, Elizabeth and her government engaged in continual efforts to convince people, particularly during royal progresses, that they were living in a Golden Age.

SOURCE 14.20 D. M. Bergeron, *English Civic Pageantry, 1558–62*, 1971, p. 44

Her ceremonial entries to Bristol and Norwich were among the high points of her provincial tours. When she knighted the mayor at Norwich, she told him that 'I have lain up in my breast such good will as I shall never forget Norwich'.

Although urban poverty undoubtedly increased, to an average twenty per cent of a town's population, people drifted in and out of this most destitute group as their own circumstances, such as bereavement or unemployment, dictated. There were also critical years, when there were plagues or poor harvests, when poverty increased overall before returning to its former level. However, in the 1590s, the atmosphere in which the decline of towns had halted changed. War with Spain, heavy taxation, forced loans, monopolies and purveyances, plus a series of disastrous harvests, caused the growing urban population to experience widespread poverty and famine and the corresponding social unrest. The government's awareness of the seriousness of the situation is shown by the 1598 Act for the Relief of the Poor which recognised that the poor needed government support and that not all of those who didn't work were unwilling to do so.

ACTIVITY

1 Copy and complete the following table, using the information in this chapter.

Towns which prospered and why	Towns which declined and why	Urban groups which prospered and why	Urban groups which declined and why	Positive effects of Elizabeth's reign on towns	Negative effects of Elizabeth's reign on towns

2 How far do you agree that townspeople were better off in Elizabeth's reign?

KEY POINTS FROM CHAPTER 14: Were people in towns prospering?

1 Not all townspeople were dependent on wages. Some, such as merchants and employers, were in a position to make a profit. It was those dependent on wages who probably saw their standard of living decline.

2 There was more poverty in towns, especially London, than in the countryside, because people crowded into towns looking for employment or help. Many urban authorities feared social unrest and wrote about the increase in vagrancy.

3 London increased in size during Elizabeth's reign and contained extremes of wealth and poverty. The fortunes of other towns rose or fell depending on their individual circumstances, although it has been argued that London grew at the expense of other towns.

4 The government did not pass legislation directly to do with towns. It was, however, concerned about controlling employment (the Statute of Artificers) and preventing social unrest (the various proclamations passed in London and in the poor relief and vagrancy Acts of the 1570s and 1590s).

5 The factors which had caused towns to decline during the reigns of Henry VIII and Edward VI were absent for the first 40 years of Elizabeth's reign, allowing a period of stability. The return of high taxation and bad harvests in the 1590s saw a revival in social unrest and riots.

Review: Did Elizabeth's government bring prosperity to her people?

Although social and economic history often appears to be a separate branch of history, to analyse the extent to which Elizabeth brought prosperity to her people, you have to examine its complex mixture of factors.

People's prosperity obviously depends directly on their ability to make money and during Elizabeth's reign income was affected, for better or for worse, by:

• population increase
• a rise in prices which led to growing inflation
• changes in agriculture, industry and commerce.

In addition, the economic wealth of the country, which determined an individual's ability to make money, was affected by:

• government legislation
• whether the country was at peace or involved in a war
• opportunities for investment and expansion.

The Elizabethan government worked very hard to convince people that they were lucky to be living in such an age. An individual's feeling of wealth does not always directly relate to their income. Some people would have looked with pride at their country's achievements:

• the establishment of the Anglican Church
• the growth of London
• the explosion of the arts, culture and learning
• overseas expansion
• the defeat of the Spanish Armada.

And of course, at the centre of this, as always, was the court and the Queen. Elizabeth extended her progresses and visited not only her courtiers on their country estates but also towns in the south east and the Midlands, where she could see and be seen by large numbers of townspeople.

Ultimately, the success of government policies depended on the acquiescence of the Queen's subjects and people were less likely to protest if they were enjoying a standard of living which, if not increasing, was at least not declining. Therefore, despite the problems caused by an increasing population and inflation and the consequent increase in urban poverty, the first 30 years of Elizabeth's reign was a period of stability and prosperity. In the 1590s, however, Elizabeth's political skills finally met their match or luck ran out or perhaps she simply paid the price for being too cautious early on. Social and economic cohesion broke down and political stability was threatened, throwing up problems to which the government had no new answers.

ACTIVITY

To test your understanding of the links between government, the economy and different social groups, read Sections 2 and 3 again. Then prepare an answer to the following question: How far was the 1590s a decade of economic and social crisis?

TALKING POINT

Do you remember the main theme of the book: the investigation into whether Elizabeth's reign was a Golden Age (see page 5)?

Was Elizabeth's reign a Golden Age for her people in terms of their individual prosperity, or do dramatic events obscure the daily realities of poverty and struggle? Or, are both of these interpretations too generalised to be helpful?

How far did religion affect stability at home?

Section 4 will focus on Elizabeth's domestic policies. It will probably form the basis of your study of Elizabeth and the questions you expect to answer in your examination. The work you have completed in earlier sections will help you considerably. You already have an understanding of:

- Elizabeth's character and her aims when she became Queen
- the problems Elizabeth inherited in 1558
- the men she chose to help her govern
- the institutions of Elizabethan government and how they worked
- the main policy areas over which Elizabeth and the governing classes disagreed.

You already know, for example, that Elizabeth and her ministers did not see eye to eye on how to deal with Mary, Queen of Scots. This section will fill in the gaps for you, by looking in detail at who Mary, Queen of Scots, was, what she did, and why she provoked such strong feelings.

As with previous sections, the main emphasis will be on the success or failure of government policies and whether Elizabeth was able to ensure the country's stability. In other words, we will continue to look at how far Elizabeth was in control.

It is easier for you to make your way through the issues if they are linked by a common theme. Since religion was, to a greater or lesser extent, involved in all the areas featured in this section it is an obvious focus for our enquiries.

- How far did religion affect stability at home?
- How far was government policy determined by religious principle or the demands of security?
- How effectively did the government react to religious opposition?

Especially after 1568, it is increasingly difficult to keep domestic and foreign issues separate. Elizabeth herself would not have done so; she had to determine policies and respond to problems as they arose on a day-to-day basis, whether they originated in the north of England or Spain. In order to keep the details manageable, foreign policy is covered separately, in Section 5, but references to events abroad will be made as they arise.

A detail from the frontispiece to Foxe's *Book of Martyrs* showing Protestant and Catholic preachers

What problems did the Religious Settlement of 1559–63 solve?

CHAPTER OVERVIEW When Elizabeth became Queen in 1558 it was widely expected that she would change the nation's religion from the Roman Catholicism of her sister's reign.

SOURCE 16.1 N. L. Jones in C. Haigh (ed.) *The Reign of Elizabeth I*, 1984, p. 31

The living symbol of her father's break with Rome, she had never been recognised as legitimate by the Catholic Church. Moreover, she believed firmly that she was the rightful ruler of all England, including its Church, and no Pope could agree with that.

In addition, Elizabeth did not want to be associated with Mary's legacy. The restoration of Roman Catholicism and the authority of the Pope were too closely associated in the minds of the English with the persecution of heretics, an unpopular Spanish consort and the loss of Calais. There was much to be gained from embarking on a new policy that would signal a break with the immediate past and enable Elizabeth to emerge as the architect of, and inspiration for, a new order.

For Mary, religious settlement had been a straightforward issue; she had imposed her own faith on her subjects. The answer for Elizabeth, who was far more aware of the political complexities of the situation, was less clear. There is now little doubt over Elizabeth's personal convictions; her own translations, her book of private devotions, her private prayers and her views on salvation, all suggest a real commitment to Protestant beliefs. But she realised that the religious choices she made would have important consequences at home and abroad. First, religious changes had caused rebellions in the reigns of Henry VIII and Edward VI and a policy of repression during the reign of Mary. Second, the issue of religion was tied closely to the question of Elizabeth's marriage as it would determine the suitability or otherwise of potential candidates. Third, it would affect relations with foreign powers and in early 1559 England was still allied to Catholic Spain in a war against Scotland and France.

As might be expected, Elizabeth's early moves were cautious, although her appointment of William Cecil as personal secretary and her instructions to Protestants to preach the first official sermons led people to believe that the English Church would not remain Roman Catholic.

A What was Elizabeth's religious inheritance? (pp. 148–50)

B What choices did Elizabeth have in 1558? (pp. 151–52)

C What did Elizabeth want? (pp. 153–54)

D Were the Act of Supremacy and the Act of Uniformity passed without opposition? (pp. 155–57)

E What form did the Religious Settlement take? (pp. 158–59)

F What did Elizabeth do next (1559–63)? (p. 160)

G Review: What problems did the Religious Settlement of 1559–63 solve? (pp. 161–62)

A What was Elizabeth's religious inheritance?

■ 16A Religion under the early Tudor monarchs

Henry VIII
Henry put an end to the Pope's authority over the Church in England after his failure to secure a divorce. Responsibility for Church DOCTRINE passed to the 'King in Parliament'. Between 1536 and 1539 some changes were introduced along moderate Protestant lines, but after 1539 Henry returned to an orthodox Catholic position on doctrine. Henry dissolved monastic institutions to seize their land and wealth. By the end of his reign many courtiers, and his son, were Protestant.

Edward VI
The Duke of Somerset introduced a Protestant prayer book and communion service, ordered the destruction of all images in churches, allowed priests to marry and decided that services should be held in English rather than Latin. The Duke of Northumberland went further with the Book of Common Prayer and the 42 Articles of 1552 which generally followed the teachings of Ulrich Zwingli and left no room for Catholic belief. The main influences behind religious changes in Edward's reign were Archbishop Cranmer and the young king himself.

Mary Tudor
Mary restored the authority of the Pope, but was unable to return the dissolved monastic lands to the Church. The Latin Mass and Catholic doctrine and ritual were all enforced. Cardinal Pole attempted to improve the standard of priests, but his measures never had time to succeed. The persecution of Protestants earned Mary the name 'Bloody Mary'.

DOCTRINE
The body of the teachings of the Church; the Church's beliefs.

ANABAPTIST
A Protestant sect which denied the act of infant baptism. It was popular on the continent. Anabaptists were attacked by all denominations for their social as well as their religious beliefs.

■ Learning trouble spot

It is important to remember that:

- **Henry VIII lived and died a Catholic but not a *Roman* Catholic**
  Although Henry VIII broke with Rome he did not change the doctrine of the Church. It remained Catholic, not Protestant, despite the influence of Archbishop Cranmer, Catherine Parr, Henry's son and many of his leading courtiers.
- **Under Edward VI, the Duke of Somerset did not permit religious toleration**
  The Prayer Book of 1549 established a Protestant form of worship but retained some Catholic ceremonial so as to be acceptable to Catholics. Somerset ordered the resignation of Bishops Bonner, Heath and Gardiner for opposing the Prayer Book for going too far, while also executing radical ANABAPTISTS who believed it didn't go far enough. Popular unrest, demonstrated by the Western Rising in 1549, occurred because the changes were too extreme for many ordinary Catholics. The inclusion of some Catholic ceremonial also produced dissatisfaction among leading Protestant reformers.

149

WHAT PROBLEMS DID THE RELIGIOUS SETTLEMENT OF 1559–63 SOLVE?

FOCUS ROUTE

I Copy and complete the table, making detailed notes on the fundamentals of sixteenth-century Catholicism, Lutheranism, Zwinglianism and Calvinism using the text on pages 149–50 and any extra research that is necessary.

	Catholicism	Lutheranism	Zwinglianism	Calvinism
Doctrine				
Organisation of the Church				
Appearance of the Church				
Communion service/Eucharist				
Relationship with the state				

2 Which of the Protestant reformers remained closest to Catholicism and which moved furthest from Catholicism?

EUCHARIST
The Christian sacrament commemorating the Last Supper, in which bread and wine are consecrated and consumed. In the Catholic Church the service is called Mass, in Protestant churches it is called Holy Communion.

TRANSUBSTANTIATION
The Catholic belief that during Mass the bread and wine is transformed into the body and blood of Jesus through the powers of the priest.

CONSUBSTANTIATION
All Protestants rejected the Catholic belief in transubstantiation, but differed over whether the communion service was simply a memorial held in remembrance of the Last Supper or whether there was a spiritual presence. Luther developed the doctrine of consubstantiation which asserted that Christ's body spiritually co-existed with the bread and wine, that they were present together. This miracle owed nothing to the presence of a priest but occurred as a result of the faithful being gathered together.

■ **Learning trouble spot**

'Communion in both kinds' does not mean that people taking communion could believe in transubstantiation and/or consubstantiation
Communion in both kinds refers to the Protestant practice of offering both the bread and the wine to all communicants. The Catholic practice was to only offer the bread to the congregation; the priest had the wine.

Protestant reformers

Martin Luther, 1483–1547
Luther, Professor of Theology at Wittenberg University in Germany, became the leader of Protestantism when he pinned his *95 Theses*, criticising aspects of Roman Catholicism, to the door of Wittenberg Cathedral in 1517. The *95 Theses* sparked national controversy and led Luther to develop his beliefs in a series of pamphlets. Luther's ideas soon spread to England. Although Henry VIII condemned Lutheranism, it continued in influence. Luther believed that:
- A man is saved by faith alone, not by good works (such as acts of charity) or the observance of the seven sacraments of the Catholic Church.
- The scriptures are the only true authority. The Pope, bishops and priests were fallible. Man could approach God directly through prayer without the intervention of a priest. Luther did, however, keep the hierarchy of the Church for the sake of convenience.
- Anything was allowable during a service, provided it did not contradict the word of God. Luther therefore retained clerical robes and singing or hymns.
- During the EUCHARIST the bread and wine were not transformed into the body and blood of Christ through the powers of the priest as Catholics believed (TRANSUBSTANTIATION), but Christ was nevertheless physically present to those who had faith. This belief is called CONSUBSTANTIATION.
- Authority over the Church should be given to the lay ruler; in Lutheran Germany this meant the local prince.

Ulrich Zwingli, 1484–1556
Zwingli was Swiss. He was educated at the universities of Basle and Vienna. As Minister of Zurich, he began to reform his Church along the lines suggested by Luther. He transformed Zurich into a Protestant centre and his writings became popular in England in the 1540s. He did not agree with Luther's tolerance of Catholic ritual or consubstantiation. Zwingli believed that:
- Practices not sanctioned by the scriptures, such as images, elaborate dress, stained-glass windows and music, had to go. Altars were replaced by tables and the bread was carried to the congregation by ministers in ordinary dress.
- The communion service was purely commemorative, in remembrance of the last supper.
- Christian communities had to follow the law of God as revealed in the Bible. Both the Church and the state shared the responsibility for enforcing moral discipline and promoting daily lectures and Bible readings. Zwingli's Church was therefore more democratic than Luther's.

John Calvin, 1509–64

Calvin was a French theologian. He was based in Geneva, where some of the Marian Exiles lived between 1553 and 1558. His beliefs were published in the *Institutes* in 1536.

- Calvin accepted various Lutheran beliefs including justification by faith alone, but added the doctrine of predestination. He believed that man had fallen so far from grace that only God had the power to decide who was to be saved; from the very beginning God had predetermined whether or not an individual was a member of 'the elect'.
- He stood between Luther's belief in Christ's physical presence during the Eucharist and Zwingli's view of the communion service as commemorative. He believed Christ's presence during the service was spiritual, but nonetheless real to the congregation.
- Unlike Luther, Calvin firmly rejected ritual and those sacraments not founded on the scriptures. Calvinist churches were plain and free of images, and the only acceptable sacraments were baptism and communion.
- Calvinist churches were not administered by a hierarchy of bishops, deacons and priests, but by a non-hierarchical ministry elected by their congregations. Pastors preached and administered the sacraments, doctors explained and preached doctrine, lay elders executed discipline and deacons cared for the sick and poor.
- The Calvinist Church and the state were separate bodies, although Calvin believed that co-operation between the two was desirable.

TALKING POINT

What effect might a belief in the doctrine of predestination have on the way people lead their lives?

SOURCE 16.2 From *The King's Psalter*, Henry VIII reading the psalms in his bedchamber, 1540

FOCUS ROUTE

Copy and complete the following table to show the likely effect of each of Elizabeth's options for the Religious Settlement.

	Effects on Elizabeth, as Queen of England	Effects on the international situation	Effects on the English people	Effects on the Church	Strengths and weaknesses of the option
Roman Catholicism (Mary Tudor)					
English Catholicism (Henry VIII)					
Protestantism (Lutheran)					
Protestantism (Zwinglian/ Calvinist)					

The religious issue could not be settled in isolation. Elizabeth had to weigh the effects each choice would have on England's relationships with other countries, the English people, and the administration and spiritual quality of the Church itself.

The situation abroad

- **Spain** was Catholic, but Philip II needed to maintain an alliance with England. His chief concern was that a combined French and Scottish attack on England might succeed, cutting off his access to the English Channel which was his communication route with the Spanish Netherlands. He was therefore prepared to support a Protestant England against the claims of Scottish Mary Stuart who, in 1558, was married to the French dauphin.

- **France** was England's traditional enemy. Peace negotiations were delayed because of England's insistence that Calais was returned, but in the treaty of April 1559 Calais stayed in French hands. Three months later, the Catholic Francis II and his 17-year-old wife Mary Stuart became King and Queen of France. Mary also called herself Queen of England.

- **Scotland** was ruled by the French regent and widow of James V, Mary of Guise, in the absence in France of her daughter Mary Stuart. Many Scottish nobles were Protestant and mistrustful of the French regent.

- **The Netherlands** were under the control of Philip II of Spain in 1558. Elizabeth needed to maintain good relations, as Antwerp was vital for the English textile trade.

- **The Pope**, as the head of the Catholic Church, could excommunicate Elizabeth, and if he officially excluded her from the Church he technically released her subjects from obeying her. He could also call on the Catholic powers in Europe to lead a religious crusade against England and its ungodly ruler.

152

WHAT PROBLEMS DID THE RELIGIOUS SETTLEMENT OF 1559–63 SOLVE?

The situation at home

The laity

- **The House of Commons** was largely Protestant, although there were a few ardent Catholics.

- **The House of Lords** was largely Catholic. The bishops were capable of blocking legislation and could usually count on the support of the conservative hereditary peers.

- **The Privy Council** was largely Protestant. It was dominated by William Cecil and his political allies. (Remember: Elizabeth decided on the composition of her council.)

- **The Marian Exiles** had fled England during Mary's reign and strengthened their Calvinist views during their time in Geneva. On their return, they expected to be given key posts in the Church and Parliament and opposed any compromise with Catholics.

- **The majority of the population** were conservative in their religious sympathies.

The Church

- **The clergy**, and particularly the bishops, were solidly Catholic. In their sermons they urged the English people to resist Protestantism. A priest in Canterbury even began arming people against religious change, raising fears of a Catholic revolt.

- **Government:** A woman as Head of the Church was unacceptable to extreme Protestants and Catholics. In addition, unless Elizabeth could persuade the Catholic bishops to remain within her Church, she would have to replace them with Protestants which would alienate her more Catholic subjects.

- **Organisation:** Despite changes in doctrine the organisation of the Church in England had remained largely unaltered. Church courts functioned as they always had and the clergy had remained hierarchical.

- **Ritual:** Changes in the Church's visual emphasis had always caused unrest. The presence or absence of images, furnishings and priests' vestments were all disputed issues.

- **Doctrine:** Conservatives wanted to retain their belief in transubstantiation, while more radical reformers saw the communion service as commemorative.

ACTIVITY

In a group, place yourselves in Elizabeth's position in 1558. Decide which features of the Church in England between 1534 and 1558 you would keep, which features of the churches of the Protestant reformers you would add, and how you would minimise opposition to your proposed changes. Review your proposals once you have completed Chapter 16.

C What did Elizabeth want?

FOCUS ROUTE

Make notes to answer the following questions.

1 What were Elizabeth's personal religious beliefs? What evidence from Chart 16C supports your answer?
2 What sort of religious settlement did Elizabeth want?

What were Elizabeth's personal religious beliefs?

This question is not as easy to answer as it would appear, mainly because Elizabeth kept her personal views private. This has enabled historians to label her as indifferent to religion and motivated solely by political considerations. It is possible, however, to reach a different conclusion.

■ 16C Elizabeth's personal religious beliefs

Elizabeth was educated by leading humanists and lived in Protestant households as a child.

Elizabeth disliked long sermons and was exasperated by the endless theological debates much loved by Protestant reformers.

In her adolescence, Elizabeth translated three texts by Desiderius Erasmus (see page 154).

Elizabeth liked clergymen to wear vestments and for hymns to be accompanied by choir boys and the organ.

Elizabeth was regarded as an example of piety during Edward's reign, and as a heretic in Mary's reign.

Elizabeth was vehemently opposed to the idea of married clergymen, particularly married bishops, and could not always bring herself to be civil to Mrs Parker, the wife of the Archbishop of Canterbury.

At her coronation, Elizabeth told priests carrying candles, 'away with those torches'. Also, the bread and wine was not consecrated during the ceremony.

Elizabeth's personal religious beliefs

Although Elizabeth attended Protestant services in English she kept crucifixes and candles in her private chapel despite the admonitions of the Archbishop of Canterbury and the Dean of St Paul's.

On Christmas Day 1558, Elizabeth walked out of her chapel when the bishop raised the consecrated bread during Mass.

In 1558, Elizabeth's Privy Council was dominated by Protestants, and Protestant preachers were invited to give public sermons.

What sort of Church did Elizabeth want?

The surviving evidence seems to suggest that Elizabeth's personal preference was for a Church with a Protestant doctrine which retained the traditional structure and Catholic ritual. Hierarchy and ritual were also preferred by the Lutherans; but as far as the doctrine of the Eucharist was concerned, Elizabeth's Church was closer to the spiritual presence of Calvinism or the commemorative focus of Zwinglianism than the physical presence of Lutheranism. In this, Elizabeth may have been motivated by her personal preferences, by broader political considerations, or even by a mixture of both. She may always have aimed to establish such a Church or may have made concessions to the opposition she encountered along the way.

Whatever the exact nature of Elizabeth's own Protestantism and her intentions, the political advantages of establishing a Church which combined Protestant doctrine and Catholic ceremonial were obvious. By appearing to be a Protestant heroine, Elizabeth could signal a break with the religious repression of Bloody Mary's reign and ensure the loyalty of the politically-active classes in England – many of whom had been in exile from 1553 to 1558 – and her Protestant allies. By maintaining an outward appearance that was familiar and comforting, the Queen could avoid the social upheavals of Edward's reign and reassure foreign Catholic powers that the Church in England had not changed so very much. They might not be fooled into thinking England was really Catholic – it was obvious that Elizabeth's Church was Protestant – but they might be lulled into thinking it was Lutheran. They would have seen a Zwinglian or Calvinist Church as a threat to stability.

By steering a middle route, Elizabeth was aiming to create a Church which was acceptable to the majority of her people. She wanted to avoid persecution and civil war. Such a Church, however, would be unacceptable to Catholic and Protestant extremists and the reality of this was demonstrated in the very first Parliament of the reign when legislation was introduced for establishing the Elizabethan Religious Settlement.

TALKING POINT

Is it necessary for a historian to have a clear knowledge of a monarch's personal religious views? Would this help us to understand their political aims?

Desiderius Erasmus

- Desiderius Erasmus was born in 1469 in Rotterdam and educated by Catholic monks.
- In 1492 he was ordained as a priest at Gilda, and then studied and taught at Paris University. In 1499 he taught at Oxford University.
- His early work concentrated on translating Latin classical texts, but during his stay in England he became more interested in translating and interpreting the Bible and analysing the teachings of Christ.
- In 1500 Erasmus published *The Handbook of the Militant Christian*, urging his readers to follow a Christianity which comes from the heart and not from the outward show of relics, rituals and ceremonials.
- In 1509, while staying at the home of his friend Sir Thomas More, he wrote *In Praise of Folly*, in which he criticised both the sterility of a clerical debate and the whole structure of monastic life.
- From 1509 to 1514, he was Professor of Divinity and Greek at Cambridge University, after which he moved to Basle, Switzerland, where he spent the rest of his life.
- In 1516 he published a Latin translation of the original Greek New Testament.
- Erasmus' views had a great impact in England, particularly on education (see pages 276–77, 279). He inspired a group of scholars who came to be known as Christian humanists, because they believed in the central importance of the humanities (the study of classical Latin and Greek) and wanted a simple religion based on a more accurate translation of the Bible. They held, above all, that religion should be concerned with internal faith and not outward appearance.
- Erasmus died in 1536.

Portrait of Erasmus by Quentin Metsys

FOCUS ROUTE

Describe the difficulties Elizabeth faced in the Parliament of 1559.

D Were the Act of Supremacy and the Act of Uniformity passed without opposition?

Elizabeth and her council planned the Religious Settlement with great care and were, not surprisingly, very cagey about its intentions. In December 1558, an anonymous pamphlet, probably commissioned by the government and entitled *A Device for Alteration of Religion,* had painted a troubled scenario of war with France and Scotland, rebellion in Ireland, riots from English Catholics, and demands for more reform from extreme Protestants if a Protestant Church were introduced. Nevertheless, this was the path down which Elizabeth and her council now felt compelled to go. Parliament was called in 1559 to determine the Queen's authority over the Church by passing the Act of Supremacy, and the form of service which her subjects were expected to follow by passing the Act of Uniformity. Although the evidence for this session of Parliament is largely missing, it would seem that events in the timeline in Chart 16D took place.

■ 16D The progress of the Act of Uniformity and the Act of Supremacy

1559

9 Feb Three separate bills are introduced into the House of Commons. One to re-establish the monarch as the Head of the Church, the other two to establish a Protestant form of worship probably based on Northumberland's Prayer Book of 1552.

21 Feb A new bill is introduced, combining the three separate ones of 9 February. It is passed by the House of Commons.

Mar The bill passed by the Commons is amended by the House of Lords to remove the restoration of Protestantism. This opposition stuns Elizabeth and her council, who debate whether or not to accept these changes and institute a religious settlement along Henrician lines.

Elizabeth arrests two bishops for disobedience.

Elizabeth reconvenes Parliament immediately after the Easter break.

Apr A new supremacy bill is introduced, giving the Queen the title of Supreme Governor rather than Supreme Head, to pacify Catholics as well as many Protestants who have serious doubts about a female claiming to be Head of the Church. It passes through the House of Commons easily, and, after heated debate, it is passed by the House of Lords.

A new uniformity bill is drafted to include concessions to Catholics. It is only passed by 21 votes to 18 in the House of Lords.

FOCUS ROUTE

Read Sources 16.4 and 16.5 and make notes to answer the following questions.

1 Which people were expected to take the oath in the Act of Supremacy?
2 What title did the Act of Supremacy confer on the Queen and why was this so important?
3 What did the Act of Uniformity lay down as the punishment for not attending church?
4 Do you think Elizabeth wanted the new Acts to be enforced strictly throughout the country?
5 Which prayer book was re-established by the Act of Uniformity?
6 Which of the sacraments were to remain unchanged from the time of Edward VI?
7 a) Which sacrament was changed?
   b) How was it changed?
   c) Why was it changed?
8 Which of the problems of 1558 was not tackled by the Act of Supremacy and the Act of Uniformity?

156

WHAT PROBLEMS DID THE RELIGIOUS SETTLEMENT OF 1559–63 SOLVE?

SOURCE 16.4 Extracts from the 1559 Act of Supremacy

*All and every Archbishop, Bishop, and all and every other ecclesiastical person . . .
and all and every temporal judge, justice, mayor, and every other lay or temporal
officer and minister and every other person having Your Highness' fee or wages
shall make a corporal oath upon the evangelist . . .*

*. . . I A. B. do utterly testify and declare in my conscience that the Queen's
Highness is the only Supreme Governor of this realm and of all other Her
Highness' dominions and countries, as well in all spiritual or ecclesiastical things
or causes as temporal, and that no foreign prince, person, prelate, state or
potentate hath or ought to have any jurisdiction, power, superiority, pre-eminence
or authority ecclesiastical or spiritual within this realm.*

SOURCE 16.5 Extracts from the 1559 Act of Uniformity

*All and every person and persons inhabiting within this realm . . . shall diligently
and faithfully, having no lawful or reasonable excuse to be absent, endeavour
themselves to resort to their parish church or chapel accustomed . . . upon every
Sunday and other days ordained . . . upon pain that every person so offending
shall forfeit for every such offence twelve pence to be levied by the church wardens
of the Parish . . .*

*. . . were at the death of our late sovereign Lord King Edward VI, there
remained one uniform order of common service and prayer, and of the
administration of the sacraments, rites and ceremonies in the Church of England,
which was set forth in one book . . . authorised by Act of Parliament . . . in the
fifth and sixth years of our said late Sovereign Lord . . . the which was repealed
and taken away by Act of Parliament in the first year of the reign of our late
Sovereign Lady Queen Mary . . . be it therefore enacted by the authority of this
present Parliament that the said Statute of Appeal . . . shall be void and of none
effect . . . and that the said book . . . shall stand and be . . . in full force and effect.*

*And further be it enacted . . . that all and singular ministers . . . be bounden to
say and use the Matins, Evensong, celebration of the Lord's Supper and
administration of each of the sacraments, and all their common and open prayer,
in such order and form as is mentioned in the said book . . . with . . . the form of
the litany altered and corrected, and two sentences only added in the delivery of
the sacraments to the communicants, and none other or otherwise.*

*And when he [the minister] delivereth the bread he shall say: 'the body of our
Lord Jesus Christ, which was given for thee, preserve thy body and soul into
everlasting life and take and eat this in remembrance that Christ died for thee,
[and] feed on Him in thine hearts by faith with thanksgiving'. And the minister
that delivereth the cup shall say: 'the blood of our Lord Jesus Christ, which was
shed for thee, preserve thy body and soul into everlasting life. And drink this in
remembrance that Christ's blood was shed for thee and be thankful'.*

What do historians think?

As you already know from the chapter on Parliament, there is considerable
controversy among historians over the interpretation of the passing of the Acts
of Supremacy and Uniformity in 1559. The theory put forward by J.E. Neale in
the 1950s, that Elizabeth was aiming for a sort of Henrician Catholicism but was
pushed into a more Protestant settlement by the 'Puritan Choir' in the House of
Commons, has been challenged by more recent historians. Dr N. Jones, in *Faith
by Statute* (1982), argued that the main opposition to the Settlement came not
from Protestants in the House of Commons but from Catholics in the House of
Lords. The effect of this was that the eventual Settlement was more of a
compromise with elements of Catholicism than had been originally intended.

FOCUS ROUTE

Read Sources 16.6 and 16.7 and make detailed notes to answer the following questions.

1 Why did J. E. Neale argue that the Elizabethan Religious Settlement was more Protestant than the Queen wanted and what evidence did he give for this?
2 How does Neale's theory about the Religious Settlement fit with his broader one on the nature of parliamentary opposition? Refer back to Chapter 7 if you need to.
3 Neale's interpretation of two events, on which he based his theory, has been shown to be wrong. What are these two events?
4 Give four reasons to explain why historians now believe that Neale's views were mistaken.

The traditional view of the Elizabethan Religious Settlement

SOURCE 16.6 N. L. Jones in C. Haigh (ed.), *The Reign of Elizabeth I*, 1984, p. 31

The oldest historiographic tradition, represented by John Foxe, William Camden, and John Strype, held that Elizabeth set out to create the Anglican Church and, despite stiff Catholic resistance, succeeded. Refined by later historians, the story of 1559 was told in this way until the early 1950s, when J. E. Neale startled his colleagues with a new interpretation of the Queen's intentions towards religion. Elizabeth, he asserted, did not wish to establish a thoroughly Protestant Church, desiring instead to return to her father's Catholicism without the Pope. Her plans were thwarted, Neale believed, by a Puritan party in the House of Commons, led by returned religious exiles. This group forced Elizabeth to compromise between her ideal of a conservative religious settlement and their ideal of a settlement modelled on the Swiss Reformation. It was this conflict, he thought, that made the Parliament of 1559 so stormy, not Catholic opposition to the change in religion. Forcefully argued, Professor Neale's vision of a conservative Queen opposed by a Puritan opposition became the stuff of text books. Recently, however, his interpretation has been challenged and rejected by several historians who have shown that John Foxe's account was generally accurate.

The revisionist view of the Elizabethan Religious Settlement

SOURCE 16.7 C. Haigh, *Elizabeth I*, 1988, p. 31

Sir John Neale suggested that Elizabeth had wanted a much more 'Catholic' Church, but, since the conservative bishops refused to accept a royal supremacy, she had to give in to the Protestant clamour for a more radical settlement. Although the evidence is inconclusive, this view appears to be wrong. Neale attached significance to the peace negotiations at Cateau-Cambresis: he thought Elizabeth had to pursue a conservative policy, at least until a treaty had been signed and England was safely out of the war. But it was Elizabeth herself who had delayed the peace, by her unrealistic demand for the return of Calais, and the negotiations did not determine her parliamentary strategy. Indeed, it is not impossible that the state of war was deliberately prolonged by Elizabeth herself to weaken the resistance of conservative peers to her religious proposal. Neale also exaggerated the political weight of the Protestant radicals in the Commons. Only nineteen Marian exiles were elected to the 1559 parliament, and some returned too late to play any active role. The radicals were not an organised pressure group able to dominate the Commons, which was usually controlled by the council and its agents. The Queen's tactics had been designed to contain conservative opposition in the Lords, not radical pressure in the Commons. Above all, the Neale version of 1559 simply does not fit with what we know of the religion of Elizabeth and her advisers. Even if the Queen herself is dismissed as a POLITIQUE, it is difficult to see that William Cecil, Nicholas Bacon, Francis Knollys, and the Earl of Bedford would have headed a regime aiming for anything less than a Protestant settlement.

POLITIQUE
A person motivated more by political than religious concerns.

TALKING POINT

Is it important to know how historians' assessments of major events change over time? Do you need to refer to this change or just to the most recent assessment in an essay?

158

WHAT PROBLEMS DID THE RELIGIOUS SETTLEMENT OF 1559-63 SOLVE?

FOCUS ROUTE

Make notes on the following:

• what the Elizabethan Religious Settlement achieved
• the problems it did not solve
• the problems it caused.

What form did the Religious Settlement take?

■ 16E The Elizabethan Religious Settlement

The 1559 Act of Supremacy and the 1559 Act of Uniformity established the Elizabethan Religious Settlement.

• They declared that Elizabeth was Supreme Governor of the Church of England with the power of visitation (the power to authorise inspections of the clergy).

• They revived the legislation which was repealed during the Parliaments of Mary's reign.

• They revoked the Heresy Acts and the Papal supremacy.

• They imposed an oath on all clergy and office holders to enforce conformity to the new Prayer Book.

• They set up a system of punishments for those who failed to use the prayer book or who publicly objected to its use.

• They ordered everyone to attend church on Sunday and other holy days and to participate in the new services. Fines were imposed on those who refused to attend.

• They set down that church ornamentation and clergy's dress should be as in the more moderate 1549 prayer book.

The Book of Common Prayer omitted the Black Rubric of 1552, which denied the real presence of Christ during the communion service, and changed the words said by the priest as he consecrated the bread and wine. This was probably done in the hope that the ambiguity would enable people of wide religious opinions to participate in the new national Church.

The Royal Injunctions of 1559, drafted by Cecil, ordered clergy to:

• observe the royal supremacy and preach against superstition and Papal authority

• condemn images, relics and miracles

• preach only with permission, which came in the form of a licence

• report recusants to the privy council or to JPs

• marry only with the permission of their bishop and two JPs

• observe the Ornaments Rubric (see page 164) laid down during Edward VI's reign.

One hundred and twenty five commissioners were appointed to visit churches throughout the country and enforce the oath of supremacy. This resulted in a great deal of destruction of church ornaments and the loss of 400 Marian clergy.

The crown restored control of Church wealth to itself. It took control of first fruits and tenths, appropriated the remaining religious foundations and allowed vacancies to occur before confirming new appointments in order to profit directly from the positions' revenues during this period. Former monastic lands remained with their owners – perhaps one of the reasons why the House of Commons supported the Religious Settlement.

Issues left outstanding by the Elizabethan Religious Settlement

Doctrine

Elizabeth's primary concern throughout had been to establish a national and legal framework for her new Church. As a result, the Religious Settlement did not mention doctrine. This caused confusion and uncertainty and dismayed Protestant reformers who had hoped for vigorous theological debate leading to statements of belief.

SOURCE 16.8 The Earl of Surrey: 'I hope you do not of purpose keep the Church in this [e]state.

The clergy

The loss of leading Catholic members of the clergy meant that Elizabeth was forced to appoint Protestants. In addition to delays caused by financial considerations, the religious confusion of the 1550s meant there was a real shortage of properly qualified clergy. As a result, the new bishops were often compelled to accept poorly trained clerics. This, coupled with the crown's policy of milking the Church for all it was worth, meant that both the physical and spiritual life of the Church were fast approaching poverty.

SOURCE 16.9 Thomas Cartwright, an English Puritan clergyman, was at a loss to state 'what was the religion which really was observed here'.

Pope Pius IV

It was expected that the Pope would excommunicate Elizabeth, an illegitimate, female, heretical ruler. His role was vital in determining the attitude of English Catholics and the policies of major European Catholic powers such as France and Spain. Although England had just signed the Treaty of Cateau-Cambresis with France, fear of a Catholic crusade led the council to make early overtures to Protestant German princes in the hope of establishing religious alliances.

SOURCE 16.10 Pope Pius IV. He was Pope from 1559 to 1565

ACTIVITY

1 Copy and complete the following table to show how different groups determined the eventual form of the Religious Settlement.

	What they did	What effect their actions had on the Religious Settlement
Elizabeth and her Privy Council		
The House of Commons		
The House of Lords		
The Marian Exiles		

2 In groups of five, prepare a script for a role play about a meeting between the following characters. Each character should express his or her opinions on the recent Religious Settlement.

- A female practising Roman Catholic
- A cloth merchant living in Cambridge
- A returned Marian Exile
- A 60-year-old parish priest
- A landowner from the north of England.

It will help if you consider how each might react to the following issues:

- the headship of the Church
- the communion service
- the quality of clergy
- the state and appearance of churches
- national issues such as security and economic wealth
- comparisons with earlier reigns.

160

WHAT PROBLEMS DID THE RELIGIOUS SETTLEMENT OF 1559–63 SOLVE?

F What did Elizabeth do next (1559–63)?

Use the following questions as a basis for making detailed notes.

1 What concessions did Elizabeth make to Catholics after 1559?
2 Why do you think Elizabeth made these concessions? How important do you think a consideration of the international situation is here?
3 What do the events of 1559–63 show Elizabeth's main aims in the Religious Settlement were?

■ 16F Religious developments between 1559 and 1563

Only the most extreme Catholic bishops were removed initially. Those who had conformed during Edward VI's reign were left in office. Commissioners were sent out to take the oath of supremacy and check on the use of the Prayer Book. By the summer of 1559 all but one of Mary's bishops had refused to take the oath and had been deprived of their office. Elizabeth delayed the consecration of the new Protestant bishops so she could transfer more Church property to the crown.

The Royal Injunctions of 1559 allowed many of the old vestments to be worn during services, and the communion table to stand where the altar had stood.

In 1560, a Latin edition of the Prayer Book allowed requiem celebrations for the dead. A Requiem Mass is a Catholic Mass for the repose of the souls of the dead.

By 1560, Elizabeth had restored a crucifix and candles to the altar in her chapel and tried to re-establish full Catholic vestments.

In 1561, Elizabeth contemplated banning clerical marriage. Eventually, she compromised and evicted the wives and children of higher clergy from colleges and cathedral closes.

Having enforced the Religious Settlement legally, Elizabeth was determined to define the doctrine of the Church of England and prevent it from changing. The 39 Articles were passed through CONVOCATION in 1563 and given statutory authority in 1571 (see Chapter 17).

ACTIVITY

In small groups prepare, then deliver to your class, a statement for Elizabeth to give to her people. It is 1560 and she wants to justify her policies, especially the Religious Settlement, and outline any future religious aims she might have.

Reaction to events in Scotland, 1559–63

■ **1559** John Knox and the Protestant Lords of the Congregation led a revolt against the French regent, Mary of Guise.
■ **1560** France pushed Mary Stuart's claims to the English throne, raising the possibility of a Catholic crusade to establish French dominance in England and Scotland.
■ **1560** Cecil and the Privy Council responded to this threat by pressurising Elizabeth into sending aid to the Protestant rebels in Scotland.
■ **1561–63** The realisation that Mary Stuart, Queen of Scots, was next in line for the English throne led to petitions for Elizabeth to marry and the opening of marriage negotiations with Habsburg suitors.

TALKING POINT

Compromises rarely succeed because they please no one. Are they worth attempting, or is it better to stick to your principles in the long run?

CONVOCATION
Convocation was the representative assembly of the Church, responsible for making ecclesiastical laws, or canons. It was composed of an Upper House (bishops) and a Lower House (clergy).

Review: What problems did the Religious Settlement of 1559–63 solve?

161

WHAT PROBLEMS DID THE RELIGIOUS SETTLEMENT OF 1559–63 SOLVE?

The Elizabethan Church of England is usually judged to have been successful because of its continued survival and because Elizabeth was able to take elements of existing doctrines and rituals and mesh them into something new, English and eventually acceptable to the majority. It was, however, a lengthy process. The Elizabethan Prayer Book was only really acceptable to those who had been brought up on it and there are many examples of people attempting to work round it.

SOURCE 16.11   D. MacCulloch, *The Later Reformation in Tudor England*, 1990, p. 172

From this story of confusion and changing direction emerged a Church which has never subsequently dared define its identity decisively as Protestant or Catholic, and which has decided in the end that this is a virtue rather than a handicap.

Yet, as successful as the Elizabethan Religious Settlement can be seen to be, it clearly did not solve all the religious problems of the day. In fact, many of these problems came to bedevil Elizabethan politics.

In addition, whether or not the Religious Settlement was more Protestant than the Queen had intended, it took all the political skill of the Privy Council to steer the bills through the Houses of Parliament. The Catholics in the House of Lords nearly ruined the government's legislative programme. The effect of this opposition is shown in Elizabeth's more conservative stance from 1559 onwards and, above all, in her refusal to permit any further discussions on the subject of religious reform.

SOURCE 16.12   C. Haigh in C. Haigh (ed.), *The Reign of Elizabeth I*, 1984, p. 47

By the time Parliament closed in mid-May 1559, the Elizabethan Religious Settlement had taken its permanent form. Not everyone was satisfied with it however, the Catholics ... could hardly like it, although ... they were not to be seriously persecuted under the new laws. Moreover, they were confused. The Pope failed to make it clear to English Catholics where their duty lay. ... This gentleness towards the Catholics and the Queen's preference for more traditional ornamentation in her churches was already worrying some leaders of her new Church, who feared that the new religion would be laxly imposed.

ACTIVITY

In groups, discuss the following question: Was the Church in England, in 1563, more conservative than Elizabeth would have wished?

162 **KEY POINTS FROM CHAPTER 16:** What problems did the Religious Settlement of 1559–63 solve?

WHAT PROBLEMS DID THE RELIGIOUS SETTLEMENT OF 1559–63 SOLVE?

1 When Elizabeth became Queen it was expected that she would change the country's religion from Roman Catholicism.

2 This would be the fourth change in the national religion to take place in 25 years. Previous changes had caused rebellions: the Pilgrimage of Grace (1536) and the Western Rebellion (1549).

3 The religious issues had to be settled within the broader context of the international situation and likely political and social implications.

4 The Religious Settlement was established by the 1559 Act of Supremacy and the 1559 Act of Uniformity, which were passed after considerable opposition from the House of Lords.

5 Elizabeth's reaction to opposition was to make more concessions to Catholics, including minimising the harshness of punishments for Catholics who did not attend church every week.

6 Although the legal framework of the Elizabethan Church had been established by the Religious Settlement, the quality of the Church's spiritual life and its doctrine had not been addressed.

7 Most contemporaries probably waited on events, such as the Pope's reaction after the Religious Settlement had been determined, before they assessed its success.

What problems did the Religious Settlement cause, 1563–72?

CHAPTER OVERVIEW Elizabeth and her government can have had no illusions about the difficulty of creating a religious settlement which pleased even the majority of her subjects, let alone the whole nation. They may have assumed, following the persecution that took place in Mary's reign, that a Protestant settlement was more acceptable to a wider range of clergy and laity. If this is so, the resistance of Catholics in the House of Lords would have been a rude awakening. Elizabeth responded by making significant concessions to placate conservative opinion. Then, having enshrined the Settlement in law, she saw no need for any further discussion on the subject of religion. This, however, proved impossible because the 1559 Religious Settlement contained no statement of faith, a deliberate omission that committed churchmen of various persuasions wanted to fill to their advantage.

SOURCE 17.1   S. Doran, *Elizabeth I and Religion*, 1994, p. 17

Elizabeth was probably content to keep silent on the issue of doctrine in 1559 as she wanted to avoid further antagonising Catholics at home and abroad, as well as taking sides in the theological disputes which were dividing Protestant Europe. Her new Protestant episcopate, however, was very keen to get down to the task of establishing the doctrine of the English Church since it believed that a statement of faith was essential to the work of teaching the gospels.

From the start, therefore, the Religious Settlement was bound to cause problems with Protestants who saw it as only the first step on the road to establishing a doctrine in line with Calvinist theology. How far the Settlement would cause problems with the Catholics depended on foreign policy issues, Elizabeth's marriage, the succession, and above all on the Pope's reaction. This chapter will look at the problems created by the Religious Settlement and will evaluate the success of the government policies introduced to deal with them.

FOCUS ROUTE

1 Read Chart 17A and make notes on the problems the government faced after the Religious Settlement had been established.

2 Carry out some independent research and make notes on:

• the Injunctions
• the 39 Articles
• the Advertisements
• the Vestments Controversy

to find out how the government dealt with these problems.

A What problems did the Religious Settlement cause, 1563–72?

■ 17A Problems caused by the Religious Settlement and the government's response

Problem	Government response
The quality of the clergy. All the Catholic bishops resigned. The lower clergy generally accepted the Settlement but many lacked religious conviction or education.	Elizabeth appointed Matthew Parker as Archbishop of Canterbury and Protestants, including Marian Exiles, to leading bishoprics. Her failure to appoint enthusiastic preachers left the way open for Puritans to do so. Consequently, she was continually at loggerheads with her bishops.
Confusion over doctrine. Protestants were disappointed and local variations of services were considerable. The services were, however, acceptable to most English Catholics.	The government published the Injunctions and the 39 Articles, and ordered commissioners to investigate breaches of the Prayer Book. The doctrine of the Church began to move in a Calvinist direction. This pleased senior clergy and councillors, but was unacceptable to Catholics.
The Marian Exiles mistakenly believed that the ORNAMENTS RUBRIC would not be enforced. This led to the Vestments Controversy.	The Advertisements (see page 198) were published, leading to the resignation of some able clergymen. The failure to make concessions to the reformers' demands led the more extreme Protestants (Puritans) to challenge the legality of Church government and turn to Presbyterianism.
The Catholics experienced growing unease over Elizabeth's claim to be Supreme Governor. Some Catholics organised the Northern Rebellion in 1569, calling for the restoration of Catholicism and the recognition of Mary, Queen of Scots, who had recently fled to England, as Elizabeth's heir.	The government put down the rebellion and executed its leaders. Mary, Queen of Scots, was imprisoned. No further rebellions took place, but the threat of plans to replace Elizabeth continued for twenty years.

ORNAMENTS RUBRIC

The 1559 Act of Uniformity stated that church ornamentation and the clergy's vestments should be those set down in Edward VI's 1549 Prayer Book. The clergy therefore had to wear Catholic vestments at the communion service and a loose white garment, called a surplice, at other services.

Matthew Parker

■ Born in 1504, educated at Cambridge and ordained in 1527. He had some links with Cambridge reformers.

■ **1535** Became chaplain to Anne Boleyn

■ **1544** Became Master of Corpus Christi College, Cambridge

■ **1552** Became Dean of Lincoln

■ **1554** He supported Lady Jane Grey in her bid for the throne and was deprived of his offices by Mary I. He went into hiding.

■ **1559** He reluctantly became Archbishop of Canterbury under Elizabeth.

■ His religious beliefs were moderate and he used his influence to keep the spread of Puritanism in check.

■ He died in 1575 and was succeeded by Edmund Grindal.

The quality of the clergy

As you will see in Chapters 19 and 20, after 1559 Elizabeth wanted to leave religious issues to her bishops. Although the Injunctions contained references to improving the clergy, this task was left to Archbishop Parker and it was not easy. The best of the lesser clergy had resigned. The Queen had made it clear that she saw the Church as a source of revenue and was therefore unwilling to support a large, well-educated and disciplined ministry. And, the higher clergy, some of whom were Marian Exiles, accepted positions within the Church so that they could continue to promote 'godly reform', a campaign which included removing all traces of Catholicism from the Prayer Book, encouraging preaching and enforcing discipline.

Confusion over doctrine and liturgy

The ambiguities of the Elizabethan Religious Settlement allowed for a great deal of local variation. The commissioners appointed to enforce the Settlement, through royal visitations, reported examples of parish churches which emphasised the ceremonial aspects of the Prayer Book, the singing of hymns accompanied by an organ, and kneeling to receive the bread and wine from a minister wearing full vestments at communion. In other parishes, ministers wore no vestments, there was no music and the bread and wine was received sitting or standing. Although the Injunctions attempted to clarify the situation, they were viewed with disappointment by many of the new bishops as they failed to remove all traces of Catholicism. Therefore, at the first opportunity, the new bishops drew up the 39 Articles, a statement of faith for the new Church. They aimed to present a united, Protestant front against the Catholics.

SOURCE 17.2 S. Doran, *Elizabeth I and Religion*, 1994, p. 18

About one third of the articles expressed ecumenical Christian beliefs, several upheld doctrines shared by both Lutherans and Calvinists, and six specifically refuted the teachings alleged to be held by the Anabaptists. ... on the issues dividing the Lutheran and Swiss Reformed Churches, the bishops tried to reach a compromise, which would satisfy both.

However, Elizabeth intervened to amend the articles her bishops had agreed upon.

SOURCE 17.3 C. Haigh, *Elizabeth I*, 1988, p. 33

She added a sentence to Article 20 on the authority of the Church, which confirmed her right to alter LITURGY ... and she deleted Article 29 ... which could be read as an attack on the real presence doctrine. From 1563 to 1571 ... Elizabeth allowed the Church of England 38, not 39, Articles.

> **LITURGY**
> a) The form of public worship laid down by the Church.
> b) The Book of Common Prayer.

> **ACTIVITY**
>
> 1 Look back at the scripts you wrote for the Activity on page 159. It is 1572.
>   a) How would each character rate the success of the Queen and her bishops in establishing the Religious Settlement?
>   b) Has the Religious Settlement lived up to their expectations? Why?
>   c) Thirteen years on, would any of the characters have altered their original opinions?
> 2 Choose which of the following views you agree with most and prepare an argument in its favour to present to the rest of the class.
>   a) Elizabeth can easily be criticised as Supreme Governor. She prevented reform, alienated her more Protestant subjects and weakened her bishops by refusing to back their initiatives.
>   b) Elizabeth must be given credit for establishing the Church of England. Her conservative approach allowed people to continue following familiar rituals on a local level, and made the transition to Protestantism acceptable to the majority of the religiously conservative population. A more aggressive approach might have caused popular unrest.

> **TALKING POINT**
>
> The initial period following change is often called a 'honeymoon' period. Are there examples of a honeymoon period occurring after the establishment of the Religious Settlement?

B How serious was the Northern Rebellion of 1569?

The Northern Rebellion was the first in a series of conspiracies centred around Mary, Queen of Scots, who arrived in England in 1568 expecting Elizabeth's support. Her arrival ended any hopes that Catholicism would wither away gently, and heralded the start of a turbulent period in foreign affairs. The English seizure of Spanish bullion ships on their way to Europe from the New World in 1568 ended the uneasy friendship between the two countries. Meanwhile, Elizabeth's failure to marry and produce a Protestant heir meant there was no guarantee that the Religious Settlement of 1559 would last. The chief fear of Elizabeth and her councillors – that a legitimate Catholic claimant to the throne might try to overthrow Elizabeth with foreign and English support – had materialised in the form of Mary, Queen of Scots.

■ 17B The personalities behind the Northern Rebellion

Thomas Howard, the Duke of Norfolk
The leading English noble, he conspired to marry Mary, Queen of Scots, to secure her succession to the English throne. He was supported by some of Elizabeth's courtiers, including Leicester, who wanted to discredit Cecil. When the conspiracy was discovered, Norfolk fled from court, urged his co-conspirators Northumberland and Westmorland not to carry out the rebellion, and threw himself on the Queen's mercy. He was imprisoned.

De Spes
The Spanish ambassador wrote to Philip II and told him he was optimistic about the successful outcome of a Catholic uprising against Elizabeth.

Thomas Percy, the Earl of Northumberland
Northumberland was willing to rise in support of the restoration of Catholicism, but he did not want Norfolk and Mary to marry. His role in the initial planning stages of the rebellion meant he was committed despite Norfolk's advice.

The Earl of Sussex
Sussex was President of the Council of the North and a friend of Norfolk. Anxious to prove his loyalty to the crown, he questioned Northumberland and Westmorland in October and was reassured by their claims of loyalty.

Charles Neville, the Earl of Westmorland
Norfolk's brother-in-law and one of the original conspirators.

Queen Elizabeth
Elizabeth was not convinced by Sussex's early reports that Northumberland and Westmorland were loyal to her. She summoned the two Earls to court, probably believing that she could force them to show their true colours, and in doing so pushed them into rebellion.

■ 17C A timeline of the Northern Rebellion

1569

9 Nov The Earl of Northumberland joins the Earl of Westmorland and his forces at Westmorland's castle at Brancepeth.

13 Nov Sussex sends out commissions to raise 1500 foot soldiers. Many men are torn between local loyalty to the Earls and national loyalty to the Queen. Few dare to join Sussex.

14 Nov The Earls march to Durham Cathedral, tear down any Protestant images and celebrate Mass.

15 Nov The rebels march south and enlist support from Richmondshire and Neville's tenants at Kirby Moorside.

16 Nov Sussex writes to the Privy Council to tell them of the difficulties he is having raising an army.

22 Nov The Earls reach Bramham Moor. Their army is made up of 3800 foot soldiers and 1600 horsemen. All the territory east of the Pennines is under this control.

24 Nov The rebels turn back to Knaresborough.

30 Nov The rebels retreat to Richmond. One contingent captures Hartlepool, hoping a Spanish army might land there to support them, while the main body besieges Barnard Castle.

14 Dec Barnard Castle surrenders to the Earls.

16 Dec The royal army, moving up from the south, reaches the River Tees. The Earls flee to Hexham.

19 Dec A skirmish takes place between the scouts of the royal army and the scouts of the rebel army. The Earls flee across the border into Scotland.

Dec– Jan 1570 Elizabeth orders the execution of 700 rebels, but because of the bad weather and her officials' reluctance, the actual figure executed is probably nearer 450. The Earl of Westmorland escapes abroad. Northumberland is betrayed by a Scottish clan and, after being imprisoned and interrogated, is beheaded at York in 1572.

SCOTLAND

Key

→ Outward march of the rebels

⋯▶ Outward march – diversion by Neville to raise his tenants at Kirby Moorside

--▶ Retreat of the rebels, including diversion to capture Hartlepool

WHAT PROBLEMS DID THE RELIGIOUS SETTLEMENT CAUSE, 1563–72?

ACTIVITY

1 You are a tabloid journalist.
   a) Design a newspaper headline for each of the events described in Chart 17C.
   b) Write an opening paragraph for each article assessing the threat posed to the government by the day's events.

2 For the same events, prepare press releases from the government underplaying the dangers.

3 Read Chart 17D and prioritise the reasons why the rebellion failed, then prepare a report on them for the Earl of Sussex to deliver to the Privy Council.

FOREIGN SUPPORT?

- The Pope did not issue the Papal Bull of excommunication until after the rebellion had been quashed, when it was too late to call on Roman Catholics throughout England to support the rebellion and depose their Queen.
- Any suggestion of Spanish support was certainly false. Philip II didn't show any enthusiasm for putting Mary on the throne, largely because of her connections with France.

REBEL ACTIONS?

- The Earls turned back when they heard rumours of a massive force being summoned against them.
- The Earls realised it was impossible to free Mary, Queen of Scots, from prison.
- The rebellion was poorly planned and lacked a coherent programme. Its support was limited geographically and Northumberland did not even have time to mobilise all his tenants.

SUPPORT FOR ELIZABETH?

- The appeals made by the Earls to the Catholic nobility completely failed. In particular, support from Lancashire and Cheshire was not forthcoming.
- Government officials, such as Lord Scrope, contained the rebellion and held the key towns of Pontefract, Berwick and York.
- There was no popular enthusiasm to replace Elizabeth with a foreigner or to restore the authority of the Pope.

ACTIVITY

There are questions to guide you through Sources 17.5–17.14 in the activity on the facing page. But you could first try to work out what caused the rebellion without using the guide questions.

What caused the rebellion?

SOURCE 17.5   An extract from the *Proclamation of the Earls*, 1569

Whereas diverse newe set up nobles about the quenes majestie, have and do dailie, not onlie go about to overthrow and put down the ancient nobilitie of this realme, but also have misused the queens majesties owne personne, and also have by the space of twelve years nowe past, set upp, and mayntayned a new found religion and heresie, contrarie to Gods word. For the amending and redressing thereof, divers foren powers doo purpose shortlie to invade thes realmes, which will be to our utter destruction, if we do not ourselves speedilie forfend the same.

SOURCE 17.6   An examination of the Earl of Northumberland, 1572

Our first object in assembling was the reformation of religion and preservation of the person of the Queen of Scots, as next heir failing issue of Her Majesty, which causes I believed were greatly favoured by most of the noblemen of the realm.

SOURCE 17.7   A. Fletcher, *Tudor Rebellions*, 1968, p. 129

Northumberland had suffered severely from Elizabeth's reassertion of the policies of her father, aimed at weakening the hold of the great magnate families on the marches. She had deprived him of his Wardenship of the Middle March and allowed him no part in the custody of Mary. In 1568 the crown had ignored his claim for compensation over the rights to the copper mine discovered at Newlands on one of his estates. Northumberland had declined in wealth as well as status ... the Earl of Westmorland was also suffering from poverty.

SOURCE 17.8   A. Fletcher, *Tudor Rebellions*, 1968, p. 93

Sir John Forster wrote on the 24 November, that he had just heard that 'the Earls have offered wages of sixteen pence a day to all that will come'. Many undoubtedly joined the rebellion because they feared for their lives and goods. On the 17 November Bowes reported to Cecil: 'they have constrined, by force, sundrie to followe them; as the people of Bishopton ... they not only forced them to go with them, but compelled the rest of the towne, armed, and unarmed, to go to Darneton.'

SOURCE 17.9 A. Fletcher, *Tudor Rebellions*, 1968, p. 94

The strength of the rebel army lay in their horsemen, who were 'gentlemen and their household servants and tenants'.

SOURCE 17.10 Lord Hunsdon writing to William Cecil in 1569

The Erle of Northumberland hathe the keepinge of Myddleham, and steward of Rychmond … whereby he hathe nowe a grete part of hys force too serve agaynst the Queen.

SOURCE 17.11 The Earl of Sussex writing to William Cecil, 17 November 1569

They persuade that their cause of seeking to reform religion is that other princes have determined to do it and this entering of strangers should be troublesome to the realm, and therefore they seek to do it before their coming.

SOURCE 17.12 A. Fletcher, *Tudor Rebellions*, 1968, p. 96

So it is the secular rather than religious tensions of northern society which now deserve serious consideration in the context of this rebellion. It may well be that political resentment at the extension of Tudor authority in the north was more important in attracting support to it than hatred of Protestantism … Elizabeth had deliberately built up the gentry clientele of Northumberland's rival Sir John Forster and had put her cousin, Lord Hunsdon, in charge of Berwick and the East March … when Elizabeth summoned the Earls to court she precipitated a crisis in northern society: the cause of Catholicism proved inadequate to sustain the rising that followed.

SOURCE 17.13 C. Haigh, *Elizabeth I*, 1988, p. 54

Elizabeth had blundered: she forced the Earls to choose between flight and rebellion, when rebellion was still (just) a realistic option. They chose rebellion, because of the Catholic enthusiasm of their followers and the scorn of the Countess of Westmorland … so the Earls rebelled, more in sorrow than in anger: men who had been planning rebellion for weeks, even months, were forced into an unplanned rising. But it was still a dangerous rising, which could use powerful slogans. The revolt was presented in traditional terms as the revenge of the old nobility against upstart evil councillors.

SOURCE 17.14 C. Haigh, *Elizabeth I*, 1988, p. 55

The rebellion was strikingly non-feudal: nine-tenths of the known rebels were not tenants of the leaders … and there was much more of a popular movement than has been supposed. Nor was the rebellion incompetent, for its leaders pursued a coherent strategy.

ACTIVITY

1 According to Sources 17.5–17.11, why did the rebellion take place?
2 Do Sources 17.12–17.15:
   a) agree with the causes of the rebellion given in Sources 17.5–17.11?
   b) suggest alternative causes?
3 What important point do Sources 17.12–17.15 agree on?
4 Both Fletcher and Haigh believe that Elizabeth made some mistakes in dealing with the two Earls. Do you think that Elizabeth:
   a) responded with her usual firm consistency? Having identified the Catholic Earls as political traitors she treated them with appropriate severity and remained in control
   b) panicked, pushed the Earls into rebellion and only defeated them because of an element of luck and factors outside her control?
   Write a mini-essay to explain your choice, using both the sources and your own knowledge.

■ **Learning trouble spot**

Most source-based AS modules have a final question in the form of a mini-essay (approximately 12 marks) which asks you to use the sources and your own knowledge to investigate an issue. A common failing here is an answer that goes through each source separately and then attempts to comment on the question in the conclusion. Instead, you should focus on the issue to be investigated and work out a list of reasons to explain your point of view. These reasons should be supported by evidence from both the sources and your own factual knowledge.

C Review: What problems did the Religious Settlement cause, 1563–72?

The Religious Settlement of 1559 was followed by refinements or decrees, issued by Elizabeth or her bishops in the next few years. A pattern emerged quite early on. Elizabeth saw the Settlement as a method to establish religious uniformity by law and she expected all her subjects to conform outwardly, using the Prayer Book and attending church. The role of enforcing the Settlement and determining future doctrine lay with her bishops. Elizabeth saw no need for her involvement in further discussions on religion; in fact, she saw any requests to discuss it as an invasion of her prerogative. The passage of the 1559 Act of Uniformity and the 1559 Act of Supremacy through Parliament made Elizabeth aware of the strength of Catholic support among the politically-active classes. She was prepared to move cautiously, turning a blind eye to priests who said Mass and the non-enforcement of fines, in order to win over – rather than alienate – the Catholic majority. Protestants who saw the Settlement as the first step to removing all traces of the Pope from the English Church resented this policy. Many of her bishops were disappointed at having to defend a Church which they still thought contained Catholic abuses, and the first conflict over vestments was a manifestation of this frustration.

By 1568, Elizabeth's policy seemed to be working. The early problems caused by the Settlement were fading. The majority of Catholics outwardly conformed and, without any leadership from the Pope, were politically loyal. Archbishop Parker and Convocation defeated, if narrowly, the Vestments Controversy. However, this honeymoon period ended in 1568 due to a number of factors which, although the government was not blameless, were not a direct result of government policies. The activities of John Hawkins in the New World, the arrival of Mary, Queen of Scots, followed by the Northern Rebellion and the Papal Bull of Excommunication, foreshadowed problems which were to dominate the rest of Elizabeth's reign.

The Northern Rebellion has been described by Christopher Haigh as 'a major threat to Elizabeth's regime ... the rising which took place had been extremely dangerous, and if Elizabeth's government had made a few small errors (such as delay in moving Mary), there could have been a disaster. Elizabeth had been very lucky' (C. Haigh, *Elizabeth I*, 1988, p. 56). Perhaps the seriousness of the rebellion is best shown by Elizabeth's reactions to it once it had been defeated. Over 450 people were executed and so much land was confiscated from leading families that traditional feudal structures in the north broke down. The Council of the North was restored and placed under the leadership of the Puritan Earl of Huntingdon, who was given wider powers enabling him to take over the government of the north in the Queen's name. Finally, Elizabeth punished the Scottish Catholics who had supported the rising by sending raiding parties across the border and destroying several castles. None of these efforts, however, solved the problem, the root of which lay in the person of Mary, Queen of Scots.

Elizabeth did not create the problem that was Mary, Queen of Scots, but, by throwing in her lot with her Protestant councillors, refusing to marry or name her successor and losing Spain's friendship by helping the rebels in the Netherlands, she contributed to a situation where Catholicism, the succession, and Spain all combined to threaten England's stability. Whether the Religious Settlement itself caused these problems is harder to assess. If Elizabeth had married a Protestant and produced a male heir would the northern Earls have still rebelled, Mary, Queen of Scots, still plotted, or Philip II still attempted to invade? Would any other religious settlement have been more acceptable to the English, met everyone's expectations and solved every problem?

FOCUS ROUTE

The Northern Rebellion was only one of the crises Elizabeth faced between 1568 and 1572. Complete the following table, listing all the crises, by:

- evaluating the seriousness of each crisis on a scale of 0–5 (0 = no threat, 5 = a very serious threat)
- assessing the extent to which each crisis was caused by government policies.

You will have to do some extra research, but use Section 4 as a starting point.

Crisis	Seriousness of threat	Was the crisis a result of government policy?
Mary, Queen of Scots, arrives in England, 1568		
Anglo-Spanish clash off the coast of Mexico, 1568		
Spanish bullion ship seized, 1568		
Irish rebels ask Spain for assistance, 1569		
Conspiracy at court to marry Norfolk to Mary, Queen of Scots, 1569		
Northern Rebellion, 1569		
Pope issues Papal Bull of Excommunication, 1570		
Ridolfi Plot, 1571		
Parliament presses Elizabeth to name an heir, 1572		
Protestant rebels in France and the Netherlands seek English support against France and Spain, 1572		
Francis Drake seizes Spanish treasure in the West Indies, 1572		

SOURCE 17.15 S. Doran, *Elizabeth I and Religion*, 1994, p. 5

When Elizabeth came to the throne in 1558 the religious situation was very difficult and complex. The country was not only divided between Catholics and Protestants, but also the Protestants themselves had different views about the nature and character of a reformed Church as a result of the varied experiences of Mary's reign. Any decision made by the new regime on the religious future of the country would bring its own problems.

SOURCE 17.16 S. Doran, *Elizabeth I and Religion*, 1994, p. 66

Through the efforts of the government, bishops and Puritan laity, a new framework for Protestant worship and devotion was erected in most English parishes, which ultimately led to a major change in religious beliefs.

KEY POINTS FROM CHAPTER 17: What problems did the Religious Settlement cause, 1563–72?

1 The Religious Settlement caused immediate problems: the Catholic bishops resigned and there was confusion over doctrine.

2 The government appointed Protestant clergy, issued the Injunctions, arranged for commissioners to make visitations and drew up the 39 Articles.

3 Puritans were disappointed with the Religious Settlement. This disappointment manifested itself in the Vestments Controversy.

4 The arrival of Mary, Queen of Scots, in England triggered the Northern Rebellion.

5 The motives for the Northern Rebellion and the extent to which it endangered the government have caused considerable debate.

6 The Northern Rebellion was one of several major threats to Elizabethan government from 1568 to 1572.

Was Mary, Queen of Scots, a major threat?

18

CHAPTER OVERVIEW

For centuries, Mary, Queen of Scots, has attracted the attention of serious scholars of history and authors of historical fiction. Her life has been the subject of many novels and films and opinion about her is firmly divided between those who see her as a tragic and misguided figure and those who see her as calculating and dangerous. As a result, Elizabeth's execution of Mary in 1587 tends to be seen as either a serious and bloody blot on the reign, or as a political necessity.

Mary Stuart was a problem for Elizabeth because of her claim to the English throne and the fact that, as she was both half-French and Catholic, recognition of her claim might jeopardise England's future political independence and its official Protestant religion. As her reign progressed, Elizabeth's failure to marry or name her successor encouraged Mary to try to win the recognition she saw as rightfully hers. The fact that, in the end, she did not succeed should not lead us to underestimate the threat that contemporaries thought she represented. Although most Catholics were not ready to support Mary as rightful Queen if Mary were to overthrow Elizabeth, since Elizabeth's right had been authorised by statute, they were anxious that Mary should be recognised as Elizabeth's heir. After 1569, when relations between England and Spain soured, Mary's presence in England was seen as more of a threat because Spain now seemed willing to support her cause.

Although this chapter will concentrate on evaluating the extent to which Mary was a threat to Elizabeth, the subject cannot be studied in isolation and you will need to look again at the chapters on the Northern Rebellion, Parliament, Catholicism and foreign policy.

A What was England's relationship with Scotland like before 1561? (p. 175)

B What was England's relationship with Scotland like, 1561–68? (pp. 175–77)

C How serious a threat was Mary, 1569–87? (pp. 178–81)

D Review: Was Mary, Queen of Scots, a major threat? (pp. 182–83)

SOURCE 18.1   G. R. Elton, *England Under the Tudors*, 1991 (3rd edn), p. 279

It remains impossible so to speak about Mary, Queen of Scots that all are satisfied; she had to the utmost the Stuart ability of attaching men's loyalties to herself despite the most outrageous and the most foolish of deeds. Of her famous beauty her surviving portraits provide little evidence. She was passionate, wilful, intelligent, given to violent moods of exaltation and depression, and entirely without common sense – one might say, entirely without moral sense.

■ **Learning trouble spot**

The existence of more than one Queen Mary in the sixteenth century is often a source of confusion. You need to remember:

- **Queen Mary I of England, Mary Tudor, 'Bloody Mary'** was Henry VIII's daughter, and half-sister to Edward VI and Elizabeth. She ruled England from 1553 to 1558.
- **Queen Mary of Scotland, Mary Stuart, Mary, Queen of Scots**, ruled Scotland from 1560 to 1568. She was Elizabeth's cousin and was imprisoned in England from 1568 until 1587 when she was executed.

Look back at the Tudor family tree (Source 1.2 on page 8) to see their relationship to each other.

SOURCE 18.2   Mary, Queen of Scots

A What was England's relationship with Scotland like before 1561?

In 1559, England and France signed the Treaty of Cateau-Cambresis, which confirmed England's loss of Calais and meant France dominated the Straits of Dover. The French also dominated Scotland, where Mary of Guise ruled as regent for her daughter, Mary, Queen of Scots. Scottish Protestants rebelled against Mary of Guise's government and forced her to flee from Edinburgh in 1559. In reality, Mary of Guise's uncles controlled policy and, in October, prepared to send troops to defeat the rebels.

Cecil convinced Elizabeth that she had to intervene to ensure the survival of the new pro-English government and to keep the French away from England's northern border. The Queen took some convincing. She hated helping subjects rebel against their divinely appointed ruler, and equated the Scottish Protestants with the Presbyterianism of John Knox. John Knox was a Scottish Protestant reformer who had worked on Edward VI's Second Prayer Book. After spending Mary's reign in exile in Geneva, he returned to lead the Protestant Reformation in Scotland. His animosity towards female rulers was highlighted in his *First Blast of the Trumpet Against the Monstrous Regiment of Women*, which was published in 1558. In 1560, Elizabeth concluded the Treaty of Berwick with the Scots and sent an English army to Scotland. Although English attempts to defeat the French garrison failed, the loss of the French task force at sea and the death of Mary of Guise led to the withdrawal of French troops.

In the Treaty of Edinburgh, both England and France agreed to withdraw their forces from Scotland and Mary, Queen of Scots, whose husband Francis had become King of France in 1559, gave up her claim to the English throne. Mary, however, never formally approved this treaty herself. The government of Scotland passed to the Protestant lords, who maintained friendly relations with England. The credit for this policy lies firmly with Cecil, who believed England had to secure its borders with Scotland and Ireland.

B What was England's relationship with Scotland like, 1561–68?

FOCUS ROUTE

Make detailed notes on:

• why Mary decided to flee to England
• Elizabeth's reaction to Mary's arrival in England
• the priorities of Cecil and the rest of the Privy Council.

In 1560, Francis II died. In 1561, Mary Stuart returned to Scotland. But it was not the same Scotland she had left at the age of five: it was now Protestant and dominated by noble factions. Her main concern, however, was to assert her claim to the English succession, and she was even prepared to ratify the Treaty of Edinburgh if Elizabeth would recognise her as her heir. She therefore accepted the Protestant ruling nobles and concentrated instead on her remarriage.

Elizabeth's suggestion that Mary should marry Elizabeth's favourite, Robert Dudley, was rejected in 1563. In 1565 Mary married Henry, Lord Darnley, son of the Earl of Lennox and grandson of her Tudor grandmother, Margaret. The marriage therefore strengthened the Stuart claim to the English throne, but it deteriorated quickly as Darnley increasingly showed himself to be alcoholic, promiscuous and unstable. In 1566, in the so-called Rizzio Affair, Darnley hatched a plot to murder Mary's secretary and close confidant, David Rizzio, by which he hoped to restore his political fortunes. Rizzio was stabbed to death and a heavily pregnant Mary roughly handled. Her child, the future James VI of Scotland, survived and was born a few months later.

In 1567, Darnley was recovering from smallpox at Kirk O'Field near Edinburgh when his house was blown up. His body was found in the grounds and there were signs that he had been strangled. The chief suspect, the Protestant Earl of Bothwell, was cleared by the Court of Assizes. In the summer of 1567 Mary married Bothwell, increasing suspicions that the two had been lovers before their marriage and were accomplices in Darnley's murder. The

Scottish lords united against Mary and raised an army. Mary was forced to abdicate in favour of her young son and a regency was established under the Earl of Moray. She was then imprisoned in the island fortress of Loch Leven.

Mary escaped from Loch Leven in 1568. Her army was defeated at Langside and she fled to England to seek protection and help against her enemies from Elizabeth. Elizabeth's immediate impulse, to meet Mary and help her regain her throne, was prevented by the Privy Council who feared that this would damage the relationship they had built up with the Scottish lords. To play for time while they decided what to do with Mary, the council asked the Scottish lords to attend a conference at York which would determine Mary's involvement in Darnley's murder. The Scottish lords agreed, claiming that they had evidence to prove Mary's guilt in the form of the so-called 'casket letters', which were denounced by Mary as forgeries and are now lost to historians.

ACTIVITY

1 Complete the table below to assess the possible solutions to the problem of Mary, Queen of Scots, and the advantages and disadvantages to Elizabeth of each option in 1568.

Possible solution	Advantages	Disadvantages	The extent to which this solution was a threat to Elizabeth and her government (0 = no threat, 5 = serious threat)
Restore Mary to her throne			
Surrender Mary into the control of the Scottish lords			
Allow Mary freedom of movement in England			
Allow Mary to go abroad			

2 In a group, prepare a memo for Elizabeth advocating the solution you believe to be the safest. Explain why she should reject the other solutions. Keep in mind her likely objections and try to counteract them and reassure her.

What happened at the York Conference?

The verdict of the conference was announced on 10 January 1569. This said that, 'nothing had been deduced against Moray and his council that may impair their honour: and on the other part there had been nothing sufficiently produced by them against the Queen their sovereign.' Moray returned to Scotland with English support, in the form of a loan for £5000. Mary's refusal to answer the charges against her left her guilty by implication, and gave the English government grounds, however tenuous, to hold her in captivity. The failure of the commission to find Mary either innocent or guilty also freed Elizabeth, who did not go to York and who never met Mary, from having to act decisively.

It is important to remember that there was never any suggestion that Mary was being accused of, or put on trial for, Darnley's murder at the York Conference. The point of the conference was to determine whether or not there was sufficient evidence against Mary to investigate the matter further. The extent to which the council and Elizabeth were staging this for their own political purposes is, however, likely to colour our view of the whole exercise.

SOURCE 18.3 J. B. Black, *The Reign of Elizabeth*, 1959

Far better it would have been if Elizabeth had allowed her discredited and defeated enemy to go whither she pleased. The Catholic world influenced by her recent behaviour would have treated her with cold contempt, she would have sunk into comparative insignificance ... but her incarceration saved her from this. As a victim of an unjust fate she became invested with a halo of martyrdom.

I am the leading Protestant noble and the effective ruler of Scotland. I am also Mary's half-brother, but I want to prevent her restoration to the Scottish throne.

Earl of Moray

There is no guarantee that a 'not guilty' verdict will restore Mary to the Scottish throne. A lot depends on the reactions of France and Spain. Whatever happens, however, I am determined to keep England's northern border secure. And the rest of the Privy Council is aware of the need to maintain friendly relations with the Protestant lords in Scotland.

William Cecil

Mary's lawyer

If the charges against Mary cannot be proved she must be restored to her throne.

Mary

Elizabeth

I recognised the validity of this conference only after being assured that I would be restored to my throne once a favourable verdict had been reached. However, I do not accept that the conference has the authority to introduce the 'casket letters', and I will take no further part in the proceedings.

I dislike the thought of a fellow monarch being overthrown by her own subjects, but I also realise the sense in my councillors' opinions. Initially I was hoping for some sort of triple alliance between Moray, Mary and myself; but I now think I should approve the introduction of the 'casket letters' to implicate Mary. Mary will either confess or refuse to discuss them, as she has already given her word as a prince that they are false – either way she will appear guilty.

ACTIVITY

1 Was Elizabeth's decision about what to do with Mary the same as the solution you advocated in Question 2 on p. 176? Do you think she made the right choice?
2 In a group discuss the following statements:
   a) The York Conference demonstrates the skill of Elizabeth's council in securing a legal solution to a complex and dangerous problem.
   b) The York Conference was a cynical propaganda exercise in which the law was used for political ends.
3 Write a brief newspaper report on the York Conference under the title: 'Verdict no surprise'.

TALKING POINT

Is Source 18.3 fair? Is it based on hindsight alone, or is it also speculative?

C How serious a threat was Mary, 1569–87?

FOCUS ROUTE

Assess the danger posed by each of the four plots against Elizabeth involving Mary, Queen of Scots. Apart from making notes on the aims of each plot, you should also try to gauge its seriousness by looking at who was involved and the government's reaction.

■ 18B Four flashpoints

The Northern Rebellion, 1569
Although probably triggered by the arrival of Mary, Queen of Scots, in England in 1568, this began as a conspiracy at court to marry the Duke of Norfolk to Mary, to have her proclaimed heir to the English throne, to overthrow Elizabeth and Cecil and to restore Catholicism. The plan was initially supported by two of Elizabeth's councillors, the Earl of Leicester and Sir Nicholas Throckmorton. In September 1569, Leicester confessed everything to Elizabeth and Norfolk fled from court. The initiative passed to the Earls of Northumberland and Westmorland, who prepared to march south to restore Catholicism. They were defeated by government forces. Spanish help, promised by the Spanish ambassador, de Spes, did not materialise.
(See pages 166–69 for more details.)

The Ridolfi Plot, 1571
Following Elizabeth's excommunication, an uprising was planned to replace Elizabeth with Mary, who would be married to Norfolk. The conspiracy involved Mary, Philip II, the Pope, the Duke of Norfolk and other English noblemen. The plan was soon discovered by Cecil.

The Throckmorton Plot, 1583
Plans were laid for French Catholic forces, backed by Spanish and Papal money, to invade England, liberate Mary and start a Catholic uprising. Throckmorton was the intermediary between Mary and the Spanish ambassador, de Mendoza. The plot also involved some Jesuit and seminary priests, including William Allen.

The Babington plot, 1586
A letter, allegedly dictated by Mary and endorsing Babington's plot to murder Elizabeth, was intercepted by Walsingham's agents.

■ 18C The government's reactions to the flashpoints

Flashpoint	The Privy Council's reaction	Parliament's reaction	Elizabeth's reaction
The Northern Rebellion, 1569	The Privy Council unanimously demanded Norfolk's execution following the Northern Rebellion.	(Parliament not called until 1571, after an interval of four years.)	Elizabeth continued to be appalled at the thought that the Scots had rebelled against their rightful sovereign, although by 1569 she no longer contemplated using force to restore Mary to her throne. In 1570–71, and again in the early 1580s, she urged the Scots to restore Mary to nominal sovereignty. But the Scottish regents, and later James VI, put obstacles in the way of Mary's return. In 1570, on the urgings of the council, Elizabeth sent forces to Scotland to subdue Mary's supporters after Moray was murdered.
The Ridolfi Plot, 1571	In 1572 the council persuaded Elizabeth to summon Parliament, citing the need to raise money. Their real purpose was to secure the execution of both Norfolk and Mary, Queen of Scots. Cecil took the lead in demanding Norfolk's execution and in drawing up two bills against Mary.	Parliament brought in two bills: one calling for Mary's execution and one barring her from the succession. Two Acts were passed prohibiting anyone bringing Papal Bulls into the country and making it high treason to deny Elizabeth her title as Queen. A decree also confirmed that any claimant to the throne who had foreknowledge of Elizabeth's assassination was to be excluded from the succession. The 1581 Act redefined treason as also applying to those who drew the allegiance of English subjects away from their Queen or her Church.	Elizabeth twice delayed signing Mary's death warrant. She finally agreed to Norfolk's execution, to placate the Commons, but would only consider the bill barring Mary from the succession – 'can I put to death the bird that, to escape the pursuit of the hawk, has fled to me for protection?' Elizabeth intervened to reduce the penalties in the 1581 Act for those Catholics who would not attend church.

Flashpoint	The Privy Council's reaction	Parliament's reaction	Elizabeth's reaction
The Throckmorton Plot, 1583	Throckmorton was tortured, then executed. Councillors established the Bond of Association, by which they undertook to ensure that, in the event of Elizabeth's assassination, none of those associated with the crime would benefit from it. Instead they would be destroyed. De Mendoza, the Spanish Ambassador, was expelled.	In 1585 an Act ordering the expulsion of Catholic priests was passed. It was now treason to become a priest, and the death penalty was passed on those who helped priests in any way. A series of questions was devised for captured priests, the sixth, 'the bloody question', asking them if they would support the Queen or the Pope if there were a Catholic invasion of England. Treason was extended to cover those, such as Mary, Queen of Scots, who were the cause of plots.	Elizabeth had reservations about the first bill for her safety and had the wording changed so that Mary's son James would not suffer by virtue of his claim to the English throne.
The Babington Plot, 1586	The Privy Council persuaded a reluctant Elizabeth that Mary must be brought to trial. The trial was held at Fotheringhay Castle, Northamptonshire. It opened in October 1586 and the commissioners found Mary guilty of 'imagining and encompassing her Majesty's death'.	Delegations from both Houses visited the Queen at Richmond to demand Mary's execution.	Elizabeth ordered that Babington and his conspirators were to be hanged, drawn and quartered, despite Cecil's protests that hanging was quite cruel enough. Elizabeth remained in London throughout Mary's trial, but sent illegible notes to Cecil which show her indecision. After hearing the verdict she twice postponed the next meeting of the House of Commons. Elizabeth expressed her regret at hearing a queen called a 'detestable traitor' and claimed Parliament had 'lain a hard hand on her'.
	The council pushed Elizabeth to sign the death warrant. Lord Howard of Effingham warned Elizabeth that her delay in dealing with the warrant was angering her councillors and subjects. The council agreed that the warrant should be sent immediately it was signed, before Elizabeth could change her mind. Mary was executed on 8 February 1587.	Parliament repeated its belief that Mary must die.	Elizabeth sent Christopher Hatton to ask Parliament to suggest other ways of dealing with Mary. She said that those who, in the past, had called her a tyrant would have more cause to complain when it was 'spread that, for the safety of her life, the maiden Queen would be content to spill the blood even of her own kinsman'. Elizabeth adjourned Parliament for two months. A letter from Mary reduced Elizabeth to tears. Spain and Scotland pleaded for Mary's life. Elizabeth sent for the warrant and signed it although she suggested to her secretary, William Davison, that it might be easier to arrange a quiet murder. On learning that the warrant had been sealed within 24 hours, she exclaimed, 'What needed that haste?' News of Mary's execution brought on an emotional outburst. Elizabeth harangued the council, banished Cecil and ordered the imprisonment of Davison in the Tower. In response to the outrage of Philip II and Henry III of France, she claimed she was not responsible for Mary's death because Davison had sent the death warrant without her authority.

The trial of Mary, Queen of Scots

SOURCE 18.4 The execution of Mary, Queen of Scots, in the great hall of Fotheringhay Castle, Northamptonshire, on 8 February 1587

SOURCE 18.5   J. E. Neale, *Queen Elizabeth I*, 1934, pp. 278–79

On the 11 October, the commissioners – 36 peers, Privy Councillors and judges . . . arrived at Fotheringhay for the trial. Mary stood resolutely upon her privilege as a sovereign, anointed Queen; but after two days of incessant argument, in which the events and mutual recriminations of past years were traversed, she consented to appear before the court, without however yielding to its jurisdiction. The trial would amaze and shock a modern lawyer, but it was conducted according to the normal procedure of the day and with less animus and more substantial proof than many another trial, of its kind. There could be no doubt whatever that Mary had been privy and consenting to a plot to assassinate the Queen and to bring an invading army into England. She frequently, vehemently, solemnly denied any knowledge of it: that was natural, for she was fighting for her life. But her denials were and are worth noting against the evidence of Babington and her two secretaries – not to mention the story of the secret post which was carefully concealed as was the forged postscript. In accordance with unswerving practice, she was not allowed counsel, but she defended herself with spirit, eloquence and ability. Voluble and impassioned, she was yet very dignified, and then, when the fierce debate was over, with characteristic suddenness her mood changed. She vowed devotion to Elizabeth, was all sweetness and forgiveness to the commissioners; and as she passed the judges and prosecuting counsel she said with a smile 'God forgive you lawyers' . . .

ACTIVITY

1 According to Source 18.6, how and why did Mary change her policy towards answering the charges against her?
2 Compare the comments made in Sources 18.5 and 18.6 on Mary's guilt and on her character. How far do you consider the conclusions to be balanced?
3 Using Sources 18.5–18.8, explain the disadvantages Mary faced at her trial.
4 Using the sources and your own knowledge, comment on the view that the commission was not a trial conducted with a scrupulous regard for English law, but a device to condemn Mary to death.
5 In a group, show how far Elizabeth's dealings with Mary, Queen of Scots, were characterised by caution and indecision.

SOURCE 18.6   C. Hibbert, *The Virgin Queen*, 1990, pp. 208–9

The Queen of Scots was behaving as her accusers had expected her to. At first she had refused to attend the trial on the grounds that she was not subject to jurisdiction in an English court and had, in any event, done nothing wrong. 'You have in various ways and manners attempted to take my life and to bring my kingdom to destruction by bloodshed,' Elizabeth had angrily responded to this characteristic protest. 'These treasons will be proved to you and all made manifest. It is my will that you answer the nobles and peers of the kingdom as if I were myself present . . . act plainly without reserve and you will then sooner be able to obtain favour of me.' Even her most ardent supporters could not maintain that Mary acted plainly: she was as devious in her answers as she was dignified in her demeanour. She was brave and passionately eloquent, it could not be denied, and most skilful in avoiding giving direct answers to questions she would prefer not to have been asked. Yet she could not convince her accusers that she was innocent; and when driven into a corner, having denied a fact subsequently proved, she could only insist that her word must be accepted since it was the 'word of a princess'.

SOURCE 18.7   Historian W. M. Taylor writing in 1884

Beautiful in person, attractive in manner, able, acute, brilliant even, in intellect, Mary Stuart had many qualities which she might have turned to good account for the welfare of her country. But, brought up in a French court her moral code was neither of the highest nor the purest; educated under the supervision of her uncles of Lorraine, she was taught to believe that the one great object of her life was to advance the interests of the Roman Catholic Church; and sister-in-law to him whose name is forever blackened by the massacre of St Bartholomew, she was not likely to be over-scrupulous as to the means which she would employ to gain her end.

SOURCE 18.8   A. Fraser, *Mary Queen of Scots*, 1969

At the forthcoming trial therefore Mary was to be allowed neither counsel nor witnesses in her defence; she was not even to be allowed a secretary or amanuensis to help her prepare her own case – her own secretaries being of course still imprisoned in London. She was to be left quite alone, a sick woman and a foreigner, who knew nothing of England, its laws, or customs, and had only begun to learn its language comparatively late in life, to conduct and manage her own defence against the best legal brains in the country. These eminent lawyers on the other hand were not even to be put to the simple task of bringing witnesses for the prosecution for none was to be called.

Yet, curiously enough, by the standards of the sixteenth century the innate injustice of the trial of Mary, Queen of Scots, lay not so much in its arrangements – the accused was never allowed counsel at an English treason trial at this date, and the barbarity of the Scottish treason trials has been sufficiently commented upon – as in the fact that the trial took place at all. How, indeed, could it ever be legal for Mary as sovereign, the Queen of a foreign country, to be tried for treason, when she was in no sense one of Elizabeth's subjects.

D Review: Was Mary, Queen of Scots, a major threat?

From the moment she arrived in England in 1568 the Privy Council and Parliament regarded Mary Stuart as a danger, whose presence, if not her activities, threatened the government and the Religious Settlement. Members of both institutions believed that Mary's death was the only solution. Elizabeth, however, was plagued by greater doubts and responsibilities.

ACTIVITY

Divide into two groups. Using the following table and your own research, one group should prepare a speech arguing that yes, Mary, Queen of Scots, was a major threat to English security, the other group should prepare a speech arguing that she was a threat but not a major one.

Remember that the background situation can be interpreted either way – to show that Mary's connection with all these issues made her extremely dangerous, or to show that the real threat to English security lay elsewhere.

Yes, Mary was a major threat to English security	No, Mary was not a major threat to security	Background situation
Mary was next in line for the English throne.	Henry VIII had excluded the Stuarts from the succession, and the English saw her as too foreign to be their Queen.	Elizabeth declined to marry and refused to name her successor.
Mary was the natural leader of the English Catholics.	Most English Catholics were loyal to Elizabeth and were scandalised by Mary's behaviour.	The Papal Bull of Excommunication and the arrival of Jesuit and seminary priests intensified the seriousness of the Catholic threat.
Mary's presence in England caused the Northern Rebellion.	The Northern Rebellion had little popular support and was basically a court conspiracy. The Papal Bull of Excommunication was issued too late to marshal Catholic support for the rebellion.	Anglo-Spanish relations broke down over the New World. From 1571 to 1583, when England was attempting to re-establish relations with Spain, Mary lived quietly under house arrest.
Mary had the support of the Guise family in France and after 1569–70 of Philip II of Spain.	The Guises and Philip were distracted by problems in their own territories.	France was plunged into civil war over religion between 1562 and 1593. Spain, despite its huge financial resources, was in debt after decades of war with France. Philip also had to deal with the threat of Islam, internally (the Moriscos) and in the Mediterranean (the Turks), as well as protecting his empire in the Netherlands and the New World.
Mary instigated the Babington Plot and intended the murder of Elizabeth.	Most English Catholics were horrified by the plot. Not many Scots wanted her back, her own son even abandoned her. Effective Catholic intervention was unlikely, because of the rivalry between Spain and France. Philip II had no wish to see an Anglo-French empire cutting off his communications with the Spanish Netherlands. France was preoccupied with her wars of religion. In addition, the council's intelligence system was so good that plots were generally uncovered at an early stage. None seriously threatened Elizabeth's life.	The murder of William, Prince of Orange, the Protestant leader of the rebels in the Netherlands, and the resulting Spanish successes against the rebels, urged England into sending an army to help the Protestants. This spurred Philip to build up an invasion force against England.

SOURCE 18.9 W. MacCaffrey, *Elizabeth* 1993, p. 351

Her attitude towards Mary had always had a schizophrenic twist to it. Fear and distrust of a rival who had asserted her claims from the first days of the reign and had never ceased to pursue them were inherent in their relationship. Elizabeth had not hesitated to checkmate Mary's designs or those of her partisans, by intrigue or by violence when necessary. Everything had been done to taint Mary's reputation, as a party to her husband's murder, as a plotter who intrigued with English rebels and foreign powers, to murder Elizabeth and bring down the English regime. Yet through all the turns and twists of Mary's melodrama, Elizabeth had never lost sight of her sacrosanct status as an anointed monarch, one of God's earthly lieutenants, and above all human judgements.

By 1587 even Elizabeth had resolved that Mary should die. Mary's involvement in plots to assassinate her destroyed any scruples Elizabeth might have had. Elizabeth's violent emotional reaction to Mary's eventual execution has been variously seen as genuine, as an act or as a mixture of both. Certainly, Elizabeth was anxious to keep public opinion on her side. She was also aware of the likely outcry Mary's execution would cause in France, Scotland and Spain. In the event, Spain's attempted invasion of England one year later owed little to Mary's execution, and her son preferred to stay on good terms with Elizabeth and safeguard his future inheritance than rush to his mother's defence. Elizabeth's advisers at the time, and historians today, agree that the execution of Mary, Queen of Scots, was a political necessity that Elizabeth could delay but not prevent. Nevertheless, the 'tragic' view of Mary's life and death has been sustained.

SOURCE 18.10 G. R. Elton, *England under the Tudors*, 1991 (3rd edn), p. 370

If she suspected that later ages, more distant from the problem and therefore better able to take the wrong view, might condemn her for the death of the unfortunate Queen of Scots, one hopes she did not let it trouble her. Whatever the moralists and the romantics may say, it is difficult to see what else could have been done about a proven danger to the state, properly and lawfully convicted of a capital crime. From the moment that Mary took refuge in England she created a situation which could not be resolved in a way that was both sensible and moral. And yet – the martyrdom of the Queen of Scots remains to stain the record of Elizabeth's reign.

TALKING POINT

Some of the films and novels depicting the life of Mary, Queen of Scots, are historically inaccurate, including, for example, a dramatic meeting between the two queens. Does this matter? Can historical inaccuracy be justified by dramatic licence, because a more interesting film might interest more people in history?

Whether Mary, Queen of Scots, was a major threat to Elizabeth and to England remains open to debate. With the benefit of hindsight it is clear that none of the plots hatched on Mary's behalf actually developed into anything serious. The danger, however, came not so much from Mary herself, but from the fact that her arrival in England coincided with a major shift in circumstances which threw England into mainstream European politics. It was now no longer possible for Elizabeth to maintain a friendly, but distant, relationship with the Catholic foreign powers while she focused on domestic issues. However much Elizabeth might have wished it otherwise, Mary, Queen of Scots, was always the focal point of concerns about Catholicism, the succession and national security.

KEY POINTS FROM CHAPTER 18: Was Mary, Queen of Scots, a major threat?

1 The Privy Council had established a good relationship with Scotland, by helping the Protestant lords overthrow the French regency. The return of Mary, Queen of Scots, to Scotland threatened this.

2 During Mary's eight-year reign in Scotland she concentrated on getting her claim to the English throne recognised by Elizabeth.

3 Mary's flight to England in 1568 placed the government in a difficult position. As the natural leader of the English Catholics she was a threat to national security.

4 During her nineteen years in captivity, Mary was involved in four conspiracies against Elizabeth. During this period English relations with Catholic Spain also deteriorated.

5 By 1587, England was at war with Spain and fighting to preserve Protestantism. Mary had been tried for treason, found guilty and executed by a reluctant Elizabeth, who had always felt that the council over-reacted in its dealing␣␣␣␣ Mary.

19

Why were Catholics penalised?

CHAPTER OVERVIEW

Elizabeth was probably sincere when she remarked that she did not want to 'make windows into men's hearts and secret thoughts' (although credited to Elizabeth, this was actually said by Francis Bacon), and that her aim was to establish outward submission to the 1559 Religious Settlement rather than examine each individual's personal beliefs. Yet even achieving this relatively low level of religious compliance throughout the country proved far harder than was originally thought.

Traditionally, historians such as A. G. Dickens and G. R. Elton have argued that, by 1558, the majority of the English people were ready to welcome the new Protestant national Church and become loyal Anglicans. A minority group of Catholics remained, but their support for the Pope and Mary, Queen of Scots, meant they could be labelled as political traitors and were therefore the legitimate targets of repressive government legislation. As a result, Elizabeth's claim that she did not penalise people for their religious opinions was valid; she reacted only to political threats. Recent works, however, have argued that this view is too simplistic because the majority of the population, especially outside London, was Catholic and not Protestant in 1559.

This raises two issues for the student of history. First, how could Elizabeth truthfully claim not to penalise people for their religious opinions when loyalty to the Religious Settlement was used as a test of political loyalty? Second, when considering how serious a threat the Catholics posed, are we talking about the majority of the English people or a few extremists?

It is also worth remembering the events of 1558–59 themselves. Although a sincere Protestant herself, the Catholic opposition in the House of Lords shook Elizabeth. Whatever her intentions in 1558, it was clear twelve months later that, despite the legal basis of the Settlement, she wanted to win over Catholics – to persuade people away from Catholicism by getting them used to the new Protestant form of service which retained Catholic visual symbols – rather than force them into submission through the full use of the law.

To have vigorously enforced the Settlement and persecuted Catholics would have driven them into open rebellion, and the Protestants were outnumbered. Besides, Elizabeth needed the support of her Catholic gentry to carry out government policies and enforce law and order in the provinces.

This chapter will assess who the Catholics were, how they reacted to the main political events of the reign, and the nature of the government's legislative reaction to any opposition. This will make it easier to define the extent of the Catholic threat at different periods in the reign and explain why Elizabeth eventually found it necessary to penalise Catholics.

Compile your own table, based on Chart 19A, identifying the different Catholic groups in England during Elizabeth's reign. Add a fifth column and rate the potential threat of each group from 0 (not serious) to 5 (very serious), giving reasons for your choice. When you have finished this chapter, check to see if your assessments were correct.

 # Who were the Catholics?

Few people in England expected the 1559 Religious Settlement to last. Clergy and parishioners alike were reluctant to remove PROSCRIBED Catholic furnishings and often hid images in the belief that Catholicism would soon be restored.

SOURCE 19.1 C. Haigh in C. Haigh (ed.), *The Reign of Elizabeth I*, 1984, p. 197

For a decade or more, the Church of England was a Protestant Church with many Catholic churches; for even longer, it was a Protestant Church with many Catholic, or at least conservative, clergy.

■ 19A English Catholics

Label	Characteristics	Numbers	Key factors
Church Papists	Church Papists were loyal to Elizabeth and were prepared to accept her as Governor of the Church, but they were also conservative and disliked radical changes to traditional patterns of worship. Above all, they believed that Mass and the other Catholic sacraments were necessary for personal salvation.	Probably the majority of the English people, especially north of London, were church Papists. This group included most of the 8000 lesser clergy who took the oath of supremacy.	Church Papists attended English church services. They may have celebrated Mass at home, or the service they attended may well have had the appearance of a Catholic service as a result of priests 'counterfeiting the Mass'. Church services began to conform only slowly to the new Prayer Book, often referring to the more ambiguous interpretations of the Royal Injunctions of 1559. Although Elizabeth ordered her bishops to enforce the Settlement by using the Prayer Book, administering the oath of supremacy to office holders and penalising those who failed to attend church, penalties were not always rigorously enforced because the bishops had been told that Elizabeth did not wish anybody to be vigorously examined over religious issues.
Recusants	Recusants refused to attend church services, although some did feel able to take the oath of supremacy. They believed in the doctrine of the Roman Catholic Church, especially the Latin Mass, and were not prepared to compromise.	It is estimated that one-third of the peerage and a sizeable section of the gentry were recusants, as were the Marian bishops. In central Lancashire, for example, Catholics still outnumbered Protestants in 1603. In 1582, the council estimated that there were 1939 known recusants.	Recusants withdrew from the life of the official Church. Recusant priests offered the Catholic sacraments to the people. Some worked as chaplains to the gentry, celebrating Mass in their houses, while others established underground churches for their former parishioners. No attempt was made by the government to identify recusants until the late 1570s.
Seminary priests	Seminary priests were English Catholics who had been trained for the priesthood at the college in Douai, Flanders, which was founded in 1568 by William Allen. Young men were taught that it was their duty to return to England to work for the salvation of souls and, if necessary, to seek martyrdom in order to re-establish Catholicism. The first seminary priests arrived back in England in 1574.	438 seminary priests returned to England. 98 were put to death.	They started arriving in 1574, determined to inspire the English Catholic community to risk their lives for their faith, and to transform this demoralised group into a strong well-organised structure capable of withstanding persecution. They were protected by the Catholic gentry. C. Haigh (1984) has recently argued that their arrival in Dover, and their consequent concentration in the south-east of England, made their task harder because this was the area with fewest Catholics.
Jesuits	The Jesuits were a Catholic missionary order, which was founded in 1534 to destroy heresy (by which was meant Protestantism). They carried out rigorous spiritual exercises designed to train and discipline the human mind. They took a special oath of allegiance to the Pope.	It is thought that there were far fewer Jesuit priests than seminary priests.	They began to arrive from 1580 onwards. They vigorously opposed compromise and denounced the laxness of the previous decades, insisting that every Catholic should obey the Pope first. They also insisted that the Catholic community should keep itself completely separate from the Elizabethan Church.

PROSCRIBED
Forbidden by law.

1 Why is it so hard to establish the numbers of Catholics and Protestants in Elizabeth's reign?
2 What types of evidence are available to help historians determine people's religious convictions?
3 How might different types of sources lead historians to different conclusions?

B Why did the Catholic threat increase after 1568?

■ 19B Events that caused an increase in the Catholic threat

1568	Mary, Queen of Scots, arrives in England. William Allen founds the first training college for seminary priests at Douai, Flanders.
1569	A rebellion breaks out against English rule in Munster when James Fitzmaurice Fitzgerald proposes asking the Spanish for support against England. The Duke of Norfolk plots against Elizabeth and, in November, the Northern Rebellion, in favour of Mary, Queen of Scots, takes place.
1570	Pope Pius V issues the Bull, *Regnans in Excelsis*, excommunicating Elizabeth and calling on all loyal Catholics to depose her.
1571	The Ridolfi Plot
1572	24 August: Protestants are massacred on St Bartholomew's Day in France.
1574	The first seminary priests arrive from Douai and establish contact with Catholic families in England.
1578	Pope Gregory XIII, who was elected in 1572, backs an expedition, under Sir Thomas Stukeley, to aid James Fitzmaurice Fitzgerald's rebellion in Munster.
1580	Robert Parsons, Edmund Campion and Ralph Emerson, all Jesuits, arrive in England. Parsons and Campion spearhead a mission to Catholic families.
1583	The Throckmorton Plot
1584	William, Prince of Orange, the leader of the Protestant rebels in the Netherlands, is assassinated by a Catholic extremist.
1585	England pledges assistance to the Protestants in the Netherlands in their revolt against Spanish rule.
1586	Philip II begins planning an invasion of England. The Babington Plot
1587	Mary, Queen of Scots, is executed.
1588	The Spanish Armada
1594	Robert Parsons publishes a document supporting the claim of the Spanish Infanta to the English throne. The Pope appoints George Blackwell as Archpriest to rule the English Catholic community. Blackwell is ordered to consult with the Jesuits. The 'Archpriest Controversy' convinces the government that it cannot be tolerant even of those priests who promised political loyalty.

ACTIVITY

1 How do you think each of the four groups of Catholics on page 185 would have reacted to the events in Chart 19B? Complete a table like the one below indicating the strength of each group's involvement in each event on a scale of 0 (no involvement) to 5 (complete involvement).

	Church Papists	Recusants	Seminary priests	Jesuits
The arrival of Mary, Queen of Scots, in England in 1568				

2 List the events in order of importance, according to how great a threat you think they would have appeared to the government.
3 Look at your table and decide:
   a) which groups were the most dangerous and why
   b) when the threat from these groups was the greatest.
   Do your findings correspond with the list you made for Question 2?

C How did the government react after 1568?

■ 19C How did the government react after 1568?

1570 John Felton is executed for displaying a copy of the Papal Bull, *Regnans in Excelsis*.

1571 Three Acts provide that:
- it is treasonable to declare that Elizabeth is not Queen
- it is treasonable to introduce or publish any Papal Bulls
- all those who have fled abroad and who fail to return within twelve months are to forfeit their property.

1577 Cuthbert Mayne, a seminary priest at Launceston in Cornwall, is executed.

1581 Parliament passes two severe Acts against Catholics, despite the Queen's intervention to modify the penalties:
- recusancy fines are increased to £20, and higher fines are imposed for hearing or saying Mass
- attempting to convert people to the Catholic faith is now a treasonable offence.

Edmund Campion and two Douai seminary priests are executed, and Robert Parsons is condemned in his absence.

1585 Parliament passes an Act against the Jesuits and seminary priests. Any priest ordained by the Pope's authority is now guilty of treason once he sets foot in England. All priests are ordered to leave on pain of death. Anyone helping or harbouring a priest is liable to suffer death.

1587 Recusants who default on the payment of fines can now have two-thirds of their land seized by the Exchequer.

1588 The government's determination to crush Catholicism results in the execution of 31 priests.

1593 The House of Commons passes legislation making large gatherings of Catholics illegal, and confining Catholics to a radius of five miles (8 km) from their homes to stop recusants moving about to avoid fines and imprisonment.

1594 The government refuses to follow a policy of toleration towards English secular Catholics who promise not to rebel against Elizabeth.

1602 A royal proclamation orders all Jesuits to leave the country. Other priests are given twelve months to leave, but are promised favourable treatment if they submit to the authorities, which thirteen do.

FOCUS ROUTE

Using Chart 19C construct a table examining:

- the government's reaction to the Catholic threat
- the events preceding the government's reaction (the threat)
- the seriousness of the threat.

Remember to look at other chapters in this book, including those on the council, Parliament, Mary, Queen of Scots, Ireland and foreign policy, so that you can explain the seriousness of a particular threat in terms of who was involved in it and why the government was particularly vulnerable at that time. The timeline above will also help you here.

Here is an example of what 1571 might look like to help you.

The government's reaction to the Catholic threat	The events preceding the government's reaction (the threat)	The seriousness of the threat
In 1571 Parliament passed three Acts stating that it was treason both to declare that Elizabeth was not Queen and to publish Papal Bulls in England. All those who had fled abroad were given twelve months to return or forfeit their property.	The Northern Rebellion of 1569 was an attempt to restore the Roman Catholic religion in England. In 1570 the Pope published a Bull excommunicating Elizabeth.	English Catholics now had to choose between Elizabeth and the Pope. The Pope had called on foreign powers to overthrow her. There was a possibility of a foreign invasion to support English Catholics against the Queen, although the failure of the Northern Rebellion suggests a lack of enthusiasm for this from English Catholics. Nevertheless, the council was worried and acted accordingly.

SOURCE 19.2 A Jesuit priest being tortured on the rack

SOURCE 19.3 Edmund Campion was one of the first Jesuit priests sent to England during Elizabeth's reign. He was executed in 1581

R.P. Edmundus Campianus. Soc: JESV, pro Fide occisus Londini in Anglia, Anno M D LXXXI. Die j. Dec:

Complete the following activity to test your understanding of the Catholic threat. The answers to these questions are discussed on page 190.

1 Catholics were not executed between 1558 and 1570 because:
   a) the Religious Settlement was not enforced.
   b) Elizabeth was too busy dealing with the Puritans.
   c) Elizabeth wanted to conciliate her Catholic subjects and encourage them to join the new Church.

2 Catholics in England did not immediately rebel against Elizabeth because:
   a) they were prepared to wait for Elizabeth's death and another possible change in the national religion.
   b) the Pope gave them no instructions.
   c) most people were illiterate and did not really know what was going on.

3 Most Catholics preferred Elizabeth to Mary, Queen of Scots, because:
   a) they did not believe Mary had a claim to the throne because Henry VIII had prevented the succession of his sister's descendants.
   b) they felt that Mary's scandalous behaviour as Queen of Scotland had forfeited any claim she had to the English throne.
   c) they preferred to be ruled by an English woman and Henry VIII's daughter, whatever the circumstances of her parents' marriage.

4 Which one of the following is not true? In the first decade of her reign, Elizabeth tolerated Catholics because:
   a) she believed English Catholicism would die out if it was not provoked.
   b) she did not want to make windows into men's souls and was satisfied if people conformed outwardly.
   c) the opposition to the 1559 Religious Settlement caused Elizabeth to move more cautiously, so as not to provoke conservative opinion.
   d) she was secure on the throne and therefore able to relax and pursue her own preferences. She had always liked Catholic ceremonial and had been pushed into a more extreme Protestant Settlement by the Puritans in the Commons.
   e) completely repressing Catholicism would have been too difficult, because so many judges and clergy were conservative.

f) there was a great deal of fear of an international Catholic League and Elizabeth was not entirely immune to it in the 1560s.

5 Elizabeth changed to a policy of persecuting Catholics in the 1580s because:
   a) she was tired of waiting for Catholicism to die out naturally.
   b) the arrival of seminary priests and Jesuits in England was strengthening Catholic resistance.
   c) it helped her image as the defender of international Protestantism, which she was cultivating as a reason for sending help to the rebels in the Netherlands.

6 Most of the Catholic priests who were executed received this punishment because:
   a) they had encouraged the English people to put the Papal Bull into operation.
   b) their commitment to the Pope's leadership was viewed as disloyal and potentially dangerous to Elizabeth.
   c) they became involved in plots to overthrow Elizabeth.

7 In the 1590s, Elizabeth refused to allow toleration even for Catholics who had previously shown their loyalty because:
   a) there was always a fear that under a more aggressive Pope Catholicism in England might revive enough to threaten her supremacy.
   b) as Elizabeth became older she became less tolerant and less prepared to do any deals.
   c) by the 1590s, the Puritans were dominant in the House of Commons and were pushing for the complete destruction of Catholicism.

8 The Archpriest Controversy was a result of:
   a) the disappointment, felt by English Catholics, that they were not being given firm leadership.
   b) rivalry between the Jesuits and the seminary priests. This rivalry came to a head when the Pope appointed an Archpriest who was linked to the Jesuits.
   c) the government's refusal to allow toleration to Catholic priests who remained loyal to Elizabeth.

9 By 1603, the number of Catholics in England had declined. This was because:
   a) many Catholics had realised that the Church of England was here to stay and had joined.
   b) the government had vigorously enforced the anti-Catholic legislation.
   c) Jesuit and seminary priests had failed in their mission to strengthen the Catholic community.

Using the information you have gathered from the Activities on page 186 and this page, add a fourth column to the table you created for the Focus route on page 187, and comment on the government's reactions to the Catholic threat between 1571 and 1602.
   Here is an example of what 1571 might look like to help you.

Comment on government's reaction
Elizabeth was forced to act after the Papal Bull was published, but was still reluctant to persecute Catholics and personally vetoed a bill to punish absence from communion. Significantly, the Catholic Northern Rebellion and the Ridolfi Plot attracted little active support in England. However, the problem of Mary, Queen of Scots, being the natural leader of the Catholics was beginning to gather momentum and the government could no longer leave Catholicism to decline naturally.

ACTIVITY (continued)

Answers to the questions on page 189

1   The Religious Settlement was enforced: commissioners were appointed to check that the Prayer Book was being used and bishops and JPs were instructed to deal with non-attendance at church. However, the degree of enforcement varied, especially in the areas where the clergy and gentry were sympathetic to Catholicism. The Puritans did not concern Elizabeth too much at the start of her reign; many became members of the Church. The correct answer is therefore **c)**.

2   The correct answer is **a)**. Catholics were uncertain how to act in 1558. Many did not expect the new Church to last and therefore waited on events, hiding Catholic images to keep them safe for the time being and keeping traditional practices alive.
     While the failure of the Pope to instruct the English Catholics at this point has been widely seen as one of the reasons why the Church of England was able to establish itself so successfully, the Pope's lack of instructions did not prevent the outbreak of the Northern Rebellion in 1569!

3   Although **a)** and **b)** are true, they probably did not bother the typical English Catholic. The correct answer is therefore **c)**. However, the role of Mary is crucial to an understanding of why relations with the Catholics began to disintegrate towards the end of the 1560s.

4   Historians such as J.E. Neale and A.G. Dickens argue that the Puritan Choir had pushed Elizabeth reluctantly into a more Protestant Settlement than she had wished. Her attitude after 1558 therefore simply showed her real conservative/ moderate views. However, modern historians, such as D. MacCulloch in *The Later Reformation in Tudor England,* have found no evidence to confirm that Elizabeth ever wanted to restore the more ambiguous 1549 Prayer Book. Her preference seems always to have been for the 1552 Prayer Book, although she was acutely aware of the need to retain the loyalty of her Catholic subjects. Therefore, **d)** is not true.

5   Before 1582 limited toleration of Catholics made good political sense. The arrival of the Jesuits and the seminary priests, however, altered the balance so that the government now suppressed what it had previously ignored (see Source 19.4). The correct answer is therefore **b)**.

6   The government was keen to show that the priests who were executed were punished, not for their religious beliefs, but as traitors to the crown (see Source 19.5). In fact, as Edmund Campion argued in 1580, the Jesuits had been specifically instructed by the Pope not to meddle in political matters. The unease of the English government was further shown by the different legal justifications for the executions (for example, Mayne was executed under the 1571 Act; Campion and colleagues under the treason statute of 1352), and the need to clarify the situation by bringing in another Act in 1585. The correct answer is therefore **b)**.

7   By the 1590s, Elizabeth had realised that it was impossible to tolerate two religions in one country. Although Catholicism was declining as pro-Catholic clergy died and were replaced by Anglicans, it still remained and Elizabeth regarded it as a potential threat to the Settlement.
     In addition, after the execution of Mary, Queen of Scots, and the defeat of the Spanish Armada, Elizabeth no longer feared a reaction from foreign powers to strict legislation and could therefore take a stronger line. Hence the passing of the 1602 Act. The correct answer is therefore **a)**, although **b)** probably has some truth in it. However, **c)** is not true: Parliaments of the 1590s were not solidly Puritan but contained MPs who were on the whole moderate Protestants opposed to extremists on both sides.

8   The correct answer is **b)**. The Archpriest Controversy is important, because the Pope's appointment of George Blackwell ended the hopes of some English priests for a compromise with the government if they promised complete loyalty in all temporal matters.

9   The missionary campaigns of the Jesuits and the seminary priests are usually seen as successful because the number of recusants actually increased while they were in England, although C. Haigh has recently challenged this view by claiming that the priests focused too much on the south of England and on the needs of the gentry class to be as effective as they might have been. Despite the length and increased intensity of government persecution in the 1580s, the number of Jesuits and seminary priests who died horrifically or who suffered heavy fines was comparatively few – although this is not to make light of their individual suffering or the dangers they faced.
     The correct answer is therefore **a)**. The 'Protestant wind' which scattered the Armada was seen as 'God's verdict', a tremendous psychological boost for Elizabeth and her people, and a vindication for her Church. This encouraged many former Catholics to accept the Elizabethan Church as a *fait accompli*.

SOURCE 19.4 C. Haigh, *Elizabeth I*, 1988, p. 38

With the inflow of Catholic seminary priests from 1574, and the arrival of the Jesuits in 1580, Catholic resistance was hardening; with a new supply of priests, the old religion was not going to die out – it would have to be murdered.

SOURCE 19.5 W. MacCaffrey, *Elizabeth I*, 1993 p. 330

The Pope had, of course, given them ammunition by the Bull of 1570, deposing the Queen. It seemed logical to argue that his agents, seeking to secure the allegiance of English subjects to his authority, were thereby conspiring to overthrow Elizabeth and her regime. Hence it was altogether just to execute them as traitors.

E Why were Catholics penalised during Elizabeth's reign?

ACTIVITY

Read Sources 19.6 and 19.7.

a) What do they tell you about what bishops were expected to do to enforce the 1559 Religious Settlement?

b) What were the bishops' main concerns about the survival of Catholicism?

c) The Archbishop of Canterbury's report was written ten years after the Act of Supremacy and Act of Uniformity were passed. Does this mean:

  • Catholicism was stronger than believed?
  • that the government was not doing its job properly?
  • other reasons in addition to these?

d) Would the continued existence of Catholicism after ten years have caused Elizabeth to change her mind about not wanting to penalise her subjects for their religious beliefs?

SOURCE 19.6 An extract from a report by the Bishop of Peterborough, 1564

Item, that straggling doctors and priests who have liberty to stray at their pleasures within this realm do much hurt secretly and in corners ...
Item, there be divers gentlemen of evil religion that keep schoolmasters in their houses privately, who be of corrupt judgements and do exceeding great hurt as well in those houses where they teach as in the country abroad about them.

SOURCE 19.7 An extract from the Archbishop of Canterbury's report on his visitation to Chichester, 1569

There is one Father Moses, sometime a friar in Chichester, and he runneth about from one gentleman's house to another with news and letters, being much suspected in religion, and bearing a Popish Latin primer.

SOURCE 19.8 An extract from the Papal Bull excommunicating Elizabeth, 1570

This very woman, having seized on the kingdom, and monstrously usurped the place of Supreme Head of the Church in all England, and the chief authority and jurisdiction thereof, hath again reduced the said kingdom into a miserable and ruinous condition, which was so lately reclaimed to the Catholic faith and a thriving condition ... declare the aforesaid Elizabeth, as being an heretic and favourer of heretics ... to have incurred the sentence of excommunication and to be cut off from the unity of the body of Christ. And moreover we do declare her to be deprived of her pretended title to the kingdom aforesaid ... and we do command and charge all and every the noblemen, subjects, people, and others aforesaid, that they presume not to obey her, or her orders, mandates and laws.

SOURCE 19.9 Walter Mildmay, one of Elizabeth's councillors, speaking to Parliament, 28 November 1584

I beseech you to consider what a change there would be if, in the place of the present rulers, those priests, rebels, fugitives, and Papists, known to be cruel and dissolute and vain, were set at the helm of the Church and commonwealth. And if any doubt what a miserable change this would be, let him but remember the late days of Queen Mary, when ... the Pope's authority was wholly restored, and for the continuance thereof a strange nation, proud and insolent, brought into this land to be lords over us.

ACTIVITY

Read Sources 19.8–19.11.

a) Why was it impossible for Catholics to be politically loyal to Elizabeth but follow the Pope in religious matters after 1570?

b) Was Elizabeth correct when she said that she was penalising Catholics because they were a political threat, not because of their beliefs?

c) Why were Elizabeth's councillors so alarmed about the Catholic threat?

d) What effect would her councillors' concerns have had on Elizabeth?

SOURCE 19.10 The Earl of Leicester, 1582

Nothing in the world grieveth me more than to see her Majesty believes this increase of Papists in her realm can be no danger to her.

SOURCE 19.11 One of Sir Francis Walsingham's secret agents, February 1585

I have revealed the miserable and perfidious design of the enemies of the state, who desire nothing but its total ruin, and to raise and stir up the people of England against their princess by a civil war. This they do by means of evil rumours and defamatory books, popish and contrary to religion, which are transported into England from France at the instance of those who are in flight from their country, and also of the Spanish ambassador and of others who favour them: such as Mass-books, other defamatory books written by Jesuits, books of hours and other books serving their purpose.

ACTIVITY

Read Source 19.12.
a) What evidence is there to show that Elizabeth was becoming increasingly hostile towards English Catholics?
b) Which Catholics in particular did Elizabeth single out as being dangerous?
c) What had happened in the 1580s to cause Elizabeth to make these comments?

SOURCE 19.12   Elizabeth's warning to James VI, 15 October 1586

I thank God that you beware so soon of Jesuits, that have been the source of these treacheries in this realm, and will have spread like an evil weed, if at the first they be not weeded out ... What religion is this, that they say the way to salvation is to kill the prince ... this is what they have all confessed without menace or torture. I swear it on my word.

SOURCE 19.13   Extracts from the Act against Jesuit and seminary priests, 1585

Whereas divers persons called or professed Jesuits, seminary priests and other priests ... have of late years come and been sent ... into this realm of England and other of the Queen's Majesty's dominions, of purpose ... not only to withdraw her Highness' subjects from their due obedience to her Majesty but also to stir up and move sedition, rebellion and open hostility within her Highness' realms and dominions ...

And be it further enacted ... that it shall not be lawful for any Jesuit, seminary priest or other such priest, deacon or any religious or ecclesiastical person ... by any authority ... from the see of Rome ... to come into, be or remain in any part of this realm or any other of her Highness' dominions after the end of ... forty days ... every person so offending shall for his offence be adjudged a traitor ... and every person which ... shall wittingly and willingly receive, relieve, comfort, aid or maintain any such Jesuit, seminary priest ... shall also for such offence be adjudged a felon without benefit of clergy and suffer death.

SOURCE 19.14   Written by a Jesuit on the English mission in 1594, while in captivity

It is a point of the Catholic faith ... that subjects are bound in conscience, under pain of forfeiting their right in Heaven ... to obey the just laws of their princes; which both Protestants and Puritans deny with their father Mr Calvin. And therefore if we were not pressed to that which by the general verdict of all ages was judged a breach of the law of God, we should never give your Majesty the least cause of displeasure.

ACTIVITY

Read Sources 19.13–19.15.
a) According to the Act of 1585, which Catholics had been judged to be political traitors?
b) Are these Catholics accused of being traitors on the grounds of their religious beliefs or their political beliefs?
c) Did the Jesuits themselves think they were political traitors?
d) Was it really possible to be loyal to both the Queen and the Pope?

SOURCE 19.15   An extract from *The Bloody Question*, written by a Jesuit in 1594 about his captivity

Turning to me they asked: 'Do you recognise the Queen as the true and lawful Queen of England?'

'I do,' I answered.

'And in spite of the fact that she has been excommunicated by Pius V?'

'I recognise that she is Queen,' I replied, 'though I know too that there has been an excommunication.'

'What would you do if the Pope were to send over an army and declare that his only object was to bring the kingdom back to its Catholic allegiance?'

Then I saw the man's subtlety and wicked cunning. He had so framed his question that whatever I answered I would be sure to suffer for it, either in body or in soul.

ACTIVITY

Choose the statement below which is closest to your own opinion and then, using the sources and your own knowledge, write a mini-essay to support it:

• Roman Catholics were penalised for their religious beliefs throughout Elizabeth's reign.
• Roman Catholics were penalised because they represented a political threat to the government.
• Roman Catholics were only penalised later on in the reign because of the international situation.

F Review: Why were Catholics penalised?

Elizabeth penalised Catholics, not for their heart-felt beliefs but for the outward practice of these beliefs. Unlike the Inquisition and Mary I in her persecution of Protestants, Elizabeth did not seek to root out heresy. As long as they appeared to abide by the Religious Settlement, Elizabeth did not view Catholics as politically disloyal. Even in the 1580s and 1590s those occasionally guilty of recusancy were welcome at court and sat in the House of Lords, whereas the Duke of Norfolk had outwardly accepted the Settlement but still plotted against Elizabeth.

For the first ten years of Elizabeth's reign, when it appeared that the Catholics had been abandoned by the Pope, legislation against them was not strictly enforced. After 1571, the situation was intensified because of the threat from abroad; Jesuits and seminary priests were, for example, treated more harshly than recusants. Yet, Elizabeth was often reluctant to follow the advice of her extreme Protestant councillors such as Walsingham. In 1581 she intervened to modify the penalties proposed in parliamentary legislation. She maintained throughout that she did not penalise religious beliefs: priests were executed for celebrating Mass and encouraging recusancy. Although Elizabeth was not prepared to allow those Catholics who, by the 1590s, had proved their loyalty, to worship, she did not introduce a Protestant form of the Inquisition. This is in marked contrast to the policies of Philip II in the Netherlands and Catherine de Medici in France, who both ordered the persecution of heretics in their states.

Elizabeth did not enforce Protestantism more vigorously after the Religious Settlement of 1559 because of the unexpected opposition she met in the House of Lords, the fear of foreign Catholic intervention, and the fact that the majority of her subjects in 1559, especially the more influential ones, were Catholic. She had no choice but to proceed cautiously, to win them over rather than alienate them. And this policy worked; by the mid-1570s Catholicism was declining as an effective force. The change in policy after this date, caused by the arrival of missionary priests and by the threat of a foreign Catholic invasion, was accompanied by a big propaganda campaign. From the 1570s onwards all Catholics were seen as potential rebels ready to welcome a foreign invader. By the 1580s, priests were being accused of treason and their work deliberately linked with attempts to overthrow the government, even when there was no proof of their involvement.

Government legislation intensified as war with Spain approached. 'In reality however, the danger from English Catholics was exaggerated. The vast majority of them were loyal to their Queen and country and simply hoped for better times when the Catholic Mary Stuart would succeed to the throne' (S. Doran, *Elizabeth I and Religion*, 1994, p. 53).

By the end of Elizabeth's reign, after the execution of Mary, Queen of Scots, and the defeat of the Armada, the Catholics were less of a political threat. Their decline in the 1590s was further accelerated by internal divisions caused by the Archpriest Controversy. Although the government did not eradicate Catholicism totally, it had become a minority sect. Christopher Haigh argues that the fact it was capable of organising itself to withstand persecution shows the widespread and popular appeal of Catholicism. Others have chosen to see the decline of Catholicism as an inevitable, if lengthy, process which, if not complete by 1603, nevertheless shows the success of the approach pursued by Elizabeth's government.

■ Learning trouble spot

When you are writing essays about the threat posed by Catholics, it is important to identify which Catholics you are talking about. Similarly, when analysing government policies, you need to identify the groups of Catholics the legislation is aimed at and the government's reasons for choosing these groups.

It was clear that by 1600 being loyal to the state meant being Protestant. Therefore, despite what Elizabeth may have hoped at the start of her reign, people were penalised for their religious beliefs; although it is true that the most severe penalties were reserved for Jesuits and seminary priests, despite the flimsiness of the evidence linking them with political activities. Perhaps it should not surprise us to learn that the majority of Elizabeth's subjects found it easier to attend church on Sunday – what they actually thought of the new service has not been recorded for posterity. A minority of devout Roman Catholics, however, found it impossible to compromise over doctrinal matters. The question, of course, is whether this made such people politically disloyal and therefore a danger to stability. The government, though not always the Queen, believed it did.

ACTIVITY

Brainstorm an essay plan to the following question: How serious a threat to Elizabeth I and her government were the Roman Catholics in England between 1570 and 1603?

SOURCE 19.16 S. Doran, *Elizabeth I and Religion*, 1994, p. 63

The long and remorseless governmental persecutions and the slow but sustained exposure to Protestantism weaned most Catholics from their faith; only the most committed became recusants; the vast majority drifted into conformity and their children or grandchildren became Protestants.

KEY POINTS FROM CHAPTER 19: Why were Catholics penalised?

1 In 1558, most Catholics were prepared to wait and see what would happen to the national religion, but were basically loyal to Elizabeth.

2 Extreme Roman Catholics did not join Elizabeth's new Church – many fled overseas.

3 For the first ten years of the reign, the government turned a blind eye to Catholic practices. Elizabeth herself seemed keen to make concessions to Catholics over dress, etc.

4 'Dual loyalty' became impossible after the Papal Bull of 1570 called on loyal Catholics to depose Elizabeth.

5 The Catholic community was strengthened from 1574 onwards when English seminary and Jesuit priests arrived.

6 From the 1580s legislation identified Catholics, and Catholic priests in particular, as political traitors, against the background of fears of foreign Catholic invasion.

7 After the death of Mary, Queen of Scots, and the defeat of the Armada Catholicism became less of a threat.

8 In the 1590s, the government refused to compromise with loyal English Catholic priests. All but thirteen were expelled in 1602.

20

Were the Puritans really a danger?

CHAPTER OVERVIEW Despite the establishment of a Protestant Church of England in 1559, there were still a number of people in England who wanted the new Church to be more Protestant and who aimed to establish a doctrine based on John Calvin's Geneva model. Some had spent Mary's reign in exile in European Protestant cities, such as Geneva, Frankfurt, Zurich and Strasbourg, where they developed Calvinist beliefs. These men were originally thought to have exerted considerable political and religious influence in 1558–59, but the traditional view put forward by J. E. Neale – that the returning exiles caused the Queen to create a more Protestant Settlement than she would have liked – has since been disputed. The severest opposition to the Act of Supremacy and the Act of Uniformity came from Catholics in the House of Lords not the Puritan Choir in the House of Commons. Nevertheless, there was a committed group of Calvinists in England, some of whom were appointed to bishoprics by the Queen, who were not prepared to conform to the Elizabethan Church and who became known as Puritans.

This chapter will examine Elizabethan Puritanism as it tried to reform the Church of England, first through the Church itself then through Parliament, before turning to popular local movements – Prophesyings and Classical Presbyterianism – and finally to separatism. The main focus will be on how great a threat the movement was to Elizabeth as Governor of the Church of England and how effectively her government dealt with the various challenges.

A How did the Puritans attempt to change the Church from within? (pp. 196–98)

B How did the Puritans attempt to reform the Church through Parliament? (pp. 199–200)

C How did the Puritans attempt to reform the Church through local movements? (pp. 201–03)

D How did the Puritans attempt to break away from the established Church? (p. 204)

E Review: Were the Puritans really a danger? (pp. 205–07)

A How did the Puritans attempt to change the Church from within?

FOCUS ROUTE

Use Sources 20.1–20.9 to help you to make detailed notes in answer to the following questions.

1 Why did leading Puritans accept the religious authority of the Queen in 1559, and how did they justify this decision?
2 Which issues were already causing concern in 1559?
3 What was the reaction of the Queen and her government to the Puritans?
4 How great a threat were the Puritans in 1559?

Many English Protestants did not regard the 1559 Religious Settlement as final, failing to recognise Elizabeth's determination that it was to mark the end of uncertainty and preferring to blame her bishops. Although there was no organised movement, there were individuals who wanted a more Calvinist form of Prayer Book and who resented the manner in which the Settlement had been imposed upon them without consultation. Some of these men accepted positions within the new Church believing it was better to reform it from within. They included:

- John Jewel, Bishop of Salisbury
- Edwin Sandys, Bishop of Worcester
- Edmund Grindal, Bishop of London
- Richard Cox, Bishop of Ely.

Inevitably these men were seen as having sold out and, by weakening the ranks, to have prevented the development of a Puritan movement backed by international support. The Scottish Calvinist leader John Knox, whose *First Blast of the Trumpet against the Monstrous Regiment of Women* attacked female rulers in general, frequently despaired of the apparent willingness of English Protestants to work with a female Head of the Church.

SOURCE 20.1 James Pilkington, Bishop of Durham and a Marian Exile, 1559

But we trust that both true religion shall be restored; and that we shall not be bothered with unprofitable ceremonies. And therefore, as we purpose to submit ourselves to such orders as shall be established by authority, being not of themselves wicked; so we would wish you willingly to do the same.

SOURCE 20.2 M. Knappen, *Tudor Puritanism*, 1939, p. 167

In a few short months the Genevan English were thus reduced from the hope of dictating terms for an alliance with the home government to a rather cheerless choice. Either they could accept whatever conditions for such a coalition the Queen cared to lay down, or they could adopt a policy of passive resistance and refuse to take office at all if her settlement proved unsatisfactory.

SOURCE 20.3 A joint Statement of Faith presented to Elizabeth by the returning Exiles who preached before her in 1559

The word of God doth not condemn the government or regiment of a woman . . . A tyrant or evil magistrate . . . is a power ordained of God and is also to be honoured and obeyed of the people in all things not contrary to God, as their magistrate and governor. It is not lawful for any private person or persons to kill, or by any means to procure the death of, a tyrant or evil person, being the ordinary magistrate. All conspiracies, seditions, and rebellions of private men against the magistrates, men or women, good governors or evil, are unlawful and against the will and word of God.

SOURCE 20.4 Edmund Grindal's advice to his followers, 27 August 1566

Not to desert our churches for the sake of a few ceremonies and those not unlawful in themselves, especially since the pure doctrine of the gospel remained in all its integrity and freedom.

SOURCE 20.5 John Jewel, Bishop of Salisbury, during the argument over clerical dress, 1561

It has been scarcely two years now since God has restored to us the free and public use of the gospel. For which reason it should not seem astonishing if our people have scarcely put themselves together again, as after a shipwreck. About the matter itself, there is no disagreement among us. Everybody is enough convinced, even the Prince who commanded these things that clothing is nothing so far as religion is concerned . . .

SOURCE 20.6   Edward Dering, a Puritan preacher, to Elizabeth, February 1570

And yet you, in the meanwhile that all these whoredomes are committed, you at whose hands God will require it, you sit still and are careless. Let men do as they list. It toucheth not belike your commonwealth, and therefore you are so well contented to let all alone.

SOURCE 20.7   John Smith, under examination by the commissioners. John Smith was a fellow of Christ's College, Cambridge who was dismissed from his preaching post at Lincoln

We remembered that there was ... a congregation at Geneva which used a book and order of preaching, ministering of the sacraments and discipline, most agreeable to the word of God; which book is allowed by that godly and well learned man Master Calvin ... and if you can reprove this book ... we will yield to you and do open penance at St Paul's cross: if not, we will stand to it by the grace of God.

SOURCE 20.8   Richard Rogers, a fellow of Christ's College, Cambridge who preached throughout Essex and published *The Seven Treatises Leading and Guiding to True Happiness* in 1603

So that no prayer may be more meet for a good Christian than this, that God would keep us in our age from the corruption of the time and of the world. For full soon a man falls to be like others.

SOURCE 20.9   An extract from a report by the Ecclesiastical Commission, 1559

We do give power and authority to you ... to enquire, hear and determine all and singular enormities, disturbances and misbehaviours done and committed ... in any church or chapel or against any divine service, or the minister or ministers of the same, contrary to the laws and statutes of this realm: and also to enquire of, search out, and to order correct and reform all such persons as hereafter shall or will obstinately absent themselves from church.

■ **Learning trouble spot**

The term 'Puritan' is difficult to pin down. It was traditionally used to define a religious movement which challenged the right of the monarch to impose a religious doctrine that contained elements of Catholicism. The Puritans' belief that they were 'the elect' and that the Church should be based on the scriptures alone brought them into conflict with the Stuart monarchs of the seventeenth century, and resulted in the Civil War of 1642–49 and the triumph of Puritanism under Oliver Cromwell. By endeavouring to show that Puritanism had its origins in the Parliaments of Elizabeth's reign, J. E. Neale extended the term to the sixteenth century. Subsequent sixteenth-century historians have used the term very loosely to mean 'left wing', 'fanatical', 'more religious than Anglicans', etc. which has caused confusion. It is also misleading to believe that all English Puritans were fighting for the enforcement of all Calvinist beliefs. The term has, in fact, been applied to a wide variety of English Protestants.

However, although the Puritans themselves saw the label as a term of abuse and preferred names such as 'the Godly', the term has remained in use, because it is a useful means of identification. It might be easiest to use the word in its literal sense, to refer to those people who wanted to 'purify' the Church of all Catholic practices and ritual and to focus instead on preaching the scriptures. The 'Puritans' were, therefore, made up of a variety of different groups and individuals – rather than a coherent opposition – within the established Church, who were united by their readiness to come into conflict with the Queen over the Protestant nature of the Church.

What was the Vestments Controversy?

FOCUS ROUTE

Make detailed notes, and include quotations, to answer the following questions.

1 Why did Puritan criticism of the Settlement lead to a campaign about vestments?
2 What was the government's response to the Vestments Controversy?
3 Why did Puritan hopes for reform from within the Church come to nothing?

Between 1559 and 1563, Puritan clergy cautiously pushed for the removal of those elements of the new Church which they thought were too Catholic. In 1563, the bishops petitioned Convocation to ask if:

- holy days could be abolished
- ministers could read services while facing their congregation
- the sign of the cross could be omitted from the baptism ceremony
- organ music to accompany hymns could be abolished
- individuals could be allowed to use their own discretion when kneeling for communion
- the surplice could be accepted as sufficient for most services.

The petition was defeated by only one vote, showing the strength of support for these views within the Church of England.

In 1566 Archbishop Parker, on his own authority, but under pressure from the Queen, issued the Advertisements which laid down fixed rules for the conduct of services and vestments. As a result, 37 of the most able and energetic clergy were removed from office. Variations over the interpretation of the new service had not been settled by either the Royal Injunctions or the 39 Articles and represented a challenge to the royal supremacy. Puritan unrest eventually centred on the wearing of the correct dress, an issue known as the Vestiarian or Vestments Controversy. Elizabeth's insistence that the exact dress be worn became a test of conformity. Although Archbishop Parker tried to persuade the Puritans that their vestments were ancient and hallowed and demonstrated obedience, to the Puritans they were 'the livery of anti-Christ'.

SOURCE 20.12 Robert Crowley, talking about the Puritan doctrine of passive resistance. Crowley was an active Protestant reformer during the reign of Edward VI. He accepted positions within the Church and clashed with the Archbishop of Canterbury, Matthew Parker, during the Vestments Controversy of 1566

First we obey God, in that both in doing and leaving undone we seek the edification of his Church. And then we obey man, in that we do humbly submit ourselves to suffer at man's hand whatsoever punishments man's laws do appoint for our doing or refusing to do at man's commandment.

SOURCE 20.13 An extract from *An answer for the tyme . . . put in print without the authour's name*, 1566

You think it dangerous for subjects to restrain the prince's authorities to bounds and limits. We think it is dangerous to enlarge the prince's authority beyond the bounds and limits of holy scripture.

Although these criticisms of doctrine went beyond differences over dress, the campaign came to nothing largely because the Puritan bishops did not resign, deciding it was better to work for reform from within the Church than desert it. As a result, after 1566, Puritan leaders tended to come from outside the Church.

B How did the Puritans attempt to reform the Church through Parliament?

FOCUS ROUTE

Make detailed notes to answer the following questions.

1 What changes did the Puritans want made to the Church of England and why?
2 How did the government react to the Puritans' requests between 1571 and 1593?
3 Who was behind the Puritan campaign in Parliament?

In the 1570s, a small, but influential, group of Puritans began to press for basic reforms in the government of the Church in Parliament. The man most associated with these demands is Thomas Cartwright (see page 200), whose programme for reform demanded that:

- the name and office of archbishop be abolished
- bishops should have a spiritual role only
- deacons should look after the poor
- the government of each church should be the responsibility of its ministers and elders
- ministers should be elected by their church congregation.

■ 20A The Puritan challenge in Parliament

Date	Event	Government reaction
April 1571	A bill was introduced by Walter Strickland to reform the Book of Common Prayer by removing those practices regarded as Catholic.	Strickland was prevented from attending the Commons by the Privy Council.
1571–72	A series of bills was introduced proposing further reforms. None was passed.	Church authorities began to be stricter with Puritan ministers, suspending some and cancelling the licences of others.
1572	A bill was introduced on rites and ceremonies to remove many practices from the Prayer Book.	The Queen intervened after the second reading to prevent Parliament from discussing religious matters further unless given permission by her bishops.
1572	The *Admonition to Parliament* was published, a biting attack on the Church which criticised its structure and doctrine for their continuing links with Catholic practices. The *Second Admonition to Parliament* was published later in the year.	The authors, John Field and Thomas Wilcox, were imprisoned. Puritan printing presses were destroyed and bishops were ordered to enforce uniformity.
1576	Peter Wentworth led a Puritan attack on clerical abuses.	Wentworth was sent to the Tower of London.
1584	Peter Turner proposed a bill to change the government of the Church to Calvin's system at Geneva.	The bill was lost from sight after a forceful speech against it in the Commons by Sir Christopher Hatton.
1587	Anthony Cope moved to introduce Turner's 'Bill and Book', and Peter Wentworth argued that MPs should have the right to discuss religious matters in Parliament.	The bill was denied a reading. The Queen ordered the imprisonment of Cope and Wentworth. The council prevented MPs from discussing the bill further.
1593	James Morrice introduced two bills to abolish oaths and subscriptions, unlawful imprisonment and restraint of liberty.	Morrice was suspended from office and imprisoned.

Thomas Cartwright, 1535–1603

- An extreme Protestant divine and author of controversial religious works, he was educated at Cambridge and was, by 1558, an avowed Puritan.
- **1565** He attacked the wearing of the surplice.
- **1569** He was appointed Lady Margaret Professor of Divinity at Cambridge.
- **1570** He was removed from his post for preaching against the Religious Settlement.
- **1571–76** He travelled first to Geneva and then to the Channel Islands.
- **1584** He was made pastor to the English congregation in Antwerp.
- **1585** He returned to England in order to become Master of the Earl of Leicester's hospital in Warwick.
- **1590–92** He was imprisoned.
- **1595–98** He accompanied Baron Zouche to Guernsey.

Mr. THO: CARTWRIGHT.

SOURCE 20.14   An extract from the *Admonition to Parliament*, 1572

Now great sins either not all punished such as blasphemy, usury, etc. or else slightly passed over . . . as adultery, whoredom, drunkenness etc. Agayne, such as are no sins (as if a man conform not himself to popish orders and ceremonies . . .) are grievously punished, not only by excommunication, suspension, deprivation . . . but also by banishing, imprisoning, reviling, taunting, and whatnot.

SOURCE 20.15   Field and Wilcox, *Second Admonition to Parliament*, 1572

We in England are so far off from being a Church rightly reformed, according to the prescript of God's word, that as yet we are not come to the outward face of the same.

SOURCE 20.16   *Admonition to Parliament*, 1572

Instead of an archbishop or lord bishop you must make equality of ministers. You have to plant in every congregation a lawful and godly seignory.

ACTIVITY

Look again at Chapter 7, pages 63–72.

1 How dangerous was the Puritan threat in Parliament?
2 How and why have historians' views on this subject changed recently?
3 What strategies did Elizabeth use to maintain control in Parliament?

C How did the Puritans attempt to reform the Church through local movements?

FOCUS ROUTE

Make notes on why, although Elizabeth kept control of Parliament and Convocation, she could not defeat Puritanism. You should include details of Prophesyings and Presbyterianism.

Despite the fact that Elizabeth maintained control over Church government and Parliament, Puritanism was not defeated. This was partly because the Queen did not have extensive powers to enforce her wishes, and partly because the Puritans enjoyed the support of leading courtiers. Having failed to achieve reform through the centre, the Puritans now concentrated on developing the reformed religion on a local level. Their campaign focused on two movements, known as Prophesyings and Classical Presbyterianism.

■ 20B Obstacles preventing Elizabeth's suppression of Puritanism

Edmund Grindal, 1519–83
- Educated at Cambridge and chaplain to Edward VI, Grindal spent Mary's reign in exile in Strasbourg and parts of Germany.
- **1558** Appointed Bishop of London, and served on the High Commission
- Enforced the Advertisements
- **1570** Appointed Archbishop of York
- **1576** Appointed Archbishop of Canterbury
- **1577** He refused to carry out Elizabeth's order to suppress Prophesyings and was suspended.

SOURCE 20.17   Edmund Grindal to Elizabeth, December 1576

And although ye are a mighty prince yet remember that He which dwelleth in heaven is mightier.

■ 20C Prophesyings and Classical Presbyterianism

	Prophesyings (1570s)	Classical Presbyterianism (1580s)
What was it?	Prophesyings were meetings where prayers and sermons were said. They originally took place as a way to improve the standards of the clergy, and were popular with the people and many bishops as a means of raising the level of clerical education. By the 1570s they were being used by Puritans to put forward their views.	Classical Presbyterianism was based on groups, or conferences, of local clergy who met regularly in secret to discuss the scriptures and common problems. Each group corresponded with others. The network was co-ordinated by John Field's London group which was also in touch with international groups. The movement aimed to re-organise the government of the Church, along the lines of Calvin's Church in Geneva.
Why did it threaten Elizabeth's supremacy?	Prophesyings were seen as potentially dangerous. Elizabeth thought they would encourage unrest and even rebellion.	It was probably the most dangerous aspect of Puritanism. It directly challenged Elizabeth's belief that Church and state government was the responsibility of the monarch.
What did the government do?	After Archbishop Parker's death, Elizabeth ordered his successor, Edmund Grindal, to suppress Prophesyings. When he refused, on the grounds that they served a useful purpose, he was confined to his house and suspended from carrying out his duties until his death in 1583.	The Queen appointed John Whitgift to succeed Grindal. He laid down regulations to improve clerical standards and uniformity within the clergy. He then set up a High Commission which, armed with a list of 24 questions, set out to determine the clergy's allegiance to the Elizabethan Settlement. Between 300 and 400 ministers were removed from office. Whitgift's methods were often attacked by the council.

John Whitgift, 1530–1604
- He was educated at Cambridge
- 1571   Appointed Professor of Divinity at Cambridge
- 1571   Appointed Dean of Lincoln
- 1577   Appointed Bishop of Worcester
- 1577–80   He was Vice-President of the Marches of Wales.
- 1583–1604   As Archbishop of Canterbury, he pursued Elizabeth's policy of enforcing religious uniformity.
- Whitgift was the only cleric to sit on the Privy Council.

FOCUS ROUTE

Make detailed notes in answer to the following questions.

1 What do Sources 20.18–20.22 show about the nature of Prophesyings?
2 Why did Elizabeth fear Prophesyings so much?
3 Why did Archbishop Grindal refuse to suppress them?
4 What conclusions can you draw from Sources 20.18–20.22 about the government of the Church?
5 Why would Puritans find the second of Whitgift's Three Articles so difficult to accept?
6 a) What does Source 20.21 tell you about Whitgift's personality?
   b) Why would this make him so indispensable to Elizabeth?

SOURCE 20.18   Commentator in 1575 at Dedham, Essex

The deep, passionate, trembling, singultive twang ... the women's sighs and the men's hawkings; at Dedham men hanging weeping on the necks of their horses after Mr Rogers's sermon had acted out a little scene in which God threatened to take away the Bible from the English people. Even the hints of rather too great a familiarity between the sexes ... many of this gadding people came from far and went home late ... both young men and young women together.

TALKING POINT

Can you think of other examples where governments have deliberately banned the discussion and spread of ideas? Is it a policy that can actually succeed in its aim?

SOURCE 20.19   Elizabeth forbids Prophesyings, 1577

By which manner of assemblies great numbers of our people, especially the vulgar sort, meet to be otherwise occupied with honest labour for their living, are brought to idleness and seduced and in a manner schismatically divided amongst themselves into variety of dangerous opinions ... and manifestly thereby encouraged to the violation of our laws and to the breach of common order.

SOURCE 20.21   Whitgift to the Puritan clergy

You are unlearned, and but boys in comparison with us, who have studied divinity before you for the most were born.

SOURCE 20.20   Thomas Wood, a Puritan preacher

For then the faithful ministers might freely tell both Prince and people their faults, but such as would do the like indeed either have their mouths stopped, or cannot be suffered to come in place where it ought chiefly to be done.

SOURCE 20.22   Article Two from Whitgift's Three Articles, 1583

That the Book of Common Prayer, and of ordering bishops, priests and deacons containeth nothing in it contrary to the Word of God. And that the same may be lawfully used; and that he himself will use the form of the said book prescribed, in public prayer and administration of the sacraments, and none other.

FOCUS ROUTE

Make detailed notes in answer to the following questions.

1 What form did the propaganda campaign carried out by the government and the Puritans take?
2 Who were the separatists and what did they want?
3 Why did the government refuse to allow the separatists what they wanted?
4 a) What powers did the Act of 1593 give the government?
   b) What choices did the Act give separatists?
   c) What does this show you about Parliament in the 1590s?
   d) Why do you think this had happened?
   e) Why else would it have been difficult for such severe action to have been taken against the Puritans earlier in the reign?

D How did the Puritans attempt to break away from the established Church?

Whitgift's efforts to enforce uniformity broke the back of Puritanism and forced its leaders underground. They increasingly realised that Puritanism would never be permissible by law and would have to be practised in secret. There was an increase in the number of Puritan pamphlets and books produced from illegal presses during the second half of Elizabeth's reign.

■ 20D The propaganda campaign

Puritan literature

Disciplinale Ecclesiale
by
Walter Travers
1573
Each congregation should have a minister, a teacher, an elder, who would govern and impose discipline, and a deacon.

Martin Marprelate Tracts
1589
A series of crude, anonymous pamphlets attacking bishops. They became popular bestsellers, although their offensive nature did not help the Puritan cause.

Government responses

Survey of the Pretended Holy Discipline Dangerous Positions and Proceedings
by
Richard Bancroft
1593
An attack on Puritanism

The Laws of Ecclesiastical Polity
by
Richard Hooker
1593
A defence of the Anglican Church

As the government destroyed printing presses and imprisoned extremists, a small minority of Puritans – the separatists – decided to leave the established Church and set up their own Church. The movement gained importance towards the end of the 1580s under Robert Browne. When Browne submitted to Whitgift, new leaders were found in Henry Barrow and John Greenwood, who were executed in 1593. In 1593 the government passed the Act against Seditious Sectaries.

SOURCE 20.23 An extract from the Act against Seditious Sectaries, 1593

If any person or persons above the age of sixteen years shall obstinately refuse to repair to some church ... to hear divine service, established by her Majesty's laws ... by printing, writing, or express words or speeches advisedly and purposely practise or go about to move or persuade any of her Majesty's subjects ... to deny ... her Majesty's power and authority in causes ecclesiastical ... or to that end or purpose advisedly and maliciously move or persuade any other person ... to abstain from coming to church to hear divine service ... that then every such person so offending ... shall be committed to prison there to remain until they shall conform ... And if any such offender shall refuse to make such abjuration as is aforesaid ... shall depart out of this realm ... shall return or come again into any of her Majesty's realm ... the person so offending shall be adjudged a felon [A felony carried the death penalty].

E Review: Were the Puritans really a danger?

Elizabeth regarded the Presbyterians as a danger to her royal authority and tended to look upon all Puritans, including the majority of them who were moderate, with suspicion. She blocked proposals for even minor reform and this intransigence made her bishops' lives almost impossible.

While the theological differences between Protestants and most Puritans was small, a minority did cause Elizabeth to perceive great danger in the entire movement. The Presbyterians wanted to model the government of the Church, not just its theology, on the Calvinist system. This was unacceptable to a sovereign who demanded uniformity for the sake of political stability and who, having established a national Church, saw no need for further debate. Nowadays, Presbyterianism is seen as less of a threat than Elizabethan propaganda made it appear in the 1570s and 1580s.

Presbyterians disgraced themselves with the abusive Martin Marprelate pamphlets, and were viewed as subversives during a time of national unity caused by the war against Spain. Elizabeth maintained control of the established Church but her refusal to consider making even minor concessions to the Puritans, while appearing eager to conciliate Catholics, may well have increased the Puritan threat; while her demands for conformity made through the Advertisements and the Three Articles drove good men out of the Church and into the Presbyterian camp. Through her refusal to support, either financially or morally, the provision of 'a godly preaching ministry' she failed to meet the spiritual needs of many of her subjects and left the way open for others to do so.

SOURCE 20.24 D. MacCulloch, *The Later Reformation in Tudor England*, 1990, p. 34

For the first generation of bishops, mostly men who had confidently expected in 1559 to lead further transformations to keep Popery at bay, this was an unwelcome, dispiriting role . . . the Queen left Archbishop Parker and his colleagues the task of bringing fellow Protestants to heel.

SOURCE 20.25 P. Collinson in C. Haigh (ed.), *The Reign of Elizabeth I*, 1984, p. 181

As for the Queen herself, she shocked Archbishop Grindal by suggesting that three or four preachers were sufficient for a shire. It was in the absence of any governmental programme for the establishment of a fully qualified, standardised preaching ministry, adequately financed, that maximum scope was allowed to a more informal and unauthorised evangelism.

In addition, until she was able to appoint men such as Whitgift who had grown up within the Church of England created in 1559, Elizabeth's defence of the Church frequently put her in opposition to many of her councillors and her bishops. Perhaps, therefore, in the final analysis, Elizabeth herself made Puritanism more of a danger than it really was.

FOCUS ROUTE

Using a table like the one below, assess how great a threat to Elizabeth each stage of Puritan development was. Make sure you include evidence to back up your judgement.

Campaign	Main features	Government response	Seriousness of the threat
Reform from within the Church			
Reform through Parliament			
Reform through local movements			
Separatism			

ACTIVITY

1 Work in pairs.
   a) Design a Puritan pamphlet explaining why they disliked the Elizabethan Religious Settlement. You can cover the campaign within the Church, in Parliament, in local movements or away from the established Church. Within your class, you should aim to cover all four areas.
   b) Produce a response, written by a government minister on behalf of Elizabeth, to explain why the government refuses to make any concessions to Puritan demands.

2 Divide into two groups. One should prepare a speech arguing that Elizabeth feared the Catholics more than the Puritans, the other should prepare a speech arguing that the Puritans were the greater threat. Then carry out a class debate.

3 Using information from this chapter and Chapter 7, brainstorm an answer to the essay question: Has the threat from Puritanism during Elizabeth's reign been exaggerated?
   You will need to include evidence that shows Puritanism was a real danger and evidence that shows Puritanism was less dangerous than it seemed, before reaching a conclusion. Remember that changing historical interpretations may have an effect on your answer.

4 To test your understanding of this chapter, match the following sentences with the correct endings. See page 300 for the answers.
   a) Calvinism was:
      • used as the basis for Edward VI's Prayer Books and was the favoured doctrine of English Protestants in 1558.
      • the preferred doctrine of the Marian Exiles, but was not widely known in England in 1558.

   b) Calvin:
      • completely rejected all the sacraments as being too Catholic.
      • wanted to keep the sacraments of baptism and communion.

   c) Calvinists believed the communion service:
      • was simply an act of commemoration.
      • possibly had a spiritual presence.

   d) Calvinists believed that:
      • a disciplined Church needed a hierarchical structure.
      • discipline should be imposed by members of the community.

   e) Calvin said that:
      • all his followers were predestined to be saved, that they were 'the elect'.
      • only God had the power to decide who was saved, that earthly actions could not determine such a thing.

   f) In 1565, the Puritans wanted to:
      • overthrow the Elizabethan Church and replace it with a Calvinist Church.
      • gradually reform the Elizabethan Church, removing all the Catholic elements.

   g) As Head of the Church, Elizabeth was:
      • unacceptable to both Catholics and Puritans because she was a woman.
      • acceptable to Puritans but not to Catholics who wanted the return of the Pope.

   h) The Advertisements:
      • promoted the new Elizabethan Church.
      • laid down rules, which the clergy had to obey.

   i) Presbyterians wanted:
      • a Church established along the lines of John Knox's Scottish Church.
      • a system of conferences, linked locally, nationally and internationally.

   j) The Admonition to Parliament was:
      • a warning from Elizabeth that the Puritans must not interfere in the running of the Church.
      • a biting attack on the Elizabethan Church.

   k) Prophesyings were:
      • predictions that disaster would befall the English Church if it did not remove all the 'papal blemishes'.
      • meetings called to discuss the scriptures.

   l) Separatists wanted:
      • toleration for all religious beliefs.
      • the right to establish their own Church alongside the official Church.

1 In 1559, most Protestants believed the Religious Settlement needed further refinement. Elizabeth did not.
2 Leading Protestants, including a number of Puritans, accepted positions in the new Church hoping to reform it from within.
3 The government's refusal to move away from its position outlined in the Royal Injunctions led to clashes over clerical dress.
4 Throughout the 1570s Puritans in Parliament attempted to introduce a Calvinist system of doctrine and Church government.
5 John Field, and other Presbyterian leaders, tried to establish Classical Presbyterianism throughout the country.
6 Elizabeth ordered the suppression of Prophesyings and suspended Archbishop Grindal when he refused to carry out her wishes.
7 Whitgift's actions, including the Three Articles, reduced the Puritan threat.
8 Puritanism declined further in the 1590s with the passing of the 1593 Act and the death of many of its patrons.

21

Review: How far did religion affect stability at home?

The following Focus route will help you to pull together the key areas that you have covered in Section 4.

ACTIVITY

Have another look at Question 2 on page 159 and Question 1 on page 165. Now you have studied the Catholics and Puritans, do you think any of the characters might feel differently about the success of Elizabeth and her bishops in establishing the Religious Settlement?

FOCUS ROUTE

1 Copy and complete the following table:

Problem	Significance (Was it a serious threat to stability?)	Government response	An evaluation of the government's response
1558–59 State of the Church			
1564–66 Vestments Controversy			
1568 Arrival of Mary, Queen of Scots, in England			
1569 Northern Rebellion			
1570 Papal Bull of Excommunication			
1571 Ridolfi Plot			
1574 Arrival of seminary priests in England			
1577 Grindal refuses to suppress Prophesyings			
1580 Jesuit missionaries arrive in England			
1583 Throckmorton Plot			
1586 Babington Plot			
1590s Archpriest Controversy			

2 a) Was each of the twelve problems above a religious threat, a political threat or both?
   b) Can you tell from the government's response what they thought?
   c) Is it possible, or even desirable, to separate religion from politics in the sixteenth century?

3 The fundamental question of how far Elizabeth was in control of religious matters continues to be the subject of heated debate amongst historians. Note down as much evidence as possible to support the following conclusions:

• Elizabeth muddled through her religious problems and was helped in this by a considerable amount of luck.
• Elizabeth instinctively knew what was politically sound and stuck to policies that she knew were acceptable to the majority of her people, despite opposition from her councillors and the clergy.

TALKING POINT

Do you remember the main theme of the book: the investigation into whether Elizabeth's reign was a Golden Age (see page 5)?

Who, if anyone, would have seen Elizabeth's reign as a religious Golden Age? Does your view of this depend on whether you take a long-term or a short-term perspective?

How far did religion affect relations with foreign powers?

Elizabeth addressing her troops at Tilbury, in 1588: a panel painting from St Faith's Church, King's Lynn

J. E. Neale, *Queen Elizabeth I*, 1934, p. 301–2

As the Armada approached the English shore, Elizabeth had thrown aside all hesitation and thoughts of peace, and had risen on the tide of popular enthusiasm to heights of true greatness ... on the 8 August 'full of princely resolution and more than feminine courage she passed like some Amazonian empress through all her army'.

ACTIVITY

What can you learn about the dangers to England in 1585 from Source 1?

SOURCE 1 Lord Burghley to Elizabeth, 1585

Dangers: 1 Great, 2 Many, 3 Imminent

Great in respect of a) the persons: the Q[ueen's] Majesty herself as patient. The Pope. The Kings of France and Spain. The Q[ueen] of Scots as the instrument whereby the perils do grow.

b) the matters: a) recovery of the tyrannous estate to the Church of Rome, which of late years has been in many parts weakened, and now so earnestly regarded by the two principal monarchies of Christendom, that is of France and Spain, as they have left all other affairs, and buried all other quarrels and have made an open profession under the title of executing the Council of Trent [1563], to recover by sword the authority of the Pope: which matter was never in such earnest and plain sort attempted in this age before now.

b) eviction of the Crown of England from the Q[ueen's] Majesty, to set it upon the head of the Q[ueen] of Scots, as a matter specially also tending to the purpose of the said two Monarch's attempts and enterprise.

The recovery of the tyrannous estate of Rome cannot be sufficiently accomplished, and to the contentment of the two monarchies, but by means of: a) wars in France to make a full conquest of all Protestants there, and the like in Flanders and the Low Countries.

b) changing of the state of England to Popery, which cannot be accomplished whilst the Q[ueen's] Majesty lives not so assuredly and plausibly compassed, as by placing the Q[ueen] of Scots in the seat of this Crown ...

The defeat of the Spanish Armada in 1588 – an event etched on our national consciousness in much the same way as the Battle of Hastings of 1066 is – has, for a long time, prevented a critical assessment of Elizabeth's foreign policy. After all, it was such an obvious success – a second league European power had taken on the mightiest empire in the world and won – that any criticism would be mere carping. As with all Elizabeth's policies, however, recent historians have taken a more objective view of her foreign policy. It will, therefore, be helpful if you keep the following points in mind as you work through Section 5.

■ **Did Elizabeth have a foreign policy at all?** Some historians argue that she simply reacted to external events in order to safeguard national interest.

■ Any consideration of Elizabeth's strategies must focus on the resources available to her: ships, munitions, man–power and above all money. Did constrained resources mean that a limited defensive policy was her only option?

■ Elizabeth was Queen for a long time and England's priorities changed during her reign. In the early years, the fear of French power in Scotland and across the Channel was her main concern, and fear of France also made Philip II continue to support England despite religious differences. This did, however, change.

■ Elizabeth's refusal to marry or name her successor had an effect on foreign policy, partly through the person of Mary, Queen of Scots, and foreign support for her claim to the throne, and partly because Elizabeth was able to use her single status as a diplomatic weapon, during the Alençon courtship for example.

■ Spain's transformation from England's natural ally into her arch enemy is the main feature of this period.

■ The growing enmity between England and Spain revealed England's development as a maritime power. Clashes with Spain in the New World are an interesting indication of how England's overseas interests had expanded, and would continue to do so.

■ It is quite possible to assess Elizabeth's foreign policy with very little reference to the role of religion. This would be to seriously underestimate the effect that differences in religion had on the way in which Catholic and Protestant monarchs dealt with each other, and to overlook the priorities of the leading Protestants in England who saw Rome, and Roman Catholic countries, as the real enemy. Just as religion, the succession and events abroad were intertwined in the minds of sixteenth-century statesmen, they should always be intertwined in your mind too.

Section 5 will focus on the shift in England's alliances, with France giving way to Spain as England's 'natural enemy', on the success of Elizabeth's foreign policy, and on the opinions of both contemporaries and historians.

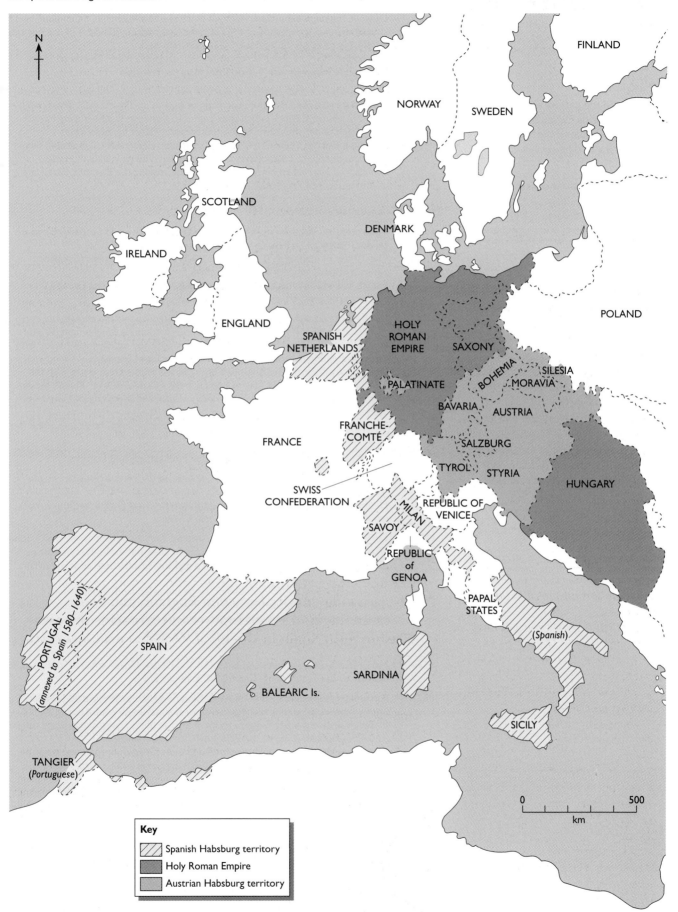

FINLAND

NORWAY   SWEDEN

SCOTLAND

IRELAND

ENGLAND

SPANISH
NETHERLANDS

HOLY
ROMAN
EMPIRE   SAXONY

POLAND

DENMARK

PALATINATE   BOHEMIA   SILESIA
MORAVIA

BAVARIA   AUSTRIA

FRANCE

FRANCHE-
COMTÉ

SALZBURG

SWISS
CONFEDERATION

TYROL   STYRIA

HUNGARY

MILAN

REPUBLIC OF
VENICE

SAVOY

REPUBLIC
of
GENOA

PORTUGAL
(annexed to Spain 1580–1640)

SPAIN

PAPAL
STATES

(Spanish)

SARDINIA

BALEARIC Is.

SICILY

TANGIER
(Portuguese)

0   500
km

Key

Spanish Habsburg territory

Holy Roman Empire

Austrian Habsburg territory

FOCUS ROUTE

Read the timeline and then answer the following questions.

1 Which countries presented the greatest danger to England and when?
2 How did the pattern of alliances change during Elizabeth's reign?
3 Was the defeat of the Spanish Armada a one-off success for England?

Keep these questions uppermost in your mind as you learn about the events in detail and you will be focusing on the main A level areas of debate.

■ The international situation, 1558–1603

1558 Catholic France is ascendant. Henry II 'bestrides the realm like a Colossus' and is 'one of the two spearheads of the Counter Reformation' (Philip II of Spain is the other). He rules on the advice of the Guise brothers.
In Scotland, Mary of Guise is regent for her daughter, Mary, Queen of Scots, who is in France with her husband the dauphin, Francis.

1559 Spain and France end decades of warfare with the Treaty of Cateau-Cambresis. England is represented at the peace conference as an ally of Spain. The French refuse to return Calais – which they captured from the English during Mary's reign – and under the terms of the treaty retain Calais for eight years.
  Philip II marries Henry II of France's daughter. Henry II is killed during the tournament held to celebrate the royal wedding. The new King of France, Francis II, is married to Mary, Queen of Scots, making the Catholic Guise family effective rulers of France and Scotland.
Scottish Protestant lords, tired of domination by a foreign Catholic power, depose Mary of Guise.

1560 To prevent the French restoring Mary of Guise to power in Scotland, Elizabeth sends an army and a fleet to help the Protestant lords.
The Treaty of Edinburgh is signed and the French withdraw from Scotland, where a council establishes Protestantism.
Francis II dies and is succeeded by his younger brother, Charles IX, and a regency is established under his mother, Catherine de Medici.

1562 Violence breaks out in France between the Catholics and the Huguenots (Protestants). The French Wars of Religion will continue for the next 30 years. Elizabeth sends aid to the French Huguenots, but they rapidly make peace with Catherine de Medici and the English are driven out of France.
England's traditional friendship with Spain, based on the cloth trade with the Netherlands and a mutual fear of France, begins to decline over Philip's tendency to govern the Netherlands as a province of Spain and bypassing its Council of State.
Calvinism continues to spread throughout the Netherlands, helping to unite the Dutch people against Spanish rule.

1563 A trade embargo is declared between the Netherlands and England.

1567 Philip sends an army, under the Duke of Alva, to the Netherlands to restore Spanish control.
Elizabeth allows the Dutch Sea Beggars (pirates) to use English harbours, from which they attack Spanish shipping in the Channel.

1568 On his third voyage to Spanish South America with a cargo of negro slaves, John Hawkins puts into the harbour of San Juan de Ulua in Mexico. Despite terms made beforehand, the Viceroy of Mexico and the Spanish fleet attack Hawkins who loses four ships and 100 men.
Two weeks later Cecil orders bullion to be unloaded from Spanish ships sheltering in English ports from pirates. Rightly or wrongly, the Spaniards think Elizabeth intends to confiscate the treasure and Alva retaliates, placing an embargo on all English property in the Netherlands.
Trade between England and Spain stops.

1570–71 Marriage negotiations between Elizabeth and Henry, Duke of Anjou, the younger brother of the French king, Charles IX, take place.

1572 A mutual defence treaty, the Treaty of Blois, is signed by England and France, both countries promising to help the other if attacked by a third party.
Elizabeth orders the Sea Beggars to leave English ports. Their subsequent return to the Netherland leads to the Revolt of the Netherlands.
A French army, under the Huguenot Admiral de Coligny, prepares to help the Dutch rebels against Spain, raising the possibility of French control of the Channel.
In August, Coligny is shot and thousands of Huguenots are killed while attending the wedding of their leader, Henry of Navarre, to the King's sister in Paris. The Massacre of St Bartholomew was said to have been arranged by Catherine of Medici, who resented Coligny's influence over her son. The event was applauded by Catholic Europe and regarded with horror by Protestant countries.
Elizabeth begins marriage negotiations with the Duke of Alençon, younger brother of Henry III. Alençon was created Duke of Anjou after Henry became King of France.

1573 Negotiations with Alva lead to the restoration of trade between England and the Netherlands.

1574	Elizabeth renews the Treaty of Blois with the new King of France, Henry III.
1577	Drake begins his voyage of circumnavigation.
1579	For the next seven years events in Scotland trouble England: nobles, particularly Esmé Stuart, an agent of the Guise, battle for control over the young king, James VI.
1580	The pro-English Scottish regent is executed and replaced by Esmé Stuart, now Earl of Lennox. Twelve months later, James VI of Scotland is seized by Protestant nobles and Lennox returns to France.
1581	Drake is knighted by Elizabeth after completing his circumnavigation of the globe.
1584	The Duke of Anjou (Alençon) dies. The French King, Henry III, has no children so Protestant Henry of Navarre becomes his heir. Henry, Duke of Guise, forms the Catholic League to prevent Henry of Navarre becoming King of France, and signs a secret treaty with Spain in which the two agree to drive Protestantism out of France and the Netherlands. William, Prince of Orange, the leader of the rebels in the Netherlands, is assassinated. The new Spanish commander in the Netherlands, the Duke of Parma, advances on Antwerp.
1585	Elizabeth signs the Treaty of Nonsuch and sends an army to help the Dutch rebels. Drake is dispatched with 29 ships to the Spanish West Indies, where he sacks Santiago and Cartagena.
1586	Elizabeth and James VI of Scotland sign the Treaty of Berwick. This mutual defence treaty guarantees James an English pension of £4000 per annum.
1587	Drake destroys the Spanish ships being constructed in Cadiz harbour, before sailing for the Azores and capturing a Portuguese treasure fleet.
1588	The Spanish Armada is defeated by the English navy in a battle off Gravelines.
1589	A massive English expedition, under the command of Sir Francis Drake, is launched. But Drake fails to comply with Elizabeth's orders and little is accomplished. Henry III of France is assassinated. The succession of the Huguenot Henry of Navarre as Henry IV leads to the renewal of civil war as the Catholic League turns against him. Elizabeth sends a small army to support Henry, under Willoughby. An English army, under Sir Francis Vere, ably supports Maurice of Nassau, son of William, Prince of Orange, against Parma in the Netherlands.
1590	Henry IV of France defeats the Catholic League at the Battle of Ivry and advances on Paris. Philip orders Parma to leave the Netherlands and defend Paris, leaving Maurice of Nassau free to capture Dutch towns and win strategic battles. Philip II of Spain renews his treaty with the Catholic League and sends 3000 men to Brittany, threatening the Channel.
1591	Elizabeth sends an army to Brittany under Sir John Norreys. A second army, under the Earl of Essex, is sent to Normandy.
1593	Henry IV converts to Catholicism and makes his peace with the Catholic League.
1595	An expedition, led by Drake and Hawkins, sails to attack Panama, the centre of the Spanish bullion route. But the Spanish have strengthened their defences, the attack fails and neither Drake nor Hawkins survives the voyage.
1596	An expedition, commanded by Lord Howard of Effingham and the Earl of Essex, sacks Cadiz. A bankrupt Philip II launches a second Armada but it is destroyed by gales.
1597	Essex is given command of an expedition to intercept a third Armada. Instead he sails to the Azores after the Spanish treasure fleet, which he misses, leaving England undefended. Luckily, the third Armada is wrecked by storms.
1598	Henry IV of France makes peace with Spain at Vervins. Philip III becomes King of Spain.
1599	The Earl of Essex is sent to Ireland with a large army to put down Tyrone's Rebellion.
1600	Lord Mountjoy is sent to Ireland with an army, to replace the Earl of Essex.
1601	A Spanish force lands at Kinsale in Ireland but is defeated by Mountjoy.
1603	Tyrone surrenders and his rebellion against English rule in Ireland fails.

22

What were Elizabeth's foreign policy priorities, 1560–72?

CHAPTER OVERVIEW

England's relationship with Europe had always depended on the priorities and personalities of its monarchs. All the Tudors had shown an awareness of certain key factors that were fundamental to English security, although the policies they followed varied considerably. These factors can broadly be summarised as:

- the protection of the cloth trade between England and the Netherlands
- the prevention of a hostile country building up a power base along the Channel or in Ireland
- the protection of the northern borders because Scotland was traditionally an ally of France.

Henry VII tried to maintain English security by using diplomacy, marrying his children to leading European ruling families, and by promoting trade; although he was prepared to go to war when necessary, for example when French control of Brittany threatened security in the Channel. Henry VIII preferred to seek personal glory through warfare to assert his claims to territory in France, although, after 1518, Cardinal Wolsey tried to use diplomacy rather than war to win his master prestige in Europe.

This chapter will focus on Elizabeth's priorities between 1560 and 1572, her response to the actions of other countries, the influences she was subject to, and, above all, the circumstances which led to the reversal of the traditional system of European alliances. It will also assess how far Elizabeth and her government were in control and the extent to which religion was the driving force behind her decisions.

TALKING POINT

Would her gender make conducting foreign policy more difficult for Elizabeth?

SOURCE 22.1 Henry VIII sought personal glory through warfare. Do you think Elizabeth was likely to do the same?

A What was the situation like in 1558?

Elizabeth was never entirely free to develop foreign policy independently, she always had to work within parameters determined by recent events at home and abroad.

Domestic factors influencing foreign policy

To fulfil the expectations of her people, and in particular her councillors, Elizabeth needed to reassert England's status after the humiliations of Mary's reign.

SOURCE 22.2 R. B. Wernham, *The Making of Elizabethan Foreign Policy*, 1980, pp. 26–27

During the decade before Elizabeth's accession much else besides the navy had been allowed to run down, and England's weakness and disunity had made it seem, in Paget's phrase, 'a bone between two dogs'.

SOURCE 22.3 R. B. Wernham, *The Making of Elizabethan Foreign Policy*, 1980, pp. 26–27

Determination to end this situation, to reassert England's independence, was the main driving force behind the policies of Elizabeth and her ministers, of William Cecil especially. This was so not only in their foreign policy, but in every aspect of affairs. It inspired the government's efforts to develop new industries, and to encourage old industries, that would make the country no longer dependent upon imports from abroad for firearms, artillery, gunpowder, copper wire for wool carding, and other necessities of defence and subsistence. It underlay the Queen's efforts to restore unity, or at least to damp down dissension in ecclesiastical matters while again breaking with Rome.

For the first two decades of her reign, foreign policy was also closely intertwined with the question of Elizabeth's marriage and the succession.

Foreign policy was a royal prerogative, but Elizabeth looked to the Privy Council for advice. Her secretary, who oversaw the letters passing to and from the Queen and her council, had a great deal of influence over decision making.

SOURCE 22.4 W. MacCaffrey, *Elizabeth I*, 1993, p. 5

The conception and initiation of policy was frequently left to the royal councillors; it became their business to devise the best possible mode of proceeding in each individual contingency of state. It remained for the Queen to accept, reject, or modify their proposals; there could be no question that the final decision remained a royal prerogative.

Elizabeth's leading councillors were Protestant, and some saw England's relationship with other European powers as part of a larger conflict between Protestantism and the forces of Roman Catholicism. For this reason they were more ready to help Protestant rebels against their divinely appointed rulers than Elizabeth was.

Apart from her council, other men clearly influenced Elizabeth and the way in which she conducted foreign policy, as is shown in Source 22.5.

SOURCE 22.5 R. B. Wernham, *The Making of Elizabethan Foreign Policy*, 1980, p. 13

For example, in the earlier years of the reign Sir Nicholas Throckmorton wrote to her somewhat avuncular discourses on policy in general, besides seeking to guide her on particular issues by his despatches during his French and Scottish embassies. Then there was John Hawkins, who persuaded her to let him transform her navy from a coast-defence force into a high seas fleet capable of operating at considerable distances from home – against the Spanish silver fleets from America, if he could persuade her to that. In later years there was Sir Walter Raleigh, with his plans for plantations in Ireland and America and his projects for winning the war against Spain. Neither he nor Throckmorton achieved their ambition to be Privy Councillor, yet their influence was not entirely negligible.

Elizabeth also learnt a lot from the lengthy audiences she gave to foreign ambassadors, and expected all English ambassadors, agents, and military commanders to write to her directly.

Last, but by no means least, Elizabeth was fully aware of England's inability to wage war in Europe for a prolonged period of time. England had a far smaller population than either France or Spain and lacked the financial resources necessary to maintain a standing army capable of fighting abroad. Although England had considerable naval power and an extensive local militia, both were primarily defensive. In the ten years preceding Elizabeth's accession, England had shown that it was incapable of conquering Scotland and holding on to Calais.

What was Europe like in 1558?

The advent of Protestantism in Europe put an end to its greatest unifying force: Catholicism. The Holy Roman Empire, the centuries-old symbol of a united Catholic Christendom, was under threat from within, and France and Scotland were drifting towards religious conflict. Henceforth, the religion of the monarch determined a country's allies and enemies. The Pope and staunchly Catholic countries, such as Spain, were committed to preventing the spread of Protestantism.

The discovery of new trade routes and overseas territories, particularly in the New World, put an end to the Euro-centric nature of national interests. Monarchs began to realise the amazing potential for power and wealth that existed in the newly-discovered continents. Religion played a part here, too, as the conversion of indigenous populations to Catholicism could give legitimate moral overtones to the violent conquest of civilizations.

Spain

The King of Spain, Philip II, ruled over Spain, the Netherlands, Franche-Comté, parts of Italy and the Spanish conquests in the New World. Spain's population was three times that of England while the treasures and silver mines of Mexico and Peru had increased Philip's income immeasurably. It was crucial that the communication routes between Spain and the Netherlands were kept open, and Philip was concerned that French control of Scotland and/or England would threaten this. He took his title of Most Catholic King seriously, but in 1558 preferred a heretic on the English throne to a French puppet. He half-heartedly proposed to Elizabeth in 1558 and persuaded the Pope to withhold her excommunication.

After half a century of fighting, mainly in Italy, Spain and France signed the Treaty of Cateau-Cambresis in 1559. Now that peace with France was possible, Philip had no wish to be dragged into a war against France to defend England, Spain's traditional ally, and he would have watched Elizabeth's activities in Scotland with unease.

England had traditionally relied on the jealousy between France and Spain to help it to maintain its independence. Peace between the two powerful countries upset the subtle balance of power. If France and Spain were to unite in a common cause against England, to uphold the Catholic religion for example, there was little doubt that England would lose its independence.

France

France was England's traditional enemy, because of its size – its population was four times greater than England's – its proximity, its alliance with Scotland and the claims of Kings of England to the French throne. France was Roman Catholic and supported the claims of Mary Stuart to the English throne because of her French blood and her marriage to the dauphin. The French monarchy had been alarmed at Spanish 'control' of England as a result of Philip II's marriage to Mary Tudor, because it threatened French communication with Scotland and increased French fears of Spanish encirclement.

In 1559, England also signed the Treaty of Cateau-Cambresis, which confirmed the loss of Calais. This small French port was captured by the English in 1347 and took on a symbolic significance as England's last surviving overseas possession from the time of the Hundred Years War. It became important for both trade and strategic reasons and was garrisoned by a small English force. It was captured by the French in 1558 when England, under Mary Tudor, intervened in France in support of Spain. With Calais in its possession, France dominated the southern shore of the Channel.

In 1559, King Henry II died in a jousting tournament and was succeeded by Mary Stuart's husband, Francis II. The new king was a puppet in the hands of Mary's uncles, the Guise brothers, who aimed to restore the control of their sister, Mary of Guise, in Scotland and advance Mary Stuart's claim to the English throne.

Scotland

In 1558 Scotland was ruled by Mary of Guise on behalf of her young daughter, Mary Stuart. In 1559, Scottish Protestants rebelled against Mary of Guise. The rebels' success was welcomed in England (despite Elizabeth's vehement dislike of those who upturned the natural order of things) because France had had access to England along the Scottish border. However, Mary of Guise seemed likely to overcome the rebels and reinforcements were sent from France.

ACTIVITY

I Copy and complete the following table to evaluate the advantages and disadvantages of the options open to Elizabeth to solve the problems she faced in 1558.

Problem	Possible solutions	Advantages/ disadvantages
The loss of Calais	• Continue the war with France • Make peace with France, and accept the loss of Calais	
Philip II's marriage proposal	• Accept • Decline	
French influence in Scotland	• Aid the Protestant rebels • Declare war against France • Recognise Mary Stuart's claim to the English throne	
England's lack of resources	• Ensure an alliance with at least one major European power • Provoke hostility between France and Spain to keep them at war • Aid the rebellions against French and Spanish rule to keep France and Spain occupied • Build up England's resources, develop new trade routes, etc.	

2 It is 1558. Draw up a memorandum, from the Privy Council to Elizabeth, outlining the foreign policies you think she should pursue.

B What were the main features of foreign policy, 1560–72?

Intervention in Scotland

In 1559 a group of Protestant lords in Scotland deposed Mary of Guise. This move was welcomed by the English government, which was pleased to see a foreign and hostile neighbour become more friendly, but it was unlikely that the French would allow the situation to remain unchallenged. Cecil, who was anxious to reduce French influence in Scotland, had to work hard to persuade a reluctant Elizabeth that she needed to aid the rebels to prevent the restoration of French power. Elizabeth finally agreed to send financial aid and then naval and military forces to the Scots, but only after Cecil had threatened to resign. This aid was confirmed by the Treaty of Berwick which was signed in 1560.

Cecil's motives arose partly from the fear of Catholicism and French links with Scotland but were also consistent with the traditional Tudor priority of securing England's borders. Whether this was purely defensive, to prevent a Catholic crusade from either Scotland or Ireland, or aggressive, in that it would leave England free to intervene in Europe, is still open to interpretation. This has been called the 'British strategy'. Cecil's policy towards Scotland was a huge success. In the Treaty of Edinburgh, signed in 1560, the French agreed to withdraw from Scotland leaving only a token force, and a new Protestant government was established under Lord James Stuart, the illegitimate half-brother of Mary, Queen of Scots.

Results

1 The Scottish problem had been resolved without war against France.
2 Elizabeth was now seen as the protectress of Protestant rebels. This new religious role would make friendly relations with France and Spain difficult to maintain.
3 Mary, Queen of Scots, religion, and the succession ensured that foreign policy became increasingly intertwined with domestic policy.
4 The success of intervention in Scotland was attributed to Cecil.

Intervention in France

In March 1562, religious civil war broke out in France, reducing the immediate threat from France. The French Wars of Religion were caused by the spread of Calvinism and by powerful feudal nobles with vast territorial influence who had no powerful monarch to keep them in check after the death of Henry II. The wars, which lasted intermittently from 1562 to 1593, were caused by the culmination of religious issues and political ambitions. The leading noble families, the Guise and the Bourbon, were divided over religion, while Catherine de Medici struggled to preserve the monarchy for her young sons.

Mary of Guise, painted by Corneille de Lyon

Mary of Guise, 1515–60

- The Guise family were the greatest Catholic noble family in France.
- Mary was sister to Duke Francis and the Cardinal of Lorraine.
- She married James V of Scotland in 1538 and gave birth to a daughter, Mary, in 1542.
- James died in 1542, after hearing of the Scottish army's defeat by the English at the Battle of Solway Moss.
- From 1554 Mary ruled Scotland as regent on behalf of her daughter.

Elizabeth came under pressure from Dudley and Throckmorton to send help to the Huguenots, who were doing badly, because a united France, under Guise control, would not be in England's interests. This time Elizabeth needed no persuading.

SOURCE 22.6 S. Doran, *England and Europe 1485–1603*, 1986, pp. 58–59

The possible recovery of Calais attracted her to the Huguenot cause at least as much as the fear of a Guise victory. For her councillors the issues were different; Cecil was most concerned with the security angle; Robert Dudley, the Queen's influential favourite, supported an interventionist policy to forward his own political ambitions. But although their priorities might have differed, the Queen and council were agreed on a policy of military aid to the Huguenots. By the Treaty of Hampton Court (September 1562) Elizabeth promised loans and troops to the Huguenots.

However, the war went badly for the English. The Huguenots were defeated in 1562 and, disappointed with the level of English support, made peace with the Catholics and joined with them to drive the English out of France at Le Havre in 1563. In the Treaty of Troyes, signed in 1564, French control of Calais was confirmed.

Results

1 Philip II complained that Elizabeth was supporting Protestant rebels.
2 Elizabeth had shown the French that she could make their life difficult, making them more likely to accept the new, Protestant regime in Scotland.
3 Elizabeth herself considered the military intervention a disaster, and returned to her policy of caution and reluctance to aid Protestant rebels.

Intervention in the Netherlands

While the deterioration of England's relationship with France in the 1560s was characterised by obvious events, such as military intervention, the decline in England's traditional alliance with Spain was harder to detect. With hindsight it is possible to identify a breakdown in communication caused by Philip II's move from the Netherlands to Madrid in 1558, a succession of weak administrators ruling the Netherlands on his behalf, and inept Spanish ambassadors being sent to England.

The key factor in England's relationship with the Netherlands was, however, trade. At least three-quarters of all England's overseas trade passed through Antwerp before being sold throughout the Low Countries, and well over three-quarters of that export trade was based on woollen cloth. Antwerp businessmen had been upset by the new Book of Rates introduced by Mary Tudor, in which duties on imports were increased by 75 per cent, and by incidents of piracy in the Channel, where privateers preyed on Flemish and Spanish shipping and disrupted trade. Philip's chief minister in the Netherlands, Cardinal Granvelle, saw Elizabeth sponsoring Protestant rebels and believed that English traders were trying to spread Protestantism in the Netherlands with her backing. In 1563, using an outbreak of plague in London as an excuse, Granvelle banned the import of all English cloth. When Elizabeth retaliated and stopped all imports from the Netherlands, trade between the two countries ceased. The economic suffering caused to both sides led to the resumption of trade within twelve months, but problems in the Netherlands were only just beginning.

An outbreak of Calvinist riots in towns in the Netherlands led to a brief period of religious toleration, but in 1567 Philip II announced his determination to crush heresy throughout the Netherlands and sent a vast Spanish army, under the Duke of Alva, to do just this. Alva's arrival led many Protestant refugees to seek exile in England, despite Elizabeth's public condemnation of the rebels. These events affected Elizabeth's view of Philip II and his intentions towards England.

SOURCE 22.7 The Duke of Alva: in this engraving he is shown trampling on his enemies

John Hawkins

- **1561–62** Navigator and slave trader
- **1564–68** Second and third slaving expeditions to the New World, culminating in the disaster at San Juan de Ulua
- **1578** Appointed Treasurer and Comptroller of the navy; set about reforming the design of English ships
- **1588** Commander of the navy during the Armada campaign
- **1595** Died at sea during Drake's expedition to the West Indies

Results

1 The danger of relying exclusively on trade in one item, to one market, was brought home vividly, and Elizabeth and her government continued to search vigorously for new markets. Trading links with the Baltic and Russia were established, and measures were set in hand which eventually led to a move from Antwerp to Emden, Hamburg, Stade and Middelburg for the Merchant Adventurers who held the monopoly over the export of English cloth.

2 Trade with Antwerp had always been one of the main reasons why England needed to maintain friendly relations with the rulers of the Netherlands. Changes in trading patterns were to have a major impact on English foreign policy in general, and England's relationship with Spain in particular.

Intervention in the New World

In 1550 Spain had conquered Mexico, Peru, Chile and the Caribbean. No alien could trade without a licence in these countries and all goods had to be registered in Seville. Although the English had participated in voyages of discovery – such as the attempts by Sir Humphrey Gilbert and Martin Frobisher to find the North-West Passage – these ventures formed only a small part of English maritime enterprise, the bulk of which was piratical or based on illegal trade with the Spanish Empire.

Silver was carried from South America to Spain in two fleets, the Flotilla which sailed from Mexico and the Galleones which sailed from Peru, both of which attracted pirates. In 1562, John Hawkins sailed to West Africa where he bought slaves which he sold to colonists in the New World. He repeated this venture in 1564, financed by Cecil, Leicester and Elizabeth, each of whom received a return of 60 per cent on their investment. This voyage, however, ended all hopes of peaceful trade with the Spanish Empire. Spain began to strengthen her defences and, in 1568, attacked Hawkins' fleet at San Juan de Ulua in the Gulf of Mexico. Hawkins returned to England with only fifteen men and open hostility broke out between the two countries.

SOURCE 22.8 Spanish territories in the New World and the principal Spanish trade routes

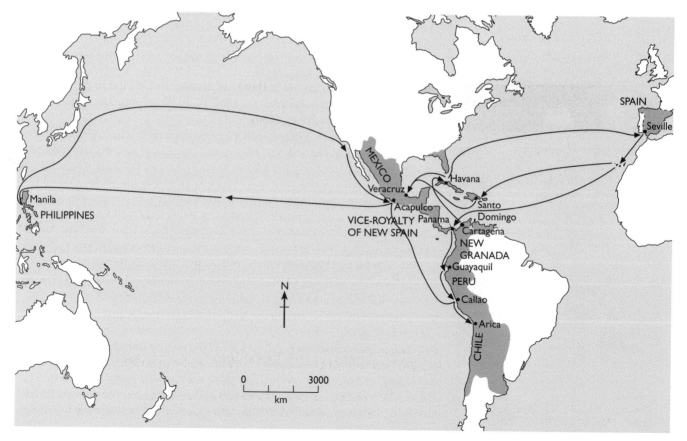

Francis Drake

- **1566–67** He accompanied his cousin, John Hawkins, on slaving expeditions to the New World.
- **1571 and 1572** He led expeditions to cut off Philip II's supply of gold and silver from Mexico and Peru. He captured the town of Nombre de Dios.
- **1577–80** He circumnavigated the globe, plundering Spanish colonies, capturing the *Cacafuego* and taking possession of California on the way.
- **1581** He was knighted on board the *Golden Hind*.
- **1585** He sailed as the Queen's Admiral to attack the Spanish West Indies.
- **1587** He 'singed the King of Spain's beard' by destroying 24 Spanish ships off the coast of Cadiz. The capture of the *San Felipe* more than paid for the expedition.
- **1588** He sailed against the Armada.
- **1589** He was court-martialled for disobeying orders after a Portuguese expedition, but was acquitted.
- **1589–95** He retired to Buckfast Abbey.
- **1595** He came out of retirement to sail with Hawkins on an expedition to defeat the Spanish.
- **1596** He died of dysentery at Porto Bello after the expedition failed.

SOURCE 22.9 The *Golden Hind*, a good example of the fast and manoeuvrable ships favoured by Hawkins

Results

1 The beginnings of the conflict with Spain is popularly seen solely in terms of English piracy, as an oceanic and colonial conflict starting in 1568. However, 'the Anglo-Spanish quarrel arose over the Netherlands, not over the West Indies. It had its origins not in Hawkins' disaster in 1568 but in the Duke of Alva's arrival at Brussels in August 1567' (R. B. Wernham, *The Making of Elizabethan Foreign Policy*, 1980).

2 John Hawkins retired from the sea after San Juan de Ulua, leaving the role of leading English seafarer to Francis Drake. His experiences in the Caribbean, however, led to his appointment as adviser to the naval board, where his insistence on the need for fast and manoeuvrable fighting ships resulted in the construction of a formidable naval force.

3 While John Hawkins built up the navy, the country's defences in general were reorganised. Thomas Gresham co-ordinated the local militia, ensuring that general musters were held. The government continued to search for ways of financing these measures, including asking for parliamentary subsidies, restoring the value of the currency after the debasements of previous reigns and attempting to stimulate industrial development.

ACTIVITY

Elizabeth had to make major foreign policy decisions as soon as she became Queen. Look again at the six events listed in Question 1 of the Focus route on page 218 and discuss in a group the lessons Elizabeth might have drawn from each event.

C Why were 1568–72 years of crisis?

FOCUS ROUTE

1 Compile a detailed timeline of events from 1568 to 1572.
2 Make detailed notes to answer the following questions.
   a) Why did Elizabeth fear the presence of Alva's army in the Netherlands?
   b) Why was Elizabeth unwilling to aid the Protestant rebels in the Netherlands?
   c) What were the dangers of an English alliance with the French?
   d) How important were events at sea for the decline in relations between England and Spain?
   e) Were the events of 1568–72 bound to lead to armed conflict between England and Spain?

■ 22A Flashpoints, 1568–72

Victory for Alva's army in the Netherlands

The presence of the Duke of Alva's army in the Netherlands, sent by Philip II to suppress the Protestant revolt, threatened English security. The deep-water harbours on the Dutch coast and the prevailing easterly winds made England an easy target for a Spanish invasion force.

By 1568, Alva had defeated the Dutch rebels, led by William, Prince of Orange. Elizabeth did not have the means to challenge Alva directly and was reluctant to send aid to the Protestant rebels. She therefore embarked on a policy of harassment. This primarily took the form of encouraging seamen, such as Francis Drake, to make life difficult for the Spanish in the New World.

Treachery at San Juan de Ulua

Hawkins' slaving voyages of 1562, 1564 and 1567 were an attempt to break the Spanish trading monopoly in the Americas. The ventures were backed by courtiers who hoped to make a handsome profit from their investments. It also seems likely that the crown had a separate reason for encouraging such expeditions. The devastating attack on Hawkins at San Juan de Ulua in 1568 increased the tension between England and Spain.

Cecil grabs Spanish bullion

In November 1568 Spanish bullion ships on their way to the Netherlands to pay the Spanish army, took refuge from pirates in English ports. The bullion was a loan provided by Genoese bankers, and Cecil may have convinced Elizabeth that the money was still technically the property of the bankers. It seems possible – although this is an area of considerable controversy – that the Queen decided to take over the loan herself to make life as difficult as possible for Alva in the Netherlands, and perhaps also in revenge for San Juan de Ulua. However, Spain's response was far more severe than anticipated and Cecil came under intense criticism for the resulting deterioration in the relationship between the two countries.

Trade embargo

The Spanish government's reaction to the confiscation of their Genoese loan was rapid and dramatic. Alva seized all English ships and property in the Netherlands, while Philip did the same in Spain. As a result a total embargo on all trade between England and Spain developed.

Growing hostilities: Spain backs Ridolfi

Between 1568 and 1572 Elizabeth and Philip looked for ways to cause each other trouble, although neither wanted full-scale conflict.

Philip authorised Alva to send financial aid to Catholics in the north of England, although he changed his mind before it got through despite the publication of the Papal Bull excommunicating Elizabeth issued in 1570. The Spanish also supported the 1571 Ridolfi Plot.

Elizabeth did nothing to prevent English seamen attacking Spanish ships and began to pursue a marriage alliance with the French Duke of Anjou. In 1572 she signed the Treaty of Blois with France, in which France and England promised to aid the other if asked.

The expulsion of the Sea Beggars

By the end of 1572 Philip and Elizabeth had agreed to settle their differences. Trade was restored in the Convention of Nymegen in 1573, and Elizabeth withdrew her support for English pirates in the Caribbean as a result of the 1574 Treaty of Bristol.

Hopes of reconciliation were, however, dashed by events in the Netherlands. In 1572 Elizabeth expelled the Dutch Sea Beggars. The Dutch Protestant privateers had been sheltering in English ports. They considered themselves at war with Philip II and had been attacking Spanish shipping in the Channel. On their return to the Netherlands they captured the port of Brill, and the Revolt of the Netherlands began.

For the next three years English public opinion and leading members of the council, particularly Leicester and Walsingham, called for Elizabeth to send help to the Dutch rebels to prevent the expected Spanish military conquest and centralisation of the Netherlands. Elizabeth continually refused to give aid officially, so as not to antagonise Spain. She did not share the enthusiasm of her subjects when the French government, under the influence of the Huguenot leader Coligny, sent an army to the southern Netherlands to support the rebels. She did, however, send a volunteer force under Sir Humphrey Gilbert to prevent Flushing from falling into French hands; but was careful to maintain good relations with the French court even after the Massacre of St Bartholomew.

In the event, Alva crushed the revolt easily.

D # What were the priorities of English foreign policy, 1560–72?

223

WHAT WERE ELIZABETH'S FOREIGN POLICY PRIORITIES, 1560–72?

TALKING POINT

Did Elizabeth have a consistent, long-term policy between 1560 and 1572 or was she reacting daily to events in Europe? Did Elizabeth really have a foreign policy at all?

FOCUS ROUTE

Make detailed notes to answer the following.

1 Using Sources 22.10–22.17, show how far contemporaries and historians agree on the aims of English foreign policy between 1560 and 1572.
2 Why was Elizabeth not keen to pursue her foreign policy aims aggressively?
3 Did Elizabeth achieve her foreign policy aims between 1560 and 1572?

SOURCE 22.10 Cecil on French intervention in the Netherlands, 1572

If ... the French begin to possess any part of ... the maritime ports, then it is like that the French ... may be too potent neighbours for us and therefore [it] may be good for us to use all the means ... to stay that course. ...

... necessary for England that the State of the Low Countries should continue in their ancient government, without either subduing it to the Spanish nation or joining it to the Crown of France ...

Let them of the Low Countries pass home to the liberty of the country; and I think it were done rather by themselves than others [the French] that percase would not suffer them long to enjoy their liberty when it should be recovered.

SOURCE 22.11 Walsingham on the Massacre of St Bartholomew, 1572

I think [it] less peril to live with them [the French] as enemies than as friends.

SOURCE 22.12 R. B. Wernham, *The Making of Elizabethan Foreign Policy*, 1980, p. 41

But neither Elizabeth nor Cecil was willing to see French aggrandisement in the Netherlands, French power spreading eastward of Calais and the straits of Dover. Nor did they trust the constancy of French policy – very sensibly, as the event turned out. So they adopted instead the policy of trying to check and control the French by co-operating with them in various more limited ways.

SOURCE 22.13 R. B. Wernham, *The Making of Elizabethan Foreign Policy*, 1980, p. 41

She wanted to retain Spain as a counterpoise to France. She wanted the Netherlands, though restored to their ancient liberties, to remain Spanish so that they would not become French.

SOURCE 22.14 R. Sloan in J. Lotherington (ed.), *The Tudor Years*, 1994, p. 313

Elizabeth knew that friendship with France would force Philip to compete for her favour. Also, as Cecil especially was aware, it might help to restrain French ambition in the Netherlands. Finally, it would stave off the possibility that the two great Catholic powers would unite against a heretical England.

SOURCE 22.15 R. Sloan in J. Lotherington (ed.), *The Tudor Years*, 1994, p. 317

Demonstrating great strength of will, she withstood all the pressure for a full and open intervention in the Protestant cause. She disliked the uncertainties of war and feared a lessening of her authority among those who would consider a female monarch unequal to the task of fighting one ... she had to consider too the financial cost of a major campaign on the continent. To pay and equip an expeditionary army would entail massive expense.

SOURCE 22.16 R. Sloan in J. Lotherington (ed.), *The Tudor Years*, 1994, p. 318

The fact that the outright defeat of Spain was not sought inevitably made Elizabeth's intervention more limited and defensive than it might have been.

SOURCE 22.17 J. Guy, *Tudor England*, 1988, p. 281

So the six principles of English diplomacy from the Massacre of St Bartholomew until 1585 were gradually formulated: **1** *England would not directly intervene in the Netherlands;* **2** *volunteers might assist the Dutch upon conditions;* **3** *a defensive Anglo-French entente would be deployed against Spain;* **4** *France would be encouraged to support the Dutch revolt, but a French conquest of the Netherlands must at all costs be prevented;* **5** *Spain should be persuaded to return the Netherlands to the semi-autonomous position they had enjoyed under Charles V; and* **6** *the entente should be couched so as to exclude French influence permanently from Scotland.*

ACTIVITY

To check that you understand the main features of Elizabethan foreign policy between 1560 and 1572, select the correct reason from the two alternatives. See page 300 for the answers.

1. a) Elizabeth was sympathetic towards the plight of Protestants in Europe, but she did not share the Calvinism of some of her councillors.
   b) Elizabeth was not very religious and therefore felt no sympathy for the Protestant rebels in the Netherlands and in France.
2. a) Elizabeth realised early on in her reign that she would eventually have to face a Catholic crusade, but she delayed the inevitable for as long as possible.
   b) Elizabeth did not feel the need to act aggressively to prevent a Catholic crusade. She believed that France and Spain would not unite against her because of their traditional rivalry.
3. a) Elizabeth did not trust foreigners because of her experiences in France in 1563.
   b) Elizabeth had an instinctive loathing of rebellion, and the experience she gained from helping the Huguenots in 1562 led her to believe rebels were not dependable.
4. a) Elizabeth had to consider the financial cost of a major campaign on the continent. Equipping an expeditionary army might well necessitate heavy taxation.
   b) Elizabeth wanted any war she became involved in to be fought on her terms, and at sea since the English navy was the best in Europe.
5. a) Elizabeth's natural inclination was to be cautious, and she was perhaps more so when faced with the prospect of leading her country to war.
   b) As a woman, Elizabeth did not grasp the strategic advantages of giving aid directly to the rebels in the Netherlands.
6. a) Elizabeth did not have any aims with regard to the Netherlands, other than the long-term aim of eventually defeating Spain.
   b) Elizabeth did not want to end Spanish sovereignty over the Netherlands because it prevented French control of the entire southern coast of the Channel. She also respected Spain's legitimate claim to the territory.
7. a) Elizabeth hated the idea of war, and was made more indecisive than usual by the fear that her own life could be in danger from religious extremists.
   b) Elizabeth believed that England's national interest would not be best served by entering a religious war.

ACTIVITY

Prepare a report reviewing the first fourteen years of Elizabeth's foreign policy, in which you highlight her successes and failures and draw up targets for her to follow in the future.

The report could be developed into a role play, with Elizabeth justifying her actions in the face of your praise and criticism.

E Review: What were Elizabeth's foreign policy priorities, 1560–72?

Elizabeth's foreign policy priorities in the period 1560–72 do not seem significantly different from those of her predecessors: she needed to preserve the Antwerp cloth trade, maintain a secure northern frontier and protect her Channel coastline. Where Elizabeth differed from her predecessors, however, was her lack of interest in matters dynastic. She realised that Calais was lost for good and that England must give up its claim to the French throne, and she refused to link national security with a dynastic policy through a marriage into a European royal family. There is little evidence that religion was a driving force behind Elizabeth's foreign policy, although it was clearly an issue for many of her councillors. Her refusal to intervene directly and send an army to help the Dutch rebels angered some members of her council and has led to criticism from historians.

According to Wernham, during the first fourteen years of her reign, Elizabeth and Cecil, although they disagreed about method, worked to re-establish England's independence from France and Spain so that, by 1572, both countries were keen to maintain England's friendship. Although this was mainly done by capitalising on France and Spain's internal problems, England had held its own and succeeded in eliminating the threat from Scotland and the likelihood of a war on two fronts by 1572. However, there was a price to be paid for this independence: a decline in England's traditional alliance with Spain. Although a lot of differences had been patched up by 1573, many Englishmen were beginning to believe that some sort of religious conflict was inevitable.

SOURCE 22.18 C. Haigh, *Elizabeth I*, 1988, p. 78

The Protestant leaders on the Council – Leicester, Walsingham, Knollys, Mildmay, and, more cautiously, Burghley – shared a common view of foreign policy. They believed that France and Spain had conspired with the Pope to extirpate Protestantism, and every move they made was seen as a step in their grand design. To Walsingham, the Catholic states were implacable enemies, and there was no point in seeking agreement with them.

SOURCE 22.19 R. B. Wernham, *The Making of Elizabethan Foreign Policy*, 1980, pp. 45–46

They tended to be obsessed with the spectre of a great international Papal–Spanish conspiracy, with its 'fifth column' among the English Catholics. This was the driving force behind many of the volunteers who trooped across to fight under William the Silent in the Netherlands . . . the sooner and more vigorously the Roman Catholic menace was opposed . . . the less likelihood there would be of having to fight it on English soil. Elizabeth did not share, or at most only occasionally half shared, these fears and these sentiments.

Elizabeth's foreign policy in the first part of her reign sprang largely from her domestic situation. She needed time, and a period of peace, to establish the new Elizabethan Church, and she had neither the resources nor the inclination to become involved in religious squabbles. The traditional English policy of playing France and Spain off against each other was not as possible after they had made peace in 1559. Faced with Spain, which was about to send an army to the Netherlands to restore its authority over the province, and France, which was occupied with religious wars within its borders, Elizabeth increasingly saw Spain as the greater threat to national security. She therefore allied herself with France and endeavoured to keep Spain occupied, because she feared that once Spain had subdued the Netherlands the Spanish army would invade England and attempt to restore Catholicism. Unfortunately, the strategies which Elizabeth used to distract Spain – attacking Spanish shipping in the New World and seizing Spanish bullion – caused Philip II to start seeing Elizabeth not as a minor irritant but as an implacable enemy. At this stage in 1572, however, perhaps alarmed by the escalation of events, both Elizabeth and Philip pulled back from the brink of war and tried to repair the damage done to their relationship.

ACTIVITY

1 Prioritise the following events in the order of their importance in the deterioration of the traditional alliance between Spain and England, and explain the significance of each.

- Elizabeth aided Protestant rebels in Scotland in 1560 and in France in 1562.
- Elizabeth stopped all imports from the Netherlands in 1563.
- The Merchant Adventurers moved from Antwerp to Emden, Hamburg, Stade and Middelburg in 1567.
- Elizabeth allowed the Sea Beggars to shelter in England in 1567, which they used as a base for attacking Spanish ships in the Channel.
- John Hawkins sailed to the New World with Elizabeth's backing in 1562, 1564 and 1567.
- Elizabeth seized bullion from Spanish ships sheltering in English ports in 1568.
- Elizabeth undertook marriage negotiations with the Duke of Anjou between 1570 and 1571 and signed the Treaty of Blois in 1572.
- Elizabeth expelled the Sea Beggars in 1572.
- Elizabeth allowed a volunteer force to go to the Netherlands in 1572 to stop the French Huguenot army from capturing Flushing.
- Elizabeth maintained good relations with France even after the Massacre of St Bartholomew of 1572.

2 These events do not look like the cautious actions of an indecisive woman.
   a) Why was Elizabeth prepared to antagonise Spain?
   b) What was happening at home between 1558 and 1572?
   c) Why did Elizabeth cause all this antagonism and yet not send direct military help to the Dutch rebels?

TALKING POINT

Elizabeth's decision to expel the Sea Beggars in 1572 has generated considerable debate amongst historians. Some believe she did it deliberately to cause trouble for Spain because it was clear that the Sea Beggars' return to the Netherlands would inflame the situation there. Others argue that Elizabeth had had enough of the Sea Beggars' unruly behaviour and wanted to make a friendly gesture to Spain. The evidence is too slight for us to know what Elizabeth's intentions really were. Does this mean that such speculation is pointless or are such controversies the very essence of history?

KEY POINTS FROM CHAPTER 22: What were Elizabeth's foreign policy priorities, 1560–72?

1 From 1560 English support helped the Protestants in Scotland drive out the French, confirmed by the Treaty of Edinburgh, but a similar attempt to aid French Protestants failed.

2 In the 1560s, English foreign policy centred on the Netherlands where a Protestant rebellion had led to the arrival of a large Spanish army. A trade embargo between the Netherlands and England was imposed.

3 Relations with Spain deteriorated as English privateers raided the Caribbean and a row flared up over the forced unloading of Spanish bullion in English ports in 1568.

4 England moved to improve relations with France: marriage negotiations began between Elizabeth and the Duke of Anjou in 1570, and the Treaty of Blois was signed in 1572.

5 Elizabeth resolved England's economic differences with Spain and expelled the Sea Beggars from English ports in 1572.

6 The outbreak of the Revolt of the Netherlands in 1572 increased the pressure on Elizabeth to send an army to aid the Protestant rebels.

7 England's alliance with France was strained by the Massacre of St Bartholomew in 1572.

23

What were the aims of English foreign policy, 1572–84?

CHAPTER OVERVIEW

Foreign policy between 1572 and 1584 usually appears as a postscript to the clash between England and Spain 1568–72, or as a prelude to the events of 1585 onwards which led to full-scale war. The result is the same from both viewpoints. These years are seen as part of the general decline in relations between England and Spain, which gives the impression that war was inevitable. By isolating these years, this chapter will examine the view that war was neither inevitable nor even desired by Philip and Elizabeth; that these years, far from being overshadowed by what was to come, were 'a period of what today would be called détente ... the high-water mark of Elizabeth's reign ... the real "spacious days of great Elizabeth"' (R. B. Wernham, *The Making of Elizabethan Foreign Policy*, 1980, p. 44).

The period 1572–84 was characterised by considerable diplomatic activity, both Elizabeth and Philip making great efforts to underplay the differences between their two countries, including the religious differences. Elizabeth tried to control English piracy and Philip expelled English Catholics from their seminary at Douai in Flanders. The ultimate reason for the failure of this détente lay in the Netherlands, where even as early as 1578 Elizabeth's foreign policy was breaking down. This has led other historians to see this period in quite a different light from Wernham.

SOURCE 23.1 S. Doran, *England and Europe 1485–1603*, 1986, p. 67

It is difficult to understand how Professor Wernham could include this period of her foreign policy in a chapter entitled 'High-water mark'.

Elizabeth's aims towards the Netherlands from 1572 to 1584 were consistent. She wanted the Netherlands to be granted their traditional liberties, but for the country to remain under loose Spanish control. She wanted the Spanish army and the Inquisition withdrawn from the Netherlands so that Philip II's subjects could exercise liberty of conscience (though not liberty of worship). French control of the Netherlands was unthinkable since it would grant France control of the southern Channel coastline. For the next ten years, Elizabeth therefore used diplomacy to encourage Philip to restore the Netherlands to a semi-independent status, while keeping a close eye on France and avoiding heavy expenditure. Her refusal to send direct support to the Protestant rebels in the Netherlands enraged some of her councillors who saw her as stubborn and prevaricating.

This cautious approach has come under attack from historians, such as Professor Wilson (1970), who argue that the situation in the Netherlands in the late 1570s was such that support from an English army would have enabled William, Prince of Orange, to unite the Dutch states and create a united Netherlands. They believe that Elizabeth misjudged the military situation and missed her opportunity. However, this presupposes Elizabeth was aiming for a Calvinist victory. In fact, she was more interested in maintaining Spanish sovereignty over the Netherlands in order to prevent possible French expansion. She also had reason to fear further trade embargoes with Spain, because the Merchant Adventurers were still not fully established in Hamburg. Above all, she refused to go to war with the mightiest European power until England's security was directly threatened. England's lack of resources and the crippling expense of war meant that Elizabeth looked for alternatives for as long as possible. Therefore, despite the protests of her councillors, 'Elizabeth remained unmoved. Her policy – if the defensive expediency of 1572–85 can be dignified with that term – attempted to reconcile conflicting strategic, commercial, and religious interests at minimum cost' (J. Guy, *Tudor England*, 1988, p. 283).

This chapter focuses on events in the Netherlands, Elizabeth's responses and her aims to explain why conflict with Spain was ultimately impossible to avoid and why it originated in the Netherlands.

A What happened between 1572 and 1584? (pp. 229–30)

B Should England intervene in the Netherlands? (p. 231)

C Review: What were the aims of English foreign policy, 1572–84? (p. 232)

SOURCE 23.2 Elizabeth to Philip II, 1575

If some speedy remedy be not taken, those countries will be at the devotion of the French King who, and his predecessor, have continually aided the Prince of Orange with money to maintain his wars and now continues the same with a monthly secret pay. As nothing can be so hurtful to the King [Philip II] and dangerous to herself as this, she earnestly desires him to divert his course now in hand by allowing his subjects to enjoy their ancient privileges and suffering them to live freely from the extremities of the Inquisition.

TALKING POINT

What can you learn from Source 23.2 about relations between England and Spain? What are the limitations of this source as evidence?

FOCUS ROUTE

1 Copy and complete the following table on events in the Netherlands between 1558 and 1584, using the information in this chapter and Chapter 22.

Date	Spanish intervention	French intervention	Indirect English intervention

2 Produce a timeline showing England's developing relationship with France, then answer the following question: To what extent was there an improvement in Anglo-French relations in the period 1558–84?

A What happened between 1572 and 1584?

FOCUS ROUTE

Make detailed notes to answer the following questions.

1 Did Elizabeth's aims towards the Netherlands change after 1572?
2 What strategies did Elizabeth use after 1572 to achieve her aims? Give examples.
3 Which of these strategies were diplomatic, and which were hostile towards Spain?
4 Why did the threat from Spain increase between 1572 and 1584 and how did this threat manifest itself?
5 To what extent was the increase in the threat from Spain a result of Elizabeth's policies?

■ 23A Events, 1572–84

1572 Religious conflict breaks out again in France. Elizabeth permits the Huguenots to use England as a base and authorises English Protestants to send munitions and a loan to the Huguenots.
Elizabeth allows Dutch refugees and English volunteers to join the Sea Beggars, then sends Sir Humphrey Gilbert and his army of volunteers to hold Flushing for the Dutch to protect it from the French army in the Netherlands.

1573 Elizabeth continues to aid the Dutch rebels unofficially, sending money and volunteers and allowing English privateers to close the Channel to Spanish ships. This policy has some success: it is indirect enough not to cause conflict with Spain but irritating enough to cause Spain to make concessions.

1574 The trade embargo between Spain and England is lifted. The two countries sign the Convention of Bristol which settles the bullion dispute, banishes English rebels from the Netherlands and allows English merchants in the Netherlands to practise their Protestant beliefs.
Spain rejects any discussion over its government of the Netherlands, although Alva is replaced by the more moderate de Requesens.

1576 The Spanish Fury – a mutiny of the Spanish army which culminates in the sack of Antwerp – unites all seventeen Dutch provinces in open rebellion against Spanish rule.
By the Pacification of Ghent, the Dutch Estates-General calls for the expulsion of all foreign troops and the restoration of their traditional liberties.
Elizabeth loans the Dutch Estates-General £100,000 and agrees to send an expeditionary force to the Netherlands. She also warns Henry III of France that if France intervenes she will use the forces against France.

1577 Don Juan of Austria arrives with a new Spanish army and begins the reconquest of the Netherlands.
Thousands of English volunteers go to the Netherlands.
Elizabeth warns Philip that he must accept the Pacification of Ghent and recall Don Juan. Philip does neither.
Elizabeth, still shying away from war with Spain, opts to finance a mercenary force under John Casimir.
Elizabeth authorises what turns out to be Francis Drake's circumnavigation of the globe, a voyage backed by financiers who have all advocated a vigorously anti-Spanish policy.

SOURCE 23.3 The Duke of Alençon, later the Duke of Anjou, painted by François Clouet

SOURCE 23.4 King James VI of Scotland, painted in 1574 by Rowland Lockey

1578 The French, Catholic, Duke of Alençon signs an alliance with the Estates-General and William, Prince of Orange, and intervenes in the Netherlands.
The problem of Scotland revives briefly when James VI becomes King and falls under the influence of an agent of the Guise family, Esmé Stuart, later the Earl of Lennox. A plot to invade England is drawn up by Stuart, but uncovered by Walsingham.

1579 The new Spanish commander, the Duke of Parma, makes considerable headway in the Netherlands.
Alençon withdraws his forces.
The southern Netherlands makes peace with Parma.
Against the wishes of her council, Elizabeth moves cautiously. She works to keep Alençon's Dutch campaigns within acceptable limits by resuming their courtship. This buys England time for Hawkins to build up the navy, but Alençon is an erratic individual and this form of control is far from ideal.
Elizabeth can still not bring herself to intervene openly against Spain.

1580 Philip II gains the kingdom of Portugal, uniting the two wealthiest oceanic empires and giving Philip a navy which comes close to matching England's in size.
Elizabeth sends Alençon £100,000 to help him to revive his campaign in the Netherlands.

1582 The Scottish Lords overthrow the Earl of Lennox and Elizabeth's agents work hard to establish a close alliance with Scotland. Elizabeth establishes an understanding with James VI of Scotland, based on their common religion and his ambition to inherit the English throne. In the Treaty of Berwick, signed in 1586, both agree to end hostilities between the two countries.

1583 Philip orders the construction of a large navy.
The Spanish ambassador, de Mendoza, involves himself in the Throckmorton Plot.
Parma reconquers most of Brabant and Flanders.
Alençon withdraws from the Netherlands. He dies twelve months later.

1584 Elizabeth expels the Spanish ambassador, de Mendoza, from England for his part in the Throckmorton Plot.
William, Prince of Orange, the leader and military genius of the Dutch rebels, is assassinated. Spanish victory in the Netherlands is virtually inevitable.
The death of the Duke of Anjou (Alençon) means the next heir to the French throne is the Protestant Henry of Navarre. To prevent a Protestant from gaining the French throne, leading French Catholics, such as the Guise, form the Catholic League and call upon Philip II for help. In the secret Treaty of Joinville Philip promises the Catholic League his protection and support.

SOURCE 23.5 The Duke of Parma

SOURCE 23.6 William, Prince of Orange

B Should England intervene in the Netherlands?

1578 Elizabeth and Leicester

English intervention would be interpreted as a hostile act by Spain.

The rebels are already doing a good job keeping Spain occupied.

If Spain is defeated, France might think about expanding into the Netherlands which would be disastrous for England.

Intervention would be very expensive.

English support would encourage all the Dutch states to rally under William, Prince of Orange.

Intervention would show England's solidarity with other Protestant countries.

France is England's ally.

The Spanish army is not making headway in the Netherlands. This is a golden opportunity to intervene and defeat them.

1584 Elizabeth and Walsingham

If the rebel cause collapses, Spain will extend its control along the entire coast and will be well placed to invade England.

The defeat of a Calvinist power would tip the scales in favour of a Catholic Europe and leave England isolated.

The death of William, Prince of Orange, leaves the rebels without an effective leader. Only England can provide a replacement.

Any intervention would strengthen Spanish support for the Catholic League.

The cost of intervention would be huge.

Spain has already restored its influence over the southern Netherlands. A rebel victory in the north would not change this. Negotiation is the only answer.

The rebels have managed for a year without a strong leader.

ACTIVITY

1 Prepare two reports to Elizabeth from her councillors. The first is to be written in 1578, the second in 1584. Both urge her to intervene in the Netherlands. You should anticipate Elizabeth's objections and offer counter arguments to them, and in the second report you should be critical of her failure to intervene in 1578.

2 Choose which of the following options you agree with most and prepare an argument to defend it. Use your argument as part of a class debate.

   a) On the whole Elizabeth's policy was unsuccessful. She missed a crucial opportunity to support William, Prince of Orange. She failed to persuade Henry III to become her ally. Alençon's campaigns were a disaster. And, in the meantime, Philip II enjoyed huge military successes in the Netherlands.

   b) In retrospect Elizabeth's policy was correct. To have openly gone to the defence of the Protestant rebels would have meant declaring war on Spain, and England was not prepared for war in the 1570s.

3 **a)** In groups, brainstorm the arguments for and against the validity of the following statement: Elizabeth did not have a definite foreign policy – between 1558 and 1584 she reacted to events outside England.

   b) If you think the statement is correct, do you think Elizabeth should be praised or criticised? Why?

C Review: What were the aims of English foreign policy, 1572–84?

Elizabeth's attitude towards events in the Netherlands attracted considerable criticism from Protestants in England and is still a cause for debate among historians. In *Queen Elizabeth and the Revolt of the Netherlands*, written in 1970, Charles Wilson criticises Elizabeth's excessive caution which he believes lost her the opportunity to exploit her advantages in the 1570s in England's long-term interests, because direct military intervention would have led to the creation of a friendly Protestant Dutch Republic. Many Englishmen felt a strong moral obligation to support their fellow Protestants against the forces of Roman Catholicism. They also felt that failure to do so would lead to the extension of Catholicism across Europe.

Elizabeth, however, remained unmoved. She continued to believe that the traditional conflict between France and Spain would always work to England's advantage, and her objectives in the Netherlands were limited. Her dislike of war, fear of unnecessary expense and distrust of rebels combined to produce a primarily defensive response to events in Europe. Even after the Treaty of Joinville was made public, Elizabeth continued to hope that the King of France would be able to contain Spanish aggression.

Yet by the 1580s the European situation had changed considerably. However minimal England's role in the Netherlands, Philip II nevertheless now saw England as the chief stumbling block preventing complete Spanish conquest. In addition, the French government had made clear that it would not intervene directly to help the rebels after the assassination of William, Prince of Orange, in a sense forcing Elizabeth's hand because without foreign support the rebels would be unable to withstand the military might of Spain. Although Elizabeth's objectives were still limited in 1585 – she did not, for instance, want to accept sovereignty over the Netherlands which had been offered to her by the Estates-General – she decided to intervene because failure to do so would in all probability result in the Spanish conquest of the Netherlands and that, her councillors were convinced, would be quickly followed by an invasion of England.

ACTIVITY

Prepare newspaper articles for the following headlines:

- 1572–84 A high-water mark for English diplomacy
- 1572–84 A weak and cautious stance drags England into war.

KEY POINTS FROM CHAPTER 23: What were the aims of English foreign policy, 1572–84?

1 Elizabeth wanted minimal Spanish control over the Netherlands. She did not want a large Spanish army there, nor did she wish for French expansion there. The presence of either force would threaten England's security.

2 The success of the Spanish army in the Netherlands led Elizabeth to embark on a courtship with the French Duke of Alençon, who was leading an army supporting the Dutch rebels, in the hope of influencing his actions.

3 The Auld Alliance between France and Scotland revived temporarily when James VI became friendly with Esmé Stuart.

4 Spain increased its military capabilities with the acquisition of Portugal, and enjoyed military successes under Parma in the Netherlands.

5 The deaths of Alençon and William, Prince of Orange, increased the demands for Elizabeth to intervene in the Netherlands to keep the Dutch rebellion alive.

24

To what extent did England's financial resources influence foreign policy?

CHAPTER OVERVIEW

To engage in warfare for any prolonged period places strain on a country's resources. Although some historians have criticised Elizabeth for not pursuing a more aggressive foreign policy, there is some justification for her hesitancy when the resources of England and Spain are compared. In addition, although Mary Tudor had begun to rebuild the economy, the job was by no means complete. Therefore, the longer the war was delayed the more time England had to build up its resources. The reigns of Henry VIII and Edward VI had shown clearly the disastrous long-term economic consequences of war, from which the country was still recovering:

- trade was disrupted
- taxation was increased
- crown lands were sold

- the coinage was debased
- the monarchy ran up massive debts.

To go to war with Spain Elizabeth needed:

- a prosperous country which she could tax – but England's trade was inextricably linked with Spain (the export of cloth to Antwerp in the Spanish Netherlands until the 1570s)
- alternative overseas markets – but all trade routes to the New World were controlled by Spain. And, although England had expanded into overseas markets not dominated by Spain, such as the Baltic, Russia, the Mediterranean, the Levant and Persia, it seemed that England's need for economic expansion was likely to hasten, not postpone, war
- a large trained army – but England didn't have a standing army and local militias were not always trained or properly equipped
- a powerful navy – but John Hawkins was only appointed to the navy board in 1578 to begin the very expensive task of building and modernising ships.

Elizabeth's foreign policy decisions need to be set in an economic context. Elizabeth and her councillors were clearly involved in a juggling act. Even after war broke out, Elizabeth was still cautious and financial considerations influenced many of her decisions for better or worse.

This chapter will therefore focus on two distinct, but linked, areas. It will look first at Elizabeth's attempts to boost the economy through the expansion of overseas trade and the impact this had on relations with Spain. It will then consider the manpower resources available to Elizabeth. This will help you to decide whether Elizabeth was simply indecisive in foreign policy – as some of her generals and admirals thought – or whether England's resources, or lack of them, prevented a more aggressive approach. This issue is relevant to any discussion on:

A What was England's trade like? (pp. 234–35)

B How did English voyages to the New World impact on Anglo-Spanish relations? (pp. 236–37)

C What were England's resources in the event of war? (pp. 238–39)

D Review: To what extent did England's financial resources influence foreign policy? (pp. 240–41)

A What was England's trade like?

FOCUS ROUTE

a) Describe how trade between England and Northern Europe developed in the years between 1559 and 1600.

b) How successful was Elizabeth in building up overseas trade during her reign?

In 1558 trade was dominated by the London–Antwerp cloth trade. The dangers of relying on a single market had already been demonstrated in the 1550s when, following the debasement of the coinage, trade with Antwerp slumped. As early as 1564, following the establishment of the trade embargo, Cecil argued for a reduction in the number of luxury imports and the diversification of the cloth market. Some attempts were made to encourage the establishment of new industries in England, such as glass making, by attracting foreign craftsmen. As clashes with Spain intensified, however, the search for new foreign trading partners accelerated.

The crown's motives were to maintain, and possibly increase, its customs revenues and support its merchant class politically and financially. New trading companies would also receive backing from Elizabeth as a private financier and she would expect to make profitable returns on her investment. The impetus for changes in trade throughout the reign therefore came from the crown and the Privy Council.

There is evidence that the government was successful in its search for new markets, especially if the number of voyages and new trading companies alone are considered. However, historians remain divided on the economic significance of these new markets.

SOURCE 24.1 England's main imports and exports before 1558

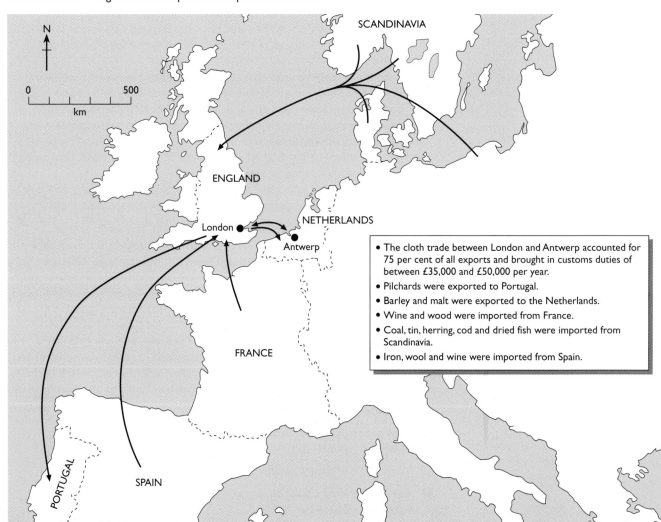

- The cloth trade between London and Antwerp accounted for 75 per cent of all exports and brought in customs duties of between £35,000 and £50,000 per year.
- Pilchards were exported to Portugal.
- Barley and malt were exported to the Netherlands.
- Wine and wood were imported from France.
- Coal, tin, herring, cod and dried fish were imported from Scandinavia.
- Iron, wool and wine were imported from Spain.

235

TO WHAT EXTENT DID ENGLAND'S FINANCIAL RESOURCES INFLUENCE FOREIGN POLICY?

SOURCE 24.3 D. M. Palliser, *The Age of Elizabeth*, 1983, p. 339

Historians used to depict the state of Elizabethan trade as buoyant and expansive, but since the 1940s the dominant view has been more sombre, stressing that the search for new markets was a desperate reaction to the stagnation of the traditional cloth trade with Germany and the Netherlands, and that the new markets accounted for only a modest share of total exports and imports.

SOURCE 24.4 Spanish ambassador to England, 1586

The whole country is without trade, and knows not how to recover it; the shipping and commerce here having mainly depended upon the communication with Spain and Portugal.

Expansion into new markets was a long-term enterprise. Many of the new trading companies would eventually thrive, while England's declining commitment to European-based trade would allow ports such as Hull, Exeter, Bristol, Newcastle and Southampton to regain some of the initiative that had been lost to London. These results, however, lay in the future. Elizabeth, like her privateers, saw the need for quick profits. Consequently she did nothing to prevent men like Drake from attacking Spain's monopoly in the New World. Although Drake vanished from the scene between 1573 and 1575, when Elizabeth was trying to restore relations with Spain, his circumnavigation of the globe in 1577 not only had royal backing but he sailed with instructions from Elizabeth, kept secret even from Cecil, to attack the Spanish empire.

Such actions – including allowing volunteers to join the Dutch rebels, financing John Casimir's mercenary force, and controlling the French army in the Netherlands via her courtship with Alençon – show Elizabeth's growing awareness that war with Spain was inevitable. Her reluctance to commit her forces until the last possible moment is understandable when England's military resources are compared with those of Spain.

SOURCE 24.2 England's trade routes by 1603

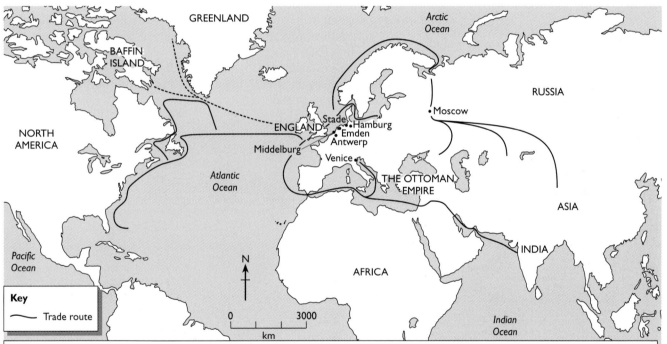

- The Merchant Adventurers transferred the cloth trade from Antwerp to Emden, Hamburg, Stade and Middelburg.

- In 1553 Willoughby and Chancellor crossed the Arctic Ocean and travelled overland to Moscow in one of the first attempts to find the North-East Passage to Asia. From 1558, overland trading expeditions under Anthony Jenkinson travelled through Russia to Asia, and the Muscovy Trading Company – heavily backed by the court – exported cloth, lead, tin, food and pewter, and imported cables, cordage, tallow, wax and furs. This trade was worth an estimated £25,000 per year.

- The Eastland Company was established in 1579 to import goods, mostly naval supplies, from the Baltic. Cloth made up 75 per cent of England's exports to the Baltic.

- From 1573 onwards, taking advantage of a dispute between Venice and the Ottoman Empire, English ships began importing luxuries such as silk, spices and oils from the Mediterranean. In 1592, the companies trading with Venice and the Ottoman Empire amalgamated to form the Levant Company, which mainly traded English cloth for raw silk, but also exported some lead and tin and imported carpets.

- The growing domestic demand for luxury goods such as sugar and spices, which generated high profits, drove men to find the North-West Passage to Asia. In 1574, Martin Frobisher reached Baffin Island and believed he had found such a passage and in 1587 John Davis explored the west coast of Greenland. These voyages produced no commercial gains, but they did provide a wealth of geographical information about the coastline of North America.

- In 1583, John Newberry and Ralph Fitch journeyed overland to India and established the East India Company. Despite the establishment of these new trade routes, 74 per cent of all imports still came from the Netherlands, the Holy Roman Empire and Spain. English maritime enterprise was more concerned with illegal trade in the New World than with legal trade in the east.

TO WHAT EXTENT DID ENGLAND'S FINANCIAL RESOURCES INFLUENCE FOREIGN POLICY?

236

B How did English voyages to the New World impact on Anglo-Spanish relations?

Copy and complete the following table to show whether England's relationship with Spain declined because of the exploits of Englishmen in the New World from 1558–84.

Date	Events in Europe	Events in the New World	Relations between England and Spain

By 1550, trade to the New World required a licence from Spain, which was rarely granted to Englishmen. The Spanish Empire was an obvious target for English privateers attracted to the two annual convoys of South American silver and to the trading opportunities with colonists who were short of many goods.

Trade with West Africa was undertaken by the Barbary Company, who traded English cloth for Moroccan sugar, and the African Company. In 1562 and 1564, John Hawkins bought slaves in Africa which he sold in America, returning to England with gold, silver and animal skins. Both these voyages were profitable. A third voyage in 1567 ended in bloodshed, when the Spanish attacked Hawkins at San Juan de Ulua in 1568.

In 1572, Drake's expedition to Panama netted £40,000 worth of Spanish silver. Drake set sail again in 1577, financed by a powerful court syndicate which included Elizabeth and Cecil.

SOURCE 24.5 Drake's circumnavigation of the globe, 1577–80

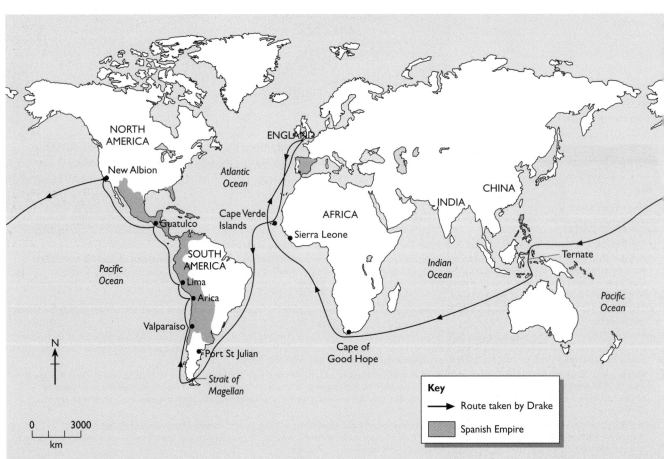

SOURCE 24.6 The *Golden Hind*, Drake's flagship, attacking the *Cacafuego*, drawn in 1603

SOURCE 24.7 Sir Walter Raleigh, from a painting by 'H' (*detail*)

During the voyage, Drake captured the *Cacafuego*, a Spanish treasure ship carrying £140,000 of treasure. In total Drake returned to England with an estimated £400,000 worth of treasure captured during attacks on the South American coast. He also signed a trade treaty with the Sultan of Ternate. These adventures elicited vigorous formal protests from Spain.

In the 1580s the colonisation of America was seen as an outlet for some of England's surplus population. Virginia in particular was thought to be an ideal place for a colony, because people believed it had an inexhaustible supply of wine, oil, sugar and flax, which might reduce England's dependence on Europe. In 1584 Walter Raleigh obtained a royal patent to establish a colony on Roanoake Island off the coast of North Carolina. The colonists did not prosper although the Virginia voyages are usually credited with introducing tobacco to England in 1586.

C What were England's resources in the event of war?

FOCUS ROUTE

Use the statistics and sources in Charts 24A and 24B to draw up your own table showing:

- England's military strengths and weaknesses in 1585
- Spain's military strengths and weaknesses in 1585
- why Elizabeth was reluctant to go to war with Spain.

■ 24A Comparison of the armed forces of England and Spain on the eve of war

	England	Spain
	• The English army was raised for a specific crisis and usually disbanded at the end of the campaigning season. • Temporary contractors, rather than a permanent structure, supplied food and clothing to the army. The supply of arms came under the control of the Ordnance Office at the Tower of London. • Lords Lieutenant had been responsible for raising local militias (whose role was primarily defensive), and maintaining a supply of arms since 1553. All able-bodied men were liable for service and there was annual training. • English armies had not fought a sustained campaign since the wars in Scotland of 1547–50. • The army assembled to meet the Armada in 1588 consisted of c. 27,000 infantry, 2500 cavalry and 14,000 sailors.	• Spain had a permanent standing army, trained in the use of firearms. It reputedly had the best infantry in the world. • Structures existed to ensure the Spanish army was properly supplied, and soldiers received medical care, marriage allowances and welfare services. • The Armada fleet of 1588 carried 8000 sailors and 19,000 soldiers. Most historians agree that its aim was to ferry Parma's army from the Netherlands to England. The army of Parma was regarded as the best equipped and trained in Europe, including crack units, and was estimated at between 20,000 and 30,000.
	• From the beginning of her reign Elizabeth maintained a small permanent fleet on the Thames and at Portsmouth. • English seamen were well trained, having been brought up in seafaring communities or worked as merchant seamen. They were not unused to smuggling or even piracy. • John Hawkins joined the permanent navy board, set up by Burghley some years earlier, in 1578. An innovative strategist, Hawkins rebuilt many of the ships, converting them to narrower, low-built galleons which were more manoeuvrable. New warships with sophisticated artillery were also developed. • By the 1580s Elizabeth had 54 men-of-war and 140 merchant ships fitted with guns.	• Only a minority of Spanish sailors had experience of the voyage to South America, which was regarded as an easier run than the voyage to northern Europe. The majority were 'fair weather' sailors whose experience was limited to the Mediterranean. The remainder had spent their lives on land and were unacquainted with the sea. • Spanish ships tended to be taller and more awkward to manoeuvre than English ships, and carried heavier artillery which had a shorter range. • Before 1580 Spain had 64 men-of-war, 24 ocean-going galleons and 130 store ships.

239

TO WHAT EXTENT DID ENGLAND'S FINANCIAL RESOURCES INFLUENCE FOREIGN POLICY?

TALKING POINT

Elizabeth's methods of funding the war led to considerable social unrest at home in the 1590s. Did she have any choice? Were there any other strategies she could have tried?

SOURCE 24.8 Giovanni Scaramelli, Venetian ambassador, 20 March 1603

The Queen's ships do not amount to more than fifteen or sixteen, as her revenue cannot support a greater charge; and so the whole of the strength and repute of the nation rests on the vast number of small privateers ... to ensure this support, the privateers make the ministers partners in the profits without the risk of a penny in the fitting out, but only a share in the prizes, which are adjudged by judges placed there by the ministers themselves.

SOURCE 24.9 G. D. Ramsay in C. Haigh (ed.), *The Reign of Elizabeth I*, 1984, p. 167

With the collapse of the Antwerp mart in 1569–73 the Queen reluctantly took up the cudgels on behalf of the rebels of the Netherlands, thereby preserving the nearby littoral of north-west Europe from complete domination by her enemies. As for the merchants, they had to risk their stock-in-trade and search out new mart towns all around the coast of the continent. In support of their solvency the Queen posed as a sincere Protestant ... She never forgot that the money she had to find to pay her soldiers or to finance her allies was derived principally from the taxes and loans supplied by the London cloth exporters, nor that the prosperity of the City of London was the mainstay of her credit and so of her authority in international affairs ... Her success is to be measured by the survival of the cloth export traffic to central Europe and by the maintenance of the Royal credit on bourses abroad, as well as by the defeat of the Armada.

Elizabeth's ordinary sources of revenue, which were annually £300,000 by the 1600s, covered her annual expenditure, and by careful economising she had also managed to build up savings. As the war with Spain accelerated she struggled to meet the financial burden, using first her savings and then extraordinary methods of fund raising such as:

- the sale of crown lands
- parliamentary taxation
- the sale of monopolies
- the use of unpaid officials
- supporting privateers in their voyages to the New World.

■ 24B The approximate cost of war

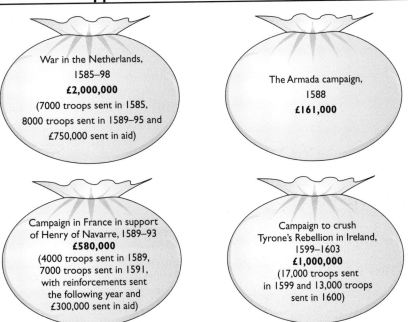

War in the Netherlands, 1585–98
£2,000,000
(7000 troops sent in 1585, 8000 troops sent in 1589–95 and £750,000 sent in aid)

The Armada campaign, 1588
£161,000

Campaign in France in support of Henry of Navarre, 1589–93
£580,000
(4000 troops sent in 1589, 7000 troops sent in 1591, with reinforcements sent the following year and £300,000 sent in aid)

Campaign to crush Tyrone's Rebellion in Ireland, 1599–1603
£1,000,000
(17,000 troops sent in 1599 and 13,000 troops sent in 1600)

SOURCE 24.10 G. R. Elton, *England under the Tudors*, 1991, p. 358

Elizabeth, it is alleged, was constitutionally incapable of conducting a war: she displayed qualities of indecision, procrastination, variability of mind, and cheeseparing parsimony which went far to ensure the failure of the various enterprises attempted. She prevented the effective use of England's resources, held up her admirals when they wished to sail, restrained them with foolishly vigorous and ill-considered instructions, and left the continental forces in the lurch when the timely despatch of reinforcements could have crowned great efforts with success. One school of commentators has concentrated on the alleged mistake of frittering away England's strength in continental expeditions, to the detriment of the war at sea where lay ... her best chance of triumph: the accusation against the Queen is that she too often neglected this side of the war, insisted on keeping the navy in home stations to protect the Channel, and wasted time on continental actions.

ACTIVITY

1. **a)** According to the Venetian ambassador in Source 24.8, what was a major consideration in the war at sea?
   b) How might this consideration have influenced decisions about strategy and the use of resources? How might this have made decisions over the deployment of forces in Europe difficult?
2. Source 24.9 suggests that, despite the transfer of the cloth market from Antwerp, Elizabeth's concern in north-west Europe was the same as the concern of her predecessors. What was this concern and why was it so important?
3. According to Source 24.10, how did Elizabeth's handling of England's resources affect her conduct in the war?

Review: To what extent did England's financial resources influence foreign policy?

It is difficult to state categorically the role England's resources played in Elizabeth's decision to pursue a cautious foreign policy, because we do not know how different her policy might have been had she possessed a large professional army and a bulging treasury. It may well be that her indecision was really based on other factors, such as a genuine dislike of war or an awareness that her control over her male advisers would be limited once war was underway. After all, similar resources had not prevented Henry VIII from attacking France in the 1540s when arguably there was less of a threat to national security.

With hindsight it is easy to point out the flaws in Elizabeth's policy. By refusing to intervene directly in the Netherlands at an early stage she missed the opportunity to establish a friendly government in the Netherlands, and instead committed England to seventeen years of warfare which was to prove a far greater drain on the country's resources. Such a view, of course, assumes that intervention in the Netherlands would have had a successful outcome, and not brought the wrath of Spain down on England. Elizabeth was never confident that England could withstand a Spanish attack and therefore saw no reason to fight before she had to.

ACTIVITY

'Elizabeth wasn't indecisive. She was right to be cautious.' Work in pairs and prepare two arguments, one for and one against this statement. Then present the argument you think is most convincing to the rest of the class.

There is no doubt that events in the Netherlands were crucial to the decline in relations between England and Spain. Few historians now believe that events in the New World would have triggered a major conflict; any problems could have been peaceably resolved had either side so wished. The Netherlands, however, was a pivotal area, vital because of its economic significance and strategic proximity, and it is possible to find the causes of the war here. The threat to national security posed by a large Spanish army across the Channel was very real, as was the desire of Elizabeth's councillors to support the international struggle between the Papacy and Calvinism. The fall of the Antwerp cloth market raised other considerations. The government's attempts to build up alternative markets elsewhere sowed the seeds for future prosperity, but did not reduce the tension with Spain. English explorers gained in confidence and expertise and quickly realised that the most lucrative area of maritime enterprise lay in the New World.

While Elizabeth delayed and worked to avoid full-scale commitment to war, she could not resist the opportunities presented by the privateers to supplement the nation's wealth. 'Privateering during the eighteen years of war brought in returns at least so great as the total value of Iberian trade before the war, and accounted for 10–15 per cent of England's total imports' (D. M. Palliser, *The Age of Elizabeth*, 1983, p. 340). In a sense Elizabeth could not lose. The privateers were not acting in an official capacity and she could easily disown them if they caused problems with the Spanish. Moreover, by delaying war for as long as possible she could use the profits generated by the privateers to strengthen England's defences. This breathing space also enabled John Hawkins to introduce a new design of ship, modify older vessels, and streamline the navy's administration.

1 One of the reasons Elizabeth did not initially endorse her councillors' plans to aid the Dutch rebels directly was her concern over England's economic and military resources.

2 Throughout Elizabeth's reign, and particularly after the Revolt of the Netherlands broke out in 1572, efforts were made to transfer the cloth market from Antwerp and establish new markets and trade routes.

3 The end of the Antwerp cloth market also added impetus to the privateering exploits of Drake and others. Drake may have been motivated in part by genuine commercial interests but there is no doubt that he was also embarking on a private war of revenge against Spain after the attack on Hawkins at San Juan de Ulua.

4 From 1573 to 1577 Elizabeth tried to curb the activities of the privateers to reduce tension with Spain. Later, still trying to avoid war with Spain, she privately backed their schemes, using the time and money to build up England's resources.

5 The activities of the privateers did not cause the war with Spain but gave Philip II another motive for attacking England.

25

How successfully did Elizabeth conduct the war against Spain after 1585?

CHAPTER OVERVIEW

Although Elizabeth's actions from 1558 to 1584 may not have been grand enough for them to be described as a 'foreign policy', she nevertheless pursued fairly clear and consistent aims. And, from Philip's point of view, there was nothing tentative about Elizabeth's actions. She had aided Protestant rebels in France and Scotland, imprisoned her Catholic successor, allowed English volunteers to help the Dutch rebels, given refuge to his enemies and encouraged raids on his empire in the New World. By 1585, Philip was stronger than ever. His army in the Netherlands was making considerable inroads against the Dutch rebels, acquisition of Portugal had added considerably to his navy and the secret Treaty of Joinville, signed in 1584 with the French Catholic League, left him free to turn against England without fearing French intervention. From 1585, although there had been no formal declaration, both Philip and Elizabeth therefore considered Spain and England at war, and Elizabeth pursued a foreign policy based on this assumption.

This chapter will examine the reasons for the length and scale of the war with Spain, and evaluate the way in which Elizabeth, her councillors, and her military advisers conducted the war. It will also examine the assessments by contemporaries and historians of Elizabeth's role and the effect of the war on England.

A Where were the main theatres of war? (pp. 243–46)

B Was Elizabeth successful? (pp. 247–50)

C Review: How successfully did Elizabeth conduct the war against Spain after 1585? (pp. 251–52)

ACTIVITY

In 1584, Elizabeth presented the Privy Council with two scenarios and asked for their advice.

If the French refused support, 'shall her Majesty take into hand to defend and protect them [the Netherlands], to recover their liberties and freedom from the tyranny and persecution of the Roman Inquisition?' But, 'If her Majesty shall not take them into her defence, then what shall she do to provide for her own surety against the King of Spain's malice and forces, which he shall offer against this realm when he hath subdued Holland and Zeeland?'

Draft the council's reply, outlining the strategies Elizabeth should adopt.

ACTIVITY

Using information from Chapters 23 and 24, prepare an eve of war statement to be delivered by Elizabeth to her people. Explain the reasons for the war, summarise England's strengths and weaknesses in relation to Spain, and outline the aims and strategies which you intend to use, and why.

243

HOW SUCCESSFULLY DID ELIZABETH CONDUCT THE WAR AGAINST SPAIN AFTER 1585?

The second of Elizabeth's scenarios suggests that she believed Philip saw England not only as a threat to his power in the Netherlands but also as an enemy to be destroyed. In fact, Philip's intentions are still a cause for debate among historians. The traditional view is that Philip wanted to secure the Channel so he could ferry an invasion force from the Netherlands to England. More recently, Susan Doran has argued that Philip's objectives were less clear, that he hoped the arrival of Parma's troops in England would either encourage English Catholics to rebel against Elizabeth or would be enough to bring about a negotiated settlement. Christopher Haigh, however, maintains that Philip instructed his commanders to drive the English army out of the Netherlands, not to conquer England.

If Elizabeth misinterpreted Philip's intentions, does that make her foreign policy incorrect?

Pull the information on pages 243–46 together into one timeline to show the events of England's war with Spain between 1585 and 1598. What were Elizabeth's main aims during this period?

■ 25A War in the Netherlands

1585	In the Treaty of Nonsuch Elizabeth agrees to send an army of over 7000 soldiers to help the rebels in the Netherlands. Leicester finally wins permission to lead the expedition, but his involvement is disastrous. Showing both arrogance and incompetence, he enrages the Queen by accepting the title of Governor-General, implying she aimed to replace Spanish sovereignty over the Netherlands. Despite financial restrictions he also wastes supplies and quarrels with his officers and the Estates-General.
1586	The English army plays a part in halting Parma's advances, preventing him from capturing Doesburg and the deep-water port of Flushing. Leicester is recalled to England.
1586–90	Harvest failures and a Dutch naval blockade cause famine in the Spanish army. After 1589 many Spanish troops are diverted to France.
1590s	The Dutch Captain-General, Maurice of Nassau, helped by a small English force of 8000 men and large amounts of English money, scores impressive military victories over Spain.
1594	The northern part of the Netherlands is secured under Dutch control while the south remains under Spain's control, acting as a buffer against French expansion.

A Where were the main theatres of war?

The Netherlands

SOURCE 25.1 Territory in the Netherlands

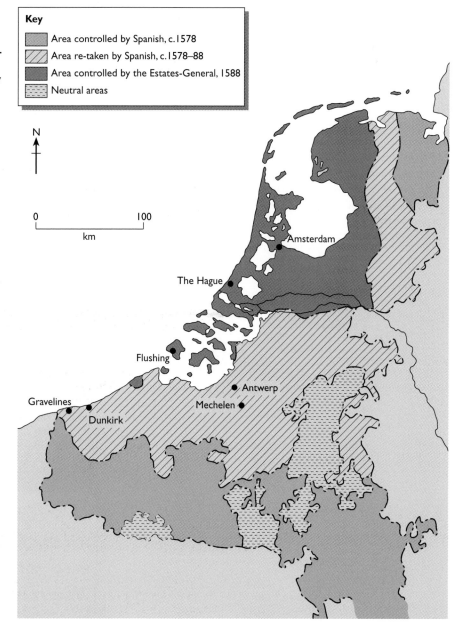

Key

- Area controlled by Spanish, c.1578
- Area re-taken by Spanish, c.1578–88
- Area controlled by the Estates-General, 1588
- Neutral areas

N

0 _____ 100
km

Amsterdam

The Hague

Flushing

Gravelines

Dunkirk

Antwerp

Mechelen

■ 25B   War in European waters

1587	Drake sails into Cadiz harbour and 'singes the King of Spain's beard', sinking 30 Spanish vessels and delaying the preparations for the Armada.
1588	130 Spanish ships carrying 17,000 men sail up the Channel to rendezvous with the Spanish army, under Parma, in the Netherlands. The Armada is met by the English navy which is only just numerically superior to the Spanish fleet, but has quicker ships and longer-range guns. The Armada sails in tight formation down the Channel and, having lost only two ships, anchors off Calais. During the night the English use fireships to scatter the Spanish fleet and defeats it next day at the Battle of Gravelines. Many Spanish ships escape northwards, but come to grief on the coasts of Scotland and Ireland. Less than half return to Spain.
1589	Drake leads a naval counter attack, but there are arguments over resources and objectives from the outset. Elizabeth wants him to destroy the remnants of the Armada. Drake wants to help Don Antonio of Portugal regain his throne from Philip II. Drake disobeys orders and, with Essex, attempts an ineffective attack on Lisbon. The expedition is a financial and psychological failure.
1596	A huge expedition is launched against Spain. Seventeen naval ships and 47 war ships, led by Essex, Charles Howard and Walter Raleigh, sack Cadiz and capture a Spanish treasure ship, costing Philip twelve million ducats.
1596–98	Subsequent Spanish Armadas are scattered by storms.

SOURCE 25.3   The route of the Armada in 1588

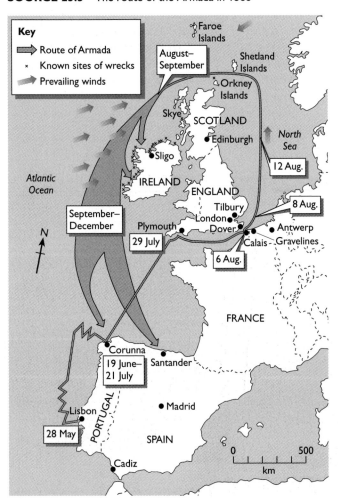

European waters

There is a tendency to overemphasise the strategic importance of England's defeat of the Spanish Armada. Its sinking was undoubtedly a heroic achievement, and a great English naval victory, but its effect was limited. Its success was not followed up and war with Spain continued for another ten years.

SOURCE 25.2   C. Haigh, *Elizabeth I*, 1988, p. 133

The defeat of the Spanish Armada in 1588 solved nothing. There was still a successful Spanish army in the Netherlands, still Spanish support for French Catholics against the Huguenots, and still a risk of Spanish invasions.

Even at the time there were criticisms. Drake and the other commanders were annoyed at their failure to capture, and therefore make profit out of, more Spanish ships and criticised Elizabeth's decision to defend the Channel rather than invade Spain.

Although English sailors continued to play an important role in the war, they were too often sidetracked by the acquisition of plunder. The navy could protect England from invasion, but it could not win the war. Ultimately events at sea were less significant than those on land. Nevertheless, the navy could prey on Spanish shipping, which helped to pay for the land war and hampered the Spanish war effort.

SOURCE 25.6   A seventeenth-century English playing card, showing Spanish ships wrecked on the shores of Scotland

ACTIVITY

1 Using Sources 25.3–25.9, explain why the Armada of 1588 failed?
2 How and why did the English government exploit the propaganda opportunities arising from the failure of the Armada?

SOURCE 25.7   F. Fernandez-Armesto, *The Spanish Armada*, 1989

Good weather . . . was essential for Spanish success. It was the least of the miracles they expected from God. They needed good weather to preserve their fragile Mediterranean shipping, calm seas to maximise the effectiveness of their galleasses, clement conditions for Parma's barges, a moderate swell to compensate for the inexperience of their gunners; and above all, an easy, speedy voyage to help keep them safe despite the lack of a northern port of refuge.

SOURCE 25.5   The Battle of Gravelines, a drawing by the Dutch artist Visscher in about 1615

SOURCE 25.9   A medal made soon after 1588 to commemorate the defeat of the Armada. The words mean 'God blew and they were scattered'

246

HOW SUCCESSFULLY DID ELIZABETH CONDUCT THE WAR AGAINST SPAIN AFTER 1585?

SOURCE 25.8 Bronze Falcon, an Elizabethan cannon, dated 1580

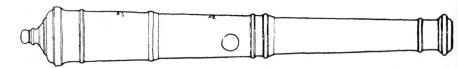

The New World
■ 25C War in the New World

1585 Drake is sent to attack Spanish shipping in the New World.

1586 Drake misses the Spanish silver fleets and although he sacks Santo Domingo and Cartagena the expedition loses £5000.

1587 After attacking Cadiz, Drake moves on to the Azores where he captures the Portuguese ship, the *San Felipe*, returning home with £140,000.

1592 The capture of the bullion ship *Madre de Dios* in the East Indies means a return of £80,000 on Elizabeth's initial outlay of £3000.

1595 A joint attack is launched by Drake and Hawkins on the West Indies treasure fleet. Hawkins dies at sea and Drake is defeated by Spain's new defensive measures in Panama. He dies of dysentery at Porto Bello.

France
■ 25D War in France

1589 Henry III is murdered and the Huguenot Henry of Navarre becomes Henry IV of France. He appeals to England for help against the Spanish-backed Catholic League, plunging France into civil war once more. Philip diverts forces from the Netherlands and Elizabeth commits herself to keeping the Spanish out of France. She sends Henry IV a loan of £20,000 and 4000 men under Willoughby.
Parma's army arrives in Paris and a second Spanish force arrives in Brittany, threatening England's Channel defences further.

1591 A force, under Sir John Norris, is sent to Brittany.

1592 Weakened by sickness and desertion, Norris' force is defeated by the Spanish at Craon.

1593 Henry IV converts to Catholicism.

1594 The Spaniards attempt to capture Brest.

Elizabeth sends an expedition of eight warships and 4000 men to push the Spanish out of France.

1598 Henry and Philip agree to a peace. England now has an ally on the French throne, who might act as a check on Spanish power in the future.

SOURCE 25.10 The Armada Portrait of Elizabeth, painted c. 1588, by George Gower

FOCUS ROUTE

Make detailed notes on the main criticisms of Elizabeth's conduct of the war.

SOURCE 25.11 Elizabeth speaking to her troops at Tilbury in 1588

I know I have the body of a weak and feeble woman, but I have the heart and stomach of a king, and of a King of England too, and think foul scorn that Parma or Spain, or any Prince of Europe, should dare to invade the borders of my realm.

Whatever arguments historians may have over the wisdom of Elizabeth's policy towards the Netherlands in the 1570s, few doubt that the decision to go to war in 1585 was correct: England could not have stood by and watched Spain extend its power throughout Europe. Yet the way in which she conducted the war has been called into question. However many stirring speeches she made to the contrary, she did not possess the aggression and daring so beloved by her male generals. Tudor propaganda worked overtime to portray Elizabeth as the heroine of her beleaguered country. But, despite her ultimate success in maintaining a war on four fronts and defeating the Spanish, Elizabeth lost the control and popularity she had enjoyed in the 1570s and England became harder to govern.

Elizabeth should have been more ambitious

SOURCE 25.12 S. Doran, *England and Europe 1485–1603*, 1986, pp. 78–79

She was only too well aware, however, of the limitations of her purse and the unpopularity of her expedients to raise necessary sums, and she cut her royal cloak accordingly. She insisted that her allies should pay their share of the cost of campaigns, and she avoided ambitious ventures. The decision to pursue a privateering war rather than to attack the Spanish navy can be seen in the same light. Dependent as she was on private enterprise for her fleets, she had to allow her captains and investors to pursue the type of warfare that would bring her profit as well as strengthen national security.

SOURCE 25.13 S. Doran, *England and Europe 1485–1603*, 1986, p. 78

Elizabeth's principal war aims against Spain, unlike those of many of her commanders and advisers, were neither the destruction of Spanish power nor the acquisition of a colonial empire. In war as in peace she sought, above all, national security. In practical terms, this meant a favourable settlement in the Netherlands, the freedom of the French Channel ports from Spanish control, and the survival of Spain and France as strong independent powers.

ACTIVITY

Read Sources 25.12 and 25.13. Why does Susan Doran argue that Elizabeth was right to follow a primarily defensive policy?

Her gender was a considerable disadvantage

SOURCE 25.14 W. MacCaffrey, *Elizabeth I*, 1993, p. 243

She was forced to take up the role of a warrior Queen who could not evade the grand responsibilities of high strategy, where and by what means to assail the enemy. In the urgencies of the campaign the movement of men or ships would not wait on her wavering hesitations ... moreover, the very nature of the decisions to be made was conditioned by naval and military expertise which Elizabeth necessarily lacked.

SOURCE 25.15 C. Haigh, *Elizabeth I*, 1988, p. 142

In council, court, and Parliament, Elizabeth could show her competence; she could beat men at their own game – if necessary by using feminine tactics. But in war she was at the mercy of her generals, who thought they knew better – and she never succeeded in persuading them that they did not. In no other area of activity or policy was there such blatant disobedience to her express orders, such scorn for her authority, such contempt for monarchical dignity. A woman could browbeat politicians and seduce courtiers, but she could not command soldiers.

ACTIVITY

Sources 25.14 and 25.15 argue that Elizabeth's gender worked against her during wartime. Do you agree?

Elizabeth was too old

SOURCE 25.16 R. B. Wernham, *The Making of Elizabethan Foreign Policy*, 1980, pp. 82–83

These men ... saw here a chance ... to destroy Spanish power ... The chief of these, the leader of what may be called the war party, was the Earl of Essex... His growing paranoia ... turned the division of opinion over policy into a bitter personal faction fight between him and the Cecils. To some extent this difference of view was one aspect of a clash of generations ... For this younger generation the frustrating thing was that some of the older less aggressive generation still hung on and still held key positions ... Most frustrating of all was the fact that Elizabeth herself, born in 1533, belonged to that older generation ... when the King of Spain had been a necessary ... ally.

SOURCE 25.17 W. MacCaffrey, *Elizabeth I*, 1993, p. 282

The difference between the horizons which bounded the world of Essex or Raleigh and those of the Queen could hardly have been wider. The spacious skies of the two men's vision looked down on a universe of far reaching splendours, rich in untold wealth, and of empires yet to be conquered. Essex dreamed of conquest, a new English empire; the Queen sought nothing more than survival.

> **ACTIVITY**
>
> Read Sources 25.16 and 25.17. Why were opinions over strategy split along lines of age?

Elizabeth was incapable of making military decisions

SOURCE 25.18 C. Haigh, *Elizabeth I*, 1988, p. 134 and p. 141

The existence of rival strategies, and the sharp divisions within the court, meant that military and naval planning was often confused and erratic, and that policies were rarely pursued to a decisive conclusion ... Elizabeth's control of her commanders was limited by her attempts to hold down costs. By taking financial partners into her initiatives, she shared her own authority and left her associates freedom of action ... Problems also arose because there was no general agreement on the strategy to be followed, and the two main approaches, land campaigns and naval strikes, were adopted by different court factions.

> **ACTIVITY**
>
> Does Source 25.18 suggest that Elizabeth was incapable of making military decisions? Are there any other reasons which might explain her inability to command?

Elizabeth did not support her generals

SOURCE 25.19 C. Haigh, *Elizabeth I*, 1988, p. 132 and p. 140

Leicester did make minor military gains in the summer campaign of 1586, but he was crippled by his own incompetence as a commander; by poor relations with more experienced deputies and the distrustful Dutch; by the inadequacies of the English recruiting and supply system; and by Elizabeth's unwillingness to spend men and money. The Queen wanted war on the cheap, and refused to recognise that there was no such thing. Leicester never had enough men ... and was given insufficient money for wages, supplies, and equipment, so desertions continued and decisive military action was impossible ... Elizabeth did keep her generals and admirals on a tight budget of men and money, and her soldiers were often underfed and badly equipped. But the sufferings of the common soldiers were as much because their commanders kept them in the field longer than had been intended, as because the initial allocations were inadequate.

A focus on events

■ 25E   Expedition by sea against Spain, 1588–89

Original plan	To attack Lisbon before proceeding against Spanish ships in the New World.
Orders issued to Drake and Norris, February 1589	• Destroy the remaining Armada ships in the Spanish ports on the Bay of Biscay • Seize the Azores as a base for further attacks against the Spanish silver fleets. Elizabeth put up £20,000 and her commanders and their backers put up £40,000. They all expected a return on their investment.

What actually happened	Essex backed the expedition heavily and joined it without Elizabeth's permission, sailing straight for Lisbon.
	   The main fleet, under Norris and Drake, sailed to Corunna where two weeks were wasted while the crews looted the city and got drunk. It then sailed to Lisbon, leaving the Armada ships untouched. It achieved nothing at Lisbon.
	   Norris and the main fleet returned to England, while Drake set sail for the Azores. He ran into severe gales and was forced to return home, having lost a total of £100,000 and 11,000 men.

ACTIVITY

Read Source 25.19 and Charts 25E and 25F. Were her generals right to be so critical of Elizabeth's management of events? How much responsibility do they bear?

■ 25F   Willoughby's expedition to France, 1589

Original plan	To prevent Philip II from seizing the Normandy Channel ports.
Orders issued to Willoughby	Henry IV of France sent a message to Elizabeth saying that English help was no longer needed. Elizabeth ordered Willoughby to stay in Dover.
What actually happened	Ignoring orders, Willoughby set off for France. During the ten-week expedition his troops engaged with the enemy five times. His men were short of food and clothing, were ill and were attacked by the French populace. Less than half of the original force returned to England in December.

ACTIVITY

1 Work in groups.
   a) Write down the main foreign policy events which took place after 1585.
   b) Draw up your own foreign policy strategies to deal with these threats. You do not have to take cost into consideration but you do need to bear in mind England's military resources.
   c) Prepare a presentation justifying your strategy:

   • How far does your strategy differ from Elizabeth's?
   • Can these differences be explained by Elizabeth's reluctance to spend money?

2 Write a paragraph attacking the following statement and a paragraph defending it: Elizabeth had no alternative but to follow the strategy she did in the war against Spain.

TALKING POINT

Consideration and compromise are now recognised as desirable attributes for managers and leaders. If Elizabeth had had to lead an aggressive group of men in the twentieth century, rather than in the sixteenth century, would her tactics have earned her respect rather than criticism?

TALKING POINT

Elizabeth had limited aims which she achieved. Why, therefore, has she been criticised?

250

HOW SUCCESSFULLY DID ELIZABETH CONDUCT THE WAR AGAINST SPAIN AFTER 1585?

I This chapter assumes that Elizabeth was free to concentrate all her efforts on foreign policy. As a reminder of the constraints upon her and the links between foreign and domestic policy, extend and complete the following table, highlighting the main issues which Elizabeth and her government had to deal with in each of the given areas. This is an excellent revision exercise which will help you to identify critical periods.

	Netherlands	Spain	France	New World	Scotland	Succession	Ireland	Religion
1560								
1594								
1595								

2 Make detailed notes on:

- the extent to which religion was a factor in English foreign policy
- the years when English security was most at risk
- the policies Elizabeth and her councillors decided on and their effectiveness.

ACTIVITY

'The negative results of the war outweigh the positive results.' Explain whether you agree or disagree with this statement.

■ 25G The results of war

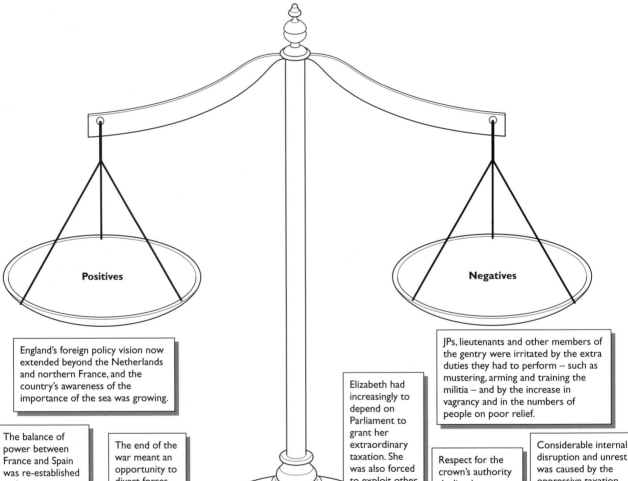

Positives

England's foreign policy vision now extended beyond the Netherlands and northern France, and the country's awareness of the importance of the sea was growing.

The balance of power between France and Spain was re-established and a strong independent Netherlands emerged. England benefited from this new European situation.

The end of the war meant an opportunity to divert forces and resources to Ireland, so Tyrone's Rebellion could finally be dealt with.

Negatives

JPs, lieutenants and other members of the gentry were irritated by the extra duties they had to perform – such as mustering, arming and training the militia – and by the increase in vagrancy and in the numbers of people on poor relief.

Elizabeth had increasingly to depend on Parliament to grant her extraordinary taxation. She was also forced to exploit other sources of revenue, which included selling monopolies and crown lands and demanding higher feudal revenues.

Respect for the crown's authority declined – illustrated by her commanders' refusal to obey orders and Essex's rebellion – as did Elizabeth's popularity.

Considerable internal disruption and unrest was caused by the oppressive taxation and extension of monopolies which were necessary to finance the war. The poverty caused by the disruption to trade was exacerbated by a series of bad harvests.

C Review: How successfully did Elizabeth conduct the war against Spain after 1585?

In the late nineteenth and early twentieth centuries it was fashionable to write stirring accounts of the daring exploits of Elizabethan seamen during their victorious war against Spain. Hollywood picked up this theme in true swashbuckling style, as the heart-throbs of the 1930s boarded Spanish galleons and indulged in inspiring displays of swordsmanship before sailing home with the booty. The emphasis today is very different. It was in the land campaigns, characterised by mud, dysentery, cold, desertion, corrupt officers and disobeyed orders, where the main advances were actually made and the war was ultimately won. Individual acts of great bravery and heroism took place at sea, but there was little strategic gain.

Although few historians challenge the validity of Elizabeth's decision that war with Spain was inevitable by 1585, they, like her generals, are critical of some of her strategic decisions. The war certainly emphasised Elizabeth's cautious and indecisive character, but England's lack of resources was a real issue. Elizabeth was never able to authorise full-scale attacks, preferring to send limited aid to her allies in the hope that they would do the job for her. She was also unable to resist the lure of New World ventures, despite the failure of most of these joint stock operations, because the capture of the *Madre de Dios* gave a tempting, if illusory, solution to the problem of financing the war. And, her concern over England's ability to finance the war was justified, given England's financial and social situation at the end of her reign after almost two decades at war.

Criticisms of Elizabeth's foreign policy can seem something of a contradiction, because her policy was ultimately successful and England's aims were by and large achieved.

SOURCE 25.20 S. Doran, *England and Europe 1485–1603*, 1986, p. 79

Ultimately Elizabeth's objectives were achieved. Spain was bloodied but undefeated. The southern Netherlands were restored to Spain on a semi-autonomous basis while the northern provinces remained free. France emerged from the civil wars with a monarch sufficiently strong to resist both Spain and the most fanatic French Catholics. Protestantism and national independence were safeguarded from foreign threats. Her policies did not achieve all this by themselves; external factors were more important, but the policies undoubtedly helped.

However, it is worth reflecting on the following points, all of which can be developed in an analysis of the effectiveness of English foreign policy.

- Since, throughout the 1570s, Elizabeth aimed to avoid war with Spain her foreign policy cannot be viewed as successful, especially when it meant a second-rate power taking on the most powerful country in Europe.
- The fact that England was ultimately successful does not necessarily mean that the war itself was conducted successfully. At three points in 1589, 1591 and 1596, the English believed a peaceful settlement was at hand, but each time Elizabeth failed to press home her advantage. The war cannot be seen as a success because of its length and its cost.
- The successful completion of the war was not necessarily due to English foreign policy. Luck (the wind direction worked in England's favour and to the Armada's disadvantage) and external factors (Henry IV's conversion, and Maurice of Nassau's military skills) may have been equally, if not more, significant.

252

HOW SUCCESSFULLY DID ELIZABETH CONDUCT THE WAR AGAINST SPAIN AFTER 1585?

SOURCE 25.23 W. MacCaffrey, *Elizabeth I*, 1993, p. 446

From that point on events more and more eluded her control, as the initiative passed to Philip, to Henry IV, and to the leaders of the new Dutch state. In these years the Queen's deficiencies as a ruler were more apparent, above all her reluctance to make decisions or to give her commanders leeway to act on the spot … Henry's triumph over his enemies was his own doing. The Queen benefited from it but could claim little credit for the outcome. In Holland she could claim a larger role; the infusion of English men and money was a substantial, perhaps essential, contribution to the state's ultimate success, but the military initiatives were theirs. None of the naval enterprises to which the Queen gave her reluctant consent realised its stated goals, but two of them triggered off ill-considered responses by Philip which finally laid the ghost of another armada.

Yet to criticise Elizabeth for not taking on Spain in the 1570s assumes she could foresee the extraordinary events of the 1580s: Philip's acquisition of Portugal, the murder of Henry III, the accession of a Huguenot to the throne of France and the assassination of William, Prince of Orange. It also ignores Elizabeth's central belief that a Spanish defeat would leave the way open for French expansion and that English security was best guaranteed by a balance of power between France and Spain. Given the situation Elizabeth found herself in, therefore, it is difficult to see how she could have acted other than the way she did.

KEY POINTS FROM CHAPTER 25: How successfully did Elizabeth conduct the war against Spain after 1585?

1 From 1585 to 1598 England was fighting a war on four fronts: in the Netherlands, in the Channel, in France and in the New World.
2 Although Leicester's campaign in the Netherlands in 1585 was a disaster, English aid eventually enabled Maurice of Nassau to establish an independent Netherlands in the north. The southern states remained under loose Spanish control.
3 The dramatic defeat of the Spanish Armada in 1588 was not followed up by any great strategic victories, although there were some stirring exploits such as the attack on Cadiz in 1596.
4 Forces were sent to France to help Henry of Navarre when a Spanish army landed in Brittany to support the Catholic League in 1589.
5 In the New World privateers continued to attack Spanish shipping. The capture of the *San Felipe* and the *Madre de Dios* encouraged such ventures.
6 Elizabeth's conduct of the war has been criticised because it was primarily defensive. Nevertheless, the strain on the country's resources caused unrest in the 1590s.

26

Review: How far did religion affect relations with foreign powers?

You have now studied the domestic and foreign policies of Elizabeth I. However, 'foreign' and 'domestic' are labels which historians use to compartmentalise events for ease of analysis. Elizabeth would not have seen issues under such neat, and separate, headings. She would have had to deal with problems daily, some of which occurred solely within England, some of which concerned foreign powers. In many cases, of course, English issues became problems because they were linked to events abroad.

■ 26A How Elizabeth's problems linked together

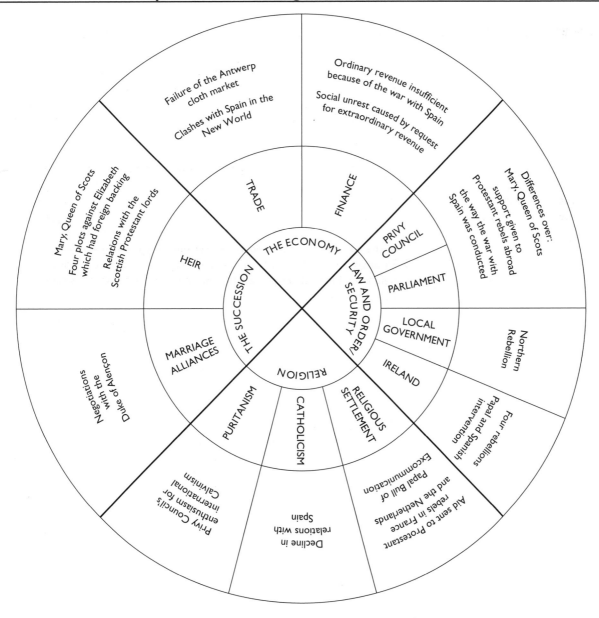

Failure of the Antwerp cloth market

Clashes with Spain in the New World

Ordinary revenue insufficient because of the war with Spain

Social unrest caused by request for extraordinary revenue

Mary, Queen of Scots

Four plots against Elizabeth which had foreign backing

Relations with the Scottish Protestant lords

Differences over: Mary, Queen of Scots; support given to Protestant rebels abroad; the way the war with Spain was conducted

TRADE

FINANCE

HEIR

THE ECONOMY

PRIVY COUNCIL

LAW AND ORDER/ SECURITY

PARLIAMENT

LOCAL GOVERNMENT

THE SUCCESSION

Northern Rebellion

MARRIAGE ALLIANCES

IRELAND

RELIGION

Negotiations with the Duke of Alençon

PURITANISM

CATHOLICISM

RELIGIOUS SETTLEMENT

Papal and Spanish intervention

Four rebellions

Privy Council's enthusiasm for international Calvinism

Decline in relations with Spain

Papal Bull of Excommunication

Aid sent to Protestant rebels in France and the Netherlands

TALKING POINT

At the end of each section there has been a Talking point relating the section to the book's overall theme: the investigation into whether Elizabeth's reign was a Golden Age (see page 5). And Section 5 is no different!

Was Elizabeth's reign a Golden Age in exploration, warfare and relations with foreign powers, or do a handful of events hide the reality of long drawn out warfare, fear of invasion and a serious impact on the economy? Does the fact that the monarch was a queen, not a king, affect our view of events and make them seem more heroic? Again, try to avoid generalisations. Were reactions different in 1585, 1588 or 1598? How might events since Elizabeth's reign have affected our view of her achievements?

SOURCE 26.1   The frontispiece to John Dee's *Arte of Navigation*, 1577

To what extent can the reign of Elizabeth be described as a cultural Golden Age?

RENAISSANCE
The re-birth of art and literature, which is often seen as heralding the end of the medieval 'dark age' and the beginning of the modern world. The movement was influenced by classical Greece and Rome, and began in fourteenth-century Italy.

The flowering of culture in Elizabeth's reign has led historians to label it a **Golden Age** or even a **RENAISSANCE**: after all, a period which produced Shakespeare must have been quite extraordinary. This perception has important implications for students of the period. Labelling Elizabeth's reign a cultural **Golden Age** implies success in other areas. It seems unlikely that artists would have flourished in an atmosphere of political instability or economic uncertainty. The picture created is therefore of a strong, stable government which encouraged achievement. As you will be aware, however, such a view is misleading because it prevents a critical analysis of Elizabeth, her government and the effectiveness of their policies. It perpetuates the 'rose-coloured' view of Elizabeth, that she was personally responsible for bringing together a set of factors whose convergence may in fact have been purely accidental.

This section will therefore encourage you to think about definitions of culture and consider whether people at the time felt that they were living in a cultural **Golden Age**. You will also need to step back and question the validity of the sources themselves – bringing you back full circle, to one of the starting points of this book – to examine how far the image of Elizabeth and her reign is the result of propaganda put about by a government faced with a female on the throne, the re-establishment of **Protestantism** and the threat, actual or otherwise, of a **Catholic** invasion.

TALKING POINT

The whole issue of cultural history is difficult to grasp. Definitions of culture are complex. Can bawdy alehouse songs, passed on from generation to generation by word of mouth, be considered as cultural when compared with a Shakespearean sonnet? To what extent is culture based on shared experiences unique to a country or locality embracing, for example, both religious tradition and pagan folklore? Does culture develop spontaneously or is it imposed by an educated elite? Is popular culture 'culture **of** the people' or 'culture **for** the people'? How can we build up an accurate picture of English cultural history during Elizabeth's reign from sources based largely on oral tradition and rituals which have long since disappeared? And, how do we know that the audience for the painting and literature that survive was anything more than a small, educated minority?

TALKING POINT

It is often said that culture flourishes only in an atmosphere of peace and prosperity. Can you think of examples from the twentieth century where the reverse is true?

TALKING POINT

The study of history is largely concerned with cause and consequence. Usually a cause (a policy, an event or a belief) will have one or more consequences. Occasionally, however, the coming together of several causes will lead to a major upheaval. Such upheavals can lead to the flowering of culture, economic changes or the overthrow of government. What examples of major upheavals can you think of?

■ **Learning trouble spot**

A level examiners frequently report that few, if any, able candidates attempt to answer the exam questions on culture. Instead, these questions are answered by desperate candidates who, studying A level English perhaps, decide to write a synopsis of one of Shakespeare's plays. Don't write off this topic, however, as being less important than foreign policy or religion. It has long been held that the test of a civilised society is the health of its creative output. There are clear links between the effectiveness of government policies and what people think about them, and popular opinion is most often found in songs, pamphlets and plays.

During Elizabeth's reign, religion and a defensive, nationalist foreign policy had a huge effect on popular culture, which was recognised and used by the government to its advantage. Far from being an area which allows little room for argument or analysis, the breadth of questions on Elizabethan culture encourages creative responses. The key to answering these questions successfully is, as always, carefully considering the evidence, breaking down the material into manageable chunks and setting out with a clear view of the direction your argument will take.

ACTIVITY

In groups, select examples of contemporary cultural achievements. Create a pamphlet which shows what these achievements tell us about society today. Your pamphlet should include:

• a definition of 'culture'
• some awareness of how culture has changed over time and the main reasons for this change in the twentieth century
• an evaluation of how far a society can be judged by its culture
• a summary of what you would expect to find in a similar pamphlet about Elizabethan England.

27

Why has Elizabeth's reign been described as a Golden Age?

CHAPTER OVERVIEW   Historians enjoy attaching the Golden Age label to periods which, with hindsight, stand out from those that came before and after. It has been applied to Elizabethan England because, from 1558 to 1603, the country enjoyed a degree of unity that enabled it to produce some of its most famous playwrights, poets and artists, and to defeat the greatest maritime power of the period, heralding the start of an era of overseas expansion and naval supremacy. The fact that all this was presided over by a woman who was something of a mystery – choosing to remain single and encouraging a semi-religious, mystical image of herself – only heightens the romance. The political chaos of the Wars of the Roses and the Civil War adds to the perception of Elizabeth's reign as an oasis of achievement.

However, it is all too easy to be swept along by the glamour, rhetoric and propaganda attached to the period. As with all history, it is necessary to take an objective and analytical look at the facts and determine whether the Golden Age label can be applied accurately. This chapter will therefore focus on the following questions:

A Who were the leading artists of Elizabeth's reign? (pp. 258–61)

B How did Elizabethan culture affect the upper classes of society? (pp. 262–64)

C How did Elizabethan culture affect the lower classes of society? (pp. 265–69)

D Review: Why has Elizabeth's reign been described as a Golden Age? (pp. 270–71)

FOCUS ROUTE

Decide which criteria you would expect to be present in a Golden Age, then, as you work through this chapter and Chapter 28, assess the extent to which these criteria were present in Elizabethan England. A table is probably the best way to record your findings. Use the one below to give you some ideas.

Criteria	Evidence that this was present in Elizabethan England	The extent to which this suggests a Golden Age
Outstanding individual achievement in the arts		
National or international recognition of these achievements		
Growth of new ideas and techniques which influence future artists		
Widespread popular interest in the arts		
Changes in popular culture		
Improvement in standards of literacy		
Increase in communication		
Increase in educational establishments and patronage		
Creation of wealth and investment opportunities		

A · Who were the leading artists of Elizabeth's reign?

Art

Nicholas Hilliard elevated the art of painting miniatures to new heights by combining the formal portraiture and use of perspective of artists such as Hans Holbein with the medieval skill of manuscript illumination. The end results were extraordinarily beautiful, a wealth of living colour and tiny intricate jewels. The Queen had her own private collection of miniatures and, by the end of her reign, courtiers pinned miniatures to their clothing. Some miniatures, set in lockets, showed English achievements such as the Armada or the Church of England. Many were of Elizabeth herself.

Music

Music was popular with all levels of society, but especially at court. The greatest composers of the period wrote religious music. Orlando Gibbons composed for the new Church of England services, while William Byrd's devotional masterpieces such as *Cantiones Sacrae* have been compared with the later works of Bach. There was also a growth in the number of secular pieces written, particularly those featuring male voices. Nearly 1500 pieces survive from the period and the most popular form seems to have been the madrigal – a part song for unaccompanied voices with a pastoral or romantic theme – many of which were composed by John Wilbye. Other leading composers included John Dowland, who wrote accompanied solo songs, and Thomas Campion, who set his own lyrics to music.

SOURCE 27.1 A Hilliard miniature of Sir Francis Drake, painted in 1581

SOURCE 27.2 A musical evening: a background detail from a portrait of Sir Henry Unton, painted *c.* 1596

SOURCE 27.3 Writer and poet Sir Philip Sidney

Drama

The growth in drama during Elizabeth's reign is usually acknowledged as the greatest cultural achievement of the period. This is due, in part, to the role played by the court and the increase in the number of theatres built; both these subjects are discussed in more detail in Chapter 28.

William Shakespeare, 1564–1616

The common assertion that Shakespeare's birthday was 23 April, St George's Day, is an indication of his place in English legend as well as English history. Born in Stratford-upon-Avon, very little is heard of him until 1592 when he appears as a well-established actor and dramatist in London. He wrote comedies, including *Love's Labour's Lost* (1592) and *The Comedy of Errors* (1593), and histories, such as *Henry VI* (1592), and *Richard II* (1595), as well as his more famous tragedies which include *Hamlet* (c.1599) and *King Lear* (c.1604). Although some of his plays were written for performance at court, Shakespeare was essentially a public dramatist, writing for the commercial theatre, and addressing himself to an audience drawn from all social classes. He retired to Stratford in 1610, where he died.

Christopher Marlowe, 1564–93

An important figure in the development of the English stage, Marlowe's first play, *Tamburlaine the Great, Part 1*, was produced in about 1587 by the Lord Admiral's Company with Edward Alleyn in the title role. Written in flamboyant blank verse it would have influenced Shakespeare who would have seen it performed when he arrived in London. Marlowe's other works include the *Tragical History of Doctor Faustus* (c.1589), *The Jew of Malta*, which may have influenced Shakespeare's *The Merchant of Venice*, and *Edward II*, which has similarities with Shakespeare's *Richard II*. Marlowe was killed in a tavern brawl, probably assassinated because of his secret-service activities.

Thomas Kyd, 1558–94

Kyd's *Spanish Tragedy* (c.1585–92) was one of the most popular plays of its day, and the prototype for many other revenge tragedies. It dealt with bloody deeds which demanded retribution, established the principle of an eye for an eye and involved much on-stage violence which easily became melodramatic. Kyd has been credited with writing other plays, now lost, which served as the basis for Shakespeare's later works, including *Hamlet*.

Thomas Dekker, 1570–1632

A poverty-stricken Londoner who was imprisoned several times for debt, Dekker was employed by Philip Henslowe in 1595 to write for the Lord Admiral's Company at The Rose Theatre. His Elizabethan works include two comedies, *The Shoemakers' Holiday* and *Old Fortunatus*. He also wrote pageants, tracts and pamphlets. Dekker's work is noted for its realistic portrayal of daily London life, for its sympathy with life's victims and for its overall note of cheerfulness.

Literature

During Elizabeth's reign, most literature was bought and read by those at court. Although the most widely read prose work was Foxe's *Book of Martyrs*, the majority combined humanist and classical principles with political commentary. Some of the best prose of the day is found in translations of the classics, leading examples of which include Sir Thomas North's of Plutarch and John Florio's of Montaigne. Sir Philip Sidney was one of the most prolific writers of the period. His *Arcadia*, while taking the form of a PASTORAL ROMANCE peppered with verse, nevertheless managed to convey the message that a state is best served by a monarch whose powers are curtailed by the noble classes. Sidney went on to write *Astrophel and Stella* and *The Defence of Poesy*: his LYRIC VERSE influenced many poets. To the modern reader, however, Sidney's prose is hard-going and more accessible writing can be found elsewhere. Richard Hooker's *Laws of Ecclesiastical Polity* (1593) is a classic example of how far literature had grown in its vocabulary, potency and structure during Elizabeth's reign. Here, as elsewhere, a confident and unique style peculiar to England had developed.

PASTORAL ROMANCE
A form of escapist literature concerned with country pleasures which enjoyed a popular revival during the Renaissance.

LYRIC VERSE
Poetry accompanied by a musical instrument.

SOURCE 27.4 Holdenby House, Northamptonshire

SOURCE 27.5 Longleat House, Wiltshire

SOURCE 27.6 Edmund Spenser, an engraving by George Vertue (*detail*)

Architecture

Elizabeth, determined to economise, did not build any new palaces or patronise architecture. She nevertheless had an indirect impact on this area. Her annual progresses encouraged her leading courtiers and nobles to construct bigger and better houses in which to entertain her. Leading examples of Elizabethan architecture include Kenilworth Castle built by the Earl of Leicester, Longleat House built by Sir John Thynne and Holdenby House built by Christopher Hatton. These buildings are characterised by their symmetry and size. The most admired interiors were light and spacious, while the grandest had brick chimneys, private living quarters, formal or state rooms and, above all, a long gallery in which to walk and converse.

Poetry

Poetry flourished throughout the sixteenth century and in Elizabeth's reign a link was forged between poetry and prose and drama. Prose writers wrote verse and dramatists wrote in verse and produced sonnets, breaking down many artistic boundaries. England already had a fine tradition of poets: men like the Earl of Surrey and Thomas Wyatt introduced the sonnet to England in the 1530s, then made it unique using personal, intense lyrics and very English themes. Edmund Spenser was the outstanding poet of Elizabeth's reign, apart from Shakespeare. His work includes the *Shephard's Calendar*, *Mother Hubbard's Tale*, *Epithalamion* and *The Faerie Queene*. The latter is an epic poem which uses rich imagery and language to portray Elizabeth as both a queen (Gloriana) and a woman (Belphoebe). *The Faerie Queene* is an allegory in which knights set out to battle against the evils of the world, each possessing the virtue necessary to defeat his particular enemy. The fluid, gracious style was to influence poets for the next three centuries. Other poets of the period include Sir Walter Raleigh and the Catholic, Robert Southwell.

SOURCE 27.7   William Shakespeare: timeless?

SOURCE 27.8   The Beatles: timeless?

B How did Elizabethan culture affect the upper classes of society?

Before the sixteenth century, culture was a unifying force in society. Based around local agrarian communities, annual events, such as harvest festival, well dressing and Plough Monday, brought local people together to celebrate. These occasions were often reinforced by the rituals of the Catholic Church. Although the more intellectual members of society had dipped into these events from time to time in the past, by Elizabeth's reign popular culture had become firmly associated with the lower classes of society. The education and learning of a small group, who held positions in the Church and in government, set them apart. There were, in effect, two cultures: the ordinary pastimes and pursuits of the majority, which included drinking, gambling and cock-fighting, and the more intellectual pursuits of the minority, which included reading the classics.

The invention of the printing press and, more importantly, the massive increase in educational opportunities had produced a new phenomenon, the gentleman, who quickly lined his shelves with the correct books and took every opportunity to show off his learning. Whether he had actually read these books is, of course, a different matter. Such a man, and they usually were male (Elizabeth's education was exceptional in an age where five per cent of women were literate compared with 30 per cent of men – see pages 276–77), now had little time for the pageants and superstitions of his less informed fellows, especially since these were often identified with Catholicism. Instead, he embraced an elitist culture, characterised by the written as opposed to the spoken word, and this was his passport to social and possibly political advancement.

Popular and elitist culture did not, however, co-exist happily. The upper and middle classes, the majority of whom were Protestant, saw their culture not only as superior but also as a means of enforcing social control over the lower classes and removing elements of Catholic ritual from their lives.

FOCUS ROUTE

Read pages 263–67 and make detailed notes on:

- the education, career path and lifestyle of a Tudor gentleman
- the pastimes and superstitions of a member of the lower classes.

Then, using a table like the one below, show how different branches of the arts were influenced by events at court and the effects such influence had on the lives of a gentleman and a commoner.

	Gentleman	Commoner
Art		
Music		
Drama		
Literature		
Architecture		
Poetry		

You may want to add to your table after reading Chapters 28 and 29.

TALKING POINT

Figures which show the percentage of the population who had literacy skills are problematic. It is likely that more people could read than could write. How can you explain this?

SOURCE 27.9   The school room at Stratford-upon-Avon Grammar School. This photograph was taken in 1954

SOURCE 27.10   C. Haigh, *Elizabeth I*, 1988, pp. 90–91

Below the level of the great, lesser men pursued their own interests and used their contacts to advantage. A host of sinecures, wardships, leases, and licences went to second-rank courtiers, and the band of gentlemen pensioners was notably successful. Brian Ansley was a gentleman pensioner from 1564 to 1603: his position at Court enabled him to gain licences to import steel and to export cony [rabbit] skins, and the office of warden of the Fleet prison, which he leased for £100 a year. Lancelot Bostock, gentleman pensioner between 1564 and 1588, acquired a grant of fines under the Pluralities Act and the constableship of Flint Castle in 1572, the constableship of Holt Castle in 1585, and lands in Ireland in 1587. Simon Bowyer was a gentleman usher of the Privy Chamber, little more than a glorified doorman, from 1569 to 1597: he gained the captaincy of a castle in Hampshire, worth £100 a year, and a patent to inquire into offences against the wool statutes (which gave huge opportunities for blackmail and the receipt of bribes).

The making of an Elizabethan gentleman

Education

A gentleman probably attended a grammar school, perhaps one of the 27 grammar schools endowed during Elizabeth's reign. The curriculum was modelled on leading schools, such as St Paul's and Merchant Taylors', where, in line with humanist principles, classical Greek and Latin were studied to promote intellectual, spiritual and personal growth.

At university all degrees involved grammar, rhetoric and logic, with compulsory lectures in mathematics, music, theology, astronomy and geometry. Only after all this could an undergraduate specialise. Most chose law, and therefore spent time at the Inns of Court.

Career

Although some were content with local prestige and influence, many gentlemen aimed to be invited to court. The main method of doing this was to enter royal employment, either in central administration or at a local level, and come to the attention of a local noble whose patronage alone would secure the gentleman an invitation to the royal presence.

Lifestyle

All gentlemen were distinguished from the lower classes by the ability to speak and write 'proper English'. A working knowledge of French, Latin and even Greek was also desirable. Social conversations were expected to be full of allusions to heroic exploits from classical literature which provided role models for leadership. A gentleman was also expected to be well versed in social etiquette, particularly good table manners, and be able to hold his own in the two aristocratic pastimes of hunting and dancing.

Hunting was not, however, just a means to an end, it was the main passion of a gentleman. He preferred to hunt deer, but hawking came a close second. Fencing, tennis and bowls also became popular during Elizabeth's reign. Despite his newly found status, a gentleman often revealed his humbler roots, continuing to watch bull- and bear-baiting and cock-fighting.

SOURCE 27.11 A gentleman preparing his hawk

Following the lead of his noble superiors, the Elizabethan gentleman lived in a brick or half-timbered building, with chimneys, which had at least eight rooms and additional servants' quarters. Household reading included the works of Erasmus, Sir Thomas North's edition of Plutarch's *Lives of the Noble Grecians and Romans*, Elyot's *The Book Named the Governor* and Hoby's translation of *The Courtier*, in addition to the more popular works of Caxton as well as pamphlets, sermons and almanacs. Elyot's book laid down strict guidelines as to what a gentleman should do and, in advising him to paint or carve only in secret, showed society's disapproval of art other than portraits or miniatures. A gentleman's walls were more likely to be covered in tapestries than in works of art, while anything which reflected Italian, and therefore Catholic, tastes was avoided at all costs. Access to court offered the gentleman the opportunity to watch tournaments, masques and drama productions, although the Queen's own company of actors did tour the country so that some of these events were nationally accessible.

All gentlemen studied music. It was thought that music not only developed character but also gave a person an insight into how things were brought together harmoniously in society. Therefore, a gentleman who had grasped the basic rules of harmony would be effective in holding public office. All the great nobles copied the court and employed household musicians, while the gentry purchased madrigal songbooks and held musical evenings where they sang complicated part-songs.

SOURCE 27.12 Kentwell Hall, Suffolk, an Elizabethan manor house

C How did Elizabethan culture affect the lower classes of society?

Huge inequalities existed within Tudor society and the majority of the population wanted pastimes which allowed them to escape for a while from the poverty, disease and natural disasters which characterised daily life. Sources 27.13–27.20 show the main recreational activities of the lower classes.

SOURCE 27.13 Inns and taverns were an important part of every social ritual. Ale was consumed regularly, even at breakfast, and statistics indicate that more was consumed in times of plague or economic depression

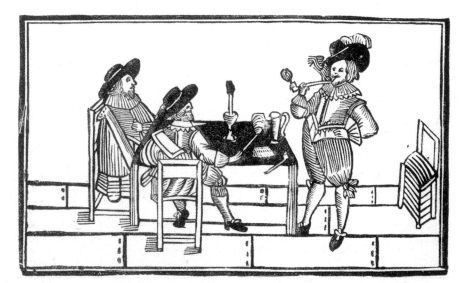

SOURCE 27.14 Tobacco was becoming increasingly popular by the end of Elizabeth's reign, although it was still expensive

SOURCE 27.15 Gambling in a London brothel: a woodcut of c. 1590. The prospect of an easy win led to widespread gambling, even among the poorest classes, on bear-baiting, cock-fighting, cards, dice and racing

SOURCE 27.16 The traditions and superstitions of the Catholic Church were believed to possess the supernatural powers necessary to ward off catastrophe. People wore amulets or charms, bought holy relics and placed great faith in the Church sacraments, despite the fact that such practices were condemned or modified by the Religious Settlement. The photo shows a gold locket made to contain the caul (the inner membrane enclosing the fetus) in which John Monson was born in 1597

SOURCE 27.17 Although lots of festivals which had their origins in England's medieval or pagan past were rejected by the Protestant Church, many continued mainly because they offered an opportunity for fun and drinking. Saints' Days, the twelve days of Christmas, Plough Monday and May Day, for example, were all celebrated throughout Elizabeth's reign

SOURCE 27.18 Ephemeral popular literature, which included popular ballads, chap books, almanacs, conduct books and sermons, was published for a new mass market with the invention of printing (see page 275). This is the frontispiece from one of George Gascoigne's books, showing the poet and courtier presenting his verses to the Queen

SOURCE 27.19 Archery and fishing were popular at all levels of society. Ordinary people also took part in wrestling and foot racing and played football. In this engraving by Crispin de Passe, spectators watch a game of football

SOURCE 27.20 The Red Bull Playhouse, Clerkenwell, London. Story telling played an important role in the lives of ordinary people. Themes of love, or good versus evil, formed the basis of most legends and tales, such as the popular Robin Hood legend. The invention of the printing press led to stories and ballads being frequently revised and reprinted. The public theatres which gentlemen attended were also attended by common folk. Whereas courtiers and gentlemen sang madrigals the ordinary people sang ballads, often adding their own lyrics to tunes composed in London

■ 27A Shakespeare's Elizabethan plays

1592	Henry VI
	Titus Andronicus
	Love's Labour's Lost
1593	Richard III
	The Comedy of Errors
1594	King John
	The Taming of the Shrew
	Two Gentlemen of Verona
1595	Richard II
	Romeo and Juliet
	The Merchant of Venice
1598	Henry IV
	The Merry Wives of Windsor
	Henry V
	A Midsummer Night's Dream
	Much Ado About Nothing
	As You Like It
	Hamlet
1602	Twelfth Night
	Troilus and Cressida
	All's Well That Ends Well

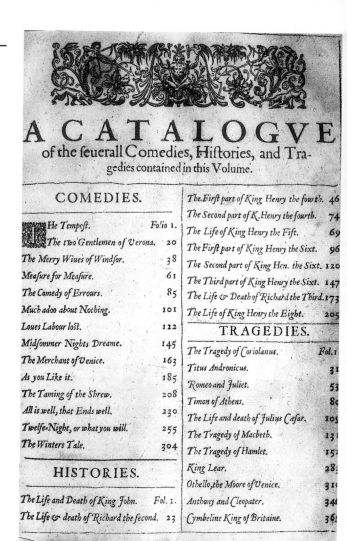

SOURCE 27.21 A list of Shakespeare's plays from the first collected edition of his works, published in 1623. Some of Shakespeare's best known plays, such as *The Tempest*, were written during James I's reign

SOURCE 27.22 A performance of *The Tempest* in Shakespeare's Globe, a modern reconstruction of the Globe theatre, in 2000. In the Elizabethan theatre groundlings stood for 1*d* in the pit. For 2*d* you could stand in the gallery and for 3*d* you could sit. The privileged classes sat on stools on the stage

The popular appeal of William Shakespeare

Although Shakespeare most admired the aristocracy and emphasised the themes of chivalry and nobility, there are references throughout his plays to professions of all sorts, to the law, to medicine (the apothecary in *Romeo and Juliet*) and to the sea, for example. His characters show his belief in the dignity of the common man. The wit of the grave digger defeats Hamlet, Bottom regains his self-respect in *A Midsummer Night's Dream* and the 'rag bags' of Henry V's army find glory at Agincourt. They are capable of a wide and convincing range of emotions. His men are strongest in action, when they confront tragedy without showing fear. His women are strongest in love, where their maturity enables them to put right a plot gone wrong because of masculine error, as in *The Merchant of Venice*.

Shakespeare based his plays on traditional, well-known stories and themes. He emphasises the need for order and structure through the triumph of good over evil, as in *Macbeth*. National pride and Christian values are also stressed, although his two main themes are sex and death as in *Hamlet*. Most of his plays focus on a leading character and are set within the context of a family or a community. The body is frequently used as a metaphor to show the links between the hero, often a king, and other members of society, as in *Corialanus*. Kingship is usually presented as a burden which involves a personal struggle, the effect of which is felt by the entire nation, as in *Richard II*.

Under Shakespeare, language reached new heights. His rich imagery stretched the imagination, while his soliloquies demanded intellectual concentration. It was probably with some relief that the audience greeted the earthy language of Bottom, Trinculo or Falstaff. Shakespeare tells a good story, where the action on stage is balanced by irony, suspense and humour. The audience is challenged and involved throughout. He was also unique amongst fellow playwrights in the extent to which his lines became assimilated into everyday language.

Shakespeare draws considerably on images from the English countryside. Flowers, birds, animals, rivers, weather and the elements are used to symbolise or emphasise emotions and to help relate the drama to the natural world. For example, a kingdom becomes 'a garden gone to riot in weeds' (*Richard II*).

ACTIVITY

A company of players is travelling from London to perform one of Shakespeare's plays at a local inn. As the editor of the district newspaper, write an article encouraging people to attend by highlighting the appeal of Shakespeare and the play. Repeat the exercise with a different play. What does this tell us about Shakespeare's appeal?

D Review: Why has Elizabeth's reign been described as a Golden Age?

When examining the extent to which Elizabeth's reign was a Golden Age the following points should be considered.

- The works of Spenser, Marlowe, Sidney, Shakespeare, Byrd, Hilliard and Dowland have not only survived the centuries but are still regarded as some of the finest examples of their genres. In each case, the artist changed the established culture of the day, developing a style which was uniquely English, and influencing future generations.
- Elizabethan culture was based on London and the court (for reasons which are developed more fully in Chapter 28). It was therefore quickly embraced by the aspiring members of the upper and middle classes who copied the cultural preferences of the Queen and her courtiers in order to advance their own political and social ambitions. Hence the Tudor gentleman consciously developed a lifestyle which proclaimed him a Renaissance man. His patronage of players, painters and architects and his desire to build up a personal library allowed artists to make a living.

SOURCE 27.25   D. M. Palliser, *The Age of Elizabeth*, 1983, p. 435

The domestic arts flourished in the second half of the century amid increasing wealth, gentlefolk being eager purchasers and even themselves creators – both embroidery and tapestry flourished on a large scale, the tapestries of the Sheldon workshops especially for wall hangings in the great country houses.

Developments in communication and centralisation – ranging from the invention of the printing press to the royal progresses, from the Bible in English to travelling players and minstrels – suggest that popular culture could not have remained immune to the cultural developments taking place in London. Even illiteracy was not a bar to knowledge, since new ideas or stories could be passed on by word of mouth or as ballads. The evidence that remains – and this is an area where sources are scarce – indicates that the ordinary people assimilated elements of elitist culture and popularised them. Thus new lyrics were sung to the tunes of court madrigals, jewelled miniature portraits were used as models for base-metal medallions, and lines from Shakespeare quickly passed into everyday language. The new popular culture existed alongside the old to such an extent that, 'The critics saw no difference between stage plays, bear-baiting, bowling alleys, and prostitution' (J. Guy, *Tudor England*, 1988, p. 428). The pressure of the Protestant Reformation, however, was to ensure that the ritual, festivals and entertainments identified with popular culture did not remain unchanged for long.

Although a classical education was still the preserve of the gentleman, new printing presses meant popular books could be published for a mass market, stimulating interest in reading and increasing the demand for education at all levels.

SOURCE 27.26   D. M. Palliser, *The Age of Elizabeth*, 1983, p. 413

Any division of Tudor culture into 'literary' and 'popular' is too simple. Gentry and clergy participated in popular festivals and rituals: a considerable minority of humble folk had access to books and could read if not write; and there were various levels of both literacy and popular culture.

The overlap between elite and popular culture is most obviously seen in the works of Shakespeare. Whereas the works of his contemporaries only slowly percolated into popular culture, Shakespeare's popularity was immediate and widespread.

SOURCE 27.27   P. Hartnoll (ed.), *Concise Oxford Companion to the Theatre*, 1972, p. 493

He came at the right moment to make full and fresh use of an emergent drama, with a novel and flexible stage for his purpose, and although some of his plays were written for performance at court, he remains primarily a 'public' dramatist, addressing himself to the demands of an audience representative of all classes, eager to listen to rich poetic utterances, keenly interested in human character, and ready to welcome both the delicacy of romantic comedy and the rigours of tragedy.

SOURCE 27.28   G. R. Elton, *England Under the Tudors*, 1991, p. 454

Even without Shakespeare it would have been an age of greatness; with him and because of him it moves into the realm of timeless magnificence.

Whether people at the time were aware of belonging to a Golden Age and whether Elizabethan artists have acquired an elevated status owing to the reflected genius of Shakespeare and the plaudits of historians are matters which remain open to debate. Perhaps of even greater interest to the historian than the question of how far Elizabeth's reign was a Golden Age, is the question which seeks to explain why it happened at all. More specifically, was the concept of a Golden Age deliberately manufactured by a government desperate to enhance the power of a female ruler or simply the result of the right factors coming together at the right time? Chapters 28 and 29 will explore these questions.

ACTIVITY

1 In a group, or as a class, discuss the following questions.
   a) Which of the achievements of the Elizabethan Golden Age had you already heard about?
   b) Which achievements are still well known today?
   c) To what extent did the Golden Age of culture impact on the ordinary Elizabethan?
   d) In order for a period to be a Golden Age, do its achievements have to be remembered?
   e) Do its achievements have to have popular contemporary appeal for a period to be a Golden Age?
2 Prepare an argument for or against the view that the Elizabethan Golden Age of culture was based solely on the plays of William Shakespeare.

KEY POINTS FROM CHAPTER 27: Why has Elizabeth's reign been described as a Golden Age?

1 The leading personalities of the Elizabethan Golden Age were Nicholas Hilliard (art), William Shakespeare (drama), Sir Philip Sidney (literature), William Byrd (music) and Sir Edmund Spenser (poetry), although there were many others.
2 The cultural achievements of the Elizabethan period had considerable impact on the educated minority who developed an elitist image of an Elizabethan gentleman.
3 The popular culture of the lower classes borrowed from elitist culture, by changing the lyrics of court songs for example, while maintaining traditional bawdier pursuits, such as cock-fighting.
4 William Shakespeare's popularity and status is partly due to his ability to appeal to all classes, to bridge the divide between popular and elitist culture.
5 The proliferation of works of art produced during Elizabeth's reign has led some historians to attach the label 'Golden Age' to this period.

28

What caused the Elizabethan Golden Age?

CHAPTER OVERVIEW

All of Europe was shaken by the Reformation and the Renaissance, which challenged the stranglehold of the Roman Catholic Church and changed the way in which people saw themselves in relation to the Universe forever. Although many decades have passed since historians routinely saw the Middle Ages as a period totally barren in achievement it was, in comparison with the period after the Renaissance, nevertheless more preoccupied with the next world and this is reflected in its painting and writings which are mainly theological in nature. It tended not to question and investigate this world, accepting the answers given by authority, the Church. Since medieval man instinctively looked for supernatural explanations where modern man would call for a scientific and rational account, the medieval Church became associated with the popular beliefs and superstitions of its day.

The overthrow of this climate of thought and belief paved the way for man to use his own reason more, to criticise more, to insist upon the rights of the individual more and to reject those features of the previous age which no longer served him. A new outlook was born, which spread rapidly in fifteenth-century Italy and then moved through the rest of Europe in the sixteenth century. The breadth of this change can be seen in the variety of features attributed to the Renaissance: the revival of classical literature, the development of a new artistic movement, the growth of science and the emergence of capitalism. As the movement spread the emphasis altered, as countries adapted Renaissance developments for their own cultural, spiritual and even political needs. This can be seen in Northern Europe's focus on scholarship.

It would have been extremely unlikely that England could have remained isolated from this dynamic cultural shift for long, and the achievements of Elizabeth's reign can be explained in these terms. Yet, they were not borrowed wholesale from Renaissance Europe. This chapter will therefore focus on the combination of forces which produced a Golden Age at the end of the sixteenth century which was uniquely and exclusively English in character.

A What factors contributed to the flowering of English culture between 1558 and 1603? (pp. 273–81)

B Review: What caused the Elizabethan Golden Age? (p. 282)

SOURCE 28.1 K. Thomas, *Religion and the Decline of Magic*, 1971, p. 35

The medieval Church acted as a repository of supernatural power which could be dispensed to the faithful to help them in their daily problems. It was inevitable that the priests ... should have derived an extra cachet from their position as mediators between man and God. It was also inevitable that around the Church, the clergy, and their holy apparatus, there clustered a horde of popular superstitions, which endowed religious objects with a magical power to which theologians themselves had never laid claim.

SOURCE 28.2 D. M. Palliser, *The Age of Elizabeth*, 1983, p. 414

Artists and craftsmen under Elizabeth displayed a strong continuity with their medieval English past, absorbing only what suited them of new continental influences.

TALKING POINT

What does Source 28.2 suggest about the wisdom of breaking down history into separate periods and studying only one or two short periods, such as the 'Renaissance' or the 'Reign of Elizabeth', rather than studying overviews of larger periods of time?

A What factors contributed to the flowering of English culture between 1558 and 1603?

FOCUS ROUTE

As you read through this chapter, make detailed notes on your own copy of the table below.

Factor influencing culture	Main developments	How they contributed to cultural growth
Royal and noble patronage		
The invention of the printing press		
The expansion of education		
The growth of London		
Wealth and stability		
Humanism		
The Protestant Reformation		
Elizabethan beliefs		

Royal and noble patronage

Royal support of the arts had a great impact on the growth of the theatre in particular. Before Elizabeth's reign, drama consisted of mystery plays or pageants performed in market squares, and classical plays performed largely in the universities. From the 1570s, the Elizabethan court began to show a real enthusiasm for plays and, as a result, companies of players were formed under the patronage of various noblemen. From 1572 onwards actors had to secure the patronage of a baron of the realm or a person of greater degree in order to gain a licence from the Lord Chamberlain. This was to give the government a degree of control over what was performed. The leading companies were:

- The Earl of Leicester's Players, established in 1574
- Queen Elizabeth's Men, established in 1583
- Lord Admiral Howard's Company which was established in 1583 and staged Marlowe's plays
- The Lord Chamberlain's Men which were established in 1594 and included Richard Burbage and William Shakespeare among their number.

The real development came when permanent theatres were established in London under royal licence. As a result of opposition from Puritans and the city authorities, these were only to be sited outside the city walls. The first two public theatres, James Burbage's Theatre and Henry Lanman's Curtain, both opened in Shoreditch to the north of the city in 1576 and 1577 respectively; they gave daily performances, except on Sundays, by one or other of the leading companies of players. When the lease on the Theatre expired, Burbage's son used timber from it to construct the Globe in Southwark. Here, a strong cast, led by Richard Burbage, premiered most of Shakespeare's plays, as well as those of other contemporary dramatists. The Globe's popularity was only rivalled by the Fortune, where Philip Henslowe's company performed.

SOURCE 28.3 A sketch of the interior of the Swan theatre, 1596, by Johann de Witt

James Burbage

- Burbage was born in 1530.
- **1572** He became one of the Earl of Leicester's Players.
- **1576** He erected the Theatre, the first purpose-built playhouse, in Shoreditch.
- **1596** He converted a building in Blackfriars into a private theatre, but died before obtaining permission to open it to the public.
- **1598** He began building the Globe using building materials from the Theatre. Work on the theatre was completed, after his death, by his sons Richard and Cuthbert.
- His son, Richard Burbage (1567–1619), played major roles in Shakespeare's plays and excelled in tragedy.

Richard Burbage

■ 28A London theatres

Theatre	Owner	Companies known to have played there
The Theatre, 1576–98	James Burbage	The Lord Chamberlain's Men
The Curtain, 1577–1622	Henry Lanman	The Lord Chamberlain's Men Queen Elizabeth's Men
The Rose, 1594–1600	Philip Henslowe	Lord Admiral Howard's Company
The Swan, 1595–1601	Langley	
The Globe, 1599–1613	Richard and Cuthbert Burbage	The Lord Chamberlain's Men
The Fortune, 1600–1621	Edward Alleyn and Philip Henslowe	Lord Admiral Howard's Company

Companies, including Queen Elizabeth's Men from 1583 onwards, also performed at court, in the stately homes of their patrons and on tour throughout the country, where provincial centres emulated London and constructed permanent wooden stages. The Earl of Leicester's Players even went with him on his Netherlands campaign in 1585. The patronage which made this flowering of dramatic art possible was not, however, without its price.

SOURCE 28.4 K. McLeish and S. Unwin, *A Guide to Shakespeare's Plays*, 1998, pp. vii–viii

In the arts, although patronage could be lavish – for example Shakespeare's company played regularly at court and had a fashionable following – royal censorship forbade explicit political or religious controversy, and any depiction of contemporary figures. In Shakespeare's year, the two or three court performances may have been the most glittering occasions, but he earned his bread and butter in the public theatres.

The invention of the printing press

SOURCE 28.5 A printing press, *c.* 1600

The first printing press was set up in England in 1476 by William Caxton who, with his assistant Wynkyn de Worde, mainly published knightly romances and religious works. The annual production of books climbed steadily over the next century, growing from 107 in the 1470s to 1040 in the 1550s. This opened up the world of learning to the laity, and to the aristrocratic and gentry classes in particular who had the means to purchase books and the learning to read them. This increased the exchange of ideas and led to what G. R. Elton has described as 'the first genuine literary movement'. He goes on to say, 'Though without the printing press there might still have been a revival in literature, it would not have been so fruitful and lavish and would certainly have been less rapid in producing perfection' (*England Under the Tudors*, 1991, 3rd edn, p. 433). John Guy talks about the printing press galvanising change so that 'in the long term, a more demanding, individualistic and better informed culture was created' (*Tudor England*, 1988, p. 419).

Although there is considerable debate about the percentage of people in Tudor England who were literate, more people living in London were literate than those living in the provinces because of their proximity to the printing presses. And, it seems reasonable to assume that the invention of the printing press stimulated the desire to learn to read at the same time as the Renaissance encouraged the re-discovery of the classics and the writing of new books for a mass market.

SOURCE 28.6 J. Guy, *Tudor England*, 1988, p. 419

Proximity to the presses encouraged people to learn to read, and those remaining illiterate could listen to others reading aloud. Also ballads and political printers transmitted their message to the semi-literate.

Although books such as Sidney's *Arcadia* remained firmly within the sphere of the educated elite, they were nevertheless now available to a far larger audience than when they were manuscripts. Ballads, chap books, almanacs, conduct books, sermons, as well as romance literature, were among the material printed for the mass market.

The impact of the printing press is best shown by the government's reaction to it. Fearful of the spread of ideas which might challenge accepted views of authority, the government maintained control over licensing and censoring the presses. The government was not, however, unaware of the potential of the presses to spread its own propaganda which, by its very use of standardised English, ensured the supremacy of the ruling, educated classes.

The expansion of education

The combined impact of the Renaissance, the Protestant Reformation, and the printing press meant that the ability to read and write became a highly desirable asset in Elizabeth's reign. The demand for education therefore grew, while the schools themselves were influenced by Renaissance ideas and made some changes to the curriculum and to teaching methods. Humanism was beginning to have an impact on what was taught in schools and there was even a flicker of recognition that interesting lessons produced better results than did beating a child. Nevertheless, most schools still believed in long hours spent in studying the classics, with strict discipline and short holidays.

In general, parish schools, which were often called petty schools, taught reading and writing in English, while the endowed grammar schools taught exclusively in Latin to prepare the sons of gentlemen for university. Not all learning, however, took place in schools: the sons of the aristocracy were tutored at home, while some apprentices and servants learned to read or write from their masters.

In 1558 there were two universities in England, Oxford and Cambridge, although the Inns of Court where lawyers trained were sometimes known as the third university. New colleges, such as Gresham which was founded in London in 1597, offered a broader curriculum with lectures on geometry, music, astronomy, medicine, divinity, geography and navigation. Many sons of the gentry attended university but did not always complete their degrees. However, the expansion of university education ensured that the government had an educated ruling class to administer its policies and ensured the status of the educated elite. By 1593, half of the members of the House of Commons were university graduates.

ACTIVITY

Using the evidence in Sources 28.7–28.17, make detailed notes on the following questions.

1 What was the Tudor curriculum and how was it delivered in Elizabethan grammar schools?
2 How far is it true to say that there was an expansion in educational opportunities for the great majority of the people during Elizabeth's reign?

SOURCE 28.7 From the statutes of Guisborough Grammar School, 1561

And the said master of the scholars shall teach freely in the said school of Jesus all scholars coming to learn ... and he shall have a register book and therein write the names of all his scholars with the day and year of their first coming and admission into the said school, taking therefore of every scholar at his said first coming four pence, and never after anything...

And to the intent the scholars of the said school may be placed in a seemly order whereby they may more quietly apply their learning, the said school shall be divided into four forms.

And in the first form shall be placed young beginners commonly called petties, until they can read perfectly, pronounce also and sound their words plainly and distinctly; the master himself shall not be bound to teach the same young beginners so long as they continue in their first form but only assign in order and course daily or weekly by his direction so many of his scholars placed in the third and fourth form as may sufficiently teach young beginners, and he himself to bestow two hours in teaching them...

In the second form shall be placed such scholars as can read and pronounce their words ... and [the master] shall teach them the introduction of grammar...

In the third form ... the master shall teach them the Latin grammar as it is set forth and used in this realm; Terence; also Aesop's Fables, Virgil and Tully's [Cicero's] Epistles ... to such scholars as he shall perceive apt to learn the same, the art of numbering by arithmetic...

The scholars of the third and fourth forms shall speak nothing in the school but Latin, saving only in their teaching of the lower forms.

SOURCE 28.8 J. Lotherington in J. Lotherington (ed.), *The Tudor Years*, 1994, p. 415

The keenly perceived moral and religious importance of education brought into question the character and status of the schoolmaster ... Nicholas Udall ... described by Haddon as 'the best schoolmaster of his time, as well as the greatest beater' ... was imprisoned in 1541 having been suspected of being involved in a robbery carried out by two of the boys ... In his great work The Schoolmaster published in 1570, Roger Ascham ... argued that teachers should encourage and teach by example rather than beat lessons into their unfortunate pupils, which could just stunt their understanding.

SOURCE 28.9 S. Atkins, *England and Wales Under the Tudors*, 1975, p. 252

That progressive schoolmaster, Richard Mulcaster of Merchant Taylors', 'grounded his pupils in Hebrew, Greek and Latin; he trained them daily in music, both vocal and instrumental, and was a convinced advocate of the study of the mother tongue and of the educational value of acting. He presented plays yearly before the court, in which his boys were the actors, and "by that means taught them good behaviour and audacity"'.

SOURCE 28.10 S. Atkins, *England and Wales Under the Tudors*, 1975, p. 252

Meanwhile up and down the country almost every corporate town had its grammar school, long since founded by some cathedral, monastery, chantry or guild, or perhaps by some wealthy fifteenth-century merchant, acting on his own. In these usually a master and an usher taught a few bright boys the rudiments of Latin. Usually these were the sons of yeomen, small gentry or burgesses. Shakespeare himself went to Stratford Grammar School, where he is supposed to have learned 'small Latin and less Greek'.

SOURCE 28.11 J. Guy, *Tudor England*, 1988, p. 420

Some 42 schools were endowed in the 1560s, and 30 in the 1570s ... Demand for schooling also increased from families below the ranks of the privileged elite; established schools in both town and country offered instruction for classes of 'petties', who were taught either by the usher or the older pupils. Likewise 'dame' schools flourished, though their efficiency was suspect.

SOURCE 28.12 J. Guy, *Tudor England*, 1988, p. 421

...although some schooling was free, more often quarterly fees were charged. In fact, the majority of 'free' schools charged for candles, coal, and educational materials ... Beyond the circle of the elite – whose children were usually tutored at home – we should probably think in terms of a shifting tide of children whose access to schooling varied according to their domestic and economic circumstances. If this is correct, a decline in both attendances and literacy rates would be expected during the 1590s.

SOURCE 28.13 J. Guy, *Tudor Englnad*, 1988, p. 422

The evidence points to an expansion of higher education across the board ... In both universities [Oxford and Cambridge] matriculants ranged from the sons of the nobility and gentry to those of husbandmen and college cooks ... Very roughly, the proportion of university students during Elizabeth's reign who came from noble and gentry families was between one-third and two-fifths.

SOURCE 28.14 William Harrison describes the contemporary expansion of the universities in *The Description of England*, 1577

In my time there are three noble universities in England ... Oxford ... Cambridge ... London ... of which the first two are the most famous...

In most of our colleges there are also great numbers of students, of which many are found by the revenues of the houses and other by the purveyances of their rich friends ... They were erected by their founders at the first only for poor men's sons, whose parents were not able to bring them up unto learning, but now they have the least benefit of them, by reason the rich do so encroach upon them.

SOURCE 28.15 A countryman, speaking in the early seventeenth century

This is all we go to school for: to read common prayers at church and set down common prices at markets, write a letter and make a bond, set down the day of our births, our marriage day, and make our wills when we are sick for the disposing of our goods when we are dead.

SOURCE 28.16 J. Lotherington in J. Lotherington (ed.) *The Tudor Years*, 1994, p. 413

The records suggest the number of students matriculating, that is officially entering the two universities, more than doubled from 300 under Henry VIII to 700 under Elizabeth ... Add to this the Inns of Court in London, which took 100 students per year in the first half of the Tudor period and 250 by the end of it, along with new institutions such as Gresham College in London, founded in 1597, and it becomes clear that higher education was becoming an ever more important qualification for those with social aspirations.

SOURCE 28.17 D. Cressy, *Literacy and the Social Order*, 1980

Illiteracy in the diocese of Durham, 1561–1631

Social group	Number sampled	Number signing with a mark
Clergy/professions	208	5 = 2%
Gentry	252	53 = 21%
Tradesmen/craftsmen	727	470 = 65%
Yeomen	1326	971 = 73%
Servants	18	14 = 78%
Husbandmen	379	345 = 91%
Labourers	176	172 = 98%
Women	706	690 = 98%

Illiteracy in the diocese of London, Essex and Hertfordshire, 1580–1640

Social group	Number sampled	Number signing with a mark
Clergy/professions	177	0 = 0%
Gentry	161	5 = 3%
Tradesmen/craftsmen	448	188 = 42%
Yeomen	319	105 = 33%
Husbandmen	461	337 = 73%
Labourers	7	7 = 100%
Women	324	308 = 95%

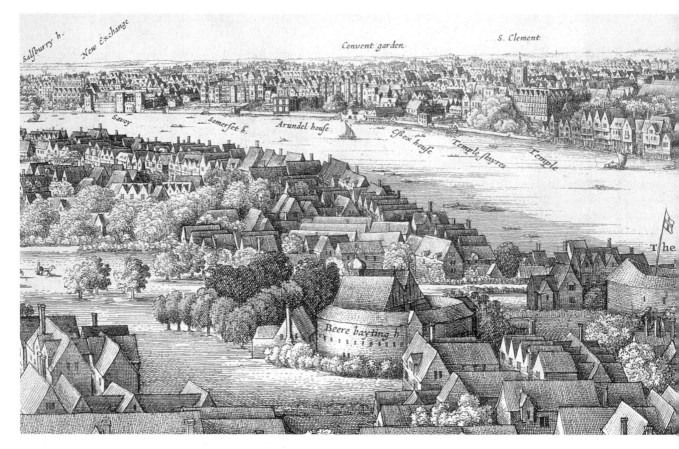

SOURCE 28.18 From Hollar's *View of London*

The growth of London

London's role in the growth of English culture is central. London was the largest and wealthiest city in the country and was therefore in a position to subsidise artistic ventures and provide a large and enthusiastic audience. It was where the court usually resided, and the court was the chief patron of, and inspiration for, the cultural achievements of the day. The first theatres were built in London and the first printing presses housed there. It was also the centre of communication because it was home to both foreign ambassadors and merchants trading with Protestant and Catholic Europe and beyond. London became synonymous with new thinking. Aspiring artists moved to London to make their fortunes. Provincial towns and local nobles followed its style. The vitality and energy of London inspired playwrights, particularly Shakespeare.

SOURCE 28.18 K. McLeish and S. Unwin, *A Guide to Shakespeare's Plays*, 1998, p. x

For Shakespeare, and his audience ... the centralising of power from regional lords to the court in London, and the self-confidence and innovative thinking engendered by ever expanding contact with the non-European world, encouraged a growing sense of 'England' and 'Englishness'. Focus on the capital was increased at the end of the sixteenth century by deforestation, enclosure of common land by rich landowners, and a series of poor harvests leading to rural discontent which penetrated even Shakespeare's Arcadia, and to the arrival in London of people from all over the country: part of the melting pot which provided his theatre audience.

Wealth and stability

Although it may seem a contradiction in a reign that experienced seventeen years of warfare and an increase in urban poverty, a growing awareness of prosperity and stability developed during this period which encouraged people to develop an interest in cultural pursuits. The following factors all played a part in fostering this 'feel good factor'.

- The increase in contact with Europe promoted the exchange of cultural ideas, while the increase in trade meant more money in merchants' pockets.

Baynards Castle

- The price rises enabled some to increase their income.
- The expansion of education and the emergence of an ideal of a Tudor gentleman encouraged those with money to invest in a certain lifestyle. Houses were built, works of art, tapestries and books purchased, and visits to the theatre made. The wealthiest citizens emulated the court and patronised players and musicians in their own households.
- The development of a uniquely English identity, as a result of the successful establishment of the Elizabethan Church, the defeat of the Spanish Armada and the longevity of Elizabeth's reign, fostered a flowering of culture as people celebrated their Golden Age.

Humanism

Humanism was an intellectual movement which sprang out of the Renaissance and influenced thinking and education throughout Europe in the sixteenth century. Originally the term meant simply the study of classical Greek and Roman literature, but it encouraged a greater interest in this world since the classical world, unlike the medieval world, was essentially 'earth bound'. Christian humanists, such as Erasmus, focused on the importance of experiencing faith rather than going through rituals for the sake of appearances and became increasingly critical of their own society which seemed riddled with corruption and meaningless superstition. Admiration for the achievements of the Ancient World encouraged a wave of optimism in man's potential, especially if he used his reason.

By Elizabeth's reign, the effects of humanism were noticeable in two ways. First, it was considered essential for anyone involved in government or politics to have a sound knowledge and understanding of classical literature. Thus grammar schools taught a curriculum based on humanist principles and Elizabethan courtiers made sure that they owned copies of Cicero, Seneca and Tacitus. Many books published in the second half of the sixteenth century were translations of the classics, such as Sir Thomas North's edition of Plutarch's *Lives* from which Shakespeare drew inspiration for many of his plays.

Second, the rediscovery of Greek and Roman culture in England led to classical and neo-classical plays, particularly the comedies of Plautus and tragedies of Seneca, being performed at court and in London by schoolboys. At the beginning of Elizabeth's reign, humanist playwrights applied the classical style to English themes, resulting in Udall's *Ralph Roister Doister*, for example. From this emerged plays with a classical structure and a real plot which also retained the English love for action and excitement. Shakespeare not only perfected this form but featured also the humanist belief in man's potential in many of his speeches:

> 'What a piece of work is a man! how noble in reason!
> how infinite in faculty! in form and moving how
> express and admirable! in action how like an angel!
> in apprehension how like a god!'
> (*Hamlet*, Act 2, Scene 2).

The same combination of classical and English tradition can be found in the work of Sir Philip Sidney who, in *The Defence of Poesy*, combined the teachings of Aristotle with Puritan beliefs.

Humanism was fundamentally important to the growth of culture in Elizabeth's reign because it freed up writers and artists to produce new and exciting work. In addition, humanist authors were quick to see the potential of the printing press and education in bringing their work to a wider audience.

SOURCE 28.19   J. Guy, *Tudor England*, 1988, p. 416

Humanist authors seeking to attract a wider audience assimilated their material to the chivalric traditions of Chaucer and Mallory. In schools and gentry households, Erasmus ... remained favourite reading ... At a more popular level Caxton's The Golden Legend *and Baldwin's* Mirror for Magistrates ... *were devoured.*

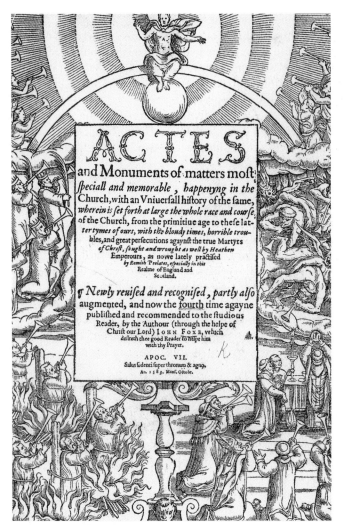

SOURCE 28.20 Frontispiece of Foxe's *Book of Martyrs*, published in 1563

The Protestant Reformation

The ideals portrayed by the life of Christ continued to inspire artists. In addition, the establishment of the Elizabethan Church had an impact on the culture and learning of the day.

The attack on the magic and superstition of the medieval Church led to the growth of a scientific and rational outlook, although accusations of witchcraft continued to be made and astrologers and fortune tellers continued to be popular. The attack on images and relics caused church walls to be whitewashed and statues destroyed. The congregation now had to focus on the words of the preacher and the Bible, rather than rely on visual images to remind them of religious ideas.

The publication of the Bible in English encouraged literacy through its use of the vernacular and influenced literature. The need to defend and explain the new Church also produced some of the finest literature of the age. Hooker's *Laws of Ecclesiastical Polity* is a good example. John Foxe's *Book of Martyrs*, published in 1563, not only ensured popular support for the new Church but also, by showing the Queen as an emperor defeating the evil Pope, used imagery and language which boosted the cult of Gloriana.

Yet, although the establishment of the new Protestant Church eventually became a source of pride and confidence, it would be wrong to explain Protestantism's influence on culture in only these terms. 'Shakespeare's England was a place not of the sunny stability often claimed for it, but of self-questioning, crisis and conflict' (K. McLeish and S. Unwin, *A Guide to Shakespeare's Plays*, 1998, p. ix). The replacement of Roman Catholicism with Protestantism caused intellectual shockwaves and questioning of the social order, as Elizabethans struggled to make sense of their world. The conflict between the new and the old orders is a central theme of many of Shakespeare's plays.

SOURCE 28.21 K. Thomas, *Religion and the Decline of Magic*, 1971, p. 78

The Protestant Reformers rejected the magical powers and supernatural sanctions which had been so plentifully invoked by the medieval Church. In Protestant mythology the Middle Ages became notorious as the time of darkness, when spells and charms had masqueraded as religion and when the lead in magical activity had been taken by the clergy themselves.

Elizabethan beliefs

The Elizabethan World Picture, by E. W. Tillyard, published in 1943, discusses the way Elizabethans saw themselves and their universe. They believed the Earth was at the centre of the Universe or Cosmos and was surrounded by ten spheres that moved around it in perfect harmony. There was a chain of being that began with God and descended through angels to mankind, to animals, to plants and to minerals. Mankind was subdivided into groups that were ranked in order from princes down to slaves. The four elements – fire, air, water and earth – existed within the hierarchical Universe and within the human body. Thus everything and everyone had a place which it had to keep to in order for the Universe to function perfectly; the whole depended on each of its parts to fulfil its role.

These beliefs influenced Elizabethan culture. For example, William Byrd's musical compositions were an attempt to bring the 'music of the spheres' to life, to show the Universe moving in perfect harmony. Spenser identifies love as the key to keeping the four elements in unity, as opposed to conflict. Again and again, Shakespeare emphasises the chaos that will follow when the natural order of things is overthrown.

'Take but degree away, untune that string
And hearke what discord follows.'
(*Troilus and Cressida*, Act 1, Scene 3)

SOURCE 28.22 The Great Chain of Being: a contemporary print showing the hierarchy of the Universe

ACTIVITY

1 In groups of eight, each choose one area of cultural achievement. Research your topic and produce a presentation for the class.

2 In groups, discuss the factors you think were most important in promoting the Elizabethan Golden Age. Prioritise the factors in order of importance.

3 Prepare an argument for or against the view that the only important factor in the cultural explosion of Elizabeth's reign was the patronage of the arts by the Queen and her court.

B Review: What caused the Elizabethan Golden Age?

It is easy, with the benefit of hindsight, to identify the factors which are likely to have caused a particular event. With movements, however, it is far more difficult to show direct links or to evaluate the comparative impact of one factor as opposed to another. And, where we can show a direct link – the court's patronage of companies of players helped to cause the Golden Age – we tend to attach more importance to that factor than to those which simply create the right climate or environment for a movement to blossom. Nevertheless, we can say that a combination of many forces, in varying ratios, created, at the end of the sixteenth century, conditions that enabled cultural achievement to take root and ensured that this achievement, although influenced by the Renaissance in Europe, was uniquely English.

ACTIVITY

Write an answer to the question: Can the flourishing of the arts in England between 1558 and 1603 accurately be described as 'A Golden Age'?

KEY POINTS FROM CHAPTER 28: What caused the Elizabethan Golden Age?

1 The Renaissance greatly changed the cultural traditions of the sixteenth century and had an impact on England, although a uniquely English culture was eventually to develop.

2 The development of English culture resulted from several factors which came together during Elizabeth's reign. These included:

- patronage of the arts by the Queen and the court
- the building of the first theatres in London
- the invention of the printing press and its impact on literature and literacy
- the growth of education
- the growth of London and its role as the centre of cultural development
- prosperity and stability, which encouraged people to spend more money on leisure and the arts
- the popularity of humanism, and its impact on education, the court, drama and literature
- the effects of the Protestant Reformation: the superstitions of the medieval Church were challenged; there was a change from an emphasis on the visual image to an emphasis on the written word; religious writings, particularly the Bible in English, made a big impact
- Elizabethan beliefs about the Universe and the structure of society, which influenced thinking and writing.

29

What was Elizabeth's contribution to the Golden Age?

CHAPTER OVERVIEW   The flowering of culture in Elizabeth's reign was the result of many different factors. The influence of the Queen herself, however, was immense. She not only took an interest in the arts but also fostered an image of royalty which inspired many artists to make her the focus of their plays, poems, songs and paintings. The fact that this was an age of great uncertainty meant that all the triumphs of the reign, from the overthrow of the Pope to the defeat of the Spanish Armada, were celebrated with all the means available to contemporary artists. Although this focus on the monarch was by no means unusual in the sixteenth century, the images of Elizabeth struck a popular chord and have led historians to create the term the 'cult of Gloriana'. The extent to which this cult was deliberately promoted by councillors and whether the government controlled culture, using it as political propaganda, is an issue still debated by historians.

This chapter will therefore focus on the following questions:

A   What was the cult of Gloriana? (pp. 284–91)

B   How did Elizabeth influence elitist culture? (p. 292)

C   How did Elizabeth influence popular culture? (p. 293)

D   Review: What was Elizabeth's contribution to the Golden Age? (p. 294)

A What was the cult of Gloriana?

From the start of her reign, in her coronation portrait painted in January 1559 (see page 1), Elizabeth used biblical slogans to emphasise the advent of a new, Protestant regime to contrast with the chaos of Catholic Mary's reign.

Elizabeth was:

- the restorer of the true religion
- the herald of a new age of harmony and progress
- the Virgin Queen who had married her people
- no ordinary woman but God's chosen instrument
- as good as any man!

Elizabeth appeared as Deborah, the judge and restorer of the house of Israel. The date of her accession, 17 November, became an annual festival in 1576. In pageants throughout the country, Elizabeth was portrayed as the Emperor Constantine, who had strengthened the Roman Empire and ensured the victory of Christianity, heralding an age of light after a time of darkness represented by a seven-headed Pope. In later poetry and paintings Elizabeth was symbolised as Cynthia the moon goddess, Venus the goddess of love, Diana the huntress and Astraea, who, according to classical legend, was one of the last of the immortals to leave Earth. Alongside these mystical images a whole array of symbols emerged, which were used in portraits of the Queen, whose meanings were obvious to Elizabethans. It is not hard to see how all these images, ceremonies and processions filled the gap left by the abolition of Catholic ritual from the English Church.

SOURCE 29.1 The Pelican Portrait, painted by Nicholas Hilliard c.1574

FOCUS ROUTE

Using pages 284–91, make detailed notes on how Elizabeth wanted her subjects to see her.

ACTIVITY

1 It is 1558 and you are an adviser to Elizabeth. Draw up a memorandum outlining the ways in which she can get her image across to the ordinary people.
2 After reading this chapter, work out which methods you and Elizabeth's real councillors agreed on.

SOURCE 29.2 The Phoenix Portrait, by Nicholas Hilliard, 1575

The Ditchley Portrait, by Marcus Gheeraerts the Younger, 1592

FOCUS ROUTE

Examine Sources 29.1–29.7 and Chart 29A, then complete your own copy of the table below.

Painting	Symbols used	Aim
The Pelican Portrait		
The Phoenix Portrait		
The Ermine Portrait		
The Armada Portrait		
The Ditchley Portrait		
The Rainbow Portrait		
The Sieve Portrait		

SOURCE 29.7 The Sieve Portrait, by Zuccari Federico

Pelican
Legend has it that the mother pelican pecks at her own breast and feeds her young on her own blood so that they might live. Elizabeth, as the mother pelican, will sacrifice her life for her people and for her Church.

Tudor rose
The emblem of the Tudor family, it shows Elizabeth's regal status and her right to the throne.

Fleur-de-lis
The royal emblem of France, it symbolises Elizabeth's claim to the throne of France which she did not renounce, despite the loss of Calais.

Cherries
This fruit represents sweetness, the fruits of paradise and the delights of the blessed.

Thornless rose
Symbolising the Virgin Mary, it suggests that Elizabeth, the Virgin Queen, was married to her country in the same way that Mary was married to the Church.

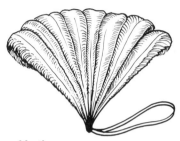

Fan of feathers
The exotic feathers, imported from the New World, represent England's overseas expansion.

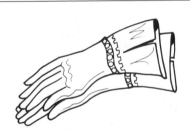

Gloves
A sign of elegance, Elizabeth was fond of holding them to show off her long white hands of which, it is said, she was very vain.

Ermine
Legend tells that the ermine was willing to die rather than dirty its pure white coat, and it therefore symbolises Elizabeth's virtue and purity.

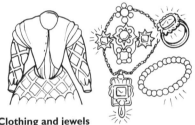

Clothing and jewels
Elizabeth's sumptuous clothing and her jewels reflect power, and the choice of colour and stone sometimes mirrors the heraldry of a particular suitor. A white dress and pearls represent chastity.

Phoenix
A mythical bird that was believed to rise from the flames unscathed, the phoenix represents the Protestant Church's rise from the flames of Mary's reign.

Rainbow
A rainbow reinforces an old Latin motto, 'no rainbow without the sun', and illustrates peace.

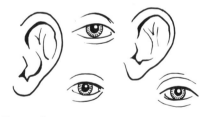

Eyes and ears
They are thought to refer to *Hymns to Astraea*, composed by Sir John Davis – 'eye of that mind most quick and clear' – and illustrate Elizabeth's ability to see and hear all.

ACTIVITY

1 Which images and themes did Elizabeth use most frequently in her portraits?
2 How would ordinary people have caught a glimpse of these royal images?
3 Why were pictures of Elizabeth so popular?

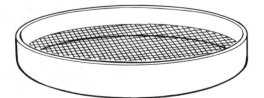

The sieve
It represents virginity: the Vestal Tuccia was accused of impurity and carried water to a temple in a sieve, without spilling a drop, to prove her innocence.

B How did Elizabeth influence elitist culture?

TALKING POINT

How far does government control of Elizabeth's image amount to censorship of the arts?

FOCUS ROUTE

Make a list of the main problems facing the Privy Council throughout Elizabeth's reign, and use it to explain why and how the council tried to control popular culture and promote the cult of Gloriana.

■ 29B How Elizabeth's image was spread through the upper levels of society

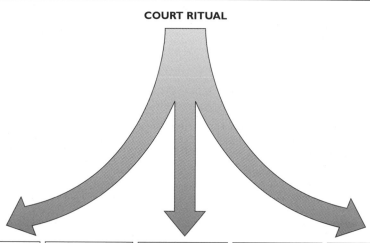

COURT RITUAL

Masques
Often anti-Papal, and with themes ranging from war against the Turks to astronomy. Masques, interspersed with mime and dancing, were regular evening entertainment at court.

Musical evenings
Elizabeth's love of music and dancing meant musicians were permanently employed at court and composers were kept busy. The achievements of the reign were usually marked with a new ditty like the following, which appeared in 1586 after the discovery of the Babington Plot:
'All English hearts rejoice and sing That fears the Lord and loves our Queen'.

Drama
Classical plays were often performed at court in the early years of the reign, usually by the choirboys of St Paul's. In the second half of the reign Elizabeth's support of actors accelerated the growth of drama and led to the establishment of permanent theatres. Leading playwrights were not able to refer to the Queen by name but nevertheless managed to bless her reign, particularly by demonstrating the chaos brought on by a weak ruler.

Miniatures
From 1586 it became fashionable for courtiers to wear miniatures or jewelled cameos of Elizabeth. Leading courtiers, including Burghley, Drake, Hatton and Walsingham, commissioned portraits of themselves wearing these signs of loyalty and devotion.

Royal progresses
Every summer the Queen and her court left London for ten weeks and undertook a stately progress, usually around the south east, staying at the homes of nobles and courtiers. This enabled her to see more of her people. It also encouraged nobles to vie with each other to build the grandest houses and some, like the Earl of Leicester, founded their own companies of actors to stage plays and pageants.

Tournaments
These became increasingly elaborate. Sir Henry Lee transformed the Accession Day joust into a spectacular pageant, in which chivalrous knights performed heroic deeds to prove their loyalty to their Virgin Queen.

Chivalry
Chivalry became the inspiration for a lot of literature and poetry. Sir Philip Sidney's *Arcadia* shows a world of shepherd knights set in an allegorical pastoral landscape. In Edmund Spenser's *The Faerie Queene*, knights set forth to champion the forces of good over evil to ensure Astraea's supremacy over political and religious divisions.

Noble patronage of the arts
Shared interests ensured the mutually supportive relationship between the Queen and her nobles was sustainable. By identifying with the monarch the ruling classes were also able to emphasise their separateness from, and superiority to, the lower classes.

C How did Elizabeth influence popular culture?

■ 29C How Elizabeth's image was spread through the lower levels of society

GOVERNMENT CONTROL

Sermons

Every week the clergy, who were licensed by the government, offered the Homily of Obedience: prayers for the Queen's safety and thanks for the blessings of her reign. The annual Accession Day was also marked by prayers and all the achievements of the reign were celebrated with specially written prayers which showed that Elizabeth was responsible for delivering England 'from the danger of war and oppression, both of bodies by tyranny and of conscience by superstition, restoring peace and true religion' (Prayer for Accession Day, 1576).

C. Haigh, *Elizabeth I*, 1988, p.159:
'The mingling of patriotic and religious sentiments had become common ... devotion to God, devotion to England and devotion to the Queen necessarily went together. This was a product of the highly influential image of the Queen as a Protestant heroine.'

Images

There was a huge popular demand for images of the Queen which, to some extent, filled the place left by the prohibition of Catholic images of the Virgin Mary. A whole domestic industry sprang up producing medallions, woodcuts and engravings. The court portraits of Elizabeth, showing an eternally youthful Queen, were copied and widely distributed. Government control over images can, however, be seen. A proclamation of 1563 made it clear that only approved versions of Elizabeth's portrait could be copied, a Book of Ordinances was issued in 1581, and in 1596 the Privy Council decided to destroy any pictures which showed Elizabeth in an unflattering light – old, in other words.

C. Haigh, *Elizabeth I*, 1988, p.148:
'The royal portrait was now a means of propaganda, not of representation.'

Printing presses

These were used by the government to publish speeches, ballads, sermons and pamphlets emphasising both the Queen's glory and her special relationship with her subjects.

C. Haigh, *Elizabeth I*, 1988, p.151:
'In 1572, on progress through Oxfordshire, Elizabeth sheltered from the rain in a barn; there, an old woman told her that the copyhold on the family's small barn was about to run out, so the Queen got her council to write to the landlord asking him to extend the tenancy.'
The story soon spread – with help from the council.

'The government maintained full powers of censorship over the presses to prevent the spread of ideas that might challenge the monarchy and therefore political stability. The only authorised presses were in London and at the Universities of Oxford and Cambridge. The power of the printed word was such that, subject to instructions from the Privy Council, the 50 or so presses in London were policed by the Stationers' Company.'

Festivals

The council encouraged festivals, the semi-religious rituals which came to take the place of Saints' Days, because they furthered the cult of Gloriana and showed Elizabeth as Protestantism's heroine in the wars against Catholicism. The most important festival was Accession Day on 17 November. In 1576, the council added the date to the calendar of Church festivals and thus, 'a popular festivity was now turned into a propaganda occasion' (C. Haigh, *Elizabeth I*, 1988, p.157).

Plays

Licences were only awarded to playwrights on condition that their plays did not contain direct references to the Queen or to the Church of England. The council, through the office of the Master of Revels, had the power to close down theatres, and patronage operated as an effective form of control. Shakespeare would have been unlikely to show the Tudors in a bad light. He preferred to concentrate, for example, on the overthrow of villainous Richard III by the upright Earl of Richmond, future Henry VII and Elizabeth's grandfather:

'O, now, let Richmond and Elizabeth [of York],
The true succeeders of each royal house,
By God's fair ordinance conjoin together!
And let their heirs, God, if thy will be so,
Enrich the time to come with smooth-faced peace,
With smiling plenty and fair prosperous days!'
(Shakespeare, *Richard III*, Act 5, Scene 5)

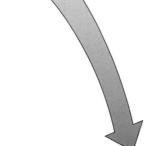

Loyalty
The cult of Gloriana compensated for Elizabeth's gender and her lack of husband and child, while at the same time emphasising her achievements. This ensured the loyalty, and probably love, of her subjects.

Review: What was Elizabeth's contribution to the Golden Age?

Pages 284–93 discuss the theory that Elizabeth deliberately created an image of royalty which was then imposed on her people by using the communication methods of the day; that this image presented both the person of the Queen and the major events and policies of the reign in a rosy glow, and that its repetition eventually brainwashed the English people and silenced any criticism of the regime. If this were the case then 'propaganda', although it is a twentieth-century concept usually used to refer to the use of mass media by dictators to control the minds of their subjects, could be used when talking about the sixteenth century.

The Tudors were a new dynasty and even the withdrawn and serious Henry VII recognised the importance of consolidating popular support through royal progresses and the use of symbolic images. Henry VIII had extended this further, using tournaments, festivals, new palaces and Holbein's portraits to emphasise Tudor stability and power. Holbein's portraits are, according to some, 'where propaganda in the modern sense of the word begins' (R. Strong, *Gloriana: the Portraits of Elizabeth I*, 1987). Henry's minister, Thomas Cromwell, faced with the need to secure popular support for the break with Rome, harnessed the power of the new printing press and used the crown's control over licensing preachers to ensure that the government's views predominated. This need to protect the royal image, and indirectly government policies, faded in the reigns of Edward and Mary. It was revived and extended under Elizabeth to deal with specific issues, primarily her single status and the Catholic threats. In other words, the aim was to enhance political stability by winning the support of, or at least reducing opposition from, her people. This seems essentially different from twentieth-century totalitarian propaganda which seeks, as a matter of policy and party doctrine, to force the individual to submit totally to the state.

SOURCE 29.8 F. Whitford, *Art and Power*, 1995, p. 5

The central message of totalitarian art and architecture was that individual identity had meaning only in terms of the larger identity of the state, embodied in the charismatic person of the supreme leader.

Perhaps, instead of using the term 'propaganda', which has negative connotations, the achievements of the Queen and the Privy Council in turning weaknesses to their advantage by promoting contemporary culture should be seen as an example of political shrewdness. Problems came only in the 1590s, when the government was unable to sustain the fiction that Elizabeth was a youthful, energetic, semi-divine ruler and the realities of prolonged warfare alienated the people and divided the council. By then, however, over three decades of political stability had guaranteed the survival of both the Church of England and the legend of the Virgin Queen.

KEY POINTS FROM CHAPTER 29: **What was Elizabeth's contribution to the Golden Age?**

1 Images of Elizabeth were used so often by artists, poets and writers that historians talk about the cult of Gloriana.
2 The rituals of the court had an impact on elitist culture. The government also exercised some control over popular culture. This has led some to accuse Elizabeth and her council of censorship and even deliberate manipulation of Elizabeth's image as a form of propaganda.

Conclusion:
The Elizabethan Golden Age – myth or reality?

SOURCE I   Glenda Jackson as Elizabeth in *Elizabeth R* in 1971

The purpose of this book has been to encourage your enjoyment of history, and to prepare you for your AS or A level examination by helping you to develop your skills of analysis and interpretation. More specifically, it has looked beyond the hype – beyond ideas of a Golden Age and the cult of Gloriana, and beyond the images of Elizabeth seen on television and in films – to find out what sort of monarch Elizabeth was, how well she dealt with the problems she faced and how successful she was in bringing prosperity and stability to her country. It has studied Elizabeth as she passed from the inexperienced politician of 1558, through the confident mistress of the 'high-water mark' in the 1570s and 1580s, to the ageing and isolated figure of the 1590s; and it has studied the insecure England of 1558 becoming the assured nation, on the brink of maritime expansion, which Elizabeth left behind her in 1603.

SOURCE 2 Miranda Richardson as Elizabeth in *Blackadder 2*, in 1984

SOURCE 3 Funeral procession of Elizabeth I, by William Camden, 1603

SOURCE 4 Cate Blanchett as Elizabeth in *Elizabeth*, 1998

ACTIVITY

In groups, discuss the following question and brainstorm an answer to it:
To what extent can the reign of Elizabeth I be seen as a blessing for her country?

FOCUS ROUTE

The table below summarises the key areas of Elizabeth's reign. It also lists some of the key events, but by no means all of them. Use your own copy of the table to record important events as you are revising. It will be a useful summary and an important tool to help you look beyond the artificial boundaries, between foreign and domestic policy for example, which are created to make studying the period possible.

	Religion	Relations with				Central and local government	The economy	Poverty	The succession
		France	Spain	Ireland	Scotland				
1558						Cecil made Secretary of State			
1559	Act of Supremacy Act of Uniformity								
1560									
1561									
1562						Dudley and Norfolk appointed to the Privy Council			
1563									
1564									
1565									
1566									
1567					James VI replaces his mother as King of Scotland				
1568			Seizure of Spanish treasure en route to Netherlands						Mary, Queen of Scots, placed in custody by Elizabeth
1569							Trade with the Netherlands broken off		
1570	Elizabeth excommuni- cated by the Pope								
1571									
1572									
1573							Trade restored with the Netherlands Corn prices regulated		
1574									
1575									

	Religion	Relations with				Central and local government	The economy	Poverty	The succession
		France	Spain	Ireland	Scotland				
1576									
1577									
1578									
1579									
1580									
1581									
1582									
1583									
1584		Treaty of Joinville	Murder of William, Prince of Orange						
1585									
1586					Treaty of Berwick				
1587									Execution of Mary, Queen of Scots
1588									
1589									
1590									
1591						Robert Cecil appointed to the Privy Council			
1592									
1593						Essex appointed to the Privy Council			
1594								Bad harvest and high prices	
1595								Bad harvest	
1596								Bad harvest	
1597								Bad harvest	
1598									
1599									
1600									
1601									
1602									
1603				Defeat of Tyrone					Cecil prepares for the accession of James Stuart

Answers to activities

Page 14

Events in chronological order	Passage
12	B
14	F
10	I
13	C
8	L
3	M
6	E
2	N
4	K
9	H
11	G
1	A
7	D
5	J

Page 15
1 c)   2 b)   3 a)   4 a)   5 b)   6 b)   7 a)   8 b)   9 a)   10 b)

Pages 30–31
  1 **b)** Elizabeth introduced many Protestants to her Privy Council, most of whom had held power under Edward VI. She also removed about 35 of Mary's councillors.
  2 **b)**
  3 **b)** Elizabeth was forced into this position because Philip II of Spain would not fight for Calais and was entering into negotiations with France. Like her father, when he had been advised to let Boulogne go in the 1540s, Elizabeth saw the loss of Calais as a blow to her honour as monarch and was reluctant to accept its return to the French.
  4 **a)** Support was only given late in 1559, with some reluctance by Elizabeth although not by her councillors.
  5 **c)**
  6 **a)**
  7 **b)**
  8 **a)**
  9 **c)**
10 **b)**
11 **a)**
12 **a)**

Page 50
The Privy Council dealt with all the cases except:
2   Court of Star Chamber
3 and 5 household
4   court
7   Court of Requests
9   Chancery
11 Exchequer
12, 14, 16 and 17 Parliament

Page 206
In each case the second alternative is the correct reason.

Page 224
1 a)   2 b)   3 b)   4 a)   5 a)   6 b) 7 b)

Bibliography and selected reading

Atkins S., *England and Wales Under the Tudors*, 1975, Hodder & Stoughton

Bergeron D. M., *English Civic Pageantry, 1558–62*, 1971, Edward Arnold
Black J. B., *The Reign of Elizabeth*, 1959, Oxford University Press

Challis C. E., *Economic History Review*, 1986
Coleman D. C., *The Economy of England 1450–1750*, 1977, Oxford University Press
Cressy D., *Literacy and the Social Order*, 1980, Cambridge University Press

Dawson I. G. W., *The Tudor Century, 1485–1603*, 1993, Nelson
Doran S., *Elizabeth I and Religion*, 1994, Routledge
Doran S., *England and Europe 1485–1603*, 1986, Longman
Doran S., *Monarchy and Matrimony, the Courtships of Elizabeth I*, 1996, Routledge
Doran S., 'Elizabeth I', *The Historian*, No. 54, 1997

Ellis S., *Tudor Ireland*, 1985, Longman
Elton G. R., *England Under the Tudors*, 1955, Routledge
Elton G. R., *England Under the Tudors*, 3rd edn, 1991, Routledge
Elton G. R., *The Parliament of England, 1559–1581*, 1986, Cambridge University Press

Fernandez-Armesto F., *The Spanish Armada: The Experience of War in 1588*, 1989, Oxford University Press
Fletcher A., *Tudor Rebellions*, 1968, Longman
Fraser A., *Mary, Queen of Scots*, 1969, Mandarin (since 1989)

Graves M., *Elizabethan Parliaments, 1559–1601*, 1987, Longman
Guy J., *Tudor England*, 1988, Oxford University Press

Haigh C. (ed.), *The Reign of Elizabeth I*, 1984, Macmillan
Haigh C., *Elizabeth I*, 1988, Longman
Hartnoll P. (ed.), *Concise Oxford Companion to the Theatre*, 1972, Oxford University Press
Hibbert C., *The Virgin Queen*, 1990, Penguin
Hoskins W. G., *The Age of Plunder*, 1979, Longman
Howarth D., *Images of Rule*, 1997, Macmillan
Hurstfield J., *Elizabeth I and the Unity of England*, 1960, English Universities Press

Ives E. W., *Faction in Tudor England*, 1979, Historical Association

Jack S. M., *Towns in Tudor and Stuart Britain*, 1996, Macmillan
Jones N., *Faith by Statute*, 1982, Royal Historical Society
Jordan C., 'Woman's Rule in Sixteenth-Century British Political Thought', *Renaissance Quarterly*, Vol. 40, 1987

Knappen M., *Tudor Puritanism*, 1939, University of Chicago Press

Lotherington J. (ed.), *The Tudor Years*, 1994, Hodder & Stoughton

MacCaffrey W., *Elizabeth I*, 1993, Edward Arnold
MacCaffrey W., *Queen Elizabeth and the Making of Policy 1572–88*, 1981, Princeton University Press
MacCulloch D., *The Later Reformation in Tudor England*, 1990, Macmillan
McLeish K. and Unwin S., *A Guide to Shakespeare's Plays*, 1998, Faber and Faber

Neale J. E., *Queen Elizabeth I*, 1934, Jonathan Cape
Neale J. E., *The Elizabethan House of Commons*, 1949, Jonathan Cape

O'Day R., *The Tudor Age*, 1995, Longman
O'Sullivan D. and Lockyer R., *Tudor England*, 1994, Longman
Outhwaite R.B., *Inflation in Tudor and Early Stuart England*, 1982, Macmillan

Palliser D. M., *The Age of Elizabeth*, 1983, Longman
Phelps-Brown E. H. and Hopkins S. V., *A Perspective of Wages and Prices*, 1981, Methuen
Plowden A., *Marriage With My Kingdom*, 1977, Oxford University Press
Pound J., *Poverty and Vagrancy in Tudor England*, 1978, Longman

Raine A., *York Civic Records*, Vol. 5, 1939–53, Yorkshire Archaeological Society
Read C., *Lord Burghley and Queen Elizabeth*, 1960, Oxford University Press
Ross, J., *Suitors to the Queen*, 1975, quoted in S. Doran *Marriage and Matrimony* (1996)

Salter R., *Elizabeth and Her Reign*, 1988, Macmillan
Servini P., *The English Reformation*, 1997, Hodder & Stoughton
Smith A. G. R., *The Anonymous Life of William Cecil, Lord Burghley*, 1990, Lampeter
Smith A. G. R., *The Government of Elizabethan England*, 1967, Arnold
Stone L., *The Crisis of the Aristocracy*, 1965, Clarendon Press
Strong R., *Gloriana: the Portraits of Elizabeth I*, 1987, Thames & Hudson

Tawney R. H., 'The Rise of the Gentry, 1558–1640', *Economic History Review*, No. 11, 1941
Taylor-Smith L. J., 'Elizabeth I: a Psycholgical Profile', *The Sixteenth Century Journal*, No. 15, 1984
Thomas K., *Religion and the Decline of Magic*, 1971, Penguin
Tillyard E. W., *The Elizabethan World Picture*, 1943, Chatto & Windus
Trevor Roper H., 'The Gentry, 1540–1640', *Economic History Review*, Supplement 1, 1953

Wernham R. B., *The Making of Elizabethan Foreign Policy*, 1980, University of California Press
Whitford, F., *Art and Power*, 1995, South Bank Centre
Williams P., *The Tudor Regime*, 1979, Oxford University Press
Wilson C., *Queen Elizabeth and the Revolt of the Netherlands*, 1970, Macmillan

Acknowledgements

Author's acknowledgements

With thanks to my editor Ian Dawson, for convincing me to undertake the book and providing reassurance and constructive advice throughout; my colleague David Cumberland, Head of History at Pensby High School for Girls, for reading the first draft and making tactful suggestions; my A level class of 1997–99, for providing the inspiration; and to Dr Susan Doran, of St Mary's University College, for undertaking her role as academic adviser with impeccable thoroughness.

Text acknowledgements

p.16 source 1.4 M. MacCaffrey, *Elizabeth I*, Edward Arnold, 1993; **p.18** sources 2.2 and 2.3 C. Haigh, *Elizabeth I*, Longman, 1988; **p.19** source 2.16 S. Doran, *Monarchy and Matrimony, the Courtships of Elizabeth I*, Routledge, 1996; **p.21** source 2.23 S. Doran, *Monarchy and Matrimony, the Courtships of Elizabeth I*, Routledge, 1996; source 2.24 C. Jordan, 'Woman's Rule in Sixteenth-Century British Political Thought' from *Renaissance Quarterly*, vol. 40, 1987; source 2.27 C. Haigh, *Elizabeth I*, Longman, 1998; **p.34** source 4.1 G. R. Elton, *England Under the Tudors*, 3rd edition, Routledge, 1991; source 4.4 C. Haigh, *Elizabeth I*, Longman, 1988; **p.36** source 4.8 R. Salter, *Elizabeth and Her Reign*, Palgrave, 1988; **p.49** source 5.5 C. Hibbert, *The Virgin Queen*, Penguin, 1990; **p.67** source 7.2 M. Graves, *Elizabethan Parliaments, 1559–1601*, Longman, 1987; **p.70** source 7.3 M. Graves, *Elizabethan Parliaments, 1559–1601*, Longman, 1987; **p.72** source 7.10 A. G. R. Smith, *The Government of Elizabethan England*, W.W. Norton and Company, 1967; **p.80** source 8.2 W. MacCaffrey, *Elizabeth I*, Arnold, 1993; **p.81** source 8.6 D. M. Palliser, *The Age of Elizabeth*, Longman, 1983; **p.85** source 9.1 D. M. Palliser, *The Age of Elizabeth*, Longman, 1983; **p.88** source 9.5 D. M. Palliser, *The Age of Elizabeth*, Longman, 1983; **p.93** source 10.1 W. MacCaffrey, *Elizabeth I*, Arnold, 1993; **p.96** source 10.3 S. Ellis, *Tudor Ireland*, Longman, 1985; source 10.6 S. Ellis, *Tudor Ireland*, Longman, 1985; **p.99** source 10.10 W. MacCaffrey, *Elizabeth I*, Edward Arnold, 1993; source 10.11 W. MacCaffrey, *Elizabeth I*, Edward Arnold, 1993; source 10.12 S. Ellis, *Tudor Ireland*, Longman, 1985; **p.102** source 11.1 C. Haigh, *Elizabeth I*, Longman, 1988; **p.103** source 11.2 C. Haigh, *Elizabeth I*, Longman, 1988; source 11.3 S. Doran, 'Elizabeth I' from *The Historian*, no.54, 1997; **p.104** source 11.4 S. Doran, 'Elizabeth I' from *The Historian*, no.54, 1997; **p.129** source 14A D. M. Palliser, *The Age of Elizabeth*, Longman, 1983; **p.130** source 14.1 S. M. Jack, *Towns in Tudor and Stuart Britain*, Palgrave, 1996, reproduced with permission of Palgrave; source 14.4 D. M. Palliser, *The Age of Elizabeth*, Longman, 1983; **p.131** source 14.6 D. M. Palliser, *The Age of Elizabeth*, Longman, 1983; **p.132** source 14.12 J. Pound, *Poverty and Vagrancy in Tudor England*, Longman, 1978; **p.157** source 16.6 R. N. L. Jones in C. Haigh (ed.), *The Reign of Elizabeth*, Macmillan, 1984, reproduced with permission of Palgrave; source 16.7 C. Haigh, *Elizabeth I*, Longman, 1988; **p.161** source 16.12 C. Haigh in C. Haigh (ed.), *The Reign of Elizabeth I*, Macmillan, 1984, reproduced with permission of Palgrave; **p.163** source 17.1 S. Doran, *Elizabeth I and Religion*, Routledge, 1994; **p.165** source 17.2 S. Doran, *Elizabeth I and Religion*, Routledge, 1994; **p.168** source 17.7 A. Fletcher, *Tudor Rebellions*, Longman, 1968; source 17.8 A. Fletcher, *Tudor Rebellions*, Longman, 1968; **p.169** source 17.12 A. Fletcher, *Tudor Rebellions*, Longman, 1968; source 17.13 C. Haigh, *Elizabeth I*, Longman, 1988, **p.171** source 17.15 S. Doran, *Elizabeth I and Religion*, Routledge, 1994; **p.173** source 18.1 G. R. Elton, *England Under the Tudors*, 3rd edition, Routledge, 1991; **p.177** source 18.3 J. B. Black, *The Reign of Elizabeth*, Oxford University Press, 1959, by permission of Oxford University Press; **p.181** source 18.5 extract from *Queen Elizabeth I* by J. E. Neale, published by Jonathan Cape. Used by permission of The Random House Group Limited; source 18.6 C. Hibbert, *The Virgin Queen*, Penguin, 1990; source 18.8 A. Fraser, *Mary Queen of Scots*, Weidenfeld and Nicolson, 1969; **p.183** source 18.9 W. MacCaffrey, *Elizabeth I*, Arnold, 1993; source 18.10 G. R. Elton, *England Under the Tudors*, 3rd edition, Routledge, 1991; **p.190** source 19.5 W. MacCaffrey, *Elizabeth I*, Arnold, 1993; **p.196** source 20.2 M. Knappen, *Tudor Puritanism*, University of Chicago Press, 1939; **p.205** source 20.25 P. Collinson in C. Haigh (ed.), *The Reign of Elizabeth I*, Macmillan, 1984, reproduced with permission of Palgrave; **p.209** (section opener) extract from *Queen Elizabeth I* by J. E. Neale published by Jonathan Cape. Used by permission of The Random House Group Limited; **p.215** source 22.3 R. B. Wernham, *The Making of Elizabethan Foreign Policy*, University of California Press, 1980; source 22.4 W. MacCaffrey, *Elizabeth I*, Arnold, 1993; **p.216** source 22.5 R. B. Wernham, *The Making of Elizabethan Foreign Policy*, University of California Press, 1980; **p.219** source 22.6 S. Doran, *England and Europe 1485–1603*, Longman, 1986; **p.223** source 22.12 R. B. Wernham, *The Making of Elizabethan Foreign Policy*, University of California Press, 1980; source 22.17 J. Guy, *Tudor England*, Oxford University Press, 1988, by permission of Oxford University Press; **p.225** source 22.18 C. Haigh, *Elizabeth I*, Longman, 1988; source 22.19 R. B. Wernham, *The Making of Elizabethan Foreign Policy*, Longman, 1980; **p.235** source 24.3 D. M. Palliser, *The Age of Elizabeth*, Longman, 1983; **p.239** source 24.9 G. D. Ramsay in C. Haigh (ed.), *The Reign of Elizabeth I*, Macmillan,

1984, reproduced with permission of Palgrave; source 24.10 G. R. Elton, *England Under the Tudors*, Routledge, 1955; **p.245** source 25.7 F. Fernandez-Armesto, *The Spanish Armada: The Experience of War in 1588*, Oxford University Press, 1989, by permission of Oxford University Press; **p.247** source 25.12 S. Doran, *England and Europe 1485–1603*, Longman, 1986; source 25.13 S. Doran, *England and Europe 1485–1603*, Longman, 1986; source 25.14 W. MacCaffrey, *Elizabeth I*, Edward Arnold, 1993; source 25.15 C. Haigh, *Elizabeth I*, 1988, Longman; **p.248** source 25.16 R. B. Wernham, *The Making of Elizabethan Foreign Policy*, University of California Press, 1980; source 25.17 W. MacCaffrey, *Elizabeth I*, Edward Arnold, 1993; source 25.18 C. Haigh, *Elizabeth I*, Longman, 1988; source 25.19 C. Haigh, *Elizabeth I*, Longman, 1988; **p.251** source 25.20 S. Doran, *England and Europe 1485–1603*, Longman, 1986; **p.252** source 25.23 W. MacCaffrey, *Elizabeth I*, Edward Arnold, 1993; **p.263** source 27.10 C. Haigh, *Elizabeth I*, Longman, 1988; **p.271** source 27.27 P. Hartnoll (ed.), *Concise Oxford Companion to the Theatre*, Oxford University Press, 1972, by permission of Oxford University Press; **p.272** source 28.1 K. Thomas, *Religion and the Decline of Magic*, Weidenfeld and Nicholson, 1971; **p.274** source 28.4 K. McLeish and S. Unwin, *A Guide to Shakespeare's Plays*, Faber and Faber Ltd, 1998; **p.276** source 28.8 J. Lotherington in J. Lotherington (ed.), *The Tudor Years*, 1994. Reproduced by permission of Hodder and Stoughton Ltd; source 28.9 S. Atkins, *England and Wales Under the Tudors*, 1975. Reproduced by permission of Hodder and Stoughton Ltd; **p.277** source 28.10 S. Atkins, *England and Wales Under the Tudors*, 1975. Reproduced by permission of Hodder and Stoughton Ltd; sources 28.11, 28.12, 28.13 J. Guy, *Tudor England*, Oxford University Press, 1988, by permission of Oxford University Press; source 28.16 J. Lotherington in J. Lotherington (ed.), *The Tudor Years*, 1994. Reproduced by permission of Hodder and Stoughton Ltd; source 28.17 D. Cressy, *Literacy and the Social Order*, Cambridge University Press, 1980; **p.278** source 28.18 K. McLeish and S. Unwin, *A Guide to Shakespeare's Plays*, Faber and Faber Ltd, 1998; **p.280** source 28.21 K. Thomas, *Religion and the Decline of Magic*, Weidenfeld and Nicolson, 1971; **p.293** chart 29C extract from C. Haigh, *Elizabeth I*, Longman, 1988.

All Longman Group Limited extracts are reprinted by permission of Pearson Education Limited. Every effort has been made to trace copyright holders and to ensure that sources are quoted correctly. If any have been inadvertently overlooked or misquoted the Publishers will be pleased to make the necessary arrangements at the first opportunity.

Index

Note: Entries in **bold** refer to historical terms explained in the glossary boxes and the pages on which those glossary boxes occur.